The New Latin American Fashion Reader

The New Latin American Fashion Reader

Edited by
Regina A. Root and Stephanie N. Saunders

BLOOMSBURY VISUAL ARTS
LONDON • NEW YORK • OXFORD • NEW DELHI • SYDNEY

BLOOMSBURY VISUAL ARTS

Bloomsbury Publishing Plc, 50 Bedford Square, London, WC1B 3DP, UK
Bloomsbury Publishing Inc, 1385 Broadway, New York, NY 10018, USA
Bloomsbury Publishing Ireland, 29 Earlsfort Terrace, Dublin 2, D02 AY28, Ireland

BLOOMSBURY, BLOOMSBURY VISUAL ARTS and the Diana logo are trademarks of Bloomsbury Publishing Plc

First published in Great Britain 2025

Selection, editorial matter, Introduction © Regina A. Root and Stephanie N. Saunders, 2025
Individual chapters © their Authors, 2025

Regina A. Root and Stephanie N. Saunders have asserted their right under the Copyright, Designs and Patents Act, 1988, to be identified as Editors of this work.

For legal purposes the Acknowledgements on p. xiv constitute an extension of this copyright page.

Cover image: Corcuera Terán's poncho by María Silvia.

All rights reserved. No part of this publication may be: i) reproduced or transmitted in any form, electronic or mechanical, including photocopying, recording or by means of any information storage or retrieval system without prior permission in writing from the publishers; or ii) used or reproduced in any way for the training, development or operation of artificial intelligence (AI) technologies, including generative AI technologies. The rights holders expressly reserve this publication from the text and data mining exception as per Article 4(3) of the Digital Single Market Directive (EU) 2019/790.

Bloomsbury Publishing Plc does not have any control over, or responsibility for, any third-party websites referred to or in this book. All internet addresses given in this book were correct at the time of going to press. The author and publisher regret any inconvenience caused if addresses have changed or sites have ceased to exist, but can accept no responsibility for any such changes.

A catalogue record for this book is available from the British Library.

A catalog record for this book is available from the Library of Congress.

ISBN: HB: 978-1-3505-1745-5
PB: 978-1-3505-1744-8
ePDF: 978-1-3505-1746-2
eBook: 978-1-3505-1747-9

Typeset by RefineCatch Limited, Bungay, Suffolk
Printed and bound in Great Britain

For product safety related questions contact productsafety@bloomsbury.com.

To find out more about our authors and books visit www.bloomsbury.com and sign up for our newsletters.

To each other

Contents

List of Figures ix
Notes on Contributors xi
Acknowledgments xv

Introduction: Reimagining Rupture and Repair
Stephanie N. Saunders and Regina A. Root 1

Part 1 Archival Considerations

1 Archives Matter: Dress Histories from Brazilian Archives
 Rita Morais de Andrade 15

2 Catholic Reliquary Lockets in the Colonial Americas: Foreign Objects with Native Presence *Alison Napier* 25

3 Manila Shawls, Trading Routes, and Global Encounters
 Inés Corujo Martín 39

4 Decolonizing Fashion, Assembling a Ruana History. Genealogies of a Resisting and Undesirable Garment *Edward Salazar Celis* 56

5 The Names of the Clothes: Cuban Fashion Brandscape, 1959–1989
 María A. Cabrera Arús 73

Part 2 Culture's Empowering Lens

6 Afro-Brazilian Styles: Dress, Race, and Coloniality in Nineteenth-Century Portraits *Alliny Maia Cabral* 93

7 Spotting Afro-Peruvian Women: A (Brief) Sartorial History in Polka Dots *Tamara J. Walker* 108

8 "Are Feminists Elegant?": Shaping Gender and Literary Style Through Fashion *Alba F. Aragón* 120

9 Imagining through Images: Clothes and Family Memories in Afro-Brazilian Identities *Hanayrá Negreiros* 136

Part 3 Social Unrest and Resistance

10 Skirting the Colonial Gaze: Indigenous Reconfigurations of
    Feminine Identity   María Claudia Andre   147

11 Fashion, Performance, and Resistance in Trans Representation
    Stephanie N. Saunders   158

12 Politics of the Clothed Body During the Social Outburst, Chile 2019
    Pía Montalva   172

13 Fashion in Distress: Cultural Fragments and Recycled Identities in
    Contemporary Argentina   Regina A. Root   188

14 From Low to High: Fashion, Reggaeton, and Latino Male Idols
    William Cruz-Bermeo   198

Part 4 Creative and Collective Agency

15 The Fashion of Face Masks in Mexico: Protest, Culture, and Identity
    during the COVID-19 Pandemic   Andrea A. Gaytán Cuesta   215

16 Transnational Experiences in Fashion: The Work of Equihua,
    Barragán and Ricardo Seco   Tanya Meléndez-Escalante   228

17 The National Movement of Maya Weavers and Neocolonialism
    in Fashion Intellectual Property   Kedron Thomas   242

18 Design as a Natural Healer   Maria Carolina Garcia   260

Index   273

Figures

2.1 Anonymous Artist. Medallón *relicario* featuring an Anonymous Saint with a Levitating Figure of *Santa Maria* (left) and *El Divino Pastor* (right) (Late eighteenth century). Painted images in a silver frame. 25

2.2 Anonymous Artist (Peru), Two-Sided *relicario* with Images of the Virgin of Carmen (Patron Saint of mestizos) (left) and the Virgin and Child (right) (Early nineteenth century) Polychrome Huamanga stone in a silver frame. 26

3.1 *Mantón de Manila* fabricated in Canton, China from 1870. National Costume Museum. Center for Research in Ethnologic Heritage, Madrid, Spain. 40

3.2 Manuel Cabral Agudo Bejarano. *El puesto de buñuelos*, ca. 1854. Collection Carmen Thyssen-Bornemisza, Madrid, Spain. 46

4.1 "Un provinciano conduciendo á su hijo al colegio" (A provincial man driving hisson to school) watercolor by Ramón Torres, *c*. 1860. 61

4.2 "Marcelino Londoño" by Fotografía Rodríguez, 1899. 65

4.3 "Chiguene gue Muisca Mantle" by Somos Mhuyscas, 2021. In the photograph, Estiven Castro wears the piece. 69

5.1 Principal themes in the Cuban brandscape. 77

5.2 Nationalist brand logos. 79

6.1 A Bahian *quitandeira* seated beside her products, 1862. 97

6.2 Portrait of a Bahian *quitandeira* depicted standing and holding a basket, 1862. Photograph from Rafael Castro y Ordoñez. *Acervo da Fundação Biblioteca Nacional – Brasil*. 98

7.1 A.A. Bonnaffé, "*La Zamacueca,*" *Recuerdos de Lima: album tipos, trajes, y costumbres dibujado y publicado por A.A. Bonnaffé en Lima, 1857*. Lima: A.A. Bonnaffé, 1857. 116

7.2 "Perfection: La Mejor Cocina a Kerosene," *El Comercio*, January 18, 1942. 117

8.1 "Balada sobre la sencillez de las rosas perfectas" (Ballad on the Simplicity of Perfect Roses) by Rubén Darío, in *Elegancias*, January 1, 1912. 125

8.2	Illustration accompanying the chronicle "¿Las feministas son elegantes?" (Are Feminists Elegant?) by Ysis in *Elegancias* May 1, 1914.	131
9.1	Party at my great-grandfather's house (center) in the 1950s. São Paulo, Brazil.	141
9.2	My grandfather wearing a tailcoat and shoes on a gala night in the 1950s. São Paulo, Brazil.	142
12.1	Greta di Girolamo covered with a hood she made herself from a lace panty and a stole inherited from her grandmother, at a protest in Plaza Italia, Santiago, Chile, 2019. Photographer: Roque Rodríguez.	180
12.2	Hooded man wears a t-shirt with the image of Argentine *guerrillero* Che Guevara to cover his mouth area and protect himself from the gas thrown by security forces cars, Plaza Italia, Santiago de Chile, 2019. Photographer: Diego Urbina.	181
13.1	Fashion confronts politics in peculiar ways during the period of State Terrorism. Photograph of the cover of *La Opinión* (20 to 26 February, 1977).	194
13.2	The Chicos del 12-na make their masks and ponchos from textile fragments. Sometimes these designs become collaborative festivals that bring together people who work together to make new collective dress to be worn by several people together at a time.	196
14.1	The image of Marco A. Jaramillo Z. gives us an idea of how local dandies of Medellín, Colombia fashioned themselves. By Benjamín de la Calle, Medellín, 1915.	201
14.2	In 2018 the reggaeton performer J Balvin collaborated with GEF, a long-standing local brand for a collection based on his sense of style. Medellín, Colombia.	207
16.1	Brenda Equihua, Tigers of the North Cobija jacket, 2018. Photographer and Stylist: Keyla Marquez. Model: Rhyan Anthony Santos.	231
16.2	Ricardo Seco, Juntos/Together jacket, FW 2017. Photographer: Enrique Figueroa.	237
18.1	This sample shows details of a single leaf of *Plectranthus barbatus*, a plant commonly found in urban gardens and sidewalks in Brazil, hand printed on felted wool.	263
18.2	*Talinum paniculatum* was the plant chosen to create a print for an augmented reality marker for Cris Romagna's song launching.	266

Contributors

María Claudia André was Emeritus Professor of Latin American and Women's and Gender Studies at Hope College, USA. Some of her publications are: *Dramaturgas argentinas de los años 20* (2010), *The Woman in Latin American and Spanish Literature: Essays on Iconic Characters* (2012), and *Escrituras extremas: Feminismos libertarios* (2016).

Alba F. Aragón is Associate Professor of Comparative Literature at Bridgewater State University, USA, where she teaches courses on Hispanic literatures and cultures. She has a Ph.D. in Romance Languages & Literatures from Harvard University. She has published articles on the significance of fashion and the dressed body in Latin American literature and culture.

Alliny Maia Cabral is a dress and fashion researcher dedicated to Brazilian dress history. She has a doctorate from the Universidade Federal de Goiás, Brazil. In her current research, she is analyzing the material and visual aspects of colonial Rio de Janeiro dress through a multidisciplinary lens.

María Cabrera Arús is an instructor in the Gallatin School of Individualized Study at New York University, USA. Her research focuses on the politics of fashion and material culture. She has published and curated exhibitions on different aspects of Cuban socialist material culture, including a special issue on "The Matter of Things: A Material Turn in Cuban Studies" and an exhibit on "Fashioning Cuban Socialism."

Inés Corujo Martín is Assistant Professor of Humanities at New York City College of Technology, The City University of New York, USA, where she teaches courses on fashion studies and Hispanic literature and culture. Her research focuses on Iberian and Latin American cultural production, gender studies and feminist theory, and visual and material culture.

William Cruz-Bermeo is a professor of Fashion Studies and Fashion History at the Universidad Pontificia Bolivariana, Colombia. He has contributed to *Latin American and Latinx Fashion Design Today—¡Moda Hoy!* (2024) and has authored the book *Medellín, medio siglo de moda: 1900–1950* (2016).

Maria Carolina Garcia is Professor of Circular Economy in the Graduate Program of Architecture, Urbanism and Design at Belas Artes University, Brazil. Her research interests focus on textiles, surface design and fashion coolhunting at the intersection of cultural sustainability, nature and technology. She publishes on fashion, design strategies, and the creative economy in Latin America.

Andrea Gaytán-Cuesta is Assistant Professor of Languages, Literatures, and Cultures at the University of North Florida, USA. Her research interests include literature, cinema, and other Mexican and Latin American cultural productions of the twentieth and twenty-first centuries derived from the intersection of science fiction, disaster studies, and border studies.

Tanya Melendez-Escalante is Senior Curator of Education and Public Programs at The Museum at the Fashion Institute of Technology, USA. She is co-editor of the book *Latin American and Latinx Fashion Design Today—¡Moda Hoy!*, which accompanied this exhibit that she co-curated, and contributing author to *Pink: The History of a Punk, Pretty, Powerful Color* (2018) and *Food & Fashion* (2023) among others. She has curated or co-curated exhibitions *Eterno Femenino* (2017) and *Julia y Renata: Moda y Transformación* (2020), among others.

Rita Morais de Andrade is Professor of Dress History and Visual Arts at the Universidade Federal de Goiás, Brazil. She has a Ph.D. in History, with specializations in Afro-Brazilian and African History and Culture and in Museology. Her scholarly focus on Brazilian and Latin American dress and textile histories is archival-informed and object-based.

Pía Montalva teaches courses on fashion, gender, and society at the Universidad Católica de Chile; and courses on contemporary fashion debates at the Universidad Andrés Bello. She has a Ph.D. in Latin American Cultural Studies from Universidad de Chile. Her books include *Morir un poco. Moda y sociedad en Chile 1960–1976* (2004), *Apuntes para un diccionario de la moda* (2017) and *Tejidos Blandos. Indumentaria y violencia política en Chile 1973–1990* (2023).

Alison Napier teaches Art History and History of Graphic Design at Virginia Wesleyan University and Tidewater Community College, USA. Her research interests focus on the role of art and material culture in shaping personal and community identity. She has presented conference papers on portrait miniatures, nineteenth-century hair work, and the role of the museum space in comics and graphic novels.

Hanayrá Negreiros is a Brazilian fashion scholar and curator, currently pursuing a Ph.D. in History at the Pontifícia Universidade Católica de São Paulo. Her research focuses on the dress histories of the African diaspora in Brazil. As a scholar, she collaborates with groups dedicated to fashion history, women's studies, and dress and textile research. She has served as fashion curator at the Museu de Arte de São Paulo Assis Chateaubriand.

Regina A. Root is an international expert on fashion studies and Full Professor of Modern Languages and Literatures at William & Mary, USA. She has authored, edited and co-edited various works, including *The Latin American Fashion Reader* (2005), *Couture and Consensus: Fashion and Politics in Nineteenth-Century Argentina* (2010), *The Handbook of Fashion Studies* (2013), and *Pasado de Moda. Expresiones culturales y consumo en la Argentina* (2016). She is the series co-editor, with Hazel Clark, of the *Fashion In Action* series with Bloomsbury Visual Arts.

Edward Salazar Celis is a doctoral candidate in Latin American and Latino Studies at the University of California, Santa Cruz, USA. He is a writer, cultural critic, and educator based in California, specializing in Latinx and Latin American arts, fashion, and visual cultures. His work straddles public humanities and academia, focusing on colonial legacies, class and race politics, history, and archives of Latinx and Latin American fashion and culture. He has authored *Nostalgias y Aspiraciones* (2021) and *Estudios de la Moda en Colombia* (2022).

Stephanie N. Saunders is Associate Professor of Spanish at Lyon College, USA. She was a Researcher in Residence at the Pontificia Universidad Católica de Chile. She has published articles and book chapters in five countries and four languages on research focusing on body studies, space studies, migration, and identity. She is the author of *Fashion, Gender and Agency in Latin American and Spanish Literature* (2021) and the novel *Covered Buttons*.

Kedron Thomas is Associate Professor of Anthropology at the University of Delaware, USA. She is the author of *Regulating Style: Intellectual Property Law and the Business of Fashion in Guatemala* (2016). Her current research interests include labor ethics, environmental sustainability, and ongoing intellectual property debates in global fashion.

Tamara J. Walker is Associate Professor of Africana Studies at Barnard College, Columbia University, USA. Her research interests focus on slavery, gender, and racial formation in Latin America, their legacies in the modern era, and global Black mobility. She is the author, most recently, of *Beyond the Shores: A History of African Americans Abroad* (2023). Her first book, *Exquisite Slaves: Race, Clothing, and Status in Colonial Lima* (2017), won the 2018 Harriet Tubman Prize. She is currently working on a book on whiteness in Latin American visual culture, and a history of slavery and piracy in the Southern Pacific.

Acknowledgments

The vision for *The New Latin American Fashion Reader* started several years ago, and such an admirable amount of support and grit has gone into its completion. Frances Arnold and her team of professionals at Bloomsbury have showed great patience and encouragement during an entire process that even spanned a global pandemic. We would like to thank Hayes Pearce and Alliny Maia Cabral for early administrative support with this project. We are grateful to Heather Dubnick and Natalya Kaza for their editorial support and to Colton Strader and Sarah Williams for continued technical support. Margaret Maynard's insightful feedback tightened our introduction. The thorough and timely feedback of our reviewers helped strengthen this project overall and ushered in other valuable perspectives. We are grateful to William & Mary and Lyon College for their support of this project.

Earlier fragments of Chapters 11 and 13 were published previously and respectively as "Recrear una conciencia social: Reciclar/reapropiar la moda en *Loco afán: crónicas de sidario* de Pedro Lemebel" (2013). *Taller de Letras*: 99–108 and as "Fragmentos culturales e identidades recicladas," Buenos Aires: Ampersand, 2017. We are thankful to the editors for the permission to reproduce facets of earlier research in translation.

We are grateful to our talented authors who encountered no small number of obstacles while working on this project, among those, a pandemic. May the spirit of collaboration and reimagining persevere as we encounter new waves of approaching fashion, and in turn, ourselves.

Our families, and in particular our partners Giuseppe Pandolfi-de-Rinaldis and Theodore Martin, have brought us good cheer and loving hope at the times when we perhaps needed it most.

Finally, dear reader, thank you for your thoughtful readings and insights you are sure to inspire.

Introduction: Reimagining Rupture and Repair

Stephanie N. Saunders and Regina A. Root

With its publication in 2005, *The Latin American Fashion Reader* began a collaborative movement to establish a more diverse and inclusive fashion register, bringing about critical explorations of historical foundations, altered cultural landscapes, ever-expanding cultural imageries, and the potential develop a more comprehensive understanding of consumption trends. The creation of multiple jobs across the globe that move these concepts forward are also finding new platforms and outlets that have amplified Latin American fashion's presence on an international stage. At the same time, an emphasis on decolonization and increased representation, political upheavals and resistance, profound climate change and a global pandemic have necessitated new ways to consider Latin American fashion's historical traditions and celebrated moments. With renewed creativity, this book explores how interdisciplinary scholars are reimagining some of the scholarly questions being posed as well as the complications that might be generated by the mere act of being a fashion scholar at this juncture.

When reimagining Latin American fashion, we might ask: How do we make meaningful design and scholarly contributions when faced with emergencies that have only magnified the many inequities of local spaces and global places? What gaps can we bridge when we find borders and disciplinary boundaries closing in on us? Having experienced challenges to our craft and scholarly pursuits, some of which are detailed here, the co-authors of this book share experiences, ideas, and knowledge, offering entry points into scholarship on Latin American fashion studies for a reader who seeks to enter the conversation and continue to build upon and reinvigorate the field.

New fashion imaginaries have long been central to diverse events throughout the Americas. Politics, fashion studies, sustainability, science and technology, innovation and education are some of the important networks facilitated by the Latin American creative industries marketplace, especially under its recent umbrella of IXEL Moda. This congress, in turn, has brought together numerous entities like design programs and universities, artisan-focused and graphic design workshops, research and business trends, social media and digital journalism, as well as administrative and diplomatic ties. Through these networks, an increasingly hemispheric approach to the innovation process guides cultural heritage tourism and diversity and inclusion initiatives. With the support of Latin American design institutions, a call for the inaugural Latin American Academic Council of Fashion[1] helped develop and ground the future of fashion studies research within its intersections of the circular economy, human rights and activism, individual and social transformation, ethics and aesthetics in fashion education, cultural appropriation and decolonization, new materials and disruptive models, bio and nano technologies and craft. With its "Manifesto of Cartagena," the Council drafted collaboratively and signed an agreement on Indigenous Peoples Day or October 12, 2019, in Cartagena de Indias, Colombia, to work towards hemispheric unity and sustainability amidst a design crisis.

The manifesto explained that the gathering's purpose unites Latin American voices in the design sectors of fashion, clothing, dress, and textiles to generate new regional imaginaries. "Understanding that we are faced with urgent challenges that require adaptive change and which will impact the training of professionals and their roles in the industry, whether in the present or future," the collective identifies three urgent objectives.[2] First, it represents an ever-expanding international network that highlights scholarly collaborations and contributions and aims to transcend borders. Second, the manifesto maintains that dialogue among members in academia, business, and society at large involves tackling current challenges in the fashion industry. Finally, this network and dialogue serve as a platform for the transfer and creation of knowledge. The years of conscientious thought and organization gained the support of design programs worldwide.

In 2020, as the world reeled with new working and living realities brought on by the COVID-19 pandemic, IXEL Moda experienced a seemingly impossible challenge: In the face of despair, should its congress for the creative industries be canceled? After all, with the new imposed blurring of private and public boundaries—brought on in part, by a Zoom boom—those with the possibility of working remotely now only had to curate their upper torso for meetings and social gatherings. Moreover, attendance options, such as "camera off" mode, allowed one to forego any fashion choices whatsoever. Companies scrambled to reassess luxury leisurewear as consumers vowed to ditch the constraints of office wear forever. As millions worried about plunging economies, unemployment, the deaths of loved ones, and a dearth of childcare, fashion appeared far from a central concern for most. Yet, IXEL Moda did not allow these dizzying realities to deter the internationally attended spaces they had cultivated over the last decade for designers and disciplines alike. Instead, as we detail, IXEL Moda worked tirelessly to move its congress to a phygital platform, allowing for increased global participation and dialogue, a sense of belonging, and creativity, at a time in which the world needed such a model for radical hope (Root & Saunders 2021).

This book, too, has built upon the foundations of a new field of knowledge, connecting an international group of scholars whose research reflected upon the past, lived fully in the present, and looked ahead to the future through visual analysis, material culture analysis, discourse analysis, and auto-ethnography. Latin American fashion reimagined itself and new ways of being and acting during this global crisis.

In other ways, the social, gender, and ethnic inequalities that were highlighted during the pandemic brought to the forefront many of the issues discussed in this book. Yet, we recognize that these are not the final word on the state-of-the-state. In *On Decoloniality*, Catherine E. Walsh observes shifts in decolonial thought and suggests, "Decoloniality, in this sense, is not a static condition, an individual attribute, or a lineal point of arrival or enlightenment. Instead, decoloniality seeks to make visible, open, and advance radically distinct perspectives and positionalities that displace Western rationality as the only framework and possibility of existence, analysis, and thought" (2018, 17). We acknowledge the rise of fashion as a marker for the Western entry into modernity (Saunders 2021, 18). According to Walsh, "Coloniality is constitutive, not derivative, of modernity. That is to say, there is no modernity without coloniality, thus the compound expression: *modernity/coloniality*" (2018, 4).

In a parallel vein to the rise in fashion demarcating a rise in modernity, and as Walsh articulates, modernity could not have existed without coloniality, one may consider the rapid speed of fashion cycles, as dependent on colonial models, since much of the fashion industry has outsourced garment production to post-colonial regions, resulting in a model of fashion/modernity/coloniality. To position ourselves within this argument, in this way, and echoing Mary Louise Pratt's charge in *Planetary Longings* "humans must reimagine themselves as 'planetary subjects' rather than 'global agents'" (2022, 10), our book projects the field of Latin American fashion studies into what has become a communal conversation.

In *Rethinking Fashion Globalization*, Cheang, Takagi, and de Greef address the need to reimagine matters of influence beyond a single scholar (1). The authors note the impact of the COVID-19 pandemic, climate-related crisis, and racial tensions and manifestations as catalyzing decolonializing debates, resulting in "a re-imagining and rewriting of the fashion system enforced by the various social, economic, cultural and economic impacts of the pandemic" (6). In *The New Latin American Fashion Reader*, we reimagine rupture and repair, or echoing Cheang, Takagi, and de Greef's call to engage with decolonial dialogues, reconsider Latin America's fashion landscape through a polyphonic discourse across geographical and generational demarcations.

For the ease of sparking what we hope will become an ongoing conversation, we have divided this book into four parts.

Part 1: Archival Considerations

Our first section takes us to the archives to re-examine how we interact with historical artifacts, what role the digital humanities might play, and how fashion may reconsider silenced voices and its terms of representation. Rita Morais de Andrade foregrounds the discussion in the tangible: How can we prioritize conservation and public access when the very beginnings of fashion archives seem compromised? After fires ravaged the National Museum of Brazil in 2018, a national call for donations to build new representative collections has inevitably offered hope, spurred debate, and altered the way in which fashion history itself might be represented. The COVID-19 pandemic placed the role of archives in the spotlight as researchers found themselves with limited access to physical documents. Rita Morais de Andrade presents us with a theoretical argument in defense of archives, even if decreased fiscal importance has threatened collections at large. Archives can take us through the interwoven stories that make up Latin American fashion history. Despite the presence of archival material, dating to the colonial period when the vigorous activity of gathering materials occurred, such categorization often resulted in the prejudicially nuanced telling of the dominant histories. Through Brazil's creation of fashion archival history, Andrade reminds us that "archives matter," and argues for a renewed commitment to a decolonizing of the archives past, present, and future.

Decolonization and the reconsideration of Eurocentrism remain at the forefront of Latin American studies. Catholic reliquary lockets, known in Spanish as *medallones relicarios*, celebrate a renewed interest in religious and commercial settings. Alison Napier explores the religious and identity-bearing implications for these intimate jewelry pieces. Considering meaning and media, Napier breaks the mold by casting Eurocentric interpretations aside to decolonize contemporary scholarship of these beloved pieces that forged native survivance alongside Catholic imagery. The Manila shawl, which Inés Corujo-Martín traces through the complex interpretations among fashion historians, emerges from Eastern roots to become fashionable in Spain and then becomes infused with further meaning in colonial and nineteenth-century Mexico. Corujo-Martín points out the hybrid nature of the garment, a perfect alchemy of Asian, pre-Columbian, European, and Hispano-Arabic exchanges. The author's reading of this well-known artifact brings to the discussion concerns such as cultural appropriation and exchange while prying into open questions of reconfiguration of the complexity of fashion objects in relation to national, racialized, and gendered identities.

The ruana—an emblematic clothing item in Colombian history consisting of a square piece with the neck slit—can trace its roots to the colonial period as a discursive interplay of colonial identity. Edward Salazar Celis accompanies us through the ruana's centuries-long, contested history. In particular, this chapter situates the article in men's fashion, recognizing the ways in which racialized men have celebrated the garment over time. Salazar Celis explores the self-fashioning and contested power of the ruana, in the face of eugenics policies outlined in the 1777 Ordinance of the Viceroy of Nueva Granada, its visual tensions with nineteenth-century projects of identity, and Jorge Eliécer Gaitán's presidential candidacy in the 1930s. Salazar Celis weaves the garment's importance throughout the twenty-first century, centering Indigenous creative labor and recognizing design projects that have reimagined the ruana as a powerful tool for both individual and collective identity.

María A. Cabrera Arús returns us to 1959 and the years leading up to the special period of 1989. While the lasting effects of the Cuban Revolution preoccupied scholars for over six decades, Cabrera Arús's thorough dive into the nationalization of department stores and fashion boutiques, alongside a rationing system uncovers and classifies the connotations of fashion brands listed in the Cuban Bureau of Industrial Property (OCPI)'s trademarks registry under the class 25 of the system of Nice, during a 30-year time span, from 1959 to 1989. Cabrera Arús delves into the powerful semiotic sword involved in naming, and provides us with the, at times, ironic twists involved in furthering a nationalist agenda.

Archival considerations provide rich visual analysis and material culture analysis across time and location by reconsidering some of the more studied of dress articles—such as the Manila shawl—while championing lesser studied articles such as the ruana and Catholic reliquary lockets. As Morais de Andrade reminds us, there is an autobiographical element to a researcher's approximation to physical and digital archives, oftentimes prompting us to revisit the powerful— and perhaps overlooked—representations that await us there.

Part 2: Culture's Empowering Lens

Our next section foregrounds the historical increase in access to photography and literary magazines as powerful tools for reaching Latin American audiences, in turn, influencing local and global perceptions of the diverse region. Alliny Maia Cabral explores photography as a means to upend the systematic invisibility of representations of Afro-Brazilian women of the nineteenth century. Through Aníbal Quijano's theory of coloniality and Nicholas Mirzoeff's approach to visuality, Cabral examines a collection of photos of Bahian women created by Spanish photographer Rafael Castro y Ordóñez to reflect on the ways in which Afro-Brazilians were stereotyped in terms of femininity, as well as the agency embedded in the act of dressing. In particular, the author analyzes various photos of *quitandeiras*, or women working as street vendors. This chapter acknowledges the problematic nature of such photography, often deemed as travel photography, steeped in the nineteenth-century obsession with categorization and in cataloging difference, as well as the nebulous means by which consent to photography was granted. In this way, Cabral highlights the societal expectations of pose, dress, and appearance as a means of control.

Tamara J. Walker analyzes the enduring use of polka-dots alongside the visual representations of Afro-Peruvian women. Beginning with A.A. Bonnaffé's nineteenth-century *costumbrista* works, this chapter takes us on a sartorial history of a clothing pattern that paralleled societal expectations of women of African ancestry, namely the depiction of women employed for domestic services. Walker laces this visual thread throughout the twentieth century when advertisements in Peru began to mirror those of the United States with nostalgic views, namely dressing formerly enslaved and descendants in polka dots, and attempting to confine female Afro-Peruvians to domestic subordination. In twenty-first-century representations, however, Afro-Peruvian populations have exemplified the centrality of their agency with the polka-dot dresses worn during traditional dances.

Alba F. Aragón explores the possibilities of the women's fashion magazine *Elegancias* (Elegances), published in Paris between 1911 and 1914. Its focus was a Latin American readership, and its literary editor was none other than the Nicaraguan poet Rubén Darío, founding figure of *modernismo*, Spanish America's first literary movement. Despite a rather dismissive attitude towards this publication, in part because of its focus on women's fashion, Aragón considers *Elegancias* as a discursive medium for positioning Latin America within the imaginary of Western modernity. The author navigates the paradoxical nature of the content, in part heavily steeped within the promotion of *modernismo* and fashion, a marker of modernity, to a female readership, and at the same time portraying women's growing role within the public sphere as a "dangerous" trend. Aragón encourages readers to consider formerly dismissed visual mediums as a means of exploring conflicting ideologies of the time.

Continuing with the medium of photography, Hanayrá Negreiros reflects on her access to a wealth of family pictures, deeming such a collection as a luxury in the face of Brazil's colonial history which deprived Black peoples of historical placement and voice. The author's grandmother, a seamstress in the 1950s, celebrated sewing as an act of creativity, and the author shares her deeply rooted relationship with clothing. The family narrative allows a dialectic site of clothing and dressing as spaces for inherited identity. Negreiros centers this analysis on the impact of scholars whose work on photography, clothing, race, and gender can serve as important pathways to broaden narratives on the African diaspora in Brazil.

Throughout this section, we see the potential of visual mediums as facilitators of culture and societal perceptions. While the nineteenth century brought increased access to photography and, in some societal circles, literary magazines, in the twenty-first century the proliferation of social media reinforced the links between fashion and image. Our next section explores how dress and fashion become vital creative expressions during times of crisis.

Part 3: Social Unrest and Resistance

Foregrounded in femme theory and transnational, queer, and fashion studies, María Claudia Andre considers resistant sites of power in fashion and femininity within the Bolivian Quechuan and Aymara women, in particular, among the *cholas* or *cholitas*. The author tackles the theoretical complexities involved in gender and sexuality, and underlines the resistance harnessed by *cholitas* and their challenge of gender roles in terms of lifestyle, motherhood, and engagement in sports and professions traditionally considered masculine. Andre examines the importance of dynamic fashion and dress choices that mark region, class, and personal style. Despite increased social and political agency and earning power, *cholitas* experience systematic discrimination. Andre examines the resistance to thrive and enter an array of political realms as a model for inventive ways of considering gender and body expressions.

Undeterred by violence and limited professional choices, fashion has often provided trans communities in Latin America with not only a creative outlet and livelihood, but also a means to increase representation and resist societal injustices. Stephanie N. Saunders offers a reconsideration of the urban chronicles of Chilean writer, performance artist, and activist Pedro Lemebel, whose depictions of the *loca* community permit a backdrop for questioning the used clothes industry. In particular, coveted haute couture items, violence against trans communities, and the AIDS epidemic ultimately springboard us to fashion's role in trans resistance throughout the twenty-first century.

In October 2019, what might seem like a brief slice of time, after an increase in the value of the Metro fare in Santiago, Chile, a three-month succession of protests shook the capital. Pía Montalva reveals the dialectic dance between officials and protesters whose dress and accessories transformed in response to societal messages and violence. This chapter highlights the artistry and design, oftentimes self-crafted, by demonstrators. Montalva underlines the interweaving of gender empowerment—one perhaps reminiscent of the pots-and-pans demonstrations representing the food shortages of the 1970s and subsequent *arpillera* workshops for the creation of shared patchwork tapestries—found through clothing, design, community, and activism.

Wrestling with design interventions that value a larger social fabric, Regina A. Root unravels the role of fashion and dress as meaning during authoritarianism and as reimagined through reconstructions of the past and recycled clothing, or fragments of found or unexpected or anonymous textiles. Growing out of earlier writings that connect style and human rights, Root looks to the role of Argentine fashion as a way of linking shared experience and a larger social collective concerned with economic inequalities, the loss of cultural identity and an ever more urgent ecological crisis.

At the beginning of the twentieth century, dandyism in Colombia experienced a wave of social scorn—especially among chroniclers such as Romualdo

Gallego—when industrialization and urbanization ushered in more urban attire and detailed self-expression among men. William Cruz-Bermeo revisits the figure of the twentieth-century dandy, highlighting the social resistance involved in dressing outside of societal norms. The author follows representations of these fashion-ready men to the presence of the late-twentieth-century and early-twenty-first-century reggaetoneros, with whom the author weaves a connective thread for their newfound urban fashions—frequently pushing socially prescribed gendered norms—and in the process, resisting and redefining subcultural styles and urban fashion that, as the author explores, celebrated global reach.

During times of social unrest and resistance in Latin America—from times of protest, to concerns of environmental devastation or violence against gender—fashion and dress bolster alternate, creative outlets for discourse and self-expression. Our final section highlights the personal and collective agency that has emerged from global crisis and, with the closing of borders and some of the most draconian lockdowns to follow, the COVID-19 pandemic. It is uncertain how fashion and dress history will integrate the sense of urgency many felt was a larger design crisis: From the taking back of centuries-old dress designs by local Indigenous groups to an exploration of how to integrate native botanical prints and dyes into one's small apartments. Design thinking that had been appropriated by the global corporate apparatus as if a colonial enterprise, even taught as a subject in prominent business schools in the Global North as if to harness economically the value of an international designer's autonomy for risk-taking, unexpected issues and failures with which to step back and reassess creatively, seemed somehow to put a value on who owned the future. And it was this call the "Manifesto of Cartagena" had sought to remedy for academic institutions and designer education until the pandemic magnified much larger issues.

Part 4: Creative and Collective Agency

In early 2020, the face mask became a constant wardrobe addition—whether by choice or obligation—across the globe. Andrea A. Gaytán Cuesta takes us to Mexico, examining the cultural history of masks from pre-colonial times to today. The author highlights masks as a metaphor for Mexican character as found in renowned essays by Octavio Paz and Carlos Monsiváis. The masked appearances of prominent *luchadores libres*, or pro-wrestlers, made public health messages a source of entertainment and education in the media. Gaytán Cuesta also explores the message-laden layers of mask-wearing and production, such as the shift of Indigenous communities' focus on tourist-driven markets for clothing and other wearables to artisanal masks. Masks inspired by the Zapatista movement (a guerrilla movement in southern Mexico in the twentieth century, named after the Mexican Revolutionary hero, Emiliano Zapata) also appear to have signified solidarity non-verbally. The author concludes with the increased focus on green labels, socially responsible brands, and the reconsideration of local production as a source of survival and expression.

Tanya Meléndez-Escalante explores fashion discourse through the provocative collections by Brenda Equihua, Víctor Barragán, and Ricardo Seco. These brands encompass the shared lived experiences of transnational and transethnic boundaries. In particular, the author applies the chicanx-term *rascuache*—usually involving negative connotations of poverty and a lack of choices regarding high style—to the aesthetic choices of Equihua, Barragán, and Seco who infuse their designs with rich, cultural imagery, in the face of racism and misrepresentation. Meléndez-Escalante's firsthand conversations with the designers transport the reader to an exciting design frontier in which borders are not merely crossed but also celebrated.

Kedron Thomas offers an insightful analysis of the ongoing fight for intellectual property rights on the part of the National Movement of Maya Weavers in Guatemala. Colorful traditional textiles that are traded in Guatemala's local markets, used by the national government to attract tourism, and taken up as inspiration by international designers, are typically created by women. In this way, the author contends, the Movement's legal concerns are also an issue of Indigenous rights and women's rights. Thomas describes the injustice of anti-Indigenous racism and patriarchy that shapes the textile trade and limits Maya women's earnings for their creations, some of which require up to three months of intense labor and expertise to produce. In analyzing the collective efforts of Maya weavers to resist deepening inequalities and assert legal and economic control over their creative work, specifying a compelling model for "the fight for Indigenous women's rights across Latin America."

The COVID-19 pandemic marked most conceivable areas of life across the globe. Textile and fashion industries navigated worker and product shortages, cancellations, and shifts in consumer needs that during the beginning stages of the pandemic lauded loungewear of bottoms-optional due to an endless stream of virtual experiences. Maria Carolina Garcia closes this collaborative book with a home-grown initiative called The Flower Punchers, "which weaves luxurious

Brazilian nature, ancestral textile techniques, garbage debris, soothing sounds of music, and cutting-edge technology into meaningful experiences." During the global pandemic, when many embraced creative endeavors to overcome fear and isolation, interactive workshops crossed national borders and reimagined an outlet to connect as community, a process that continues today. This sustainable project encouraged participants to recycle and reuse plants and textiles around them, and once printed, the author would lay out augmented realities, hybrid models, and even the metaverse to "enable biodiversity to thrive through technology."

The New Latin American Fashion Reader reimagines rupture and repair and posits scholarly roles within a dynamic storytelling process, much like thinking and writing itself. Seen in this light, unpacking single sentences becomes a profound act that may be as political as they are cultural. When we began this book, many of us were unknown to one another and have ended this book as friends. We are grateful for this time to reflect and learn together. With an ambitious eighteen chapters, we are still humbly aware that many alternative research paths lie ahead, from facilitating the body with border-jumping tennis shoes that tie themselves, to scientifically created textiles that protect the human form in space. Since we connect in different ways now, and a few of us did in real time with artificial multi-dimensional form and style, perhaps it is indeed the moment for *The New Latin American Fashion Reader*.

Notes

1 This call by the Latin American Academic Council of Fashion, which unites Latin American design schools, programs, and universities in the wake of massive change, was co-authored by Carolina Agudelo, Adriana Betancur, Maria Carolina Garcia, Laura Novik, and Regina A. Root.
2 Translated from the original: "Comprendiendo que enfrentamos con urgentes desafíos que requieren la adaptación al cambio y que afectarán a la formación de profesionales y su actuación en el sector, en el presente y con mirada prospectiva."

Bibliography

Cheang, Sarah, Erica De Greef, and Yōko Takagi. 2021. *Rethinking Fashion Globalization*. London & New York: Bloomsbury Visual Arts.

Concilio Académico de Instituciones de Moda. 2019. "Manifiesto de Cartagena." Cartagena de Indias, Colombia.

Mignolo, Walter D. 2018. *On Decoloniality: Concepts, Analytics, Praxis*, edited by Walter D. Mignolo and Catherine E. Walsh. Durham: Duke University Press.

Pratt, Mary Louise. 2022. *Planetary Longings*. Durham: Duke University Press.

Root, Regina A. 2005. *The Latin American Fashion Reader*, edited by Regina A. Root. Oxford: Berg.

Root, Regina A. and Stephanie N. Saunders. 2021. "Refashioning Collaborations: Crossing Border During the Pandemic." *MARLAS* 5 (1) June: 88–96.

Saunders, Stephanie N. 2021. *Fashion, Gender and Agency in Latin American and Spanish Literature*. Woodbridge, Suffolk, UK: Tamesis.

Walsh, Catherine E. 2018. *On Decoloniality: Concepts, Analytics, Praxis*, edited by Walter D. Mignolo and Catherine E. Walsh. Durham: Duke University Press.

Part 1

Archival Considerations

1

Archives Matter: Dress Histories from Brazilian Archives

Rita Morais de Andrade

One can never quite imagine the impact of the loss of two major historical museums. The Paulista Museum of the University of São Paulo closed its doors to the public in 2013, as its building was in danger of collapse. The museum reopened with a modernized and expanded building in 2022, in celebration of Brazil's independence from Portugal. The destruction by fire of the National Museum, a 200-year-old building containing a collection of twenty million historical and scientific artifacts, housed a significant collection of pre-Columbian textiles. A campaign to rebuild this museum's collections with donations from individuals and institutions, as this site experiences renovations, represents a foreseeable future born out of devastation and crisis to create a full Brazilian and global register (Kellner 2021). The Iny-Karajá peoples,[1] among the first to respond to this call, have viewed their visibility in museums as a strategy to combat cultural erasure. In this renewed effort to transcend the profound loss portrayed by the press as a national tragedy, there emerge pathways for greater participation in curatorial decisions, which present new, more dialogical relationships that offer valuable opportunities for learning. (Duarte Cândido 2013). New venues for examining Brazil's dress history through a decolonial lens ultimately demonstrate that archives do matter—a point this chapter aims to explore.

The development of public archives and museums in Brazil, and Latin America more widely, has deep historical roots dating back to the colonial period and reflects both European and local influences. During colonization, the need to record administrative, legal, and religious aspects of the colonies led to the creation of public archives to store official documents, while the first museums were influenced by European national museums and cabinets of curiosities. With the process of independence and the consolidation of nation-states, these institutions became integral to nation-building and the preservation of historical memory. Such is the case of the National Museum, one of the oldest and most important institutions, founded in 1818 in Rio de Janeiro, with significant collections in natural history, anthropology, and ethnography. In 1838, the establishment of the National Historical Archive marked the beginning of a central repository for Brazilian govermental documents related to administrative records, royal decrees and Brazil's independence. It was followed by the founding of the Paulista Museum in 1895, which concentrated on preserving and documenting São Paolo's history and culture, now featuring collections that span from Brazil's independence to artifacts that tell us about daily life in the colonial and imperial periods. Although these institutions underwent a modernization and expansion process in the twentieth and early twenty-first centuries, they continue to face challenges such as the need for more inclusive representation and insufficient funding, all while striving to become more dynamic and accessible spaces for researchers and the general public.

Black and Indigenous peoples[3] and their dress histories are frequently overlooked or misrepresented in mainstream culture. These histories are often reduced to a single, dominant narrative, as Adichie (2014) points out. Krenak (2019)[4] further highlights the colonial legacy of museums and archives, which perpetuate Eurocentric views and suppress diverse cultural expressions. Fashion, in this context, is a complex tool. It can be used as a means of domination, as traditional dress is often appropriated and commodified. However, it can also be a powerful tool of resistance, allowing marginalized groups to reclaim their cultural identity and challenge oppressive norms.

In his September 4, 1987, speech during the Constituent Assembly, Krenak was forbidden to dress in the manner of his people. He then wore a conventional Western-style suit and painted his face with genipap tint, a traditional pigment extracted from fruit, in an act many would consider provocative and performative.

Archives and museums have historically failed to systematically preserve diverse forms of dress—whether Indigenous or not—as records of national identity and cultural heritage. Furthermore, European art collecting practices led to the expatriation of Brazil's cultural assets. During the colonial period (1500–1822), many culturally valuable objects, such as artifacts, artworks, and historical documents, were taken through various means, including pillaging during military conquests, unequal trade exchanges, scientific expeditions, and even through coercive and violent practices. The expatriation of cultural assets had profound impacts on Brazil's Indigenous communities, resulting in the loss of a significant part of their cultural and historical heritage. Many of these cultural assets were incorporated into private and institutional collections in Europe, often without proper acknowledgment of their origin and significance to their communities of origin. The expatriation of cultural assets is an important part of the colonial legacy and has been the subject of contemporary debates and efforts for the repatriation and preservation of Indigenous cultural heritage (Oyarce ed. 2013; Tello 2017; Saldaña and Goñi 2019). Two recent events demonstrate this well. Brazilian Indigenous ceramic dolls called *ritxoko*, dressed in Indigenous but also Westernized fashions, have been identified and located in Portuguese, French, German, and US archives by a multicultural and multidisciplinary research project called "Karajá Presence" (Duarte Cândido et al. 2021). One Tupinambá cloak, which has been housed at Denmark's National Museum since the seventeenth century, considered an *Encantado* (an ancestral) to the Tupinambá people of Brazil, has been successfully repatriated following extensive negotiations. Brazilian Indigenous activist and artist Glicélia Tupinambá, through her performance art, played a key role in facilitating the return of the seventeenth-century Tupinambá traditional cloak, known as the Tupinambá cloak (*Assojaba* in the native language), from the Nationalmuseet in Denmark to Brazil in 2024 (Silva 2024).

When the National Museum of Brazil went up in flames in 2018, the loss of the dress archives was utterly devastating. With the global COVID-19 pandemic that followed, the pivotal role these museum collections had played in reconstructing diverse dress archives were only accentuated. Efforts to diversify and digitize collections gained renewed significance as these addressed colonialism and modernization, among others, as temporal categories and spatial markers within museums. This fashion history archive seemed a more dynamic space through which to engage historical, anthropological, and ethnographic perspectives. Proposing a paradigm shift, this archive advocated a set of proactive measures to fortify its fashion register, emphasizing the resilience and diversity of collections. Part of these collections were poorly documented as gathered, which does not allow for an accurate view of the formational history of textile and dress collections (Andrade 2016).

While there is no standardized framework for archive-based research in fashion studies, the utilization of archival material is gaining significant traction. Lou Taylor (2002, 2004) details how the systematic use of different archival and museum materials contribute to advancing and consolidating this research field. The approaches vary from the typology of objects to the research methodology, and thus, she lists perspectives based on artifacts; visual analysis of paintings, drawings, cartoons, photographs, and films; economic and social history, ethnography, and the use of literary sources, all unique ways in which to engage sound methodological research. *Understanding Fashion History* (Cumming 2004) complements this view, locating the origins of fashion history as a field and highlighting the creation of clothing collections in seventeenth-century English museums as a foundational aspect. Daniela Calanca (2019) discusses the making of Italian fashion history and historiography by assessing archival material dating from 1911 to 1961 from the Archivio Istituto Luce online. Valerie Steele (1998) argues that a museum of fashion has a rationale that transcends and cannot be compared to fashion shopping. Amanda Vickery (1994) enlightens the field with a detailed account of a woman's inventory of eighteenth-century England. Lesley Miller (2017) offers a perspective of object-based research in her biography of Balenciaga culled from the designer's business archives. *The Handbook of Fashion Studies* (2013, 231–346) dedicates a section to material culture —"Fashion and Materiality"— in which artifacts become part of an investigative methodology of great potential, highlighting its inseparability from immateriality as a research problem. Isabel Alvarado Perales and Verónica Guajardo Rives (2018) have long worked from the dress collections of Museo Histórico Nacional de Chile with a particular interest in women's fashions from the nineteenth century, while Teresa Cristina Toledo de Paula (2006) has addressed the nature and origin of the textiles collection and conservation sector at the Paulista Museum. Lastly, I recall working at Casa Mappin's business archives in São Paulo in the 1990s and could never imagine that a private archive would be acquired by Museu Paulista's library decades later (Andrade 2005). Articles, book chapters and *Dissertações de Mestrado and Teses* have been foregrounded in research based on archival materials and museum collections.[5] Since the origin of fashion and dress studies, the use of these materials in understanding and assessing historical perspectives has been paramount.

Making these historical materials accessible from Brazilian archives creates the potential to challenge and reshape fashion history and historiography. The oldest book published in Brazilian Portuguese on the history of fashion is *Três Séculos de Moda* by João Affonso (1923); it is unclear whether or not the author used archival materials. The book's illustrations do not have accompanying captions or references and are perhaps based on images from other fashion histories—common practice in publications of the time (Tétart-Vittu 2009, 6–15). Sophia Jobim, founder of the Chair of History of Costume at the Escola Nacional de Belas Artes in Rio de Janeiro of the 1950s, appears to be the first Brazilian researcher to publish on the significance of archives and museum collections. In an open class in 1960, she stated that Brazil stood in need of the collections it required for a comprehensive study of its costume and dress history (1960, 169–176). In that same period, Gilda de Mello e Souza (1951) defended at the University of São Paulo what became a seminal work on the history of nineteenth-century Brazilian fashion, using photographs from different public and private archives, which would take thirty more years to see print (Mello e Souza 1987).

While the subject of Brazilian fashion history and archives became ostracized between the 1960s and early 1980s, publications in the 1970s and 1980s stayed close to the history of the textile and clothing industries and the topic of Brazilian identity. Stanley Stein's work that had been published in English in 1957 was translated as *Origens e evolução da indústria têxtil no Brasil, 1850–1950* (1979). Gilberto Freyre, a Brazilian anthropologist, published *Modos de Homem and Modas de Mulher* in 1987. Both works would integrate documents from company archives and personal objects, though without an accessible or accurate record of research references. As Brazilian universities inaugurated fashion and design courses for undergraduates in the 1990s and early 2000s, educational materials were composed largely of translated titles, many of which are still in use today, such as James Laver's *Costume and Fashion: A Concise History* (1969) and François Boucher's *History of Costume in the West: From the Origins to the Present Day* (1987).

Given the pivotal role of archives, researchers revisit their significance in Brazilian dress and fashion histories. Problematizing these collections and their utilization from a decolonial standpoint has caused researchers to adopt a more dialogical and inclusive approach, particularly towards Black and Indigenous communities. Embracing inclusivity has allowed researchers to foster a more diverse internationalization of the field and, as implied in this book's title, to establish a critical framework for reimagining Latin American fashion. Numerous obstacles have often hindered the archival and museum-based research process in Brazil, reflecting challenges in other regions worldwide, where dress and fashion archives have been erratic and fragmented when viewed through a Western-centric lens of collection.[6] Understanding the archival organization and categorization has been vital for researchers investigating dress and fashion in Brazil. Through the study of these dress collections and their construction, researchers have addressed issues of social and cultural representation, while also examining inconsistencies in terminology contributing to the invisibility of dress within museum contexts (Andrade 2016). One Indigenous feathered vest from the National Museum, for instance, had been considered and documented in the museum files as featherwork,[7] not as dress, clothing, or vest. Ribeiro (1994) explains that locating dress can represent a significant feat. One relevant problem is that the concept of dress and its meanings and functions can vary across cultures.

The creation and consolidation of Brazilian archives and museums accelerated in the twentieth century. The nationalism and nationalist motivation at the root of these events ran through independent countries. Initiatives to strengthen Brazilian cultural heritage as a way of consolidating a national identity became evident during the first half of the twentieth century, though rarely mentioning dress and fashion (Fragelli 2020). Nonetheless, the first attempts to collect dress in a systematic way are traceable back to the 1940s and 1950s. Such is the case of Museu do Traje e Indumentária de Salvador, Bahia, and Sophia Jobim's assessments, currently housed in the National Historical Museum, Rio de Janeiro, which include drawings, books, and dress.[8] Similarly, the Paulista Museum holds historical dress and a range of related documents such as photographs, diaries. and inventories, ranging from children's, women's, and military clothing from the nineteenth to twentieth centuries and objects related to the history of dressmaking.[9] Others, such as the Petrópolis Museum, house costumes of the Portuguese royal court and the Brazilian imperial family, while museums like Casa da Hera in Vassouras, Rio de Janeiro, and the Ema Klabin Museum in São Paulo showcase French haute couture. Specialized collections, such as the Museu do Traje e do Têxtil de Salvador, include rare, printed skirts from the late nineteenth and early twentieth centuries, along with wedding dresses, underwear, and children's clothing. Despite the diversity of clothing items in museums, there still needs to be a comprehensive and critical approach to their foundation and history, and a reassessment of its content in light of decolonial theories and practices. The museums' statute law (*Estatuto de Museus – Lei* 11904/09, 2009) imposed responsibilities on institutions to inventory collections—an effort that is interpreted both as a mechanism of social control over national material heritage and as a tool for promoting inclusivity and social justice.

Despite ongoing efforts, such as the those mentioned previously, multidisciplinary and intercultural work is key to determining a cohesive research methodology, as the presence, omission, alterations, and deaccessioning can reveal a prioritization of certain themes and conservation practices.[10] Archives can foster agency for individual and collective identities. They support interpersonal, intergenerational, and cross-cultural relationships by weaving together a narrative thread of stories and experiences represented by documents and objects, just as it has been done in an online exhibition on traditional dress of Iny Karajá women.[11] This narrative thread is meaningful and continually reshaped by those who work with archives and collections, their visitors, and the communities whose cultures and histories are represented in the artifacts they display and house.

Reflecting on how Brazilian fashion and dress are preserved as history in museums and archives—often out of sight—it becomes clear that Brazil's rich cultural heritage can carry multiple meanings when it comes to representation, exhibition, and conservation. As researchers apply different methodologies to explore decolonial theories within their field, archives offer a platform for cross-cultural dialogue and exchange. They also highlight the importance of objects in shaping and affirming identity and culture. (Duarte Cândido et al. 2021). If this shift in perspective is embraced as a decentering act rather than a performative one, it represents a significant reimagining of Latin American fashion—one that highlights the need for inclusive and diverse representations in the discourse surrounding cultural identity and heritage.

Acknowledgements

The author acknowledges the support of PROAP/CAPES through the Postgraduate Program in Art and Visual Culture at the Federal University of Goiás, Brazil.

Notes

1 Iny Karajá is the denomination of Indigenous populations living today mainly in Goiás and Tocantins states in Brazil. See more on Iny Karajá dress and material culture in Andrade and Duarte Cândido (2022).
2 Archives Matter derives from "Black Lives Matter" (BLM), a social movement that originated in 2013, following the verdict of the Trayvon Martin case, a Black teenager who was killed in Florida. Its founders, Alicia Garza, Patrisse Cullors, and Opal Tometi, created the hashtag #BlackLivesMatter in response to George Zimmerman's acquittal, the man who killed Trayvon Martin. The hashtag quickly evolved into a social and political movement that seeks to highlight the violence and discrimination faced by the Black community in the United States and beyond (Leach 2022).

3 A modern understanding of race in Brazil integrates Lélia Gonzales's view (1982), emphasizing interconnected oppressions and Black community resistance. Lilia Moritz Schwarcz's perspective (2018) adds depth by exploring historical racial imagery complexities.

4 Ailton Krenak is a Brazilian Indigenous leader from the Krenak ethnic group, who mainly inhabit the region of the Rio Doce Valley in Minas Gerais, Brazil. They are part of the Macro-Jê group, which includes several Indigenous ethnicities in Brazil.

5 In Brazil, master's theses are known as dissertations and doctoral dissertations are known as theses. It is common to mistake one for the other since the order is inverted.

6 See Valerie Cumming (2004) on the history of dress collections in Europe, Teresa Cristina Toledo de Paula (2006) on textiles and its conservation in museum collections in Brazil, Rita Morais de Andrade on dress collections in Brazil (2016), and Berta Ribeiro (1994) on the lack of documentation and conservation of ethnographic and historical documents of Brazilian Indigenous cultures and ethnomuseology.

7 I saw this vest when visiting the National Museum archival storage in 2013. It is unclear whether or not the vest has been lost in the fire. I could not find information on it or locate any image, unfortunately.

8 More on this collection can be found in Volpi (2016) and on the Museu Histórico Nacional (Brasil) website available at: https://mhn.museus.gov.br/index.php/mhn-disponibiliza-online-desenhos-e-aquarelas-de-sophia-jobim/.

9 More on Museu Paulista collections can be found in Paula (2005, 2006) and Almeida (2001).

10 Deaccessioning in museums refers to the process of removing an object or artwork from a museum's permanent collection. This can occur for various reasons, such as if the object no longer aligns with the museum's mission or collecting policies, if it is found to be a duplicate or in poor condition beyond repair, or if it needs to be sold or exchanged to acquire funds or other artworks that better serve the museum's goals. Deaccessioning is typically done with careful consideration, following ethical guidelines and often involving a formal review process by the museum's curatorial and governing bodies.

11 The exhibition "Vestires: Traditional Attire of Iny Karajá Women," available at https://www.vestiresmulheresinykaraja.com/, presents an audio visual and informative content of the cultural significance, craftsmanship, and stories attached to traditional dress. The curators are both Indigenous and non-Indigenous researchers.

Bibliography

Adichie, Chimamanda N. 2014. "The Danger of a Single Story." In *We Should All Be Feminists*, 43–52. New York: Anchor Books.

Affonso, João. 1923. *Três Séculos de Modas*. Belém: Tavares Cardoso Portuguese.
Almeida, Adilson J. 2001. *Uniformes Da Guarda Nacional (1831-1852): A Indumentária na Organização e Funcionamento de uma Associação Armada*. Anais Do Museu Paulista: História E Cultura Material 8, no. 1: 77–147. doi.org/10.1590/S0101-47142001000100004.
Andrade, Rita M. 2005. "Mappin Stores: Adding an English Touch to the São Paulo Fashion Scene." In *The Latin American Fashion Reader*, edited by Regina A. Root, 176–187. 1st ed. N.p.: Berg Publishers.
Andrade, Rita M. 2016. "Indumentária no Brasil: A Invisibilidade das Coleções." *Musas* 7: 10–31.
Boucher, François. 1987. *History of Costume in the West: From the Origins to the Present Day*. New York: Thames and Hudson.
Brasil. 2009. "Estatuto dos Museus." In *Lei 11904/09*. Jusbrasil.
Calanca, Daniela. 2019. "Moda e patrimônio cultural entre imaginários sociais e práticas coletivas, na contemporaneidade." *Revista História* 1 (28): 1–28.
Cumming, Valerie. 2004. *Understanding Fashion History*. London: Batsford.
Duarte Cândido, Manuelina M. 2013. *Gestão de Museus, um Desafio Contemporâneo: à Diagnóstico Museológico e Planejamento*. 1st ed. Porto Alegre: Mediatriz.
Duarte Cândido, Manuelina M., Lu d. Mendonça, and Nei Clara Lima. 2021. *Caderno De Resumos—I Seminário Do Projeto Presença Karajá*. Goiânia: Virtual Books.
Fragelli, Pedro. 2020. *Tradição e revolução: Mário de Andrade e o patrimônio histórico e artístico nacional*. Revista do Instituto de Estudos Brasileiros 75 (April): 144–161.
Freyre, Gilberto. 1987. *Modos de homem and modas de mulher*. São Paulo: Global.
Gonzales, L. 1982. *Lugar de negro*. São Paulo: Marco Zero.
Jansen, Angela M. 2020. "Fashion and the Phantasmagoria of Modernity: An Introduction to Decolonial Fashion Discourse." *Fashion Theory* 24 (6): 815–836.
Jobim, Sophia. 1960. "Palestra da Prof.ª Sophia J. Magno de Carvalho." *Arquivos da Escola Nacional de Belas-Artes* VI (August).
Kellner, Alexander. 2021. "Apresentação do 'novo' Museu Nacional do Rio de Janeiro." YouTube: Home. https://youtu.be/heeuh8WOHwE.
Krenak, Ailton. 2019. "Discurso De Ailton Krenak, Em 04/09/1987, Na Assembleia Constituinte, Brasília, Brasil." *GIS—Gesto, Imagem e Som—Revista de Antropologia* 4 (1): 421–422. doi.org/10.11606/issn.2525-3123.gis.2019.162846.
Laver, James. 1969. *Costume and Fashion: A Concise History*. New York: Harry N. Abrams.
Leach, C.W. and Teixeira, C.P. 2022. "Understanding Sentiment Toward 'Black Lives Matter.'" *Social Issues and Policy Review* 16: 3–32. doi.org/10.1111/sipr.12084
Mello e Souza, Gilda de. 1987. *O Espírito das Roupas: A Moda no Século XIX*. São Paulo: Companhia das Letras.
Mello e Souza, Gilda R. 1951. "A moda no século XIX. Ensaio de sociologia estética." *Separata da Revista do Museu Paulista* V (5): 7–94.
Miller, Lesley E. 2017. *Balenciaga: Shaping Fashion*. London: V&A Publishing.

Oyarce, S., ed. 2013. *Arqueología, patrimonio y comunidad indígena en América Latina*. Quito: Ediciones Abya-Yala

Paula, Teresa C. 2005. "O tecido como assunto: os têxteis e a conservação nas revistas e catálogos dos museus da USP (1895–2000)." *Anais do Museu Paulista* 13: 315–371.

Paula, Teresa C. 2006. *Tecido e sua conservação no Brasil: museus e coleções*. São Paulo: Museu Paulista da Universidade de São Paulo.

Perales, Isabel A., and Verónica G. Rives. 2018. "Una metodología para el estudio de colecciones de vestuario en el Museo Histórico Nacional de Chile." *Acervo* 31 (2).

Ribeiro, Berta G. 1994. "Etnomuseologia: da coleção à exposição." *Revista do Museu de Arqueologia e Etnologia*, no. 4, 189–201.

Root, Regina A. 2013. "Mapping Latin American Fashion." In *The Handbook of Fashion Studies*, edited by Sandy Black, Joanne Entwistle, Agnes Rocomora, Regina A. Root, Helen Thomas, and Amy De La Haye, 391–407. London: Bloomsbury.

Saldaña, J. M., and Goñi, R. A. 2019. *Repatriación de bienes culturales indígenas: Conceptos, estrategias y retos en América Latina*. Santiago: Ediciones Universidad Alberto Hurtado.

Schwarcz, L. M. 2018. *Racism in Brazil: Academic Perspectives*. São Paulo: Companhia das Letras.

Silva, G. de J. da. 2024. "O Voo do Manto e o Pouso do Manto: Uma Jornada pela Memória Tupinambá em um relato sobre a exposição Manto em Movimento." *dObra[s]—revista da Associação Brasileira de Estudos de Pesquisas em Moda*, [S. l.], n. 40: 162–188. DOI: 10.26563/dobras.i40.1817.

Steele, Valerie. 1998. "A Museum of Fashion Is More Than a Clothes-Bag." *Fashion Theory* 2 (4): 327–335.

Stein, Stanley. 1979. *Origens e evolução da indústria têxtil no Brasil, 1850-1950*. Rio de Janeiro: Campus.

Taylor, Lou. 2002. *The Study of Dress History*. Manchester: Manchester University Press.

Taylor, Lou. 2004. *Establishing Dress History*. Manchester: Manchester University Press.

Tello, M. 2017. "La Repatriación de bienes culturales indígenas en América Latina: Un análisis desde la perspectiva del derecho internacional." *Revista de Derecho* 28 (2), 251–269.

Tétart-Vittu, Françoise. 2009. "Auguste Racinet´s Le Costume Historique: a monumental 19th-century achievement." In *The Costume History*, edited by Auguste Racinet, 6–15. N.p.: Taschen.

Vickery, Amanda. 1994. "Women and the world of goods: a Lancashire consumer and her possessions, 1751-81." In *Consumption and the World of Goods*, 274–301. 1st ed. Abingdon: Routledge.

Volpi, Maria Cristina. 2016a. "Sofia Jobim e o ensino da indumentária histórica na E.N.B.A." *Revista Maracanan* 12, no. 14 (junho): 300–309. doi.org/10.12957/revmar.2016.20876.

Volpi, Maria Cristina. 2016b. "The Exotic West: The Circuit of Carioca Featherwork in the Nineteenth Century." *Fashion Theory* 20, no. 2: 127–151. doi:10.1080/1362704X.2016.1133542.

2

Catholic Reliquary Lockets in the Colonial Americas: Foreign Objects with Native Presence

Alison Napier

Medallones relicarios are a type of Catholic devotional jewelry worn throughout colonial Latin America. Their formal composition typically consists of miniature painted or low relief images enclosed in glass with a silver or gold frame or bezel. *Medallones relicarios* can be single- or double-sided, and they are worn suspended from a pin or a chain as a pendant for personal adornment (Figures 2.1 and 2.2). The term *medallón relicario* translates as "reliquary locket," but this is somewhat inaccurate since the colonial Latin American versions of these objects do not contain actual relics. Instead, practitioners of Catholic Christianity in the Ibero-American colonies believed that the images themselves embodied the spiritual

Figure 2.1 Anonymous Artist. *Medallón relicario featuring an Anonymous Saint with a Levitating Figure of Santa Maria (left) and El Divino Pastor (right)* (Late Eighteenth Century). Painted images in silver frame. Image from the collection of author.

essence of the holy personage or event depicted. These renderings, believed to have an innate power to guide and protect the wearer, functioned like traditional relics despite the lack of any material remains of a saint or sacred object. Christians throughout the region believed the images could heal, protect, and/or guide those who wore them as well as intercede with God on their behalf. Owners of *medallones relicarios* wore these personal adornments to commune with the important religious figures that they featured as well as publicly perform their personal piety, social status, and group affiliations. As personal possessions worn by the diverse colonial population in the Latin American contact zone, each locket reflected the preferences of its artisan and/or patron. Examining the significance of these artistic choices reveals the contribution of *medallones relicarios* to the survival of Indigenous cultural practices in colonial Latin America.

Figure 2.2 Anonymous Artist (Peru), *Two-Sided Relicario with Images of the Virgin of Carmen (Patron Saint of mestizos) (left)* and *the Virgin and Child (right)* (Early Nineteenth Century). Polychrome Huamanga stone in a silver frame. Image from the collection of author.

Although small in size, *medallones relicarios* symbolize the enormous impact of European colonial projects in the Americas. They reveal not only the intricacies of religious devotion and identity formation for the diverse populations of this colonial contact zone, but they also provide evidence of Native American survivance strategies in their media and techniques. This chapter seeks to decolonize current scholarship and restore Indigenous voices to the analysis of *medallones relicarios* by revealing how Native American materials and techniques functioned as an integral part of their creation.

Most historiographies of Latin American conquest have promoted European narratives of colonization. These accounts frequently fail to acknowledge the sophistication of the Indigenous cultures that existed prior to contact and survived despite conquest, instead extolling European colonial endeavors as noble causes, and reflecting their sense of cultural superiority as well as a savior complex. Cultural influence and transmission is never unilateral, yet versions of acculturation in the Americas that focus on the hegemonic imposition of culture by European powers have neglected to consider the impact and the survival of native cultural practices within colonial regimes. In "Arts of the Contact Zone," historian Mary Louis Pratt examines material culture production in "social spaces where cultures meet, clash, and grapple with each other, often in contexts of highly asymmetrical relations of power, such as colonialism [and] slavery" (1991, 34). As cultures collide and co-mingle, so too do their material forms. Objects created in contact zones use artistic strategies such as mediation and parody to create new versions of old forms. These new hybrid forms reflect not only the power dynamic of the contact zone, but also the negotiation of cultural priorities among the groups wrestling for control in these spaces.

It is important to note that interaction is the rule for cultural groups, not the exception; examples of truly isolated societies are extremely rare. So, given that contact zones are conventional spaces resulting from social exchanges, it is the nature of that contact and the subsequent interactions that really determine the level of cultural dominance one group has over another. In her essay "Mutations of the Contact Zone: From Human to More-than-Human," Pratt (2022, 129) updates this framework after its thirty years of application by students and other scholars in the field. Pratt asserts that discourses related to contact zones focus on performativity and the improvisation of identity in embodied events. Through words and actions, members of coexisting cultural groups in a contact zone perform their identities to varying degrees, which are largely defined by the established power structure. In contact zones where power relationships are unbalanced, dominant groups often impose their identities on other cultural groups to assimilate them. This imposition of cultural identity from above occurs through both hard and soft power strategies. Regardless of the power mechanism deployed, dominated groups seek assimilation into new cultural dynamics in order to survive, and hopefully thrive, in the contact zone. As new cultural identities are performed and improvised, the result is imperfect semblances of the dominant cultural group.

The Americas were already a contact zone when the Europeans disembarked. Indigenous groups had engaged each other in a variety of ways that included trade, warfare, and intermarriage for centuries. As ruling groups rose and fell, subjugated Indigenous Americans assimilated different cultural influences, practicing both performativity and improvisation as survival strategies to adapt to the demands of presiding cultural groups and to coexist with them. Resulting cultural mixtures were imperfect versions of the dominant cultures as well as those that were subjugated. Dominant groups like the Aztecs of Mexico, the Incas of Peru, and the Maya of Guatemala and Yucatán used hard power strategies to conquer their geographic regions. Once in power, however, they ruled over subordinated cultural Others using soft power strategies, such as extracting tribute and taxes. Instead of trying to eradicate the beliefs and practices of the conquered societies, the Aztec, the Inca, and the Maya were comfortable with cultural heterogeneity as the status quo. As a result, Indigenous Americans were inherently receptive to performing identities and improvising daily life as power dynamics shifted, creating their own imperfect versions of the dominant ruling cultures as they blended cultural traditions.

The Europeans, however, were not so open-minded in their conquest endeavors, and they leaned on brute force and hard power strategies to subjugate Indigenous peoples and colonize their lands. The Spanish, for example, entered the Americas hardened by years of battling the Moors to regain control of their homeland and reestablish Christianity as the one true faith. Their intense brand of Catholicism was intolerant of the Indigenous populations' religions, violently destroying material culture objects associated with "pagan" practices. The Spanish regents Ferdinand and Isabella dispatched the conquistadors to the Americas under the banner of "God, Glory, and Gold" with the goals of obtaining lands for the Spanish empire, claiming Indigenous souls for the Christian faith, and filling both Spain's and the Church's coffers with New World treasures. Native American groups that did not succumb to European diseases found themselves forced to adopt new languages, a new faith, and countless new customs to perform new identities deemed acceptable by the Europeans. Indigenous Americans improvised their daily existences in the new world order of the colonial contact zone, imitating Europeans and their cultural models, and then creating their own imperfect versions by adapting Indigenous cultural practices. Through performativity and improvisation, Indigenous peoples found ways for their own cultural beliefs and practices to survive despite the oppression of European colonial regimes.

In the "Aesthetics of Survivance: Literary Theory and Practice," Anishinaabe cultural theorist Gerald Vizenor defines Indigenous survivance in the Americas as "an active resistance and repudiation of dominance" (2008, 11). Vizenor explains that "the practices of survivance create an active presence, more than the instincts of survival, function, and subsistence." Native people are and have historically been actors with agency who have sought to define themselves and preserve their own cultural traditions within the confines of colonized power systems. So, as Indigenous societies used performativity and improvisation to grapple with European customs, they devised surreptitious ways of maintaining their own cultural practices as strategies of survivance and cultural continuity.

It is important to clarify the difference between Indigenous strategies of survivance and the use of cultural appropriation as a tool of colonization. Native survivance is not imposed from above, so the arrogation of Indigenous cultural forms to facilitate the goals of the conquistadors and missionaries is not survivance. To demonstrate this assertion, consider the relationship between Indigenous Earth Goddesses and iterations of the Virgin Mary in Christian conversion efforts in colonial Latin America. The Franciscan, Dominican, and Augustinian friars who accompanied the conquistadors led the early attempts to convert the native population. They met resistance in their missions as they preached to Indigenous groups and had varying degrees of success in conversion. One strategy for converting Native peoples from their polytheistic religions involved mapping Christian themes and symbols onto elements of Indigenous religion. In "From Coatlicue to Guadalupe: The Image of the Great Mother in Mexico," Patrizia Granziera explains how the Virgin Mary played a pivotal role in these early conversion efforts and establishing an American Catholic faith.

Mary's association with flowers, gardens, trees, and water made her compatible with the Nahua's views of sacred power. When the Spanish invaders suppressed the Nahuas' public religion and offered the cult of their mostly venerated "Immaculate Virgin" in exchange, Mary became the most important sacred female available for Indigenous adaptation. Coming from a tradition in which female divinities were significant players and the sacred was conceived in terms of deified forms of the cosmic human and vegetal cycle, Nahuas were predisposed to grant importance to the only major female figure presented to them by Christianity (Graziera 2004, 269). This type of religious syncretism occurred throughout the Americas and facilitated conversion by giving Native deities a European makeover. Transforming powerful Earth Mother goddesses like the Inca Pachamama and the Aztec Coatlicue into versions of the Virgin Mary aided the friars in their push to replace "pagan" beliefs and practices with Christianity.

Different iterations of the Virgin Mary, therefore, allowed in part for the survival of native forms since she functioned as a vestige of an Earth Mother deity as well as the mother of Christ. Cultural appropriation and analogous assertions, however, are not the same as survivance. It is important to recognize that the co-opting of the Indigenous deities was the strategy of a colonizing group to assert religious dominance; it was not an attempt by subordinated native cultures to survive and resist this domination. Subversion, whether purposeful or unintentional, forms the foundation of survivance. Indigenous peoples replicated the practices and material culture forms of the Europeans, using performativity and improvisation to mediate and undermine the dominance of their colonizers. The narratives constructed by the missionaries, however, were an assertion of that dominance, not an attempt to facilitate the survivance of Indigenous practices and cultural forms.

Again, survivance is not compelled from above. It develops as a tactic to subvert imposed cultural forms by injecting them with Native presence. In material culture objects, survivance manifests itself in hybrid objects, but the perceptibility of Indigenous presence fluctuates depending on the type of object, its function, and the context of its production. In their article "Hybridity and Its Discontents: Considering Visual Culture in Colonial Spanish America," art historians Carolyn Dean and Dana Leibsohn (2003, 24–26) examine the phenomenon of cultural hybridity and its varying degrees of visibility in material culture forms.

> Cultural hybridity, then, should be understood as a perhaps obvious subaltern strategy for coping with dominant and dominating cultures. It should also be understood as a perhaps obvious strategy utilized by dominant cultures to incorporate subalterns. In turn, recognizing colonial hybrids is—or ought to be—a profoundly political act, for hybridity is inherent to the process of colonization.... Much of the force of hybridity stems from the fact that there are multiple kinds of mixing and interacting—some of which are more tolerable and less disturbing than others. Hybridity that is treated as though it leaves only a visible trace in objects, and thus concerns only style, iconography, form, composition, and materials has not been particularly problematic—or

interesting—because it is quite tolerable.... The more embedded forms of hybridity—those related to manufacture, audience, meaning, and use—which are not necessarily visually, or easily, recognizable are more dangerous because they are perceived as somehow deeper and more consequential. Again, these are the hybrids that appear to have mattered.

Colonization and conquest create asymmetrical power dynamics among groups in a cultural contact zone. This power structure establishes a social hierarchy with the conquering group at its top, and other cultural groups in the contact zone in lower-ranking (i.e. subaltern) positions. In colonial Latin America, Indigenous peoples were subaltern groups using performativity and improvisation to emulate the Europeans and survive their rule.

Dean and Leibsohn, like Vizenor, recognize the production of hybrid cultural forms as an Indigenous assertion of presence in the asymmetrical power dynamic of the colonial Americas. Creating hybrid forms could be interpreted as political acts since Native Americans were actors performing and possibly subverting the forms of the dominant cultural group, but there also existed cases of hybridity that were visually discernible. The existence of this hybridity represents an improvisation of European models that resulted in the "imperfect" hybrid cultural forms in Latin America. The visible presence of Indigenous materials and techniques in these improvised forms were considered "tolerable" by the Europeans because they made practical sense and/or were aesthetically novel and pleasing. Within the distinct category of objects identified as *medallones relicarios*, a continuum of hybridity is present ranging from highly visible to imperceptible. Variations in subject matter and media reflected the artistic traditions of both European and Indigenous cultures while simultaneously asserting a connection to the Christian faith.

The first *medallones relicarios* entered the Americas with explorers from the Iberian Peninsula, who brought with them a number of different religious items and images for their individual devotions and the Christianization of new lands. Contemporary accounts confirm that Hernán Cortés, leader of the Spanish conquest, wore a *medallón relicario* featuring an image of the Virgin and Child on one side and John the Baptist on the other when he landed on the Yucatán Peninsula in 1519 (Díaz del Castillo [1568] 1955, 557). To create the miniature images encapsulated in European versions of *medallones relicarios*, artists used transparent and opaque colors on small disks of vellum, cardstock, ivory, or copper (Johnson 1990, 14). Through their Catholic subject matter and their European materials and techniques, these jewelry items symbolized a direct connection to their European heritage and its intense brand of Christianity.

Although these specific jewelry forms entered the continent with the conquistadors, the practice of wearing pendant-style objects featuring religious personages did not. The material culture records of Indigenous societies such as the Aztec, the Inca, and the Maya provide a variety of evidence demonstrating their rich image-making traditions and their creations of pendants and pectorals featuring ancestors or important deities. While Europeans and Native Americans shared this tradition of personal adornment, the materials they used to create their pendant and pectoral forms differed, as did reverence in which those materials were held. In many Indigenous societies, each material substance possessed its own spiritual essence that communicated significant meaning. For Native artisans, the materials used to create these objects were as important as the subjects they rendered.

As cultures and practices collided in the colonial contact zone, Native Americans wore *medallones relicarios* as strategies of both survival and survivance. As a tactic of survival, wearing one of these lockets openly signified allegiance to the Europeans and their faith. An Indigenous member of colonial society adorning themselves with a *medallón relicario*, therefore, could have demonstrated conversion to Christianity in earnest or employed the reliquary locket as form of mimicry. Regardless of the premise, opting to wear the fashion of their conquerors served as a strategy of survival. Donning this Christian jewelry deflected the surveillance of both political and religious authorities and facilitated Indigenous existence under colonial rule. *Medallones relicarios* also provided an opportunity for the survivance of Indigenous material cultural traditions. Indigenous artisans had their own methods for creating sacred objects and jewelry items, and these practices reflected a Native reverence for both materials and techniques that connected them to their cultural roots.

The material culture records from the pre-Columbian period demonstrate a long artisan carving tradition in the Americas. Skilled in working with a range of materials, Indigenous artisans sculpted large-scale reliefs and freestanding works as well as personal adornments and miniature forms from durable natural substances. According to Mary Strong (2012) in *Art, Nature, and Religion in the Central Andes: Themes and Variations from Prehistory to Present*, the stone carving tradition dates back to Chavín, one of the earliest known Andean civilizations, and passed from cultural group to cultural group over the centuries.

> The civilization of Tiahuanacu likewise produced extraordinary carving on stone plaques and enormous statuary in incised and bas relief styles that artists incorporated into the architecture. The Huari inherited Tiahuanacu designs and

incorporated them into their own stonework. The Huarpa and Huari cultures of the ancient Huamanga region used Huamanga stone [i.e. alabaster] in their art and may have dyed some of their work with materials available in the local natural environment, as contemporary people do. The Huanca, Huanta, and Chanca cultures inherited this alabaster-working tradition. When they in turn became part of the Inca empire the tradition passed on to this new dominant culture.

(315)

For Indigenous peoples, the earth and its material resources possessed an innate spirituality that needed to be respected, and this imbued these materials with significance.

Native American artisans used a variety of stones in creating jewelry items and small-scale figural sculptures. In the Andean region, alabaster enjoyed great popularity for several reasons, including its availability and its hard, yet still malleable, consistency. It was also white in color and receptive to pigmentation. Deposits of alabaster exist throughout Peru, and it was heavily quarried near the city of Huamanga during the colonial period, earning it the name of Huamanga stone. Huamanga stone was widely used for creating Indigenous ritual figures known as *conopa*. Archaeologist Bill Sillar (2017) explains the significance of these objects in "Animating Relationships: Inca *Conopa* and Modern *Illa* as Mediating Objects."

> *Conopa* were not simply stone figurines or whimsies. In the Andean highlands a *conopa* was considered to be an animate entity that was an active participant in the preparation of offerings. The objects themselves were thought to be alive, forming part of people's communicative relationship with the sacred geography of the Andes. Spanish Colonial priests considered these "cult objects" to be a dangerous focus of idolatrous practice which they were trying to eradicate. *Conopa* and objects like them, which are now more commonly referred to as *illa*, continue to play an active role in ritual offerings and are an emotive expression of Andean ideals and aspirations.
>
> (141)

Accessibility and facility were practical reasons for using Huamanga stone to create *conopa*, but Strong discusses that electing to fashion objects from stone also exhibited the cultural priorities of their artisans.

For the Incas and their ancestors, stone is a sacred material. The mountain gods, or *apus*, are of stone. Small stones are the *apus'* children. Special stones like *illas*, carved or uncarved stone *conopas*, or *ultis*, and stone plaques incised with symbols for making prophecies have a special power among stones (Strong 2012, 315). Andeans viewed the natural world and its features in religious terms, and their stonework, regardless of scale, showed respect for the actual material and its source. The choice to craft objects from Huamanga stone was partially pragmatic, but the process of physically working the sacred substance also showed reverence to the *apus* and their children. Shaping the stone into *conopa* reinforced the spiritual significance of both the material and resulting ritual figure.

Pre-Columbian artisans in South America created *conopa* from other materials as well. In *La extirpación de la idolatría en el Perú*, Father Pablo José de Arriaga recounts early Spanish efforts to convert the Indigenous population of Peru ([1621] 1999, 36). He describes *conopa* throughout his account as small ritual idols in the form of humans, llamas, maize, and potatoes used by the Indigenous population. The majority of *conopa* discussed are created from stone, but he also cites examples made of other material, such as wood and metal. The archaeological record also confirms the existence of *conopa* created from other media. In his report on the Milagro-Quevedo culture, which thrived around 500 CE near Guayaquil, Ecuador, anthropologist Olaf Holm includes drawn examples of the *conopa* created from tagua found in the region to illustrate his findings (1981, 21–22). Tagua is the nutlike seed of the *Phytelephas* palm that grows throughout the tropical regions of South America, and it shares physical similarities with Huamanga stone: white in color, hard, shiny, smooth, easy to carve, and receptive to different pigments. These properties have earned it the nickname "vegetable ivory." The nuts range from 1.5 to 3 inches in diameter, an ideal size for creating small figural sculptures, pendants, and personal adornments. Tagua is harvested by hand without harming the tree, showing respect for the source of the material and the earth that produced it (Acosta-Solís 1948, 46). It is difficult to know with certainty how Indigenous Americans viewed tagua or interpreted its intrinsic spiritual properties, but given its physical parallels to Huamanga stone, the substance may have also been associated with the *apus*. In some cultural groups, each member of the society or tribe received a tagua pendant to wear, reflecting the Indigenous belief that wearing this substance ensured a life of harmony filled with the love of friends and family. As the fruit of a palm tree, tagua also had associations with the maternal, the sacred feminine, and the life-giving power of the earth (Cultural Elements 2021).

Regardless of the material used, recovered *conopa* are consistent in style, scale, and subject matter. The variety of materials used to create them demonstrates the importance of carving as an Indigenous artisan tradition as well as the versatility of the pre-Columbian craftsmen, who adapted stone carving techniques for different media. Native American artisans built on their material culture traditions in fashioning their versions of *medallones relicarios* in the materials and techniques they elected to use. They improvised their versions using the European exemplars present in the colonial contact zone, retaining the pendant locket featuring a miniature rendering of Christian imagery. The European lockets typically contained images in a two-dimensional painted format (Figure 2.1), but those of Indigenous facture incorporated carved miniature reliefs created from Huamanga stone (Figure 2.2) and tagua. By using natural materials that had Native religious significance to create their own versions of *medallones relicarios*, Indigenous Americans created objects to help them perform Christian identity and undermine European attempts to eradicate their cultural practices. The improvised versions of *medallones relicarios* that they created depicted Christian subjects and imbued them with Native religious meanings.

Given the symbolic meaning of Huamanga stone and tagua nut for Indigenous artisans in the pre-Columbian South America, it makes a great deal of sense that they selected these materials to create the Christian images contained in *medallones relicarios*. Quarried and extracted from the ground, Huamanga stone was directly connected to the earth mother goddess Pachamama, as well as the power and spirituality of the stone *apus* (mountain gods). As plant matter, tagua shared this association with the earth as well as feminine energy, love, and existential harmony. The qualities inherent in these media conjoined perfectly with the values and beliefs asserted by the Christian faith, which promised the unconditional love of a powerful god that could bring a faithful believer peace in this world and the next. Huamanga stone's and tagua's connections to the power of Mother Earth made it perfect for rendering images of the Virgin Mary, a common subject of these reliquary lockets. *Medallones relicarios* were jewelry items worn to provide support, guidance, and protection for faithful and pious Christians. Devoted Catholics believed they contained "true images" of holy personages that possessed the power to mediate on their behalf and help them navigate the trials and tribulations of daily life. Like *conopa*, they possessed an innate spiritual power that allowed them to function as intercessors between a deity and a human and facilitate ritual practice. Employing "the living matter" of Huamanga stone or tagua as the medium to create the "true images" contained in these reliquary lockets conjoined Indigenous cultural beliefs with Christian religious practices.

Indigenous *medallones relicarios* made from Huamanga stone and tagua demonstrate visible hybridity. Their presence in the material culture record has a few implications. First, it indicates their colonizers accepted the use of these materials in the Indigenous versions as tolerable and acceptable "imperfections" when compared to the European models. From the European perspective, the fact that Native Americans created and wore *medallones relicarios* signified their successful conversion, making *medallones relicarios* an important aspect of Indigenous performativity. The material differences also had social implications since huamanga stone and tagua adornments were symbolically connected to Christians of Indigenous descent, and this helped reinforce race and class identity in the socially stratified colonial contact zone. *Medallones relicarios* created by artisans working in the European tradition, whether imported or created in the Americas, likely would have been more expensive and prestigious than those created with Indigenous materials. Their European origin enhanced their monetary value and their symbolic value as luxury items of the dominant class. European and Creole Christians living in the contact zone would have elected to wear reliquary lockets created with painted images in the European style to publicly display their wealth and their connection to the Iberian Peninsula, relegating those created with Huamanga stone and tagua as fashion signifiers of a subaltern segment of the colonial population.

There is, of course, another perspective that needs to be considered in this analysis to facilitate the decolonization of centuries of scholarship: that of Indigenous Americans. The existence of Huamanga stone and tagua *medallones relicarios* are evidence of Indigenous performativity and improvisation in the contact zone. These materials demonstrated continuity with the South American tradition of creating pendants, personal adornments, and ritual miniatures from this material. The hybrid or improvised versions of *medallones relicarios* created from Huamanaga stone and tagua nut objects are evidence that Native American artisans were actors making conscious choices about their materials as a strategy of survivance that instilled their versions of these reliquary lockets with Indigenous presence. Native beliefs regarding the spiritual properties inherent in these materials worked in tandem with the images of the holy personages they were used to create. Christian believers attributed renderings of the Virgin Mary, Christ, and the saints with having the power to intercede on their behalf, help them navigate the trials of daily life, and protect them from harm. Creating their likenesses from materials associated with Indigenous religion and spiritual practice enhanced the significance of these images for Native populations. From an Indigenous perspective, blending old and new religious traditions in a hybrid *medallón relicario* was an acceptable form of cultural heterogeneity that ensured their cultural survivance. It is possible that from their perspective, using

Huamanga stone or tagua also made the Indigenous versions of these reliquary lockets more spiritually potent than those of their European counterparts as they encompassed the power and spirituality of both Indigenous and European religious traditions.

Medallones relicarios were common devotional items throughout colonial Latin America, but they have received very little scholarly attention. When they appear in academic texts, they are discussed only tangentially and identified as minor arts and decorative objects, serving as ancillary evidence of Catholicism in the Ibero-Americas or as examples of the diverse corpus of Latin American painting or sculpture. Analyses of these objects largely fail to address their roles in Indigenous performativity and improvisation in the contact zone, nor do they address their visible hybridity that displays Native materials and techniques. Indigenous groups throughout Latin America fashioned their own *relicarios* out of local and traditional materials, such as tagua, Huamanga stone, bone, and other substances that had Indigenous cultural significance. Overall, *medallones relicarios* are a highly diverse group of objects, indicating an array of cultural traditions and practices existing throughout colonial Latin America. The diversity of their materials of manufacture demonstrates a broad continuum of hybridity that reflects the diverse population of this colonial contact zone and their strategies for performing identity in the colonial contact zone.

With the onset of independence movements across Latin America in the early 1800s, wearing *medallones relicarios* fell out of fashion because of their association with European colonialism. Today, the practice has come full circle, manifesting in modern times as patron saint medals. These medals still signify the devotion and piety of their wearers, but as modern manifestations of religious pendants, their cast relief images do not openly exhibit the hybridity of their colonial counterparts. Although they do not reflect Indigenous carving techniques or material choices, it is important to acknowledge, however, that they do reflect the survivance of Indigenous metallurgy traditions and the adaptation of European Christianity in the legacy of colonialism. Furthermore, the survivance of Indigenous traditions and cultural forms are alive and well. Despite European efforts to eradicate the "idolatry" of the Indigenous population through the destruction of *conopa*, Native American artisans and craftsmen still carve tagua and Huamanga stone into these small figures for their personal use as well as for tourist consumption, and this reflects not only the importance of carving as artistic practice, but also the continuing significance of these materials to Indigenous groups in the Americas.

Bibliography

Acosta-Solis, M. 1948. "Tagua or Vegetable Ivory: A Forest Product of Ecuador." *Economic Botany*, 2 (1): 46–57.

Cultural Elements. 2021. "Tagua Nut: Vegetable Ivory of South America." https://medium.com/@townsonr025/tagua-nut-vegetable-ivory-of-south-america-b2da0a5f52c4.

De Arriaga, Pablo Joseph ([1621] 1999). *La extirpación de la idolatría en el Perú*. Translated by Henrique Urbano. Cuzco: Centro de Estudios Regionales Andinos Bartolomé de las Casas.

Dean, Carolyn and Dana Leibsohn. 2003. "Hybridity and Its Discontents: Considering Visual Culture in Colonial Spanish America." *Colonial Latin American Review* 12 (1): 5–35.

Díaz del Castillo, Bernal. ([1568] 1955). *Historia verdadera de la conquista de la Nueva España*. Mexico, D.F.: Editorial Porrúa, S.A.

Egan, Martha J. 1993. *Relicarios: Devotional Miniatures from the Americas*. Santa Fe: Museum of New Mexico Press.

Graziera, Patrizia. 2004. "From Coatlicue to Guadalupe: The Image of the Great Mother in Mexico." *Studies in World Christianity* 10 (2): 250–273.

Holm, Olaf. 1981. *Cultura Milagro-Quevedo*. Guayaquil: Impreso en los Talleres del Museo Antropológico y Pinacoteca del Banco Central del Ecuador.

Johnson, Dale T. 1990. "An Introduction to the History or American Portrait Miniatures." in *American Portrait Miniatures in the Manney Collection*, 11–12. New York: The Metropolitan Museum of Art.

Pratt, Mary Louise. 1991. "Arts of the Contact Zone." *Profession*, 33–40.

Pratt, Mary Louise. 2022. *Planetary Longings*. Durham: Duke University Press.

Sillar, Bill. 2017. "Animating Relationships: Inca Conopa and Modern Illa as Mediating Objects." In *The Inbetweenness of Things: Materializing Mediation and Movement between Worlds*, edited by Paul Bascu, 141–161. London: Bloomsbury.

Strong, Mary. 2012. *Art, Nature, and Religion in the Central Andes: Themes and Variations from Prehistory to Present*. Austin: University of Texas Press.

Vizenor, Gerald. 2008. *Survivance: Narratives of Native Presence*. Lincoln: University of Nebraska Press.

3

Manila Shawls, Trading Routes, and Global Encounters

Inés Corujo Martín

Few garments in the history of women's fashion conjure up such a mixture of notions and cultural meanings as the *mantón de Manila* (Manila shawl), as evidenced by costume historians and cultural critics.[1] Valued for its rich, lavish embroidery with macramé fringes, decorative embellishments, and sumptuous silk, its emergence in the Hispanic world is inextricably linked to the maritime route of the Manila Galleons established in 1565. The merchant ships crossed the Pacific Ocean from Manila, the commercial hub of the Spanish Philippines, to Acapulco and, from there, sailed the Atlantic from Veracruz to the port of Seville—a journey that lasted six months, the longest recorded in the history of world navigation.[2] The treacherous route of the Manila Galleons lasted almost 250 years, coming to an end in 1815 with the outbreak of civil strife throughout Latin America and the subsequent wars of independence from Spain. The trade was then limited between the ports of Manila and Seville until 1898, when Spain lost the Philippines to the United States in the Spanish–American War and saw the definitive downfall of its colonial empire.

The luxury goods brought from the Philippines for the Spanish Peninsular and Latin American markets included ivory, sandalwood, muslin, tea, porcelain, spices (Mindanao cinnamon), rugs, tapestries, and other fine goods. The Manila Galleons carried wooden boxes containing delicate gauze, Cantonese flowered crepes, velvets, taffetas, damasks, and exquisite brocades decorated with exuberant designs of gold and silver thread. Alongside shawls, scarves, fans, jewelry, combs, and all sorts of accessories, these luxurious items revolutionized sartorial customs and spurred the craze for oriental and exotic trends (Tinajero 2005, 68). Silk was by far the most highly coveted product of the cargoes, and the Manila Galleons were often referred to as *barcos de seda* (galleons of silk) and their course the "silk trade route," as several colonial documents show (Sierra de la Calle 1999, 25).

Despite its name, the *mantón de Manila* was primarily manufactured in the prosperous center of Canton in southeastern China, from where it was transferred to Manila and then carried across the Spanish Empire.[3] The square-shaped women's shawl was made of fine satin or silk and could reach up to 200 centimeters in length. It was lavishly decorated with exquisite fringe ornaments hanging from its ends, a trace of Hispano–Arab influence. *Mantones*, made exclusively for export, showcased bright and exotic flowers, butterflies, fountains, and birds, and incorporated all kinds of South-Asian decorative motifs. Even though the *mantón* could be worn in numerous ways, it was usually wrapped around the upper body or folded over the head (see Figure 3.1).

Although the donning of the *mantón de Manila* in Spain and the Americas can be traced back to colonial times, it turned into a quintessential accessory in Spanish women's wardrobes from all social strata during the second half of the nineteenth century—a period that coincides with the Spanish nation-building process and the rise of nationalism. Regardless of its oriental roots, the *mantón*

Figure 3.1 *Mantón de Manila* fabricated in Cantón, 1870. 169 x 171 cm, CE092934. National Costume Museum. Center for Research in Ethnologic Heritage. Madrid, Spain. © Photograph: Munio Rodil Ares.

became a symbol of traditionalism and national purity on Spanish soil, playing a decisive role in the invention of national dress. Concurrently, in the Viceroyalties of New Spain, particularly in Mexico, the Chinese shawl brought from the Philippines merged with pre-Hispanic and European motifs and designs, originating unique garbs like the *rebozo* (Mexican scarf), an emblem of the newly formed Mexican state.

At the cultural crossroads between East and West, the *mantón de Manila* was prompted by colonialism, imperialism, and global networks to evolve, blending Asian, pre-Columbian, European, and Hispano-Arabic ingredients in the process. As such, it illustrates an exemplary case study of "hybrid" fashion, since it is not fully Asian, Latin American, or Spanish, but rather an item of dress formed by an amalgam of elements from diverse cultures.[4] As an accessory traded on a global scale, it constitutes a multifaceted garment fraught with layered meanings, embodying the concept of "object in motion" theorized by Daniela Bleichmar and Meredith Martin (2015, 612). The *mantón* traveled great distances, passing through various regions and cultures, gaining new meanings and functions, and undergoing both physical changes and shifts in interpretation along the way. That is why there is no one version of the *mantón*, but multiple, and each convey different meanings.

The case study of the *mantón de Manila* in the Hispanic world reveals how fashion accessories function far beyond their decorative and embellished qualities, and how they can operate as key drivers for cultural and societal change. In this regard, recent research has drawn attention to the crucial role that accessories have played throughout cultural history, in spite of the lack of scholarly attention given to them. For instance, Susan Hiner comments that fashion accessories are fraught with complex meanings, and in nineteenth-century France they "became primary sites for the ideological work of modernity" (2010, 1–2). In a similar vein, Marni Reva Kessler looks to artistic depictions of the female veil in Paris during the late 1800s, arguing that studying veils sheds light on debates surrounding the ways in which modern life was constructed, including those about public health, imperialism, and modernist art practices. As Kessler points out, accessories are "always politically, socially, and culturally determined" (2006, xxx).[5] In relation to this, as theoretical approaches associated with the "material turn" within the fields of literary and cultural studies have shown since the 1980s, objects can be vital cultural symbols. Several scholars from this critical trend not only discuss the role of the material and the non-human in creating and shaping human subjectivity, they also seek to highlight the vital role that objects, artifacts, and things—often disregarded as trivial—play in everyday life and social history.[6] In the same vein, fashion is both a material and immaterial phenomenon. Recent research in the field of dress and fashion has proposed a new approach known as the "material culture of fashion," which seeks to study the object itself, in conjunction with the social and cultural meanings embedded in it (Riello 2011, 2).[7]

Drawing upon the aforementioned works and methodologies, the objective of this chapter is to examine the multiplicity of values and associations that women's fashion accessories convey over time through the lens of the *mantón de Manila*. As I argue in what follows, by putting an object, like the *mantón*, into various historical contexts in conjunction with other forms of culture, we can grasp a multifaceted understanding of the ideals and narratives that circulated in a given time and helped forge a distinct way of seeing the world. Because they are human-made artifacts, accessories reflect the anxieties of the individuals who wore and interacted with them, revealing by extension the concerns and beliefs of the culture at large. Indeed, tracking the transnational paths and modifications of the *mantón* sheds light on concepts such as cultural appropriation and exchange through a global lens. At the same time, it draws attention to broader questions, such as the complex significance of fashion objects in the reconfiguration of national, racialized, and gendered identities.

Although several studies have illustrated the profound juncture of gender and the nation during the constitutive phase of modern nationalism,[8] collective volumes such as *Fashioning the Body Politic: Gender, Dress, Citizenship* (ed. Wendy Parkins) and *The Politics of Dress in Asia and the Americas* (eds. Mina Roces and Louise Edwards) have demonstrated in detail the significance that dress plays in this dynamic. Contrary to trivializing opinions of the intersections between fashion, womanhood, and nationalism, these publications provide a vital key to understanding fashion as a prominent site for political struggle that can help shape a gendered construction of national identity. This chapter adds to the ongoing scholarship by reinforcing the centrality of women's accessories within nation-building processes and highlighting their cultural significance in the redefinition of critical categories of class, gender, and race. Finally, this chapter generates productive insights for the fields of Iberian and Latin American transatlantic and global studies, opening the path to future object-based research that delves into the rich material culture that was transferred across oceans.

As costume manuals, paintings, postcards, and travelogues from the last quarter of the nineteenth century amply evidence, the *mantón de Manila* evolved from an exotic luxury to a ubiquitous accessory in Spanish women's fashion, as well as a repeated motif of *costumbrista* (costumbrism) art.[9] In its beginnings donned solely by the wealthy, upper classes, the piece progressively expanded to different regions and to women of all social strata, becoming a staple element of the Spanish female wardrobe and strongly associated with traditional practices.

The propagation of the *mantón* coincides with the reconstruction of Spanish national identity after the imperial dismemberment in the Americas during the 1820s and can be linked to the evolution of Spain from a global empire to a nation-state. As scholar Susan Martin-Márquez explains, this period in Spanish history lasted until the independence of the last colonies (Philippines, Cuba, Guam, and Puerto Rico) in 1898, and it was characterized by a deep national identity crisis (2008, 17). Several investigations argue that this complex process of national reorganization was conceived in colonial and imperialist terms and was profoundly marked by the empire's definitive end.[10] Within this context, the *mantón de Manila*, at first an exotic, valuable item employed to mark high social rank, transformed into one of the most popular and fashionable women's accessories (Zanardi 2019, 201; Gutiérrez Garcia 2005, 28–29). Interestingly enough, the garb's democratization took place alongside the above-mentioned historical events. Its spread started in the early 1820s, when the Peninsular trade with the Philippines centralized in Seville—the capital city of Andalusia—soon after the independence of New Spain (Stone 1998, 35). Once Seville reopened its ports to trading ships in 1821, the importation of Chinese shawls tripled, transforming the port city into a crucial site of its trade (Stone 1998, 50). Nevertheless, as costume historians describe, the *mantón* didn't reach its heyday until the last third of the nineteenth century, coinciding with the years leading up to the outbreak of the Spanish–American War of 1898. With the definitive loss of the Philippines to the United States, the first workshops and treadle looms were established in Seville, which turned into the epicenter of the production and manufacture of *mantones* in the Iberian Peninsula.[11]

During this same period the shawl was frequently and richly displayed in the cultural imagery of the Iberian Peninsula. Featured in *costumbrista* paintings, novels, and *zarzuelas* (Spanish operettas); in bullfighting posters, advertisements, and prints, the *mantón de Manila* performed an integral role in identifying women as Spanish, while symbolically paying homage to the last bastion of Spanish colonial power.[12] In this regard, the Manila shawl was not only in charge of adorning the female wearer's shoulders and torso, but it was also a fashion object that embodied within its materiality imperial anxieties and nostalgia, helping shape a collective national sentiment.

It is important to mention the strong associations of *mantones de Manila* with Andalusia, the southern part of Spain which became a fundamental signifier in discourses on Spanish national identity at the time. Although this connection existed previously, it took on greater meaning within the national redefinition phase and, as Luis Fernández Cifuentes points out, any attempt to analyze the advent of modernity in Spain should pay attention to the decisive role played by the images produced of Andalusia in the construction of national identity (2007, 133). The *mantón de Manila*'s popularity and spread over the course of the nineteenth century, both in visual and textual accounts, can thus be understood in the light of orientalist discourses focused on Andalusia to reformulate and shape national values. As art historian Tara Zanardi illustrates, the *mantones* added a sartorial component that was recognizable to both local and foreign audiences, identifying women as definitively Spanish and participating in a visual construction of Spanish feminine identity that positioned Andalusian women as paradigmatic bearers of cultural heritage or exemplars of tradition (211).

Furthermore, the case study of the *mantón de Manila* draws attention to the pivotal role of dress during nation-building projects. It shows how the complex invention of "national dress" often took place on the global stage and blurred the distinctions between East and West. Indeed, as Mina Roces and Louise Edwards argue, national costumes are transnational projects that showcase oriental elements typical of "cultural otherness" (2008, 5). As both historians explain, "National dress was, and is, hybrid dress—variously a combination of the colonized and colonizing nations' points of contact or the competing political forces such as gender, class or ethnicity within a nation, or even an adaptation from an exotic but culturally influential non-colonizing power" (2008, 5). The *mantón de Manila*'s evolution exemplifies this common phenomenon by which the appropriated, foreign accoutrement serves as a privileged platform to craft a distinct idea of national identity.

Nonetheless, over the course of the nineteenth century, the shawl was profoundly altered on Spanish soil and appropriated to suit specific tastes and needs. Many motifs favored by the Spaniards included carnations, roses, daisies, and other botanical details instead of dragons, temples, or peacocks, which were popular in southern China. For its part, the *mantón*'s fringe, which was added after it left Asia to cater to the consumer preferences of Spaniards, was an element inspired by Moorish sartorial trends that remained popular in Andalusia, presumably as a result of the long and fertile Hispano-Islamic cultural exchange produced in the region (Stone 1998, 67). The *mantón*'s fringe grew longer throughout the 1800s, reaching almost 30 centimeters in length. There was an exceptional variety of patterns, colors, textures, and motifs of shawls across the

Spanish territory. This infinite array of combinations is typical of objects moving across cultural and geographical borders, making the *mantón* an object in flux, always in the "process of transforming or being transformed" (Bleichmar and Martin 2015, 612). Paradoxically, despite its variety and pronounced regional distinctions, the *mantón* helped articulate a unified and cohesive notion of the Spanish state.

The cultural appropriation of *mantones de Manila* reflects the longstanding Western fascination with the exotic. The European craze for Chinese luxury goods at the start of the eighteenth century—a phenomenon known as *chinoiserie*—revolutionized sartorial trends globally throughout the nineteenth century (Purdy 2020, 105). *Mantones* in the Hispanic world participated in this broader trend, but also diverged from it. While they embodied their Chinese origins in their materiality and designs and insisted upon their exotic origins, they simultaneously declared their Spanish adaptation. Through the transnational process of crossing borders, *mantones* became disconnected from their original context and material narrative, and manufacturers directed their designs toward the Spanish style and market. Through this process of dissemination and transformation, the *mantón de Manila* became "Spanishized" to exude Spanish traditional values, asserting an idealized notion of authentic Spanishness and evoking the extinct global empire. In this regard, Valerie Steele and John S. Major point out that the integration of Asian motifs, shapes, and iconography in Western design can go beyond the mere purpose of exoticism. On the contrary, this phenomenon can reflect profound cultural meanings and allude simultaneously to several referents, such as the shift of critical identities during times of political instability (1999, 70–71). This interpretation perfectly applies to the case study of the *mantón*. Far from interpreting it solely as an exotic or superfluous accoutrement adorning the female body, it can be viewed as a performative object through which Spanish women seemed capable of expressing national allegiance.

Abundant *fin-de-siècle* textual and visual depictions of *mantones* contributed to the characterization of Spanish women, particularly those from southern Spain, as orientalized and exotic. Artists from the period exaggerated Andalusian women walking, flirting, or dancing while sporting dynamic and bold shawls with large floral and avian motifs. These visual accounts of women wrapped in colorful *mantones* at bullfights, *sevillanas*, and local markets put on display exquisite fringes extending down their bodies and color-gradated silk shimmering while they moved. Artists often emphasized southern Spain's ethnic variety and showcased different skin tones in their paintings. This can be

Figure 3.2 Manuel Cabral Agudo Bejarano, *El puesto de buñuelos*, ca. 1854, oil on canvas, 63.5 x 50 cm. CTB.2002.1. Collection Carmen Thyssen-Bornemisza.

seen, for instance, in *El puesto de buñuelos* by Manuel Cabral Agudo Bejarano (1854)—one of the leading *costumbrista* painters (see Figure 3.2).

In other instances, artists depicted embroidered *mantones de Manila* to highlight the Moorish cultural background of the wearers and the mixture of ethnicities in the Andalusian region.[13] This connects with recent research that points out that *fin-de-siècle* Spanish national discourses were grounded in the positive valuation of racial hybridity and miscegenation, an ideology that went against the grain of northern European theories (Blanco 2016, 101). According to cultural critic Alda Blanco, racial intermixing is a principal feature of the intellectual and political project of envisioning the future of the nation in Spain and Latin America (2016, 85). The positive valorization of racial hybridity is often reaffirmed through the *mantón de Manila* in textual and visual accounts. As can be seen in Cabral's *El puesto de buñuelos*, all women, regardless of their socio-economic or racial background, wear the same accessory, which suggests the shawl's ability to classify each woman as Andalusian, and by extension, Spanish. Even though there were differences in fabrics and embellishments depending on social rank, through the sporting of the *mantón*, all women became equally part of the nation and wore it to assert a communal sense of national pride.

The spread of *mantones de Manila* throughout the Hispanic world was not restricted to the Iberian Peninsula, and they were widely transported from the Philippines to various Latin American regions. In fact, the earliest textual accounts of *mantones* hail from the Americas where it was embraced during the seventeenth and eighteenth centuries due to the immediate commercial contact of the Viceroyalties of New Spain with the Philippine archipelago.[14] Between 1565 and 1815, all commercial contact between the Spanish Empire and the Philippines happened through the ports of Acapulco and Veracruz, which explains the early, rich influence of Asian products on Mexican soil, in particular textiles, accessories, and apparel (Vázquez-Parladé 1992, 58). Silk and shawl embroidery were also important industries in the Mexican economy from early colonial times (Randall 2008, 47; Schurz 1939, 390).

Even though eighteenth-century women and men in Mexico dressed in fabrics from Asia regardless of their social origin, silk was primarily worn by the *mestizo* (mixed blood) population. Due to the strict sumptuary laws and sartorial decrees in the Viceroyalties of New Spain, this social group was not allowed to wear indigenous, creole or Peninsular clothing. As the studies of historians Magali Carrera, Rebecca Earle, and Chloë Sayer investigate, clothing played a crucial role in colonial Mexico and operated as a marker to differentiate social and racial castes. Silk *mantones de Manila* were already sported by *mestizo* women in Mexico by the 1830s—decades before they became a staple garment in Spain—and they were a common motif in nineteenth-century media forms such as paintings, prints, posters, postcards, and advertisements. The Mexican clientele opted for different kinds of patterns and a distinct length from that in Spain. For instance, *mantones de Manila* in their adaptation to Mexican local customs often incorporated Indigenous motifs into their predominantly Asian-inspired design (Zanardi 2019, 201).

Apart from the expansion of the *mantón de Manila* across New Spain,[15] a distinct female shawl emerged in this region as a synthesis of European, pre-Hispanic, and Asian influences—the *rebozo*. The *rebozo* is a large, rectangular shawl, made of cotton, silk, wool, or rayon threads—depending on the wearer's wealth—that wraps around the women's shoulders and across the waist. An average size is 26 inches (66 centimeters) wide by 28 inches (71 centimeters) long, with an additional 32 inches (81 centimeters) of fringe hanging from each side. For the *mestizo* population, *rebozos* had multiple functions beyond embellishment and adornment, such as protecting the wearer from the climate, carrying objects or babies, and covering the head for church.[16]

From its origins, the *rebozo* shared similarities with *mantones de Manila* in terms of design and production techniques, which solidifies the theories that associate their emergence with the Manila Galleon trade route (Davis 2010, 68; Armella de Aspe 1992, 32). Silk *rebozos*, in a similar manner to *mantones de Manila*, displayed gold and silver threads as well as elaborate Asian-embroidered motifs, including flowers, trees, birds, and fountains. Moreover, the silk *rebozo* was fabricated using the Asian *jaspe* or *ikat* technique, by which a design is bound on threads that are then dyed before weaving. Many silk *rebozos* resembled Manila shawls, featuring fringes on both ends and following the Spanish–Arabic trend that had flourished in Andalusia (Castelló y Martínez del Río 1971, 7).

Initially associated with *mestizo* cultures, mid-nineteenth-century paintings portrayed women from a wide range of ethnic and social backgrounds, including women from the upper classes, sporting *rebozos*. This indicates the democratization of the garment and its greater accessibility among women at the time. What differentiated them was the material and artistry of the shawl. There were also many different styles and patterning that reflected regional preferences.[17] So popular became this garment that *rebozo* producing centers developed in several areas, particularly Michoacán, Oaxaca, and Puebla, with the most highly rated from Santa María del Río (San Luis Potosí). In a likeness to the *mantón de Manila*, the *rebozo* constitutes a prime example of "hybrid" female fashion and "object in motion" as it travelled across all parts of the Mexican territory, crossing boundaries of race and class, while absorbing elements and motifs from various cultures in this process.

During the second half of the nineteenth century, *rebozos* began to manifest values of purist *mexicanidad*, contributing to the sense of national identity developed during the Mexican nation-formation process. In this period, the *rebozo* became strongly associated with the costume of the *china poblana*—the popular, lower-class female archetype of both ideal femininity and Mexican nationalism. Although the *china poblana* (and her male counterpart, the *charro*) evolved during the colonial era, it gained greatest cultural relevance starting in the second half of the nineteenth century, paradoxically coinciding with the beginning of her disappearance (Earle 2007, 173). Throughout this time, romantic and *costumbrista* references to young women wearing *rebozos* were artistically incorporated into poems and popular songs and it became a repeated, recognizable motif in Mexican imagery. Concurrently, an enormous number of paintings and lithographs circulated in Mexico and Europe, portraying *chinas poblanas* sporting *rebozos*, which contributed to spread the female national symbol beyond Mexican borders.[18]

Remarkably, the *china poblana* is characterized by her *mestizo* identity, an idea manifested in her attire. As Kimberly Randall explains, the *china poblana*'s costume was "comprised of a skirt in contrasting colors, a ruffled or embroidered blouse, and the ubiquitous shawl or *rebozo*, which would be artfully manipulated to cover and reveal the neck and arms" (2005, 44–45). The colorful and exotic clothing was complemented with sequins, silk shoes, and white stockings, in addition to layers of tinkling jewelry. The distinctive attire of the *china poblana* is thought to have developed over time and been inspired by the clothing worn by lower-class *mestiza* women in several parts of Mexico in the early nineteenth century and by the Spanish peasant styles from Andalusia (Lynch et al., 2014, 198; Randall 2005, 54). Although there are multiple explanations around the term *poblana*, which can either refer to a person from the state of Puebla (region established by the Spanish Empire in 1531 and key in the trade route), or derive from the word *pueblo* (village), various fables connect the term with the arrival in Puebla of an oriental princess in the seventeenth century. In this regard, the name's origin, despite its mystery, hint at Asia's long-term influence on Mexican culture. The myth and symbolic role around the *china poblana* can thus be understood in the light of *mestizaje* (a culture of mixed races) and the interactions produced between classes and races in nineteenth-century Mexico.

Although the relationship between Spanish *mantones de Manila* and Mexican *rebozos* is an ongoing subject of inquiry that needs further study, their common Asian roots are evident. They lie in an unparalleled convergence of cultures and reflect racist stereotypes of cultural hybridity. Both garments, enmeshed in traditional and everyday local practices from the nineteenth century onwards, performed a pivotal role in nation-building processes on both margins of the Hispanic Atlantic, epitomizing the relevance of clothing in establishing national and gendered identities. *Mantones de Manila* and *rebozos* experienced a comparable process of hybridization due to transcultural exchanges dating back to the sixteenth-century Manila Galleons trade. *Mantones de Manila* and *rebozos* still function today as emblems of national sentiment and purist traditionalism and are deeply ingrained in national dress. While Spanish *mantones* are worn today in solemn acts in Andalusia like Holy Week, *Feria de Sevilla* (the Seville Fair), and Corpus Christi festivities, the *rebozo* is considered the most typical and representative Mexican female garb of all since the 1930s (Pérez Monfort 2003, 48).

Both the *mantón de Manila* and the *rebozo* reveal the vital role that women's accessories acquire in the construction of national, racialized, and gendered identities during periods of national formation. Through their symbolic and material capacity, these accessories fostered a specific notion of national unity in Spain and Mexico, while serving as markers of femininity. They are globetrotting objects marked by their travels across continents and their multiple transformations, bringing together Iberian, Latin American, and Pacific histories. Studying *mantones* and *rebozos* expands our understanding of transatlantic and transnational cultural exchanges in the age of Spanish colonial expansion and collapse. As material embodiments of cultural contact and global commerce, both female garments ultimately serve as distinctive objects for cultural analysis on both sides of the Hispanic Atlantic. Their transformations demonstrate how fashion objects are an important tool for the creation of historical narratives, fostering social change and inhabiting the intersection of multiple aspects of identity.

Notes

1. On this subject, I refer to the collective volume *El mantón de Manila* organized by the Museo Municipal de Madrid (1999).
2. On the importance and longevity of the Manila Galleon trade route, see works by William Lytle Schurz, Shirley Fish, and Carmen Yuste López.
3. Seminal publications like Caroline Stone's *El Mantón de Manila* maintain that Chinese shawls were also produced and manufactured in Manila.
4. For more on the notions of "hybrid" and "hybridity" applied to dress, see Mina Roces and Louise Edwards.
5. For further information on this subject, see *Accessorizing the Body*, edited by Cristina Giorcelli and Paula Rabinowitz (2011).
6. Among the large list of authors related to the "material turn" in the humanities and social sciences, see Arjun Appadurai (*The Social Life of Things*); Bruno Latour

(*Matter, Materiality and Culture*); Bill Brown (*A Sense of Things*); and Barbara Johnson (*Persons and Things*).

7 For an overview of this research methodology, see Heike Jenns and Viola Hoffman (2019).
8 For more on the intersection of gender and national construction, see Blom et al. (2000); Sharp (1996); Heng (1997); and Yuval-Davis (1997).
9 On this phenomenon, I refer to Tara Zanardi.
10 On this subject, I refer to Alda Blanco's *Cultura y conciencia imperial en la España del siglo XIX* and the collective volume *Empire's End. Transnational Connections in the Hispanic World*, edited by Akiko Tsuchiya and William Acree (2016).
11 For an extension of this topic, see Encarnación Aguilar Criado (1999).
12 The Spanish National Library in Madrid holds several *zarzuelas* around the common theme of *mantones de Manila*. In prominent novels from the period like Benito Pérez Galdós's *Fortunata y Jacinta* (1887) *mantones de Manila* also take center stage. Leading *costumbrista* Spanish artists like Manuel Cabral and Joaquín Sorolla, as well as foreign artists visiting Spain like Mary Cassatt and John Singer Sargent amply depict *mantones de Manila* and the strong cultural values invested in the garment become clear. For an overview of this phenomenon in Spanish Peninsular visual arts, see Zanardi.
13 Andalusia, formerly Al-Andalus, was part of the Moorish territory for almost 800 years (711–1492), which has left an outstanding cultural legacy in southern Spain. Andalusia's Muslim past and its geographic and cultural proximity to Morocco are all aspects that define Andalusia's difference and racial uniqueness in contrast to the rest of the areas in the Iberian Peninsula. For a thoughtful and thorough overview of *andalucismo*, see José Acosta Sánchez.
14 The oldest known literary mention of the Manila shawl appears in the travelogue *Pérégrinations d'une paria* (*Pilgrimages of a Pariah*) written by French-Peruvian author Flora Tristán in 1838—the grandmother of the painter Gauguin, who, in 1833, went to the city of Lima, Peru, in search of her paternal family. Historian Joaquín Vázquez Parladé states that the Chinese shawls started to be worn firstly and more strongly in Mexico. On the impact of Asian influences in Latin American fashions, see Araceli Tinajero.
15 According to references found in archives and historical documents, the Manila shawl was also incorporated into Peruvian female dress and gained immense popularity during the second half of the nineteenth century.
16 For a comprehensive study of Mexican *rebozos*, see Gámez.
17 For instance, in Michoacán and Tlaxcala they are embroidered; in Guanajuato they are decorated with colored fringe; and in Santa María del Río, over the past 300 years, they have been worn for weddings, made of such fine silk that the *rebozo*, it is said, may pass through the bride's ring.
18 On this subject, see Magali Carrera (2007).

Bibliography

Acosta, Sánchez José. 1978. *Andalucía: Reconstrucción de una identidad y la lucha contra el centralismo*. Barcelona: Anagrama.

Aguilar Criado, Encarnación. 1999. *Las bordadoras de mantones de Manila de Sevilla. Trabajo y género en la producción doméstica*. Sevilla: Ayuntamiento de Sevilla.

Almazán, Marcos A. 1971. "El Galeón de Manila." *Artes de México* 143: 4–19.

Anthias, Floya and Nira Yuval-Davis. 1989. Eds. *Woman-Nation-State*. Basingstoke: Macmillan.

Appadurai, Arjun, ed. 1986. *The Social Life of Things: Commodities in a Cultural Perspective*. Cambridge: Cambridge University Press.

Armella de Aspe, Virginia and Guillermo Tovar de Teresa. 1992. *Bordados y Bordadores*. México: Grupo Gutsa.

Blanco, Alda. 2012. *Cultura y conciencia imperial en la España del siglo XIX*. Valencia: Universidad de Valencia.

Blanco, Alda. 2016. "Theorizing Racial Hybridity in Nineteenth-Century Spain and Spanish-America." In *Empire's End. Transnational Connections in the Hispanic World*, edited by Akiko Tsuchiya and William G. Acree, 84–106. Vanderbilt: Vanderbilt University Press.

Bleichmar, Daniela, and Meredith Martin. 2015. "Introduction: Objects in Motion in the Early Modern World." *Art History* 38 (4): 605–619.

Blom, Ida, et al., eds. 2000. *Gendered Nations: Nationalisms and Gender Order in the Long Nineteenth Century*. Oxford/New York: Berg.

Brown, Bill. 2003. *A Sense of Things: The Object Matter of American Literature*. Chicago: University of Chicago Press.

Calvo Serraller, Francisco. 1999. "La pérdida de Manila y el triunfo pictórico del mantón." In *El mantón de Manila*, 11–17. Madrid: Museo Municipal de Madrid.

Carrera, Magali. 2003. *Imagining Identity in New Spain: Race, Lineage, and the Colonial Body in Portraiture and Casta Paintings*. Austin: University of Texas Press.

Carrera, Magali. 2007. "Fabricating Specimen Citizens: Nation Building in Nineteenth-Century Mexico." In *The Politics of Dress in Asia and the Americas*, edited by Mina Roces and Louise Edwards, 215–235. Portland: Sussex Academic Press.

Carrillo, Abelardo y Gariel. 1959. *El traje en la Nueva España*. Mexico: Instituto Nacional de Antropología e Historia.

Castelló Yturbide, Teresa and Margarita Martínez del Río. 1971. "El Rebozo," *Artes de México*, vol. 142, año XVIII.

Davis, Virginia. 2010. "The China Poblana." In *Encyclopedia of World Dress and Fashion*, edited by Margot Blum Schevill vol. 2, Latin America and the Caribbean, 66–71. London: Oxford University Press.

Earle, Rebecca. 2007. "Nationalism and National Dress in Spanish America." In *The Politics of Dress in Asia and the Americas*, edited by Mina Roces and Louise Edwards, 163–181. Portland: Sussex Academic Press.

Fernández Cifuentes, Luis. 2007. "Southern Exposure: Early Tourism and Spanish National Identity." *Journal of Iberian and Latin American Studies* 13, no. 2–3: 133–148.

Fish, Shirley. 2011. *The Manila-Acapulco Galleons: The Treasure Ships of the Pacific. With an Annotated List of the Transpacific Galleons 1565-1815*. Central Milton Keynes: AuthorHouse.

Fisher, Abbey Sue. 1992. *Mestizaje and the Cuadros de Castas: Visual Representations of Race, Status, and Dress in Eighteenth-Century Mexico*. Ph.D. diss., University of Minnesota.

Gámez, Ana Paulina. 2009. *El rebozo estudio historiográfico: origen y uso*. Tesis de maestría en Historia del arte, Universidad Nacional Autónoma de México.

Giorcelli, Cristina and Paula Rabinowitz, eds. 2011. *Accessorizing the Body. Habits of Being*, vol. 1, Minneapolis: University of Minnesota Press.

Goode, Joshua. 1990. *Impurity of Blood: Defining Race in Spain, 1870-1939*. Baton Rouge: Louisiana State University Press.

Gutiérrez Garcia, María Ángeles. 2005. "Un mundo burgués y la moda en la obra de Benito Pérez Galdós." In *De crinolinas y polisones*, edited by María Paz Soler et al., 8–41, Murcia: Museo de Bellas Artes de Murcia.

Heng, Geraldine. 1997. "A Great Way to Fly: Nationalism, the State, and the Varieties of Third-World Feminism." In *Feminist Genealogies, Colonial Legacies, Democratic Futures*. Eds. Mohanty, Chandra Talpade and Alexander, M. Jacqui. New York: Routledge.

Hiner, Susan. 2012. *Accessories to Modernity: Fashion and the Feminine in Nineteenth-Century France*. Philadelphia, PA: University of Pennsylvania Press.

Ibarra, Rogelia Lily. 2014. "Mexican Tourist/Souvenir Jacket." In *Ethnic Dress in the United States: A Cultural Encyclopedia*, edited by Annette Lynch and Mitchell D. Strauss, 198–200. London: Rowman & Littlefield Publishers.

Jenns, Heike and Viola Hoffman. 2019. *Fashion and Materiality: Cultural Practices in Global Contexts*. London: Bloomsbury.

Johnson, Barbara. 2008. *Persons and Things*. Cambridge, MA: Harvard University Press.

Jones, Carla and Ann Marie Leshkowich. 2003. "Introduction: The Globalization of Asian Dress. Re-Orienting Fashion or Re-Orientalizing Asia?" In *Re-Orienting Fashion. The Globalization of Asian Dress*, edited by Carla Jones, Sandra Niessen, and Ann Marie Leshkowich, 1–48. New York: Berg.

Kaplan, Karen, Norma Alarcón, and Minoo Moallem eds. 2007. *Between Woman and Nation: Nationalisms, Transnational Feminisms, and the State*. Durham: Duke University Press.

Kessler, Marni Reva. 2006. *Sheer Presence: The Veil in Manet's Paris*. Minneapolis: University of Minnesota Press.

Latour, Bruno .2005. *Reassembling the Social: An Introduction to Actor-Network Theory*. Oxford: Oxford University Press.

Lynch, Annette et al. 2014. *Ethnic Dress in the United States: A Cultural Encyclopedia*. Lanham, MD: Rowman & Littlefield Publishers.

Martin-Márquez, Susan. 2008. *Disorientations: Spanish Colonialism in Africa and the Performance of Identity*. New Haven: Yale University Press.

Metzger, Sean. 2014. *Chinese Looks. Fashion, Performance, Race*. Bloomington: Indiana University Press.

Parkins, Wendy, ed. 2002. *Fashioning the Body Politic. Dress, Gender, Citizenship*. Oxford & New York: Berg.

Pérez Monfort, Ricardo. 2003. "La china poblana como emblema nacional." *Artes de México* 66: 40–51.

Purdy, Daniel Leonhard. 2020. "Chinoiserie in Fashion: Material Images Circulating between China and Europe." In *Fashion and Materiality. Cultural Practices in Global Contexts*, edited by Heike Jenns and Viola Hofmann, 105–122. London: Bloomsbury.

Randall, Kimberly. 2005. "The Traveler's Eye: Chinas Poblanas and European-Inspired Costume in Postcolonial Mexico." In *The Latin American Fashion Reader*, edited by Regina A. Root, 44–65, Oxford/New York: Berg.

Riello, Giorgio. 2011. "The Object of Fashion: Methodological Approaches to the History of Fashion." *Journal of Aesthetics & Culture* 3 (1): 1–9.

Robinson, Natalie V. 1987. "Mantones de Manila. Their Role in China's Silk Trade." *Arts of Asia* 17 (1): 65–75.

Roces, Mina, and Louise Edwards eds. 2010. *The Politics of Dress in Asia and the Americas*. Brighton: Sussex Academic.

Ruiz Olmedo, Antonio ed. 1999. *El mantón de Manila*. Madrid: Museo Municipal de Madrid.

Said, Edward. 1979. *Orientalism*. New York: Vintage.

Sayer, Chloë. 1985. *Costumes of Mexico*. Austin: University of Texas Press.

Schmidt-Nowara, Cristopher. 2006. *The Conquest of History: Spanish Colonialism and National Histories in the Nineteenth Century*. Pittsburgh, PA: University of Pittsburgh Press.

Schurz, William Lytle. 1939. *The Manila Galleon*. New York: E. P. Dutton.

Sharp, Joanne P. 1996. "Gendering Nation. A Feminist Engagement with National Identity." In *Bodyspace. Destabilizing Geographies of Gender and Sexuality*, edited by Nancy Hall-Duncan, 97–108. London: Routledge.

Sierra de la Calle, Blas, 1999. "El galeón de Acapulco y las sedas de Oriente." *El mantón de Manila*, 21–29. Madrid: Museo Municipal.

Steele, Valerie, and John S. Major. 1999. *China Chic. East Meets West*. New Haven: Yale University Press.

Stone, Caroline. 1998. "El mantón de Manila." *El Mantón de Manila*, 31–85. Granada: Fundación Caja de Granada.

Tinajero, Araceli. 2005. "Far Eastern Influences in Latin American Fashions." In *The Latin American Fashion Reader*, edited by Regina A. Root, 66–76. Oxford/New York: Berg.

Vázquez Parladé, Joaquín. 1992. "Los mal llamados mantones de Manila (eran de China)." *Buenavista de Indias* 1 (1): 58–78.

Yuste López, Carmen. 1984. *El comercio de la Nueva España con Filipinas 1590-1785*, México, D.F.: Instituto Nacional de Antropología e Historia, Departamento de Investigaciones Históricas.

Yuval-Davis, Nira. 1997. *Gender and Nation*. London: Sage.

Zanardi, Tara. 2019. "From Global Traveler to *Costumbrista* Motif. *The Mantón de Manila* and the Appropriation of the Exotic." In *Visual Typologies from the Early Modern to the Contemporary. Local Contexts and Global Practices*, edited by Tara Zanardi and Lynda Klich, 200–213. New York: Routledge.

4

Decolonizing Fashion, Assembling a Ruana History: Genealogies of a Resisting and Undesirable Garment

Edward Salazar Celis

The history of the ruana, a quintessential Colombian poncho-like piece that traces its roots to South American Indigenous and Spanish garments, attests the colonial narrative of what counts as fashion. The hegemonic definition of fashion relies on a modern/colonial paradigm that centers fashion history, dress practices, as well as bodily experiences and their legitimacy in Europe. The extensive colonization process in the Americas has been displayed through the dressed body since the "discovery" of the so-called "new land." Colonization created a racial division between the Indigenous adornment and dress practices, which were viewed as inferior, and the white European practices viewed as civilized and modern. These assumptions and hierarchies persist in fashion history across the Americas, and this explains why, despite its omnipresence in the Colombian visual landscape, the ruana has been excluded from fashion history and memory.

The absence was especially noticeable at the 2018 exhibition *The Museum Within the Museum*, organized by the National Museum of Colombia. It was a major display regarding nation, modernity, and culture in the Colombian nineteenth and twentieth centuries, where at first a ruana was not available for exhibition. Samuel León and Ángela Gómez, the exhibition curators, had already acknowledged the significance of showing the object. They borrowed Samuel's grandfather's ruana to fulfill the absence. Looking at his family memories in Bogotá, inside the family archive, a 1950s piece, handmade woven wool, was found and displayed in the exhibition. This event reveals how museums preserve the aesthetics of colonialism informed by whiteness (Mirzoeff 2017) in the lack of particular pieces, but also offers the possibility to interrogate and interrupt the silence around the ruana.

In this chapter, I propose to develop a genealogy of this Colombian garment, from the Viceroyalty of New Granada to the twenty-first century, to demonstrate how ruana's pervasiveness challenges the temporalities and evolutionary sense of hegemonic fashion, its colonial power and its white gaze. Although elites have used the ruana for leisure activities and for claiming national identity, this chapter focuses on its primary users and producers: poor, racialized as non-white and peasant people. Also, the chapter delves into the actions that colonial/modern authorities enacted in attempting to eradicate the ruana, which I interpret as a manifestation of coloniality of power (Quijano 2020): the pervasive racialized asymmetrical power that deemed the ruana incompatible with the aspirations of whiteness and civility.

I focus the attention on men's dress practices due to the representational predominance of men wearing ruanas through visual and narrative documents I gathered to compose this archive. Women have also been involved in producing and wearing the ruana, but I focus on racialized non-white men because their fashionable practices have been overlooked in the field of fashion studies, essentializing the relationships between fashion and femininity. Racialized peasants and impoverished men have embraced the ruana in everyday life or special occasions as a garment that speaks about modesty, pride, elegance, progress, style, and belongingness, among other multiple relations. I observed this with the 1970s ruana worn by Saúl, my grandfather, a peasant who arrived in Bogotá during the mid-twentieth century. Despite seeing his ruana for decades, I denied his heritage, reproducing my self-prejudices through the garment.

To start, a ruana is commonly a square piece of woven wool with a gap in the middle to insert the head. The sides are not sewn together. In its basic definition, the ruana is closely related to several pieces in the Autonomous Period,[1] the colonial period and its aftermath. The discussion of traditional garments such as the ruana tends to frame whether they are authentic autonomous pieces or produced by the material encounter with Europeans. For example, Inca's *unku* was a one-piece and knee-length tunic, with sides sewn together, called *camisa* (shirt) by the Spanish invaders. The Mapuche male mantle *makuñ—trarikan makuñ* when it is with pattern designs—is an Autonomous Period square piece with the neck slit. Combined with the medieval Spanish *balandre*, it further produced the poncho that became the *chamanto* (Lacoste and Lacoste 2018).

Due to the ruana's similarities with *trarikan makuñ*, Colombian sociologist Orlando Fals-Borda (1953) reclaimed the Andean roots of the garment by stating that the ruana is derived from the Yanaconan Quechuas[2] poncho in the sixteenth and seventeenth centuries, derived from Mapuche-Huilliche Indigenous poncho from actual Chile. Anne Pollard Rowe also argued that "the poncho appears to have arrived in Ecuador from the south" (2011, 314) from the Mapuche poncho. Moreover, Martínez-Carreño (1995) argued that the ruana is an authentic mestizo piece derived from the Autonomous Indigenous mantle that had been worn from Mexico to Peru, and the Spanish *capisayo* that gave its distinctive central gap. However, the Spanish garments were not the only ones with a gap, which can also be observed in Autonomous Period Mapuche and Inca attires.

I argue the question should not be exclusively if the ruana is a "true" Autonomous/Indigenous garment, but how the piece speaks about whiteness, power, and coloniality, and also how racialized and impoverished people exercised creativity and opposition through dynamic material culture. The impoverishment that Indigenous people faced due to the invader's destruction of their lives also shaped the ruana's material, racial, and political circumstances. In 1583, Don Diego de Torres, the Cacique of Turmequé, traveled to Spain where he had an audience with King Felipe II the following year not only to reclaim the right of his *cacicazgo* (chiefdom) as Indigenous Muisca descendant, but also to advocate for a collective cause against the violence and precarious conditions the royal authorities inflicted on Indigenous peoples in the new kingdom (Restrepo 2010). Along with their steeled jewelry, said Don Diego de Torres, Indigenous clothes revealed a precarious and violent situation: "They are so poor and miserable that, being unable to dress as they used to with cotton clothes, which is all they have, they now cover their bodies with mantles they made from wool while they lived in misery and endured hard labor" (Rojas 1995, 437).

Clothing underwent a long and sustained process of precarity in the following centuries. The demand for cotton mantles and their exchange value increased to an extent that made it impossible for impoverished Indigenous people to afford, even though cotton mantles were made and designed by Indigenous weavers (Martínez-Carreño 1995). Mantles had significant value and material richness in Indigenous populations in the Autonomous Period, which developed a rich textile culture that was decimated by the invaders. From the late sixteenth to eighteenth centuries, the piece started being made with sheep wool, an animal brought to the Americas during colonization. The establishment of *Obrajes* (forced textile workshops) and the increasing availability of sheep led to a shift from using cotton to wool in Indigenous clothing (Alzate 2007).

Black people also wore ruanas as coverage attire amid enslavement.[3] In the plantations, enslavers gave enslaved Black people fabrics to make their ruanas as coverage against the cold weather. Merchants also sold ruanas and other commodities to Black enslaved people in the Real Mines. As a consequence, in the eighteenth century, the ruana flourished among Indigenous and impoverished people, solidifying its connection with wool as the main material. This shift also fabricated a cultural identity around sheep and wool mediated by the ruana, amid the ongoing process of dress control and prescription that favored the European appearance as a means of civility.

This process needed to be broadened within the Bourbon Reforms, which emanated from Spain in the second half of the eighteenth century with the intention of bolstering profit and control in the colonies. The reforms were a series of mandates based on the Enlightenment ideals of civilization and progress. In the New Granada, the Bourbon Reforms also served as a control strategy used by local elites to diminish local traditions and intervene in the body—more precisely, the racialized body (Alzate 2007). Associated with backwardness and dirtiness, eradicating the ruana was conceived as a strategy of civilization and moral control. Although the discourse against the ruana was not novel, it is essential to recognize the ongoing efforts of local authorities to exert colonial power through clothing as a whitening tool. In 1777, the Viceroy of New Granada, Manuel de Guirior, promulgated an Ordinance to regulate artisan labor associations while simultaneously prescribing the appearance, specifically targeting the ruana as part of eugenic politics:

> The use of ruanas in these Kingdoms is most likely a result of lack of cleanliness: it covers the upper part of the body, and the people who cover themselves don't care whether they are clean or dirty underneath. From feet to legs, everyone is seen barefoot, and only with the cover of the ruana, which, although indeed a very appropriate garment when traveling on horseback, should be eliminated for all other uses and, therefore, teachers and parents should strive to completely remove it from their pupils and children.
>
> de Rueda 1995, 97

The Ordinance shows how colonized bodies and spaces were divided between the lines of class and race. The problem was not only being poor but looking like a poor non-white individual. Thus, the Bourbon Reforms were a project of the coloniality of power based on modernity and the Enlightenment (Cardona 2017) where clothing was one of the tools to acquire whiteness (Castro-Gómez 2010). The ordinance pressed to adopt the European dress by stating that craftsman apprentices must wear "shoes and short dresses such as sayos, Anguarínas or casacs," meaning Spanish dress. By stating that sons and disciples should avoid its use, the authority suggested that the ruana would disappear from everyday life in the next generation and that education was fundamental in that endeavor.

Although Colombia gained its independence from Spanish rule in 1810, the colonial mentality persisted. The republic inherited colonial race and class structures amidst discourses of independence and modernity that influenced the perception of the ruana in a new nation governed by creole elites, predominantly comprising white and *mestizo* subjects. The local elite viewed the ruana with a dual perspective: as a threat to national progress but also as a potential symbol with which to identify the new republic. In the nineteenth century, the ruana was marked by this dichotomy.

In schools, the ruana was prohibited by national regulation in 1899, a gesture that evoked the mentioned 1777 Viceregal ordinance. According to Aldana, the ruana was considered in school as an enabler of laziness and untidiness, as well as a way to hide poverty. In consequence, the ruana should be fought against as much as possible. As the place to educate future national citizens, the school was a privileged site for that endeavor. An 1865 school regulation declared: "all the students must be clean and cannot be at school or in the streets without proper and perfectly clean dress. The ruana is prohibited, unless in the countryside where its use is allowed" (Berrío 1865, quoted in Aldana 2017 translation mine).

In the same vein, around 1860 artist Ramón Torres painted a telling lithography about a peasant and his son. The image title stated *Un provinciano conduciendo a su hijo al colejio* ("A provincial man driving his son to school") (Figure 4.1). Father and son wore identical shirts, ties, pants, and shoes. However, the son replaced the peasant hat with a modern Western top hat and the undesirable ruana for a frock coat. The boy wears a fashionable suit, while his father mixes modernity and tradition. There is no doubt that the father is also a modern citizen, judging by his elegant pants, bowtie, leather shoes, and Black umbrella, and because both are light-skinned subjects. However, the ruana was not considered as fashionable as the frock coat. The evident generational shift was symbolized by the abandonment of the ruana and the hat. The lithograph suggests that the substitution of the non-modern piece must be taught by the father—described as a provincial man potentially because of his ruana—especially for attending school. The ruana and the school were unsuited.

I argue that, in daily life, the ruana was incompatible with the national project. However, simultaneously, the new Republic sought to develop a national identity through local symbols and cultural production, in which the ruana played a

Figure 4.1 "Un provinciano conduciendo a su hijo al colegio" by Ramón Torres, c. 1860. Source: Banco de la República, Colombia.

prominent role. As a symbol, the ruana was ubiquitous and widely associated with modesty and poverty among Indigenous, Black, peasant, and impoverished populations. Additionally, the ruana was romanticized as a "natural" part of the nation and was closely associated with the racialized population. A watercolor of Carmelo Fernández for the Chorographic Commission[4] presents an idyllic image: a barefoot Black man, resting in a cacao tree, wears a white striped ruana and white pants in an idealized rural scene. The ensemble is modest but clean. The pose reveals some comfort, even confidence. His sharp eyes return the painter's gaze. The painting gave dignity and importance to the ruana, a national symbol in the aftermath of the independence. Likewise, in a description of another of Fernández's watercolors, similar to the aforementioned piece, Lázaro María Girón wrote in 1891 about two Indigenous lovers. Girón described the man as a gallant wearing a rough but clean ruana and patched pants, gazing at a young Indigenous woman with love and mischief from a beautiful guava tree. Those depictions connected the ruana to decency and pulchritude amid modesty while portraying it as a natural garment of rural, Andean, or tropical life. The images foster a narrative of national pride and heritage through a piece that should exist in the countryside but outside modernity.

In *Peregrinación de Alpha* ("Alpha's Pilgrimage"), the travel diaries of the intellectual Manuel Ancízar between 1850 and 1851, the "eternal ruana"—as he named it—appears multiple times. In a poetic tone, the author described leaving the capital city in search of a scientific and literary narrative of the northern lands of the Republic of New Granada. The ruana was omnipresent in almost all small towns he visited, appearing in a range of ambiguous uses as a garment that was both rich yet rural and racialized. Ancízar depicted honest workers, prosperous peasants, and gentlemen wearing the attire, while stating that the ruana's people—the poor and ordinary land workers—were the Republic's true "foundation and hope" (2016, 359). At the same time, the intellectual affirmed that mestizos, "the truly national type," do not wear ruana. Amid these divergent affirmations, Ancízar concluded that "the ruana, this national uniform, sometimes clean and elegant, sometimes worn, heavy, and stained with misfortune" (ibid., 498), symbolizes the Andean nation. Like Ancízar, national politicians and intellectuals defended whitening the population as the way to achieve sustained civilizational progress for the new Republic.

During his visit to the country between 1897 and 1898, writer and traveler Pierre d'Espagan wrote a romantic and idyllic depiction of the tropical lands and populations. His narrative made clear the widespread presence of the ruana across the national territory. He described the piece as a simple but practical rectangle that falls in folds around the shoulders. The apparent simplicity of the garment contrasts with its always-reported variety. He observed it in various climates and lands: a brown ruana—red on the inside—in Villeta, two musicians in colorful ruanas in Magdalena, a horse rider guitarist in a ruana, and a peasant in his Black ruana close to Medellín.

The ruana was visible in the city, but regarded by the elites as a suspicious object. In *Reminiscencias* ("Reminiscences"), José María Cordovez's chronicles of Colombia's capital from the mid-nineteenth to early twentieth centuries, the ruana appeared primarily in crime scenes. Men wearing it were involved in violent or conflictive situations, mostly against respectable citizens. In the urban space, the garment was criminalized and created a stereotype based on the dressed body. In his account, social classes were also divided between those with ruana and the elegant *cachacos* as those male subjects from Bogotá that wore a modern Black frock coat. Other nuanced uses were described in Cordovez's chronicle, as in the case of a political club that gathered law students and artisans from the liberal party. The members of the club are described wearing big blue ruanas to their feet as if to indicate their political affiliation through the blue color, and their social class and potentially racial provenance through the ruana.

All these narratives and visual depictions recognize the wide variety of ruanas, which prompts an inquiry into their rich materiality and uses. Therefore, the ruana was not as homogeneous and strictly traditional as assumed in the Colombian imaginary. What elements could explain such variety, and how might they reveal practices of self-fashioning?

During the eighteenth and nineteenth centuries, an emerging national textile industry competed with imported textiles, offering cheap goods primarily to Indigenous people, peasant, and artisans. Nevertheless, the whole population was not just guided by low prices. As demonstrated by Ana Maria Otero-Cleves (2017), their "purchasing choices were subject to product quality and texture; tactile engagement was key for peasants and laborers in choosing among fabrics" (445). Indeed, "they were able to express their dissatisfaction over foreign products if needed and sought various alternatives to access the products they liked and preferred" (449). In the case of importations, she suggests that by the late nineteenth century, national importers were demanding ponchos and ruanas with specific and better design features, prettier fringes, and brighter colors from their European suppliers. "Such detailed instructions regarding designs and colors were the norm in order placed by merchants and shopkeepers at midcentury," thereby acknowledging the specific demands of ruana buyers (2024, 89). Racialized individuals expressed their taste by acquiring these imported goods, revealing that some of the ruanas depicted in nineteenth-century images might be imported objects.

This hypothesis could explain the wide variety of colors and patterns in the ruanas. Furthermore, it also recognizes the emerging patterns of social mobility and diverse economic conditions among Indigenous, Black, peasants, and *mestizo* populations. For example, artisanal labor jobs were predominantly performed by racialized individuals, and prosperous merchants were also numerous within these social and racial lines. Their ruanas were often crafted from valuable imported materials and styled with leather shoes and buttoned shirts. In the southwestern region of Colombia, educated artisans utilized fine cloth for their ruanas, while women created ornamented ruanas with colorful patterns and religious imagery (Rodríguez 2002).

Writings and visual representations also emphasized the stylistic richness of the piece. Ruanas varied by territory (e.g., Guascan, Pastusa, or Ecuadorian ruanas), came in various sizes with rounded or tasseled borders, and offered a rich color palette (for example, blue, green, brown, black, white, gray). Some ruanas were designed with inner red or yellow linen, enriching their materiality. One with a red interior and the other with a blue interior can be observed in the watercolors by Ramón Torres Méndez and Manuel María Paz, and these colorful interiors were also described by chroniclers across the Andes. The variations of striped patterns were equally so vast that it feels like no two striped ruanas are ever alike.

Moreover, users stylized them by putting an edge on the shoulder to show the colored interior to indicate quality and worth, or by selecting the proper ruana according to the social occasion. In one of those occasions, for example, leave on the ruana meant that the gentleman was not going to dance, just as leaving the hat on for women implied their preference for remaining seated. Also, the ruana was used as formal attire to highlight the social position of the user. The traveler's chronicles describe some ruanas as elegant, alluring, and splendid, adjectives that offer a small space to imagine its material richness and splendor. If fashion is about codes, manners and details, then the ruana has been a fashionable garment in rural and urban Colombia. Hence, the racial and class valuation of the piece was not inherent; it depended and still does on who gazes upon the ruana.

Figure 4.2 depicts what I consider to be the most striking and lesser-known image of a ruana from the late nineteenth century. New prosperous men, especially artisans, developed an appearance aligned to the modern performances of elegance and simplicity that would shape male fashion in the following century. The ruana was permeated by these fashionable ideals, and once again, its materiality transformed. Photographs captured both continuity and change in the piece. Consequently, the ruana meant not only a traditional garment but also a basic piece in the sense that fashion understands basic—as something timeless or classic.

Marcelino Londoño was photographed in 1899 in Medellín. The Black man is depicted wearing a soft, plain, dark ruana with subtly adorned V-shaped slits. He lifts his head in a gesture and gaze that elevate his appearance, conferring him dignity and confidence. Marcelino wore a crisp white shirt with a fashionably wide collar, buttoned with seemingly delicate metal buttons. The dark ruana contrasts with the impeccable shirt, making a visual statement of modern elegance that continuously refashions traditions. Visiting a photographic studio was also a performance of appearance and subjectivity, in which the photographed subjects composed a curated and elevated image of themselves. The choice of the ruana as part of this polished look situates the object as an esteemed piece full of beauty and pride.

Figure 4.2 "Marcelino Londoño" by Fotografía Rodríguez, 1899. Source: Biblioteca Pública Piloto.

Craftsmanship had historically been a racialized labor, a link that traces its roots back to colonial times. But it was also a guild that allowed for social upward mobility. In the nineteenth century in Medellín and Antioquia, Black and biracial individuals conducted the majority of artisan labor, and some of them achieved prosperity in these endeavors (Mayor 1997). Alberto Mayor also demonstrated that artisans wore fine ruanas that cost the same as a Spanish *casaca* (a type of jacket) made with fine woolen fabrics. Moreover, he described artisans wearing ruanas with two interchangeable faces, and in some cases, the ruana's V-neck revealed the gleaming gold buttons of the impeccable white shirt. Reputed tailors such as José María López wore a ruana of the best "cloth neatly folded and resting over the left arm," a style that the author called "Artisan Fashion" (ibid., 150). The preference for English woolen cloth highlighted the taste, refinement, and choices of men, as well as their pursuit to acquire some characteristics of European taste while creating a novel approach to elegance and masculinity through the ruana.

Another photograph also taken by the studio Fotografía Rodríguez of a man called Pedro Londoño in 1892 reveals a less lavish ruana compared to Marcelino's piece. The fabric shows some loose threads. To elevate the outfit, Pedro wore a white detachable collar, a fashionable piece "mass marketed to men in the US and internationally from the 1840s, [which] were among the earliest mass-produced consumer items" (Turbin 2002, 472). The detachable collar was also a piece tied to middle-class identities and men's social aspirations. By pairing the detachable collar with the ruana, Pedro Londoño actively produced a deliberate appearance with national and international fashionable elements. Londoño completed his look with a well-groomed curly hairstyle and a polished mustache, allowing me to interpret the ruana as a fashion piece. To conclude this argumentation, it is essential to note that in Colombia the ruana has not traditionally been associated with Black people. However, these images, among several others in the archives, prove otherwise.

Throughout the twentieth century, modern/colonial authorities continued to reject the ruana due to its perceived incompatibility with the racialized notion of modernity. In the 1930s, the prominent and assassinated political leader and presidential candidate Jorge Eliécer Gaitán refused to wear a ruana. Despite facing discrimination due to his Indigenous heritage and skin color, Gaitán intended to eliminate ruanas because he considered them unclean garments that hid even greater dirt (Braun 1997). The politician saw the ruana as a symbol of backwardness, distant from the values of urban progress based on the ideals of mestizaje, modernity, and whiteness (Salazar 2021). He sought to eliminate all marks of precarity and moral indecency by controlling the body through eugenic and racial politics.

Nevertheless, the ruana was still visible in rural spaces and in the city. Impoverished people, prosperous merchants, and a growing middle class of rural migrants continued wearing the ruana in the following decades, although in big cities its uses were slowly narrowed to the private sphere. Simultaneously, in the field of fashion design the ruana started to be employed as a national design piece. The "Red Ruana" became the symbol of Avianca Airlines to represent the company and Colombian-ness of the stewardess outfit. The red ruana with a high collar was inspired by the colors of the airline and designed by Arturo Tejada (*c.* 1950), the founder of the first Colombian fashion school. In the following decades, Avianca's commercial routes in Colombia and Latin

America greatly increased the use of the ruana in its uniforms and advertising campaigns, mostly worn by light-skinned women. Avianca used the ruana as a symbol of Colombian fashion for local and global audiences and as a marker of South America's finest hospitality.

In the ongoing circle of admiration and rejection, the interiorized colonial power persisted in refusing ruanas along more elusive class and racial lines. In 1973, the journalist and pioneer fashion disseminator Gloria Valencia de Castaño stated in *Cromos*, the most popular and fashionable Colombian magazine: "Our Seven Avenue is a disaster. The reign of the maxi-ruana as unisex fashion is something utterly grim. At any given moment, one doesn't know whether the person coming toward you has stumbled by accident, or if the person is going to pull a menacing shove or a swift hand from beneath the folds, snatching your wallet or watch" (Cromos 1973: no. 2878).

Paradoxically, Valencia wore ruanas in her public life as a fashion expert, such as in 1962 in Italy at an art opening show. Cromos reported Valencia and her ruana by saying that "Our ruana causes fascination. It wouldn't be rare for one of the famous designers to feature it in their next collection. Something similar has already happened in the United States" (Cromos 1973: par. 3). Perhaps, she did not have concerns with the ruana but with the politics of its use. Ruanas can be the national symbol of modernity and heritage, or as this shows, a suspicious object depending on their users' race, economic background, and social position.

However, the historical account acknowledges that power has not eliminated this ever-changing and resisting fashionable garment. In the twenty-first century, the ruana gained prominence within the national fashion system amid the increasing search for a national fashion that began in Latin America in the 1950s. Nevertheless, the fashionable use and production of the ruana were not created by the fashion system and are not sustained entirely by it. Instead, it is the result of collective actors who create and experiment with its materiality while centering the cultural and affective labor behind the garment.

Stable and profound relationships are essential to the creative process that challenges the concept of a fashion brand within capitalism, demonstrating that economic prosperity does not have to come at the expense of human and non-human connections. Building on this premise, Francisco Gómez and Silvino Patiño founded the brand Tejidos Rebancá. Silvino, an Indigenous Muiscan descendant, though not formally affiliated with any Indigenous Council, emphasizes his heritage: "I am Muisca because I know it. A tree doesn't have to say it's a tree."[5] He inherited weaving skills from his family and developed a special affinity for wool due to its significant presence in the Andean region. Francisco, an artist from Bogotá with roots in Boyacá, the same Andean region as Silvino, grew up observing his grandfather wearing the ruana in Bogotá. As an art student devoted to Andean textile traditions, he incorporated the ruana into his everyday attire.

Silvino Patiño and Francisco Gómez shared a profound connection with the material, seeking to explore innovative designs featuring the ruana's dense wool fabric and distinctive square shape. This exploration has involved altering its traditional form, experimenting with sizes, shapes, embellishments, and natural colors extracted from plants. Their strong connection to the roots of the ruana led them to establish the brand's atelier outside the capital city, choosing to make their home in the Andean town of Iza, Boyacá.

Likewise, as an Indigenous designer of the Muisca Council of Cota, Estiven Castro started his design inquiry through the mantle worn by Indigenous people before colonization, a piece highly regarded in Muisca culture. Estiven recognizes the close ties between the mantle and the ruana. Since everyone in the Council developed a craft, he wondered which he would pursue. The Cabildo's governor gave him a needle to start learning weaving, guided by an experienced woman from his community. Estiven traveled to Bogotá to study graphic design, where he created the brand Somos Mhuyscas (We are Mhuyscas), an effort that brought him back to the Council's weavers and other artisans from Cundinamarca. It was also his journey to understand the connection between weaving and spirituality and weaving within the urban space. "Weaving is a language composed of three threads: the spiritual, the earthy, and the self."[6]

Through his work in Somos Mhuyscas, Estiven Castro is interested in blending the relationships between the ruana and the mantle by using wool thread to remember the sheep and the peasant component of indigeneity, and a cotton thread as the material used in the rich mantles made by his ancestors. The third thread over the piece depicts pictograms and fauna close to the Council's land, a gesture that enriches the design. Furthermore, the brand adopted an aesthetic of ruanas and hats that Estiven Castro remembered as the visual language of his grandfather's dress. The brand's name, Somos Mhuyscas, proposes a collective dialogue and creative process, a bridge between urban/rural spaces and producers/consumers. "The word Muisca means 'human being with red blood' as everybody is one," said Estiven.

The rich presence of the ruana in the Colombian national imagination is a testament to the ongoing resistance and creativity primarily enacted by racialized and impoverished people in the country. In those long centuries,

Figure 4.3 "Chiguene gue Muisca Mantle" by Somos Mhuyscas, 2021. Courtesy of Estiven Castro. In the image, Estiven wears the piece.

from the 1777 viceregal ordinance to the 1973 complaint in a fashion magazine, it is thanks to their primary users and creators that the ruana remains visible and maintains its national significance until the present. Thanks to them, the ruana occupies a fundamental place in Colombian fashion culture, within and beyond the fashion system, reminding us that the decolonization of fashion practices and knowledge must be viewed as a verb rather than a noun derived solely from academia (Mignolo and Walsh 2018). As with the ruana, the contours of fashion, tradition, design, and craftsmanship must be challenged, blurred, or even collapsed. This is a collective call to disrupt fashion's colonial power structures.

Acknowledgements

This work was supported by the Summer Publishing Institute, an initiative of the Department of Latin American and Latino Studies at the University of California, Santa Cruz, funded by the UC-Hispanic Serving Institutions Doctoral Diversity Program. A special thanks to Jennifer González for most generous feedback.

Notes

1 Following Aubrey Hobart's (2018), Autonomous Period "refers to that period of history during which the Indigenous people of the Americas governed themselves without interference from any other continent" (14).
2 Ruana is a Quechua voice that means Quechua people. However, it is not possible to establish a connection between the voice and the garment.
3 See Borja and Rodríguez 2011 and Posada 2021.
4 Chorographic Commission, 1850–1862, the ambitious enterprise for documentation and knowledge production of the new republic inhabitants and territories, to state the foundations for a modern nation.
5 Silvino Patiño, interview with the author, Zoom call, September 4, 2023.
6 Estiven Castro, interview with the author, Zoom call, September 1, 2023.

Bibliography

Alzate, Adriana. 2007. *Suciedad y orden: Reformas sanitarias borbónicas en la Nueva Granada 1760–1810*. Bogotá, D.C: Editorial Universidad del Rosario.

Aldana, Alexander. 2017. "Cuerpos vestidos, apariencias aseadas y lujo maldecido: hacia una estética corporal en la escuela colombiana." *Praxis & Saber* 8 (18): 35–56.

Ancízar, Manuel. 2016. *Peregrinación de Alpha*. Bogotá: Biblioteca Nacional de Colombia.

Borja, Jaime and Pablo Rodríguez. 2011. *Historia de la vida privada en Colombia*, Bogotá: Taurus.

Braun, Herbert. 1997. "Jorge Eliécer Gaitán y la modernidad: en política, señaló la falta de equilibrio entre lo privado y lo público." *Credencial Historia* 96: 139–147.

Cardona, Hilderman. 2017. "Colonialidad del poder y biopolítica etnoracial: Virreinato de Nueva Granada en el contexto de las Reformas Borbónicas." *Boletim do Museu Paraense Emilio Goeldi. Ciências humanas* 12 (2): 571–594.

Castro-Gómez, Santiago. 2010. *La hybris del punto cero: Ciencia, raza e ilustración en la Nueva Granada (1750–1816)*. 2nd ed. Bogotá: Pontificia Universidad Javeriana.

Cordovéz, José María. 2015. *Reminiscencias escogidas de Santafé y Bogotá*. Bogotá: Biblioteca Nacional de Colombia.

Cromos: Cromos. 1970. "Gloria Valencia de Castaño, editorial column," *Cromos*, 2878, n.p.

D'Espagnat, Pierre. 1942. *Recuerdos de la Nueva Granada*. Colombia: Ministerio de Educación Nacional.

De Rueda, Martha. 1995. "Instrucción general para los gremios." Santa Fe, 1777." *Ensayos: Historia y Teoría del Arte* (1): 188–215.

Fals-Borda, Orlando. 1953. "Notas sobre la evolución del vestido campesino en la Colombia central." *Revista Colombiana de Folklore* (2): 139–147.

Hobart, Aubrey. 2018. *Treasures and Splendors: Exhibiting Colonial Latin American Art in U.S. Museums, 1920–2020*. Santa Cruz: University of California Press.

Lacoste, Pablo and Michelle Malén Lacoste Adunka. 2018. "Chamantos, Ponchos y Balandres en Colchagua y Rancagua (siglos XVII–XIX)." *Estudios atacameños* (57): 97–118.

Martínez-Carreño, Aida. 1995. *La prisión del vestido: Aspectos sociales del traje en América*, 1st ed. Santa Fe de Bogotá, D.C.: Planeta Colombiana Editorial.

Mayor, Alberto. 1997. *Cabezas duras y dedos inteligentes: Estilo de vida y cultura técnica de los artesanos colombianos del siglo XIX*. Colombia: Instituto Colombiano de Cultura.

Mignolo, Walter, and Catherine Walsh. 2018. *On Decoloniality: Concepts, Analytics, Praxis*. Raleigh, NC: Duke University Press.

Mirzoeff, Nicholas. 2017."Empty the Museum, Decolonize the Curriculum, Open Theory." *The Nordic Journal of Aesthetics* 25, (53): 6–22.

Mirzoeff, Nicholas. 2023. *White Sight: Visual Politics and Practices of Whiteness*. Cambridge: MIT Press.

Otero-Cleves, Ana. 2017. "Foreign Machetes and Cheap Cotton Cloth: Popular Consumers and Imported Commodities in Nineteenth-Century Colombia." *Hispanic American Historical Review* 97 (3): 423–456.

Otero-Cleves, Ana. 2024. *Plebeian Consumers Global Connections, Local Trade, and Foreign Goods in Nineteenth-Century Colombia*. Cambridge: Cambridge University Press.

Posada, Sara. 2021. "Esclavitud y vida cotidiana en los Reales de Minas de Popayán, siglo XVII." *Quirón Revista de Estudiantes de Historia* Special Edition: 64–84.

Quijano, Aníbal. 2020. *Cuestiones y horizontes. De la dependencia histórico-estructural a la colonialidad/descolonialidad del poder*. Buenos Aires: CLACSO.

Restrepo, Luis. 2010. "El Cacique de Turmequé o los agravios de la memoria." *Cuadernos de literatura* 14 (28): 14–33.

Rodríguez, Pablo. 2002. *En busca de lo cotidiano: Honor, sexo, fiesta y sociedad, s. XVII–XIX*, Bogotá: Universidad Nacional de Colombia.

Rojas, Ulises. 1995. *El cacique de Turmequé y su época*. Boyacá: Imprenta Departamental.

Rowe, Anne Pollard. 2011. "Conclusions." In Rowe, Anne Pollard, and Lynn Meisch, eds., *Costume and History in Highland Ecuador*. Austin: University of Texas Press.

Salazar, Edward. 2021. "Beauty has no age anymore: Fashion and youth in Colombia (1970–99)." *International Journal of Fashion Studies* 8 (1): 67–84.

Turbin, Caroline. 2002. "Fashioning the American Man: The Arrow Collar Man, 1907–1931." *Gender & History*, 14 (3): 470–491.

5

The Names of the Clothes: Cuban Fashion Brandscape, 1959–1989

María A. Cabrera Arús

January 1, 1959, stands as a pivotal date in Cuban history. It not only heralded the start of a new year but also inaugurated a transformative political era, as the triumph of the Cuban Revolution brought far-reaching changes that permeated every aspect of life, fashion included. The government's March 1959 campaign *Consumir lo que el país produce es hacer patria* (To Consume what the Country Produces Builds the Fatherland) encouraged the patriotic consumption of Cuban-made goods. The creation of the Tiendas del Pueblo stores in June enhanced clothing accessibility for rural populations.[1] A legislation introduced in July sanctioned a 30 percent surcharge on luxury goods, aimed at curtailing foreign spending on products associated with wealth and status. The year 1960 saw further changes as the state monopolized imports and assumed control over the textile industry, centralizing the production and distribution of clothing and footwear. The following year's endorsement of Marxism-Leninism solidified this trajectory, culminating in the almost complete socialization of the textile and footwear industries by 1962.[2]

In 1963, the introduction of a national rationing system for industrial goods, encompassing clothing and footwear, turned consumption into a process mediated and mostly controlled by the state, reducing consumer agency in an economy increasingly marked by scarcity (Rodríguez Balari 1990). As the fashion industry evolved into a potent channel for state propaganda, it also became a conduit for communicating narratives of nationalism, collectivism, and progress that were instrumental to the legitimation of the state socialist regime. At the same time, fashion was criticized as an instrument of capitalist exploitation and class division, with the industry pivoting towards producing workwear and uniforms for various state-led programs and mass organizations. As the influence of the Soviet Union grew, fashion discourses increasingly diverged from the actual material reality present in stores, resulting in the proliferation of elaborate fashion imagery and branding that contrasted sharply with the tangible products available to consumers (Cabrera Arús 2019a; Cabrera Arús 2019c).

This chapter delves into the meanings embedded within the 366 local fashion brand names licensed under Class 25 of the Nice Classification—which specifically pertains to clothing and footwear[3]—by Cuba's National Office of Inventions, Technical Information, and Trademarks (ONIITEM) between 1959 and 1989. The timeframe spans from the revolution's rise to power to the fall of the Berlin Wall, an event that precipitated the collapse of the Eastern European state socialist regimes and the disintegration of the Soviet Union, which were Cuba's major allies and trading partners. These global shifts necessitated significant economic adjustments in the country, profoundly impacting the fashion and apparel industries.

In the absence of available data on consumer perception, this chapter adopts a semiotic approach (Niesing 2015) to brand identity. The primary focus is on the brand names and, where applicable, their logos, ignoring information on producers, styles, and target consumers. The purpose is to decipher the underlying cultural, social, and political messages embedded in fashion brands as they were conceptualized by state enterprise creators, under the premise that such an exploration reveals profound insights into the politics of fashion—namely, into how brands were intended to be experienced and interpreted by consumers.

All data were sourced from the Cuban Bureau of Industrial Property (OCPI), which succeeded ONIITEM in 1997.[4] This methodological choice constrains the study to focus solely on licensed brands, excluding potential trademarks that were not registered. In some instances, licenses were issued retrospectively, with the official grant date preceding the date of the application submission. To avoid accounting for this and other irregularities, the analysis is based on the filing dates of each brand's application, with meanings derived solely from the author's interpretation.

In understanding brands not merely as distinguishing marks for products, but as semiotic engines capable of generating a multitude of meanings and values (Heilbrunn 2006; Lury 2004), other studies have recognized their incidence in modern political imaginaries (Askegaard 2006; Schroeder and Salzer-Mörling 2006). However, while national and country brands have been widely acknowledged as instruments of diplomacy and soft power (Niesing 2015; Rojas-Méndez and Khoshnevis 2023), commercial brands have rarely been considered tools of statecraft. In the state socialist countries of Eastern

Europe, where most facets of social life were subject to politicization, anthropologist Krisztina Fehérváry posits that brands acted as a language that endowed state-produced goods with "rich sociocultural and ideological 'captioning'" (2009, 452). However, while her research offers valuable insights into the politics of consumption in socialist Hungary, it does not address the politics of commercial brands under socialist regimes.

This chapter contributes an analysis of the "captioning" aspect of Cuban socialist brands, focusing on the narratives conceived by state producers. This approach not only enriches existing knowledge about Cuban fashion but also illuminates the broader interplay between fashion and politics in a Latin American state socialist regime.

In terms of brand licensing, the Cuban Revolution brought a long pause as no licenses were filed for national brands between 1959 and 1965.[5] By the time two national fashion brands applied for licenses in 1966, many private brands had vanished from the by-then-state-owned fashion scene. Paradoxically, 39 footwear brands filed for and obtained licenses in 1967, followed by 29 clothing and footwear brands in 1968. This increase in licensing activity occurred during a period characterized by "extreme idealism" in government policies, where there was a concerted effort to dismantle traditional market mechanisms (Mesa-Lago 1978, 30).

Likely contributing factors to this surge are the expiration of licenses issued before 1959, which may have led state enterprises to secure legal protection for the brands they had appropriated, and the Ministry of Domestic Commerce's initiative to develop new brand names, logos, and marketing campaigns aimed at enhancing consumers' perceptions of domestically produced goods.[6] Whatever the cause, the uptick in brand licensing was short lived. In 1968, when the government's Revolutionary Offensive intensified state control and eliminated any remnants of private ownership in the industrial and service sectors, the rate of fashion brand licensing decelerated dramatically. From 1969 to 1978, only three footwear brands and three apparel brands were granted licenses, one of them specializing in work clothes.

By 1979, brand registration experienced a notable resurgence, remaining consistent throughout the following decade. Remarkably, nearly three-quarters of the 366 brands licensed from 1959 to 1989 were licensed in or after 1980.[7] This boom occurred amidst the expansion of the state-owned free market, a cautious yet progressive opening towards foreign capitalist partnerships and international tourism, and a marked increase in media attention and press coverage focusing on consumer issues (Mesa-Lago 1978; Salinas Chávez and Salinas Chávez 2017).

In 1983, coinciding with the enactment of Decree-Law No. 68, which required the registration of trademarks for products designated for both domestic and international markets, 36 new licenses were granted.[8] Prior to the implementation of this decree, ONIITEM had undertaken efforts to educate the public about the significance of trademarks, including the publication of various booklets designed to inform both producers and consumers of the importance of brand identification and protection.[9] Yet the largest peak in brand licensing occurred in 1989, when Cuban enterprises licensed 68 brands, some of them of foreign origin. This surge in licensing activity coincides with the unfolding of political and economic turmoil in Eastern Europe and the Soviet Union, a situation that led Cuba to actively pursue new partnerships and alliances in Latin America and Western Europe, and to place a stronger emphasis on international tourism (Mesa-Lago 1984).

In analyzing brand meanings, anthropologist Arjun Appadurai's notion of "scapes" comes in handy. Coined to describe the fluid and dynamic nature of global cultural flows and their "deeply perspectival" nature (1996, 33)—shaped by historical, linguistic, and political contexts—it aptly describes the multifaceted cultural constructs brand names create (Oyama 2009; Oswald 2012; Klingmann 2007). Factors such as the nationalization of the fashion industry, a significant decrease in foreign tourism, a shift in foreign trade partners, the introduction of rationing for clothing and footwear within the domestic market, and a general scarcity of consumer goods shaped the Cuban fashion brandscape, influencing not only the availability and distribution of fashion products but also the circulation and logic of fashion branding.

In this context, the meanings of the national fashion brands licensed between 1959 and 1989 can be grouped into five main categories (Figure 5.1), with the most prevalent theme corresponding to demographic characteristics, particularly gender and age (127 brands). This is followed by themes evocative of foreign imaginaries (111 brands), nationalist (103 brands), denoting beauty and highbrow culture (79 brands), and expressing socio-political status (47 brands). Other thematic groups, although less numerically dominant, include brands with military connotations or direct links to state socialist institutions (25 brands), brands associated with the modern imaginary (23 brands), those reflecting elements of popular culture (23 brands), and sports-themed brands (16 brands).

These categories are not mutually exclusive, with several brands embodying meanings that span multiple themes. For example, Cacique draws its name from the title of Taino aboriginal leaders in precolonial Cuba, resonating with nationalist sentiments, targeting a male demographic, and implying an elitist

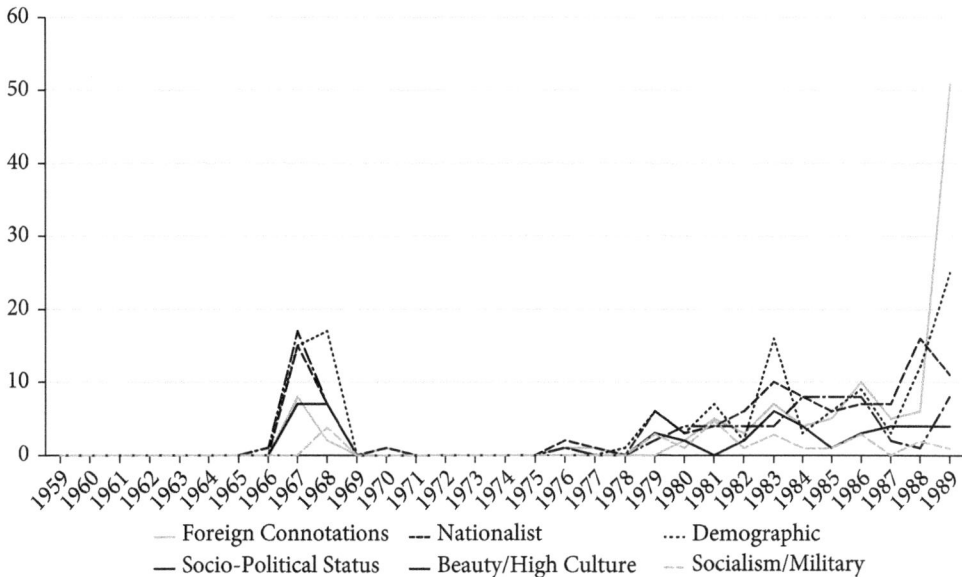

Figure 5.1 Principal themes in the Cuban brandscape. Graph made by author with OCPI's data.

status-oriented product. Similarly, Estrella, meaning "star" in Spanish and a common woman's name, interweaves references to a female target demographic with nuances of beauty and status. This nuanced role of fashion branding presents brands as not just a mere commercial tool, but a potent medium for articulating various aspects of identity, culture, and political discourse.

An analysis of the brand themes reveals that brands with demographic connotations are salient in 1968 and the early 1980s. These brands mostly feature proper names and, to a lesser extent, gender-specific nouns such as Futura, a feminized, non-standard Spanish adaptation of the word "future," and Favorita, a favorite female. This category also includes diminutives, onomatopoeias, and nicknames commonly associated with children, such as Caballito (little horse), Bamby (a variation of "Bambi"), Bambino (Italian for "child"), Chama (Cuban slang for "child"), and Kikirikí (the onomatopoeic name for roosters used in child-related contexts). The diverse range of languages and spellings as well as the use of inventive or colloquial terms in this theme indicates a strategic approach to resonate with specific consumer demographics.

Brands that evoke foreignness are primarily names with foreign spellings or referents. For example, Yak, Ruby, First Lady, Golden Pigeon, Flamingo, Letty, Lyn, Olimpic, Flexil, Delta, Continental, Magnum, Tiffany's, Anatomix, Karla,

Buffalo, Euphon, Yin-Yu, Scarlett, Línea Internacional (international line), Gotcha, Ivanhoe, and Renegade. This theme gained significant traction in 1986 and, most saliently, in 1989, when an astounding 51 of the 68 licensed brands depicted foreign elements, accounting for 48 percent of the meanings in that year's fashion brandscape. Many of these were international trademarks, such as Franco Pugi, Justin Charles, O de la Renta, Paco Rio, Pierre Balmain, and Mc. Kay, registered under Cuban enterprises, likely due to legal caveats.

The numeric relevance of brands with foreign connotations highlights the persistent association of fashion with influences from abroad, despite governmental efforts to promote localized production and consumption (Pérez 1999). Notably, the fact that many of them are English names reflects the enduring cultural influence of the United States on the Cuban sartorial imagination, also indicating their possible commercialization in dollar stores, which catered mainly to foreign tourists and diplomats—the boom of this theme coincides with the promotion of foreign capitalist tourism.

The nationalist theme appears particularly significant in the late-1960s, the late-1970s, and the 1980s, reaching a peak in 1988 when 16 of the 47 brands licensed that year bore nationalist connotations, accounting for 23 percent of the total meanings identified in that year's brandscape. This theme arises from various sources that often overlap and interrelate, predominating among them meanings associated with the countryside. Numerous brands are named after rural inhabitants, such as Llanero (a plainsman), Payito (a village boy), Montuno (a hillbilly), and Serrano (a highland dweller). Others encompass broader connections to rural life, like Agro (denoting farmland and agriculture), Hato (meaning both "herd" and "ranch"), Palma (a palm tree), Jiquí (a local timber tree), Yarey (a species of guano used in traditional peasant hats), Catey (a local parakeet), and Trocha (a path through bushes or forest). Additionally, some brands reflect occupations and tools typical of the countryside, as seen in Cazador (a hunter), Montero (a hunter), Arico (a derivative of "*aricar*," meaning "superficial plowing"), and Zagal (a shepherd boy).

The significant presence of the rural imaginary in Cuban nationalist fashion brands is likely to be connected to the fashion industry's focus on producing workwear for agricultural activities and state-run programs such as the boarding schools in rural areas, where students engaged in agricultural work, among other initiatives that mobilized urban workers and students for agricultural labor (Luke 2018; Hynson 2019). The infusion of rural motifs in Cuban fashion brands can be attributed as well to the geographical expansion of the industry, as new textile mills were established in provincial towns, and to attempts to infuse brand identities with regional character and lore.[10]

Figure 5.2 Examples of nationalist connotations in Cuban brand logos. Images obtained from OCPI.

Other nationalist brands feature toponyms, mostly derived from aboriginal origins or spelling. Examples include Soroa, Caisimú, Caujerí, Jagua, Cajío, Cauto, Caonao, and Cubanacán. Another group comprises names with historical connotations, often referencing elements of pre-Columbian history or connecting to colonial-era imagery. Examples in this category are Cacique (a Taino tribal leader), Taína (a Taino woman), Atabey (a Taino goddess), Guamá (a Taino cacique known for resisting Spanish colonization), Caonex (a word of Arawak spelling), Criolla (a Creole woman), Colonial, and Quitrín (a type of Cuban colonial cabriolet). A final group is formed by brands that incorporate national symbols or reference sports events organized in the country, such as Habana '91, coined prior to the 1991 Pan American Games celebrated in Havana.

Nationalist connotations in Cuban fashion brands extend beyond names, also appearing embodied in logos drawn from aboriginal or colonial imagery (Figure 5.2). For example, Judex, a brand specializing in children's sleepwear, features a logo depicting a crawling child adorned with a feather hat reminiscent of indigenous headwear. Similarly, Jurey, a brand of guayabera shirts, is represented through a flint ax, an aboriginal tool. Recreo and Diana utilize logos featuring large clay pots, echoing the colonial-era pottery traditions prevalent in Cuba's central region (Hernández Fusté 2014). These logos serve not only as brand identifiers, but also as visual representations of the rich cultural and historical influences that shape national identity.

At this point, it is worth noting the paucity of Afro-Cuban cultural references. Only Rumba, a popular Afro-Cuban dance, yet also a variant of Spanish flamenco, and Batá, a type of drum integral to religious ceremonies of African origin, distinctly embody this aspect of Cuban heritage. Comparatively, imagery stemming from the Spanish colonial period is more prominent, although this falls short compared to the prevalence of aboriginal motifs.[11] The Latin American imaginary, while present, is not prominent either. Only a few brands, such as Abey (a jacaranda tree typical of Latin America and the Caribbean), Caribbean Sea, and Continental, explicitly reference the continent or its regions. This selective emphasis within the brandscape paints a nuanced picture of the country's historical narrative, highlighting its aboriginal and Spanish heritage while featuring much less prominently the African and broader Latin American elements that were also integral to Cuban culture.

In general, the wide-ranging nationalist themes present in brands and logos indicate governmental efforts to use fashion as a medium to articulate and strengthen national identity and infuse socialism with a distinct Cuban flavor. The nationalist theme in fashion emerges as a potent form of both cultural expression and political validation of the Cuban socialist model. While not as dominant as the demographic, foreign, and nationalist themes, notions of beauty and culture also hold relevance within the Cuban fashion brandscape. This theme came to the forefront in 1967 when 17 of the 65 brands licensed that year—slightly more than a quarter—expressed ideas of beauty or culture. This theme saw a resurgence in the mid-1980s, when a similar proportion of brands embodied similar connotations.

Within this theme, a subset of brands features names directly evocative of beauty and its varied symbols. For instance, Encanto ("charm"), Primor ("darling" or "a fine thing"), Ensueño ("fantasy"), Cisne ("swan"), Gacela ("gazelle"), Silueta ("silhouette"), Bella ("beautiful" in the feminine form), Gaviota ("seagull"), and Venus, the Roman goddess of beauty and love. Another group within this theme derives inspiration from high culture, as illustrated by brand names like Sonata, Vinci (likely alluding to Leonardo da Vinci), Giselle, Ballet, Mona Lisa, and Coppelia. These names not only highlight elements of classical beauty and elegance but also draw connections to the broader realms of art and high culture, enriching the cultural depth of the Cuban fashion brandscape.

The relative prominence of the beauty and cultural theme within the Cuban fashion brandscape reflects governmental efforts to extend access among the working class to traditionally elitist forms of presentation and overall culture. This was manifested in the establishment of a sewing school in 1961 for peasant girls, where they were taught to make sophisticated dresses, headgear, and suits (Guerra 2012).[12] It was also expressed in the founding of cultural institutions like the Cuban National Ballet, the National Institute for Cinema Art and Industry, the National Art Schools, the National Symphonic Orchestra, and the Imprenta Nacional, a publishing house that was inaugurated with an ambitious 100,000-copy print of *Don Quixote* under the Biblioteca del Pueblo (People's Library) collection, featuring illustrations by Gustavo Doré and Pablo Picasso.[13]

Closely related to the theme of beauty and culture, the theme of status comprises brands with names that suggest distinction and class. Examples include Cónsul (consul), D'Gala, D'Lis, Sello Azul (blue stamp), Elegante (elegant), Premier, Oro (gold), Canciller (ambassador), Jade, Royal, La Maison, and Quitrín. The presence of status symbolism strikingly contrasts with an official discourse critical of class disparities and luxury (Castro 1959; also in Pérez 1999), and highlights the persistent role of fashion as a means of expressing and signifying social distinction (Kapferer 2006), even during periods characterized by political idealism and radicalism, such as the late-1960s in Cuba.

In contrast, brands allegorical to popular-class culture constitute just over half of those conveying status. They typically represent common idioms, environments, and entertainment forms, as in the case of Rumba, Pepito (a character from popular jokes), Camping (a low-budget vacationing option promoted in the 1980s as hotel capacities were redirected towards foreign tourism), Rodeo (a popular rural spectacle and sport), and Alamar (a prefabricated housing project in Havana). The limited presence of popular culture themes in the fashion brandscape suggests that the government's critique of luxury might have been more rhetorical than reflected in the promotion of a genuinely popular fashion narrative.

In general, the presence of themes relating to beauty, culture, and status within the Cuban fashion brandscape points to the official appeal to cultural sophistication and social distinction in the commercialization of fashion, despite the prevailing rhetoric of modesty and function over form that accompanied the fashion industry's reorientation towards producing practical and utilitarian apparel (Rodríguez Balari 1985). This ambivalence most likely served the government to not only stimulate consumer interest and drive the purchase of domestically produced goods but also foster participation in the broader socio-political project. Such a complex interplay suggests that despite the overarching emphasis on functionality, there was still room for fashion to be leveraged as a tool for both economic stimulation and social mobilization.

In this context, brands reflecting revolutionary and socialist ideals are comparatively scarce, especially when considering the prominence of revolutionary and socialist narratives in the country's political ethos. These themes are represented in brands such as Trinchera (trench), Fortín (bunker), Paladín (defender), Caravana (caravan), Triunfo (triumph), and Victoria (victory), which reflect the growing militarism that distinguished the Cuban Revolution and state socialist regime (San Martín and Bonachea 1984; Vellinga 1976). They are also represented in brands that resonate with socialist institutions and programs, such as Heroína (a female hero and an exemplary female worker within the socialist emulation system), Pionero (a member of the Soviet-inspired organization for school children), Vanguardia (a status of distinction awarded to outstanding workers and students), and Monitor (a student supervisor).

These themes resonate with another set of brands that embody modernity. Names like Nueva Línea (new line), Lo Nuevo (the new), Futuro (future), and Avance (move forward), which anticipate the dawn of a new era and embody a progressive, forward-thinking mindset. As well as brands such as Cometa (comet), Órbita (orbit), and Radar, which are drawn from the lexicon of space exploration that also distinguished the Soviet and Eastern European brandscapes, and which present Cuban socialism as technologically advanced, wrapped in a futuristic vision (Cabrera Arús 2019c).

This interplay between politics and modern aspirations is also manifested in the design of brand logos. As an example, the brand Futura's logo features the symbol of the atom, an emblem of modern science and technology that contrasts with the actual product: basic shirts with only five buttons, crafted from thin, plain-colored polyester blends. The use of a technologically evocative logo on an otherwise unremarkable garment underscores the use of fashion brands to symbolize the country's alignment with modern scientific progress, despite clear limitations in material quality and design.

In addition to their individual significance, various themes intersect into individual brands, resulting in multiple overlapping narratives. For example, the shoe brand Cacique, licensed in 1967, encapsulates both nationalism and a sense of status, while Mariposa, a brand of women's shoes licensed in 1967, blends themes of gender and beauty with undertones of rural nationalism that position its product as both aesthetically appealing and an embodiment of authentic local craftsmanship. On the contrary, the footwear brand D'Gala conveys a sense of foreignness and status, not only through the inherent exclusivity suggested by the word "gala" but also through the use of the foreign prefix "D," which adds a touch of international flair to the brand.

Similarly, Gulliver, a brand of sports pants for young men licensed in 1968, blends foreignness with cultural connotations, while targeting a male demographic. Another example is Jaruquito, a brand of ranch pants for boys licensed in 1980, which embeds rural nationalism via a place name while also signaling the gender and age group of its target market. Lastly, Heroína, a brand of women's work shirts licensed in 1983, intertwines elements of the revolutionary-socialist narrative with indications of both political status and female demographics.

This multifaceted nature of branding is also highlighted by the design of brand logos. For example, while Cubartesanía and Batos, both licensed in 1988, connote nationalist themes, the radar-like imagery in their logos introduces a modern technological dimension to this narrative. This branding strategy honors the country's heritage while projecting the socialist fashion industry as ambitiously forward-thinking.

Ultimately, the meanings of brands were affected by the inherent quality and style of the products they represented. In the cases of the late-1980s brands La Maison and Quitrín, their elite connotations are reinforced by the product craftsmanship, based on techniques like lace and embroidery that give them an image of exclusivity and sophistication while also rooting the brands in Cuban traditions. Their commercialization in dollar stores presents this high-end nationalist branding approach as geared towards positioning the products as premium options for foreign visitors.

By contrast, the brand Órbita, licensed in 1980 for men's work shirts, blends the theme of technological advancement under socialism (it references the USSR launching an artificial satellite into orbit) with the practicality of working-class apparel. This brand not only represents a socialist future characterized by scientific and technological progress, extensive to outer space, but also symbolically places the working class at the forefront of this futuristic vision. The brand Jiquí, launched in 1977 for Cuban-made blue jeans, addresses a different kind of transformation. After more than a decade of official discourse presenting blue jeans as a symbol of moral deviance and capitalist influence (Cabrera Arús 2015; Cabrera Arús 2017), the garment's nationalist branding facilitates its assimilation into the local milieu, acting as a vehicle for the reinterpretation of the denim apparel as an emblem of national identity.

Besides these caveats, substandard quality affected the perceived value and meanings associated with many brands (Delgado Lamela 1993). A government study conducted in 1985 revealed that as much as 7 percent of manufactured goods were deemed unsellable because of poor quality.[14] Another study conducted in 1989 revealed that dissatisfaction with the quality and style of items obtained from state stores was prevalent.[15] Factors such as the rationing system and the Black market, among others, are also expected to have played a role in shaping the actual meanings of brands.[16]

The various examples analyzed highlight the government's strategic use of fashion branding as an instrument for political communication and social influence, presenting the fashion industry as a complex interlocutor between state policies, cultural expression, and economic ambitions. Cuban socialist fashion branding was, in essence, a political performance meticulously crafted to communicate and reinforce the government's agenda under fashion guise.

After 1989, the fashion brandscape underwent a radical transformation in response to shifting economic policies. As the country ventured towards a mixed economy, embracing capitalist elements and increasingly depending on foreign tourism, factors such as the legalization of foreign currency, the expansion of the private sector, and the opening of dollar stores to Cuban citizens transformed fashion production and commercialization (Hernández Morales 2005). In the new economic context, many brands licensed in the previous three decades either ceased production or faded away while new private brands timidly began to emerge.

In 2019, Ana Gabriela Valdés, a visual arts student, created the brand Nawe, stemming from a colloquial term used to denote friends or, most often, people from the countryside.[17] Nawe's branding delves into Cuba's heritage, drawing significantly from Indigenous influence, as evinced in the brand's logo, which incorporates aboriginal pictograms, and the name itself, which resonates with pre-Columbian phonetics.[18] These elements align Nawe with the nationalist theme prevalent in the socialist fashion brandscape, attesting to the reinterpretation and reinvigoration of the nationalist narrative within a modern context in which new private brands are protagonists.

Nawe is part of a process that media scholar Jeannine Diego describes as "an undeniable *movida*" or fashion boom, characterized by a flourishing scene that includes "catwalks, fashion weeks, fashion magazines, fashion designers, fashion photographers, models, modeling agencies, boutiques, influencers and bloggers" that largely operate outside state control (2021: 50).[19] At the forefront of this *movida* is Clandestina, a brand that proudly positions itself as Cuba's "first independent, international fashion label" (O'Connell 2021).[20]

A partnership between a Cuban graphic designer and a Spanish entrepreneur, Clandestina debuted in 2015, when the US and Cuba participated in conversations that led to the restoration of diplomatic relations. This timing proved advantageous as, in the year following its inception, cofounder Idania del Río was invited to meet with President Barack Obama during his visit to Cuba, consolidating the brand's position and facilitating its appeal to the US public. With this goal, Clandestina set up an online sales platform on a website with Colombian domain extension (.co), marketing its t-shirts as "designed in Cuba and printed in the US."[21] In a strategic expansion of its physical presence, the brand launched pop-up sales points in New York and Washington, DC, in 2019, a move that was followed by the establishment of a permanent outlet in The Canvas, a multi-brand store situated in Brooklyn, New York (Cabrera Arús 2019b). Most recently, Clandestina opened a permanent store in the Oculus Center, an upscale shopping location in Downtown Manhattan.

Clandestina's brand semiotics conveys a narrative of female ownership while portraying the brand as irreverent, anti-establishment, and non-conforming, attributes stressed by the incorporation of slogans from movements such as Occupy Wall Street into its branding strategy (Diego 2021). This ethos, which co-founder Leire Fernandez defines as a pursuit of "high social impact," resonates with consumers who are socially conscious and eager for meaningful change.[22] In doing so, Clandestina echoes strategies distinctive of the socialist brandscape, innovatively flipping the script. Whereas the Cuban state had used commercial branding as a conduit for its political agenda, Clandestina packages politics as a commercial product. The driving force behind its branding is neither an anticapitalist nor an antisocialist revolt (Diego 2021) but profit accumulation through the commercialization of socially conscious meanings. Such an approach may be deemed revolutionary in the context of Cuba's fashion industry but only because of the country's unique brandscape and socio-political backdrop.

Notes

1 "Las Tiendas del Pueblo," *INRA* 1, no. 3 (March 1960): 107.
2 For historical analyses on these developments, see Díaz Castañón 2004; Guerra 2012; Thomas 1971.
3 World Intellectual Property Organization, "Nice Classification," 11th edition (2021), www.wipo.int (accessed November 23, 2023).

4 www.ocpi.cu/marcas (accessed November 22, 2023).
5 By contrast, four foreign brands received licenses during this period, including two in 1959.
6 Wilfredo Benítez, interviewed by author, August 3, 2012, Havana, Cuba.
7 This trend is also observed among the 222 foreign brands licensed in the three-decade period, a significant number of which originated from capitalist countries, with the United States leading with fifty brands and the United Kingdom contributing twenty-two. A mere twelve originated from communist regimes.
8 "Decreto-Ley No. 68 (14 de mayo de 1983) de invenciones, descubrimientos científicos, modelos industriales, marcas o denominaciones de origen," http://extwprlegs1.fao.org/docs/pdf/cub111622.pdf (accessed November 22, 2023).
9 Publication titles included "Do you know what a brand is?" (1981), "Designs of national trademarks" (1982), "Trademarks in Cuba" (1982), and "Objectives and main functions of the ONIITEM" (1982).
10 Gabriela Rodríguez, "La nueva tecnología soviética en la Industria Textil," *Ellas en Romances* 40, no. 490 (1977): 38–40.
11 Colonial influence manifests in brand names such as Criolla, Hato (a term for land used for cattle raising), Colonial, La Villa (referring to the early cities established by Spaniards), Quitrín, and Goleta (a type of sailing vessel).
12 Also in "Escuela para Campesinas Ana Betancourt," *Mujeres* 8, no. 8 (August 1970): 30–32; M.R.C., "El arte de las modas y el diseño," *Mujeres* 2, no. 4 (February 15, 1962): 108–109.
13 "Entregan edición cubana de El Quijote a museo español," *CiberCuba* May 31, 2010, www.cibercuba.com/noticias/2010/05/31/entregan-edicion-cubana-de-el-quijote-museo-espanol (accessed November 5, 2023).
14 ICIODI, "La consistencia de la oferta a la población," MEP/CH: IG-68 (1985), Dirección de Investigaciones Globales.
15 ICIODI, "Informe Final. Tema #3: La demanda y el consumo de la población en la esfera del vestuario, el calzado y otros artículos" (1989), Departamento de Vestuario y Artículos de Uso Personal.
16 From 1978 to 1982, a significant portion of clothing was either produced domestically or acquired from private seamstresses. Even following the expansion of the parallel market in 1983, a considerable amount of apparel continued to be sourced from informal channels or the Black market (Hernández Gómez 1984).
17 Ana Gabriela Valdés, Instagram message, January 6, 2024.
18 https://nawecraft.com/ (accessed March 13, 2024).
19 The author borrows the term from the post-Franco Spanish *movida* or cultural boom.
20 See also "Clandestina, la primera marca de ropa cubana que llegó a la revista Vogue," *BBC* January 31, 2018, www.bbc.com/mundo/noticias-42878541 (accessed March 17,

2024); Brooke Bobb, "These Slogan Tees Are Creating a Dialogue Around Fashion in Cuba," *Vogue* November 10, 2017, www.vogue.com/article/cuba-designers-clandestina (accessed September 12, 2023).
21   https://clandestina.co/ (accessed September 13, 2023). Cuban domains are not available to private businesses.
22   Ibid.

Bibliography

Appadurai, Arjun. 1996. *Modernity at Large. Cultural Dimensions of Globalization*. Minneapolis, MN: University of Minnesota Press.

Askegaard, Soren. 2006. "Brands as a Global Ideoscape." In *Brand Culture*, eds. Jonathan E. Shroeder and Miriam Salzer-Morling, 91–102. New York: Routledge.

Cabrera Arús, María A. 2015. "Pañoletas y polainas: Dinámicas de la moda en la Cuba soviética." *Kamchatka* 5: 243–260.

Cabrera Arús, María A. 2017. "Thinking Politics and Fashion in 1960s Cuba: How not to Judge a Book by its Cover." *Theory & Society* 46 (5): 411–428.

Cabrera Arús, María A. 2019a. "Beauty and Quality for All: A Vision of Fashion under Cuban Socialism." In *The Oxford Handbook of Communist Visual Cultures*, eds. Aga Skrodzka, Xiaoning Lu, and Katarzyna Marciniak, 455–474. Oxford: Oxford University Press.

Cabrera Arús, María A. 2019b. "Clandestina *mainstream*." *Hypermedia Magazine* November 27, https://hypermediamagazine.com/sociedad/clandestina/.

Cabrera Arús, María A. 2019c. "The Material Promise of Socialist Modernity: Fashion and Domestic Space in the 1970s." In *The Revolution from Within: Cuba 1959–1980*, eds. Michael Bustamante and Jennifer Lambe, 189–217. Durham, NC: Duke University Press.

Castro, Fidel. 1959. *Una sola bandera, un solo ideal: Cuba*. Havana: Ministerio de Estado.

Delgado Lamela, Miguel A. 1993. "Los elegantes prefieren Bulnes. Diseño de calzado cubano." Bachelor's thesis, Instituto Superior de Diseño Industrial.

Díaz Castañón, María del P. 2004. *Ideología y revolución. Cuba, 1959–1962*. Havana: Ciencias Sociales.

Diego, Jeannine. 2021. "Fashion in Cuba as Revolt, and the Horror of the Nonproductive." *Fashion Theory* 27 (1): 43–83.

Fehérváry, Krisztina. 2009. "Goods and States: The Political Logic of State-Socialist Material Culture." *Comparative Studies in Society and History* 51: 426–459.

Guerra, Lillian. 2012. *Visions of Power in Cuba: Revolution, Redemption, and Resistance, 1959–1971*. Chapel Hill: University of North Carolina Press.

Heilbrunn, Benoît. 2006. "Brave New Brands: Cultural Branding between Utopia and A-topia." In *Brand Culture*, edited by Jonathan E. Shroeder and Miriam Salzer-Morling, 103–117. New York: Routledge.

Hernández Fusté, Yelanys. 2014. "Historia de tinajones." *On Cuba* November 20, https://oncubanews.com/cuba/sociedad-cuba/tradiciones/historia-de-tinajones/.

Hernández Gómez, Ángel R. 1984. "Características y dinámica de la moda en Cuba." *Demanda* 6: 3–43.

Hernández Morales, Aymara. 2005. "Las reformas descentralizadoras cubanas de los noventa: Diseño, implementación y resultados." *Revista Liminar* 3: 39–53.

Hynson, Rachel. 2019. *Laboring for the State: Women, Family, and Work in Revolutionary Cuba, 1959–1971*. New York: Cambridge University Press.

Kapferer, Jean-Noël. 2006. "The Two Business Cultures of Luxury Brands." In *Brand Culture*, edited by Jonathan E. Shroeder and Miriam Salzer-Morling, 67–76. New York: Routledge.

Klingmann, Anna. 2007. *Brandscapes: Architecture in the Experience Economy*. Cambridge, MA: MIT Press.

Luke, Anne. 2018. *Youth and the Cuban Revolution: Youth Culture and Politics in 1960s Cuba*. Lanham, MD: Lexington Books.

Lury, Celia. 2004. *Brands: The Logos of the Global Economy*. London: Routledge.

Mesa-Lago, Carmelo. 1978. *Cuba in the 1970s: Pragmatism and Institutionalization*. Albuquerque: University of New Mexico Press.

Mesa-Lago, Carmelo. 1984. "The Socioeconomic Performance of Cuba." In *Cuban Communism*, fifth edition, edited by Irving L. Horowitz, 13–42. New Brunswick, NJ: Transaction.

Niesing, Eva. 2015. *Latin America's Potential in Nation Branding: A Closer Look at Brazil's, Chile's and Colombia's Practices*. Hamburg: Anchor. https://search-ebscohost-com.proxy.library.nyu.edu/login.aspx?direct=true&db=nlebk&AN=1006931&site=eds-live.

O'Connell, Mark J. 2021. "'Y Sin Embargo Te Quiero' (And Yet, I Love You): An Ethnographic Study of Economic Policy and Colonial Hegemonies Encoded in the Recommodification of Used Garments," *Textile*. DOI: 10.1080/14759756.2021.1909207.

Oswald, Laura R. 2012. *Marketing Semiotics: Signs, Strategies, and Brand Value*. Oxford: Oxford University Press.

Oyama, Shinji. 2009. "The East Asian Brandscape: Distribution of Japanese Brands in the Age of Globalization." In *Cultural Studies and Cultural Industries in Northeast Asia*, edited by Chris Berry, Nicola Liscutin, and Jonathan D. Mackintosh, 135–150. Aberdeen: Hong Kong University Press.

Pérez, Louis Jr. 1999. *On Becoming Cuban: Identity, Nationality, and Culture*. Chapel Hill: University of North Carolina Press.

Rodríguez Balari, Eugenio. 1985. *Cuba–USA, palabras cruzadas*. Havana: Ciencias Sociales.

Rodríguez Balari, Eugenio. 1990. "The Supply of Consumer Goods in Cuba." In *Transformation and Struggle: Cuba Faces the 1990s*, edited by Sandor Halebsky and John M. Kirk, 157–172. New York: Praeger.

Rojas-Méndez, José I., and Mozhde Khoshnevis. 2023. "Conceptualizing Nation Branding: The Systematic Literature Review." *Journal of Product & Brand Management* 32 (1): 107–123, DOI: 10.1108/JPBM-04-2021-3444.

Salinas Chávez, Eduardo, and Eros Salinas Chávez. 2017. "El turismo en Cuba: Planificación y desarrollo." In *Desarrollo del turismo en América Latina: fases, enfoques e internacionalización*, ed. Noemí Wallingre, 118–157. Bernal: Universidad Nacional de Quilmes, https://ridaa.unq.edu.ar/bitstream/handle/20.500.11807/1022/desarrollo_del_turismo.pdf?sequence=1&isAllowed=y.

San Martín, Marta, and Ramón L. Bonachea. 1984. "The Military Dimension of the Cuban Revolution." In *Cuban Communism*, 5th edition, edited by Irving L. Horowitz, 585–616. New Brunswick, NJ: Transaction.

Schroeder, Jonathan E., and Miriam Salzer-Mörling. 2006. "Introduction: The Cultural Codes of Branding." In *Brand Culture*, edited by Jonathan E. Shroeder and Miriam Salzer-Morling, 1–12. New York: Routledge.

Thomas, Hugh. 1971. *Cuba: The Pursuit of Freedom*. New York: Harper & Row.

Vellinga, M.L. 1976. "The Military and the Dynamics of the Cuban Revolutionary Process." *Comparative Politics* 8 (2): 245–271.

Part 2

Culture's Empowering Lens

6

Afro-Brazilian Styles: Dress, Race, and Coloniality in Nineteenth-Century Portraits

Alliny Maia Cabral

In contrast to other regions affected by the Atlantic slave trade, Brazil possesses unique characteristics. Overall, the period of slavery in Brazil lasted more than 350 years. It stood out as the foremost importer of enslaved Africans and was the last country in the Americas to abolish slavery on May 13, 1888 (Schwarcz and Gomes 2018). Even after attaining freedom, Black individuals and their descendants faced the precariousness of free-wage labor, leaving them vulnerable to marginalization. Therefore, Brazilian social dynamics were significantly shaped by slavery, which perpetuated models of servitude, dependency, and the subordination of Black[1] individuals.

Owing to the protracted duration of slavery, the image records of the enslaved and their descendants were able to benefit from developments in photographic technology, which improved the conditions for documenting everyday life. That, coupled with the interest in documenting Black bodies for a lucrative market that promulgated such images in Brazil and abroad, culminated in the creation of a diverse and extensive archive of photographs of Black subjects during the nineteenth century.

Due to what is described as a "policy of exceeding invisibility" coupled with an "inflated visibility" (Schwarcz and Gomes 2018, 31), Black women, despite being marginalized, found their images commodified and extensively exploited for economic and political purposes. Portraits of Black women, including studio photographs of enslaved and free individuals and ethnographic photography, depict how they fashioned their bodies, underlining a keen interest in registering their ways of dressing.

Drawing from Quijano's theory of coloniality and Mirzoeff's approach to visuality (Quijano 1992; Mirzoeff 2016), this chapter examines a series of photographs featuring Bahian Black women, captured in the nineteenth century by Spanish photographer Rafael Castro y Ordóñez. These photographs echo a recurring theme found in the works of other photographers active in Brazil during that period, showcasing a fascination with depicting Black women engaged in urban scene activities. Castro's depiction of these women, known as *quitandeiras*, showcases meticulously crafted attire, including dress items distinctly associated with Black women's fashion styles, such as headwraps.

Scholars across disciplines including art history, cultural studies, social history, anthropology, and sociology, have frequently interpreted the gaze of this type of visual representation as emblematic of masculine, imperialist power. However, they have often overlooked the images as evidence of the pivotal social, cultural, economic, and political roles that dress played in those photographs, which may function as a tool of submission and, significantly, as a form of resistance. I apply an interdisciplinary framework from my perspective as a dress researcher trained in visual culture to interpret these images underscoring the importance of photography in studying fashion and dress history, demonstrating how dress—and the images it materializes—shapes social perceptions. That is particularly relevant when exploring Black women's dress practices, which have often been misrepresented and poorly preserved in Brazilian museum textile collections due to the historical marginalization of subaltern social groups (Paula 2006).

Photography, especially portraits, was used as a means of shaping the colonial and postcolonial social idea of African presence in Brazil, often depicting Black subjects as exotic and primitive. Analyzing these images demands critically examining strategies often used to represent, regulate, and integrate the Black body within preexisting conceptual frameworks related to colonial thought. In terms of terminology, it is important to acknowledge Tulloch's definition of "style," defined as "part of the process of self-telling, revealing an aspect of one's autobiography through clothing choices," or "style narratives" (Tulloch 2010, 276). Building on Tulloch's definition, it is argued here that although Black women had their style narratives utilized within the colonialist representational agenda to construct an idea of Black femininity that situated them within anthropological and political hierarchies of difference, these women were still able to assert their agency and resistance when depicted as portrait subjects. By fashioning their bodies, they managed to express themselves and demonstrate their defiance against the unequal power relations in which they were entangled.

According to Quijano (2010), an essential aspect of social thought originating from colonialism involves the categorization of society based on race, leading to ethnic and national discrimination that was supported by nineteenth-century scientific theories. This perspective extends beyond colonialism alone and persists as a hegemonic structure known as coloniality (Quijano, 1992), which represents enduring power dynamics even after political independence. Coloniality continues to maintain processes of limitation and subordination across Latin America, particularly affecting Indigenous peoples, Africans, and their descendants. In the cultural sphere, coloniality perpetuated racial ideas through artistic productions, thereby shaping the national imaginary.

In the nineteenth century, Brazilian photographic production operated within a specific visuality regime influenced by the epistemic hegemony that regarded European knowledge as superior. This stance facilitated the widespread acceptance of the work of European photographers, allowing them to imprint their gaze and interests onto the images they produced. The photographers' role often mirrored that of "an extension of the anthropologist, visiting natives and bringing back news of their exotic doings and strange gear" (Sontag 1977, 33). Consequently, the gaze of European foreigners dominated photographic production, resulting in an extensive archive depicting subaltern people and positioning them as others.

Among the various photography formats that were produced within that context, portraiture was a widespread genre. Portraits served as a means of conveying the power of members of dominant social classes who used the Black body to corroborate their political agenda through visuality. Furthermore, through practices such as collecting and disseminating images, they began to take on new social dynamics. As a result, reproducing and commercializing Blackness became especially interesting to photographers and their clients.

Ethnographic photographs, mostly produced as *cartes de visite* and typology images, emerged as a particularly popular type of portrait. These images were intended for sale both in Brazil and abroad or served as scientific evidence supporting theories that classified individuals from non-Western countries as underdeveloped, positioning them at the lower end of a supposed racial hierarchy. For the composition of commercial images, photographers often created staged scenarios to depict the subjects engaged in work activities, using painted backdrops to simulate outdoor settings and incorporating scenographic objects to mimic the traditional portraiture techniques borrowed from painting. Conversely, scientific images were characterized by simplicity, sometimes depicting subjects with minimal clothing.

Ultimately, these photographs served similar functions in depicting imagined customs of people associated with specific material elements within particular cultural contexts. Therefore, dress, including clothing and body adornments, consists of a relevant element in constructing these visual narratives, reflecting social and material culture aspects. This is particularly evident in nineteenth-century photographs, considering how cultural perceptions and social status were heavily influenced by appearance at that time, making dress elements a visible marker of distinction.

The pair of photographs examined in this chapter falls under the category of typology images. Like many others in this genre, these portraits depict Black women engaged in staged urban commerce activities, captured in the studio setting. They feature simple backgrounds, highlighting the focus on dress compositions. Both images were produced under the lens of the Spanish photographer Rafael Castro y Ordoñez, who lived between 1834 and 1865 and was the eighth member commissioned to participate in the scientific expedition to the Pacific as a photographer-designer.

The expedition was organized during the reign of Isabel II of Spain (1833–1868) and sent a group of scientist naturalists to study and document the fauna, flora, and customs of South America, Central America, and California from 1862 to 1865. The project was designed to carry on the great illustrated expeditions of the eighteenth century; thus, it is primarily romantic and nationalist (Puig-Samper 2003, 22). Castro's participation "constitutes another reflection of his harmony with the interests of the State and judging by the success of travel photography at that time, of his hopes of adding one more commercial product to his business" (Badia-Villaseca 2016, 4).

It is noteworthy that Castro was not one of the most well-known photographers in Brazil, and his stay was brief, which may have contributed to the fact that he did not become well-known there. On the other hand, Castro's images from the expedition were widely circulated in Europe, particularly in the illustrated periodical *El Museo Universal*, to which he contributed chronicles from the Americas for nearly two years. In Brazil, the most prominent record of Castro's work is an album produced in 1862 and given as a gift to Emperor Dom Pedro II, the last ruler of the Empire of Brazil (1831–1889), before it transitioned from monarchy to republic.

Understanding the expeditioners' subjects of interest is crucial for grasping the photographer's scientific and political agenda, primarily focused on nature (especially cataloging different species) and human types. Manuel Almagro, an anthropologist and member of the expedition, provided detailed descriptions of the city of Bahia's landscape, economy, and population in his travel narrative. Notably, he emphasized racial aspects, describing the population as exceeding 100,000 people, comprising mostly Black people, both enslaved and free individuals, with many Europeans, particularly Portuguese and Germans (Almagro 1866). Castro's photographs from the expedition show how he was drawn by the idea of a recently "discovered" land with a great number of Indigenous and Black individuals whose customs differed remarkably from those of Europe.

The images examined in this chapter belong to an album of 51 photographs which constitutes a portion of the expedition's photographic output that remained in Brazil. It was presented to Emperor Dom Pedro II as a gift after the completion of the expedition. Remarkably, this album was later included in the Biblioteca Nacional catalog as part of the Thereza Christina Maria collection.[2] Two photographs depicting Black women, allegedly street vendors, who were part of the Bahian urban scene were chosen from the album. These photographs were probably numbered (as displayed at the bottom of each image) by the photographer, following an archiving logic that reproduces the position of each image in the album. They were also accompanied respectively by the following captions: "a Bahian *quitandeira*" (Figure 6.1), and "Bahian *Quitandeira*" (Figure 6.2 (Losada, Puig-Samper, and Domingues 2013, 27).

Figure 6.1 A Bahian *quitandeira* seated beside her products, 1862. Photograph from Rafael Castro y Ordoñez. *Acervo da Fundação Biblioteca Nacional—Brasil.*

Figure 6.2 Portrait of a Bahian *quitandeira* depicted standing and holding a basket, 1862. Photograph from Rafael Castro y Ordoñez. Acervo da Fundação Biblioteca Nacional—Brasil.

While originally intended for the expedition's objectives, the images stand out for depicting a specific type of representation: portraits of Black women referred to as *quitandeiras*. These portraits are reminiscent of the works of painters and illustrators like Henry Chamberlain and Jean-Baptiste Debret, who worked in Brazil during the first half of the nineteenth century. From the mid-nineteenth century onwards, depictions of *quitandeiras* were widely reproduced in photography.

The term *quitandeira* was used to describe Black women both free and enslaved who worked selling food products on the streets. Such items were known as "*quitandas*," a term derived from the word *kitanda*, which originated from a set of languages spoken in Africa belonging to the Bantu linguistic branch. *Kitanda* refers to the objects used for the exhibition of food at free markets as well as the free markets themselves, which constituted a widespread commercial practice in African countries such as Angola and Luanda that was adapted in various ways in the African diaspora (Lifschitz and Bonomo 2015, 194).

Quitandeiras worked in Brazil during the nineteenth century as food vendors in a similar manner to women in Africa during the same period, particularly in Luanda (Soares and Gomes 2002:8). However, while the role of *quitandeira* was exclusively female in Africa, men also engaged in selling such goods on the streets in Brazil, although to a much lesser extent. Nevertheless, in terms of visual representation, the figure of the *quitandeira* was supremely feminine, based on depictions of Black women dressed in a specific way.

In particular, this way of dressing corresponds closely to the ceremonial dress belonging to *Candomblé*, which is very representative of the Afro-Brazilian culture.[3] It can be seen in Castro's images, consisting of long and full skirts, a short-sleeved blouse, a shawl called *pano da costa*, and a headwrap.[4] This combination of items, closely linked with the *quitandeira* figure, represented a specific dress composition worn by Black women in Bahia, where the presence of *quitandeiras* was quite notable. This association is evident in Castro's photographs, where the women are labeled as both Bahian and *quitandeiras*. In the social imaginary of the time, the images of Bahian women and *quitandeiras*, primarily constructed through dress, merged into a stereotype of Black women's style disseminated within and beyond Brazil through these images.

As Burke (2004) notes, it is critical to consider the images' flaws as documentary sources before using them as historical evidence. For instance, when examining racialized representations, the images' focus on stereotypical characteristics rather than the individual's unique traits is problematic (Burke 2004). The goal of Castro's portraits was to classify rather than identify. Hence, the subjects' interests were not considered while these photographs were produced. Instead, the Black women captured in the images often faced coercion, whether as enslaved individuals or as socially vulnerable free women.

To study this type of photograph, it is necessary to keep in mind that the meaning constructed through images goes beyond what they visually project; therefore, it is essential to acknowledge the elements that remain hidden under the demands of the conventions that made these portraits acquire meaning within a given canon. Thus, it is critical to engage them to comprehend the images beyond the instrumental functions they were created to have. By doing so, a gesture of noncompliance takes place, supported by the desire to see beyond the presuppositions and have a broader comprehension of the meanings intentionally and not intentionally conveyed.

To look at the images and engage them that way, it is necessary to question their narrative and the perspective they reproduce. This exercise is facilitated by the fact that, although assessing them through the lens of their period, we no longer represent the original observers for whom they were created. Consequently, we can examine the portraits more critically, focusing on the women depicted instead of just the regime of visuality in which they found themselves. This approach raises pertinent questions: Who were those women exactly? Were they actually vendors or were they just depicted as such? Did their clothes belong to them, or were they arranged to create the scene? Were the women enslaved or free? Were they compensated or forced to pose for the photos? Were *quitandeiras* in fact dressed that way, or is the image just a stereotypical representation?

Many of these questions have become increasingly challenging to address solely through the information presented within the images over time. Nonetheless, despite the limitations, examining the portrayal of dress offers an avenue to surpass certain visual constraints. Photographs offer a window into the social significance of dress, furnishing intricate details on its usage across diverse settings. Moreover, they shed light on the spectrum of dress items prevalent in specific places and periods, situating the subject within the broader context of material culture while unveiling nuances of "national, regional, and local differences" (Taylor 2002, 115).

To conduct a thorough analysis of these aspects, it is essential to initially observe the image in a broader context. Concerning Castro's portraits, both photographs feature a simple backdrop, drawing attention to the sitters themselves. Objects such as a chest and a basket help characterize the sitters based on their presumed occupation. However, a narrative inconsistency arises in the first image with the presence of the chest, as its contents suggest manufactured products from Paris rather than food items, typically associated with the occupation. Nonetheless, despite this inconsistency, the visual composition suggests that the woman's skin color and attire alone are enough to identify her as a street vendor and a native of Bahia.

In the second image, although the woman and the setting differ, the *quitandeira* theme persists. She is dressed very similarly to the woman in the previous photograph. However, the setting in this image features an object distinct from the chest seen in the first. The small basket in her hand serves as a reminder of her role as a *quitandeira* who carried her goods. Its diminutive size suggests it was likely just a prop. Compared to the baskets depicted in other similar images, taken outdoors without studio manipulation, this one seems incongruous with the volume of goods typically carried by these women, which were usually contained in larger baskets and often balanced on their headwraps.

In essence, the images appear to have been created by someone attempting to depict what was perceived as typical of that social context, such as the *quitandeira* image. However, it seems that the photographer lacked sufficient familiarity with Brazilian culture to accurately capture scenes representative of everyday life in a studio setting. It is noteworthy that the tradition of photographing Black women engaged in work-related activities played a significant role in perpetuating a socially and hierarchically inferior status for Black women, emphasizing their association with physical labor (Conduru 2007).

Although Castro's portraits reflect his superficial perspective, the dress styles depicted in them are similar to those seen in photographs of other Black women, both taken outdoors and in studios. The dress composition worn by both subjects is an element that goes beyond the photographer's control over the images, as he relied on the Black women's knowledge for the selection of specific items and their combination. While Castro intended for these women to be represented dressed according to Afro-Brazilian style narratives, he did not have sufficient knowledge to fabricate them. Therefore, details such as the combination of a full skirt and white blouse, the use of striped *panos da costa* worn over the shoulders, the presence of accessories like bead bracelets, and, finally, the use of white headwraps with voluminous and well-crafted ties demonstrate the agency of these women in constructing their own image.

In addition to the images, written documents from the period confirm that the dress styles depicted were not merely fabricated by the photographer, as their elements were part of style narratives of Black women that were widely recognized and meticulously described. Therefore, beyond visual interpretation, the dress compositions seen in the images align with descriptions found in runaway slave advertisements from that period. These advertisements are particularly valuable for the study of dress because they aimed to be precise, containing descriptions that could easily define and be recognized by contemporary readers. By providing historical documentary support, these documents help fill in some of the gaps in meaning present in the photographs. To contrast the data found in these documents with the interpretation of the photographs, a survey was conducted among 620 Brazilian periodicals published and circulated throughout Brazil from 1840 to 1880, seeking information on dress.[5]

One of the advertisements found describes a woman called Francisca who had run away in Bahia. It states:

[...] fugio no dia 27 de maio levando vestida camiza de zuarte, saia de xita já desbotada, pano da costa velho, de nome Francisca, Nação Nagó, ladina maior de 40 annos, alta, magra, pés pequenos, tornozellos grossos, signaes de sua terra no rosto, tres golpes em cada lado.

[...] ran away on the 27th of May, wearing a *zuarte* shirt, faded chintz skirt, old *pano da costa*, named Francisca, Nação Nagó, wily over 40 years old, tall, thin, small feet, thick ankles, signs of her nation on the face, three scars on each side.[6]]

O Guaycuru: Os principios são tudo, os homens pouco, 1846, 4

Francisca's advertisement followed a standard format for fugitive notices that appeared in that newspaper and other periodicals at the time. The description emphasizes how she was dressed the last time she was seen, revealing how dress was regarded as a distinguishing feature. Francisca was dressed in a combination of a shirt, skirt, and *pano da costa*, which is similar to how women were dressed in Castro's portraits. Her occupation was not stated, so it is unknown whether she worked on the streets like the *quitandeiras*. It is sufficient, however, to show that Black women could be seen in Bahia dressed in styles similar to those depicted in the portraits. The way the dress items are put together, as well as details like patterns, colors, and shapes, are all socio-culturally significant elements that are closely associated with the women's Afro-diasporic experiences.

Following, there is another advertisement that circulated in Rio de Janeiro:

Recommenda-se aos Srs pedestres a preta Bernarda, Cabinda, ladina, boa estatura, pelle lisa, signaes da sua terra nas costas, lenço na cabeça á moda da Bahia, vestido branco, ou de chita de cores, com babado e cordâo, e chale de barege, ou de lãs: anda pelas ruas circunvizinhas do largo do Capim até á da Quitanda, fingindo-se quitandeira, ou compradora com samburá; é do Cattete n. 136.

[It is recommended for pedestrians[7] the Black Bernarda, Cabinda, wily, good stature, smooth skin, signs of her nation on the back, headwrap in the Bahian mode, white or colored chintz dress, with ruffles and cord, and a barege or wool shawl: she walks through the surrounding streets from *Largo do Capim* to *Quitanda*, pretending to be a *quitandeira* or shopper with a *samburá* basket; she belongs to Cattete street n°136.]

Diário do Rio de Janeiro, 1848, 4

Bernarda was a woman who, according to the document, pretended to be a *quitandeira* or shopper on the streets, carrying a *samburá* basket. This advertisement stands out for several reasons, beginning with her fugitive strategy of resistance. The way she used the headwrap is mentioned very specifically as belonging to a supposed Bahian dress tradition described as a "Bahian mode." However, even though she was identified as an Angolan woman, and lived in Rio de Janeiro, the passage does not mention her contact with Bahia. It shows how the Bahian woman, the Black woman, and the *quitandeira's* image were merged into an indistinguishable idea fashioned through dress.

Due to coloniality, the assumption of cultural and ethnic homogeneity was widespread, and to some extent, it still persists. Thus, women were often labeled as "quitandeiras" or "Bahians." While this classification served the typification function of the images, it failed to accurately depict the complex relationship these women had with dress and work. For example, Bernarda's dress description includes some distinctive items not commonly worn by women in her social condition, such as the wool shawl and the dress with ruffles. This suggests that there was no fixed formula or singular style adopted by them.

Similarly to dress, the work activity was another layer of categorization used to define them. However, it was common for a *quitandeira* to also engage in other occupations such as washerwoman or cook, depending on the demands of her owner or the need to generate income, particularly for free women. As Reis notes, "the majority of Blacks in urban Bahia, both enslaved and free, worked either in the streets or partly in the home and partly in the streets" (1997, 455). This highlights the diverse and multifaceted nature of their labor and challenges the oversimplified classifications imposed upon them.

Another notable aspect of the portraits that is related to the social context is the subjects' anonymity, which served the typifying function. The absence of the subjects' names in the image captions underscores how they were perceived: as Black women engaged in work, rather than as individuals with unique identities. Despite their lack of identification, we can challenge the power dynamics embedded in these images by recognizing that the portrayal of the Bahian *quitandeira* was only made possible by the presence of these women. By acknowledging this, we move beyond attributing the creation of the images solely to the photographer's gaze and recognize it as a product of a collaborative negotiation between representational authority and the meaningful subjectivity of the women themselves.[8]

The presence of the women in these images becomes apparent through various visual elements, including their facial expressions, body posture, and dress choices. As Gage's research on Bahian women's dress and identity reveals, attempts to represent them through stereotypical dress styles failed to capture the deeper significance of their attire, which conveyed a profound sense of pride and cultural connection (Gage 2016). Engaging with the images beyond their superficial meaning, however, allows us to see how the portraits show intricate style narratives shaped by the women's selective adoption of European, indigenous, and distinctly African elements, reflecting their diasporic experiences and identity formation.

Furthermore, it is crucial to recognize that dress in these images goes beyond mere visual representation as it serves as a direct extension of the wearers' bodies, intimately intertwined with their physical form. As Kutesko (2016) argues, dress possesses both material and visual dimensions, with its appearance in images reflecting the tactile experience of the wearer. This perspective underscores the complexity of interpreting visual representations, as viewers engage with the images based on their own experiences with dress, mobilizing meaning through their understanding of the sensory relationship between textiles and the body.

Therefore, examining specific details within the images, such as the appearance of the skirts and the materials used, provides further insights into the women's dress practices. For instance, the use of chintz fabric for skirts, deduced from the runaway ads and the textile's appearance, implies affordability and practicality within their socio-economic context. Considering the tactile quality of this fabric, we can infer that it was lightweight and comfortable, albeit lacking the softness of more delicate and expensive textiles commonly used during that period, like silk.

Moreover, the loose silhouette of the clothes depicted is consistent with *quitandeiras*' daily lives, as they would enable women to engage in their work activities without hindrance. Additionally, the headwraps, meticulously designed to create a unique shape and volume, symbolize an essential aspect of their identity and cultural expression. This attention to detail in their appearance underscores their resourcefulness and cultural pride despite facing social and economic constraints.

Castro's portraits serve as a compelling case study for exploring how Black women's identities were asserted, and visually codified. Interpreting them showed that beyond their surface narrative, the dress elements depicted in the photographs signify resistance against processes of objectification, and stereotyping perpetuated by the prevailing political system. Moreover, it is important to mention that besides being conformed to a specific visuality regime, the elements comprising the *quitandeira*-style narratives played a significant historical role in fostering a sense of community among Black women in Brazil. This went beyond their role in the workplace, becoming integral to how they negotiated and expressed their cultural identities in both private and public spheres. Furthermore, items such as the *pano da costa* and headwraps held not only visual significance but were also imbued with symbolic and spiritual meaning. The headwrap, in particular, continues to be viewed among Black women in Brazil as a symbol of cultural resistance and African heritage.

Notes

1. In Brazil, the process of societal formation was deeply influenced by racial mixing, a phenomenon commonly referred to as miscegenation. This historical background of the nation significantly shaped the interpretation of race, ethnicity, and identity formation. Therefore, in this chapter, individuals are referred to as "Blacks" rather than solely "Afro-Brazilians." While "Afro-Brazilian" traditionally denotes individuals of African descent, the preference for "Black individuals" acknowledges their African ancestry while recognizing the intricate interplay of racial and ethnic diversity within Brazilian society. Therefore, it is worth noting that "Afro-Brazilian" is employed here to refer to cultural practices resulting from African and Brazilian influences rather than to individuals themselves.
2. That collection had its cultural value internationally recognized when it was added to the UNESCO International Memory of the World Register in 2003.
3. *Candomblé* is an Afro-Brazilian religion with African and Catholic influences. It involves rituals, dances, and worship of orishas, embodying cultural resistance and community solidarity.
4. According to Torres (2004), the expression was adopted in places that traded with Africa in reference to pieces of cloth used by Black women to compose their dress styles. The name "da costa" refers to the African goods route that ran along the coast.
5. The archival research was conducted using the digital newspaper database of the Biblioteca Nacional, a Brazilian institution that also owns the photographs featured in the chapter. This database is searchable by keyword and includes Brazilian newspapers from the early 1800s to the late 1990s.
6. Due to the period of circulation of this type of advertisement, the publications were written in archaic Portuguese. Therefore, some sentences may seem fragmented.
7. The fact that the ad was "recommended for pedestrians" means that it was directed to this audience so that, while walking through the city, they would be alert to the possible appearance of the woman described.
8. For more information on the issues involving image negotiation and the colonial gaze, see: Eileraas, 2003.

Bibliography

Almagro, Manuel de. 2012. *Breve descripción de dos viajes hechos en América por la Comisión Científica enviada por el Gobierno de S.M.C. durante los años 1862 a 1866: acompañada de dos mapas y de la enumeración de las colecciones que forman la exposición pública*. Alicante: Biblioteca Virtual Miguel de Cervantes. www.cervantesvirtual.com/nd/ark:/59851/bmc3f4n6.

Badía-Villaseca, Sara. 2016. "Las fotografías de California de Rafael Castro y Ordóñez, miembro de la Expedición Científica del Pacífico (1862–1866): discurso y circulación." *Asclepio* 68 (2). https://pesquisa.bvsalud.org/portal/resource/pt/ibc-158650.

Burke, Peter. 2004. *Testemunha Ocular: história e imagem*. Translated by Vera Maria Xavier dos Santos. Bauru: Educs.

Castro y Ordóñez, Rafael. 1862. *A quitandeira of Bahia* [Photograph]. Salvador, Bahia, Brazil: Acervo da Fundação Biblioteca Nacional, Brasil. www.loc.gov/item/2021669425/.

Castro y Ordóñez, Rafael. 1862. *Quitandeira of Bahia* [Photograph] Salvador, Bahia, Brazil: Acervo da Fundação Biblioteca Nacional, Brasil, 1862. www.loc.gov/item/2021669492/.

Conduru, Roberto. 2007. *Arte afro-brasileira*. Belo Horizonte: Editora C/Arte.

Eileraas, Karina. 2003. "Reframing the Colonial Gaze: Photography, Ownership, and Feminist Resistance." *French Issue* 118 (4): 807–840. www.jstor.org/stable/3251988.

Gage, Kelly. 2016. "Moda da Bahia: An Analysis of Contemporary Vendor Dress in Salvador." *Fashion Theory: The Journal of Dress, Body & Culture* 20 (2): 153–179. https://doi.org/10.1080/1362704X.2016.1133543.

Kutesko, Elizabeth. 2016. "Fashioning Brazil: Globalization and the Representation of Brazilian Dress in National Geographic since 1988," *Fashion Theory: The Journal of Dress, Body & Culture* 20 (2): 181–207. https://doi.org/10.1080/1362704X.2016.1133547.

Lifschitz, Javier and Juliana Bonomo. 2015. "As quitandadeiras de Minas Gerais: memórias brancas e memórias negras," *Revista Ciências Sociais Unisinos* 51 (2): 193–200. https://doi.org/10.4013/csu.2015.51.2.09.

Losada, Janaina, Miguel Puig-Samper, and Heloisa Domingues. 2013. "Álbum Fotográfico." In *Um álbum para o Imperador: A comissão científica do Pacífico e o Brasil*, eds. Losada, Janaina, Miguel Puig-Samper, and Heloisa Domingues, 9–67. Rio de Janeiro: MAST; Uberlândia: EDUFU.

Mirzoeff, Nicholas. 2016. "O direito a olhar." *ETD Educação Temática Digital* 8 (4): 745–768. https://doi.org/10.20396/etd.v18i4.8646472.

Paula, Teresa Cristina Toledo de. 2006. "Tecidos no museu: argumentos para uma história das práticas curatoriais no Brasil." *Anais do Museu Paulista* 14 (2): 253–298. https://doi.org/10.1590/S0101-47142006000200008.

Puig-Samper, Miguel. 2003. "La expedición en la historia de la ciencia española." In *Historia de un olvido: la expedición científica del Pacífico (1862-1865)*, ed. Esteban, Carmen, 22–27. Madrid: Ministerio de Educación, Cultura y Deporte.

Puig-Samper, Miguel. 2013. "A Comissão Científica do Pacífico no Brasil e o presente fotográfico para Pedro II." In *Um álbum para o Imperador: A comissão científica do Pacífico e o Brasil*, ed. Losada, Janaina, Miguel Puig-Samper, and Heloisa Domingues, 67–100. Rio de Janeiro: MAST.

Quijano, Aníbal. 1992. "Colonialidad y Modernidad/Racionalidad." *Perú Indíg*. 13 (29): 11–20. www.lavaca.org/wp-content/uploads/2016/04/quijano.pdf.

Quijano, Aníbal. 2010. "Colonialidade do Poder e Classificação Social." In *Epistemologias do Sul*, ed. Santos, Boaventura de Sousa and Maria Paula Meneses, 73–118, São Paulo: Cortez.

Reis, João José. 1997. "The Revolution of the Ganhadores: Urban Labour, Ethnicity and the African Strike of 1857 in Bahia, Brazil." *Journal of Latin American Studies* 29 (2): 355–393. https://repositorio.ufba.br/handle/ri/8349.

Schwarcz, Lilia Moritz. 2018. "Sobre as imagens: entre a convenção e a ordem." In *Dicionário da escravidão e liberdade: 50 textos críticos*, ed. Lilia Moritz Schwarcz, and Flávio Gomes, 18–41. São Paulo: Companhia das Letras.

Schwarcz, Lilia Moritz, and Flávio Gomes. 2018. "Introdução." In *Dicionário da escravidão e liberdade: 50 textos críticos*, ed. Lilia Moritz Schwarcz, and Flávio Gomes, 18–41. São Paulo: Companhia das Letras.

Soares, Carlos Eugênio Líbano and Flávio dos Santos Gomes. 2002. "Dizem as quitandeiras . . .: ocupações urbanas e identidades étnicas em uma cidade escravista: rio de janeiro, século XIX." *Acervo - Revista do Arquivo Nacional*, 15 (2): 3–16. https://revista.an.gov.br//index.php/revistaacervo/article/view/21.

Sontag, Susan. 1977. *On Photography*. New York: Farrar, Straus & Giroux.

Taylor, Lou. 2002. *The Study of Dress History*. Manchester: Manchester University Press.

Torres, Heloísa Alberto. 2004. "Alguns aspectos da indumentária da crioula baiana." *Cadernos Pagu* 23: 413–467. https://doi.org/10.1590/S0104-83332004000200015.

Tulloch, Carol. 2010. "Style-Fashion-Dress: From Black to Post-Black." *Fashion Theory: The Journal of Dress, Body & Culture* 14 (3): 273–304. https://doi.org/10.2752/175174110X12712411520179.

7

Spotting Afro-Peruvian Women:
A (Brief) Sartorial History in Polka Dots

Tamara Walker

A watercolor completed by French artist A.A. Bonnaffé around 1856 features a pair of dancers, frozen mid-movement (Fig 7.1; Bonnaffé 1857). The male half of the pair has his back to the viewer: his right foot is poised to tap the ground beneath him, and his right hand holds aloft the handkerchief that serves as a central prop in the performance of the *zamacueca*, a courtship dance originated by enslaved Afro-Peruvians, performed to the beat of a *cajón*, or box drum, and characterized by a flirtatious push and pull between paired performers (Romero 1988, 274–276).[1] His partner in this scene faces the viewer: her right foot arches slightly off the ground, her right hand holds her own handkerchief, and her left hand gathers the folds of an off-the-shoulder pink dress covered with red polka-dots. Although seemingly unremarkable, especially in relation to the handkerchiefs and kinetic energy emanating from the dancers despite their being frozen in place, the polka dots nonetheless merit careful attention. Thanks to their regular presence across more than a century of visual representations of Afro-Peruvian women, polka dots—both the pattern itself and their pattern of repetition in the realm of visual discourse in everything from nineteenth-century watercolors to twentieth-century product advertisements—have much to offer to our understanding of the place of African-descent women in the Peruvian national imagination. In exploring these interrelated subjects, my chapter seeks to use fashion as a critical lens through which to examine the construction of race-based inequality in post-abolition Peru.

When A.A. Bonnaffé arrived in Lima sometime in 1845, he entered an artistic realm that was increasingly dominated by *costumbrista* artists whose drawings and watercolors depicted Lima's denizens in their everyday lives, customs, and attire. The city's popular classes figured heavily in the genre, including street vendors, manual laborers, and household servants, who appeared at work with the tools of their respective trades. They were also represented as they attended dances, religious celebrations, or engaged in moments of rest and leisure. Perhaps the most high profile of these artists was Francisco "Pancho" Fierro, who had been born into slavery, freed at a young age, and taught himself to paint (Palma 1935; Cisneros Sanchez 1975; and León y León Duran 2004). His background dovetailed with that of the populations he depicted in his work, a fact which set Fierro apart from the other prominent *costumbristas* of the era, including French artist and diplomat Léonce Angrand, and German artist Johann Moritz (Juan Mauricio) Rugendas. Together with Fierro—and soon Bonnaffé—these artists saw their work grow in demand among patrons throughout the city. It adorned the walls of private residences, murals along city streets, and the entrances to rodeos, celebrations, and cockfights.

In Bonnaffé's case, his work also filled the pages of a two-series book titled *Recuerdos de Lima: tipos, trajes, y costumbres*, in 1856 and 1857. The images in the volume provide a particularly useful source base for visualizing Afro-descendant women in the nineteenth century because of the ways the images both typify and depart from the genre of *costumbrismo*. Like his fellow *costumbristas*, Bonnaffé zeroed in on his human subjects in ways that evoke for viewers the experience of looking through a viewfinder that frames out the surrounding buildings or landscapes, like the Plaza de Armas, Plaza de Toros, and the Rimac river, all of which figured heavily in other portraits from the era, to allow the humans to command full attention. This, in turn, endows the images with a kind of timeless, placeless quality since they are not easily situated in a particular historical context or geographic setting. At the same time, unlike his fellow *costumbristas* whose work features individuals, pairs, groups, and urban vignettes, up close and at a distance, Bonnaffé's work focuses almost exclusively on close-range shots of individuals (one rare image of a pair is *La Zamacueca*, in which the male subject is nonetheless faceless). Consequently, his portraits allow for a detailed analysis of the subjects and their clothing, which, perhaps paradoxically, helps to root them in their time and place and makes it possible to consider matters of sartorial history like polka dots.

In addition to his depiction of the *zamacueca* performers, Bonnaffé also produced other images of Afro-Peruvian women, including an image titled *La Chichera* (not pictured; Bonnaffé 1857). It centers on a female vendor of *chicha*, a fermented beverage made from corn that had roots among Indigenous populations in the pre-conquest era. The woman, whose dark skin tone suggests African (and possibly formerly enslaved) ancestry, balances an earthen jug of liquid on her head and carries a basket, most likely filled with cups to drink from, in the crook of her left arm. Her right hand holds a cane to steady her balance, perhaps due to old age or to the physical demands of a job carried out over an extensive period. And, just as the *zamacueca* dancer had done, the *chichera* wears a yellow dress covered in red polka dots. In fact, the two dresses are nearly identical: they both feature short sleeves, low necklines, and layers of ruffled hems near the bottom. Where the dresses differ is in their color and styling. The *chichera* wears the sleeves of her yellow dress pulled up at the shoulders, with an apron tied around her waist to catch any spills from the bright purple liquid that was her stock in trade. For her part, the *zamacueca* dancer wears the sleeves of her pink dress pulled down to expose her shoulders, and a crinoline underneath the skirt to give it more volume. Perhaps during her own workday, she wore the dress like the *chichera* did, with her shoulders covered to protect against the sun's punishing rays or cold snaps, and later prepared for her night out by untying the apron, adding the crinoline for a fashionable detail, and pulling the sleeves of her dress past her shoulders. The latter would have facilitated the dance movements that involved raising her arms above her head, kept her cool during these kinds of physical exertions, and allowed her to showcase a bit of sex appeal as well. In other words, it was a dress that went easily from work to play with just a few clever tweaks.

While further research is needed to determine whether there was anything inherently or explicitly racialized about polka dots in nineteenth-century Lima, and, if so, how that process of racialization took shape, Bonnaffé's watercolors offer compelling suggestions of an enduring relationship between pattern and people. In both *La Zamacueca* and *La Chichera*, the artist visually links polka dots to women of apparent African descent, to the folkloric dance tradition of their ancestors, as well as to race- and gender-based forms of labor. And he was not alone in doing so. These links would persist across various modes of image production and last well into the twentieth century.

By the 1940s, the *Zamacueca* began to be called to *La Marinera* in honor of the Peruvian navy (as a way of honoring sailors as masculine and deserving of flirtatious female attention), and consequently came to serve as the national dance of Peru. While the process by which the dance made its way from the world of the enslaved to the national stage merits the kind of scholarly attention that scholar Robin Moore has given to the process of "nationalizing blackness" in early twentieth-century Cuba (Moore 1997). Such work has the potential to enhance our understanding of how the process of the dance's incorporation into national culture seemed to simultaneously result in the relegation of the dance's African-descent progenitors and even its more recent practitioners to the folkloric past.

A product advertisement from a December 1946 edition of the Lima-based *El Comercio* newspaper for a brand of alcohol called Aguardientes Vargas, illustrates this point (not pictured).² The advertisement features a scene within a scene. The first depicts a duo of apparent African descent engaged in a flirtatious, handkerchief-waving dance while surrounded by musicians and fellow revelers. That scene is bordered by a picture frame, with an engraving that says "Bailando 'La Marinera'" ("Dancing the Marinera"), and forms part of the second scene as a wall hanging before which stand two white-presenting men who hold glasses of aguardiente while gazing and gesturing at the painting. The effect produced by the second scene is that the dancers appear as objects of study, as though in a museum for relics of a bygone era. In turn, the dancers are reduced to folkloric human types who seem to have no place in modern Peruvian society but are instead reminders of the past and the customs that came out of it.

The advertisement had parallels in contemporaneous discourses in Peru that sought to minimize the place of people of African descent within the modern nation, instead relegating them, along with Indigenous populations, to the distant past while emphasizing the country's mestizo identity (Sanchez 2008; de la Cadena 2000). These assertions were supported by census data, which in 1940 purported that African-descent Peruvians made up just 2 percent of the population despite the country's long history of African slavery. But as in other regions of Latin America, the data said more about attitudes about race in Peru, where identifying as African-descent (rather than mestizo, for example) was often perceived as a socio-economic liability, than anything about the country's actual racial makeup (Cozart 2017).

In the 1940s, when the US-based Perfection Stove Company (which made its debut in the 1880s with a patented "lamp stove" that derived heat from the same kerosene oil that fueled streetlights and household lanterns and marked the beginning of a revolution in home cooking since it allowed for faster, more even heating than did cooking with wood or coal) introduced a new model of stove that improved upon earlier iterations that had just a single tank fitted beneath a small cast-iron plate that served as a cooking service, requiring either the preparation of one-pot meals or the careful planning of when to cook what. The newer versions had multiple tanks that were installed in a steel-framed case outfitted with a large surface to allow for cooking multiple dishes at once. A January 1942 advertisement in Lima's *El Comercio* newspaper promoted one such product (Figure 7.2; *El Comercio* January 13, 1942).³ The Black-and-white ad features two women flanking the stove. Behind it stands a white-presenting woman who wears a densely patterned, short-sleeve collared shirt, an ankle-length skirt, and high heels. With her hair carefully coiffed and lipstick perfectly applied, she looks dressed for an afternoon out on the town rather than one spent toiling near a hot stove that would certainly have made her curls fall and makeup melt in minutes. Better suited for the task of attending to the multiple steaming pots on the stove is the woman standing right in front of it. She has dark skin and wears her hair tied back in a scarf to protect it from the smoke, smells, and sweat that were and remain a common byproduct of laboring in the kitchen, and an apron around her waist to protect her clothes from food stains. Underneath the apron is a similar outfit to the one worn by her lighter-hued counterpart: a short-sleeve collared shirt, an ankle-length skirt, and shoes with a modest heel. The main differences lie in the fit of the clothes, with the dark-hued woman at the stove wearing looser-fitting materials to allow for ease of movement around the kitchen, and in the polka-dotted pattern of her shirt.

Alongside this assortment of visual cues, the text accompanying the advertisement further clarifies the relationship between the two women, as well as between the two women and the stove. "Te gusta la nueva cocina?" ("Do you like the new stove?"), asks the woman standing behind it. "Claro Señorita, Ahora sí da gusto cocinar" ("Of course, ma'am. Now cooking is so enjoyable"), responds the woman standing in front of it. In other words, the woman behind the stove is an *ama de casa*, or lady of the house, and the woman in front is a domestic servant hired to cook for the lady and her family, and possibly clean after them as well (the Perfection Stove Company was also there to help on that front, as they sold other household products, like water heaters, to facilitate doing laundry and other cleaning tasks.) Here, then, is a stove that was being marketed to ladies of the house so that they—or, more likely, their husbands—could purchase them for the women responsible for carrying out the actual work of using them.

Those women were nearly always of African or Indigenous ancestry, and they occupied similar roles in the early twentieth century that their ancestors had for generations before them. As early as the sixteenth century, both groups toiled in urban and rural households alike, providing services that included cooking, the work of laundering, ironing, and sewing clothes, nursing children (particularly in the case of African-descent women), and various other forms of housework (Graubart 2007; Aguirre 2005; Arrelucea Barrantes 2009). This work involved being in close physical proximity to male and female heads of household and slaveholders, exposing Indigenous and African-descent women, in turn, to sexual assault and to punitive physical violence for supposed infractions such as working too slowly, failing to show enough deference, or mistakes made by other people (if they were indeed mistakes at all) (Walker 2020).

Owing to a combination of racism, gendered expectations, and limited opportunities for economic mobility, these roles and dynamics persisted well into the modern era. African-descent and Indigenous women learned at a young age to master domestic tasks such as cooking, cleaning, and minding younger children. These skills enabled them to provide support for their own families while their parents worked outside the home, to care for their own households when the time came to start them, or to find live-in domestic work in nearby and distant cities. Indigenous women from the Andean highlands were recruited into the latter via family members, godparents, teachers, priests, and the recruiting agents who were growing in prominence in Peru and particularly in Lima in the 1940s (Radcliffe 1990).[4] This kind of work regularly isolated African-descent and Indigenous women from their social networks, as they worked long hours and made scant wages (if they made any at all, since financial abuse and the withholding of wages was rampant) that further hindered their mobility and ability to nurture social ties.

In the twentieth century, as in centuries past, African-descent and Indigenous women nearly always worked for middle- and upper-class families of European or mestizo (or Indigenous-European) ancestry. The early twentieth century saw the rise of white-collar work in accounting, banking, and commerce on the high end, and retail clerking and sales on the lower end; across this spectrum emerged a shared "middle-class culture and consciousness" that was built around the idea of belonging to a class of *gente decente* ("decent people"). They defined themselves in opposition to *las masas* ("the masses") both through the things they did, such as join social clubs and play sports like cricket and tennis, and by the things they did not do, like work outside the home, if they were women, or do any kind of housework (Parker 1992). Doing one's own housework carried the implication of not being able to afford to pay for outside help, and the risks of association with the masses who had no choice but to clean up after themselves and their own households. Indeed, just as domestic workers of African and Indigenous ancestry were following in their ancestors' footsteps, so too were middle- and upper-class mestizo and white limeños. Their ideas about who should and should not do housework had roots in the colonial period, when housework was the domain of people of African and Indigenous ancestry.

The Perfection Stove Company advertisement both exemplifies these local labor histories while also evoking transnational ones as well. For example, the advertisement shares several features in common with the *Aunt Jemima* advertisements that proliferated in the United States of the early twentieth century. There, the figure of *Aunt Jemima* provided the brand's target demographic of white female homemakers with a nostalgic vision of slavery, which had been abolished just two decades earlier. The "Aunt Jemima" character conjured up memories of the domestic slaves who labored in both Southern and Northern households, and who were keepers of the recipes that many white female homemakers were now attempting to recreate on their own. Without the help of the Black women who had for so long been pressed into their service, these homemakers needed guidance. That, at least, was what the brands who courted them seemed to suggest. With her wide smile and the generic uniform that defined her entirely in terms of her labor, "Aunt Jemima" seemed to say to these women that even though slavery was over, she was still there to help.[5] In other words, the character served both an evocative and encouraging purpose. Here was a new kind of kitchen helper for the late nineteenth and early twentieth century, who not only supplied recipes but who—when she performed live demonstrations, beginning with the 1893 World's Fair and later at county fairs and club bake offs and on live television—provided a set of guiding hands.

These kinds of product advertisements spoke a language that consumers—in both the United States and Peruvian contexts—would have clearly understood. They both invoked the roles that African-descent women had long played in domestic service under the institution of slavery, and both offered nostalgic views of that history, not just from the apparent perspectives of the ladies of the house (the ones pictured or simply imagined) but from that of the African-descent maids as well, whose smiling presence suggested that there was no lingering resentment on the part of the formerly enslaved and their descendants, and instead a happy occupation of the same roles and place in racial dynamics as their distant forebears. It was a fantasy that would have been at odds with the more complex emotional terrain navigated by the domestic workers, who may have felt a mixture of sadness and frustration at belonging to such a long line of Afro-Peruvian women laboring in service to white households.

It is also worth noting the presence of the polka-dotted scarf adorning Aunt Jemima's head, as well as the use of the pattern on all four members of "her rag doll family," which were available for purchase. The polka dots also, of course, find parallels in the Perfection Stove Company advertisements and the Bonnaffé watercolors. This would not have been by accident, as the late nineteenth and early twentieth centuries were periods when Latin American consumers were gaining increased exposure to US popular culture, thanks to newspapers, radio programs, films, and performers bringing news, entertainment, and social discourses from and to the north. As historians such as Matthew B. Karush and Louis Pérez have shown, included among these US cultural exports were racist depictions and caricatures of African Americans (Karush 2012; Pérez 1999). The Aunt Jemima advertisement would thus have been familiar to the creators of the Perfection Stove Company advertisement and perhaps even to some of their consumers.

So, too, would it have been familiar to the creators of another product advertisement, this one from the latter part of the twentieth century and for a brand of laundry detergent called *Ña Pancha*.[6] It features a smiling Black woman wearing a polka-dotted apron and headscarf, holding a package of detergent that, according to the copy, is "unique for its whitest whitening" ("unico por su blancura blanquisima"). The copy is clearly meant to play up the ironic contrast between the woman's own dark skin and the whitening properties of the product. Perhaps her smile is meant to suggest that she is in on the joke, but more likely it is meant to echo the smile worn by the domestic worker in the Perfection Stove Company advertisement, to suggest the pleasure she takes in her work. The implication embedded in the image, which forms part of a long visual discourse made up of the images discussed so far in this chapter (among others), is that work is on behalf of other people.

Of course, answering the question of *how* Latin Americans gained exposure to figures like Aunt Jemima is not the same as addressing *why* they found such resonance in them. One possible answer is that the invocation of Aunt Jemima served to link Afro-Peruvian women to transnational forms of blackness and the forms of labor that traditionally accompanied it (and perhaps, in turn, to link mestizos and whites in Peru to transnational forms of whiteness and all the privileges that traditionally accompanied it). But, unlike the United States, where African Americans were impossible to erase through census data or national discourses, these advertisements served to confine Afro-Peruvians to a place where they were properly subordinated and subsumed within mestizo and white households, alienated from their own communities and, by extension, unable to engage in their own forms of social and biological reproduction. Thus, when taken together, the Aguardientes Vargas, Perfection Stove Company, and the Ña Pancha advertisements all worked together as if to say: if Afro-Peruvian women cannot be relegated to the past, they can at least be relegated to the kitchen.

It is one thing to acknowledge the biases embedded within the images at the center of this chapter and highlight the myriad ways they disregarded the full humanity of their subjects. But that is not the same as meaningfully considering the perspective of the subjects depicted in the images themselves. Such work is hindered by the forms of image production themselves, which each present their subjects as human types rather than individual portrait subjects (in the case of

Figure 7.1 A.A. Bonnaffé, "*La Zamacueca*," *Recuerdos de Lima: album tipos, trajes, y costumbres dibujado y publicado por A.A. Bonnaffé en Lima, 1857*. Lima: A.A. Bonnaffé, 1857.

the watercolors) or paid spokespersons (in the case of the product advertisements). But adopting an analytical gaze that ignores the real people who inspired such imagery carries the danger of reproducing dehumanizing tropes, however inadvertently. How do we navigate around this in ways that remind us of the human beings who were, and will always remain crucial to processes of image production, and to highlight the tension that often existed between those human beings' own self-regard and their manners of representation? One way is to engage the ethnographic present. For example, YouTube is filled with videos of Afro-Peruvian performers dancing to *La Zamacueca/La Marinera*, and one,

Figure 7.2 "Perfection: La Mejor Cocina a Kerosene," *El Comercio*, 18 January 1942.

uploaded on November 29, 2016, and titled "Zamacueca canto y baile Peru" provides a compelling place to start.[7] In it, we see a quartet of Afro-Peruvian dancers, two men and two women, all holding handkerchiefs and smiling flirtatiously at one another as they pair off and move towards and around one another. We also see the two women wearing dresses evoking the same polka-dotted pattern that adorned the women in the images discussed in this essay. But more than anything, we see a scene of modern Afro-Peruvians alive, well, and keeping the culture that sustained their ancestors out in the open, all while celebrating their own humanity, sexuality, and the fact that they are not going anywhere.

Notes

1 Romero traces the origins of the *zamacueca* to the Congo-Angola region of Africa which, the author notes, helps explain the similarities between the Peruvian

zamacueca and its counterparts in other slaveholding regions such as Cuba, where it was known as the "samba de cajón."

2   "Aguardientes Vargas," *El Comercio*, December 19, 1946. *Photograph taken by and courtesy of Roxana Escobar.*
3   Reproduction by and courtesy of Roxana Escobar.
4   Radcliffe (1990) also shows that Indigenous women from the Andean highlands were recruited into domestic work via family members, godparents, teachers, priests, and the recruiting agents who were growing in prominence in Peru and particularly in Lima in the 1940s (236–241).
5   "I's in Town Honey." Taken from, Jon Schlosberg, "The untold story of the real 'Aunt Jemima' and the fight to preserve her legacy," *ABC News*, August 12, 2020. https://abcnews.go.com/US/untold-story-real-aunt-jemima-fight-preserve-legacy/story?id=72293603.
6   Advertisement taken from Arkiv Peru. https://arkivperu.com/prefiero-na-pancha-1964/
7   Afro-Peruvian performers dancing to *La Zamacueca/La Marinera*, November 29, 2016, entitled "Zamacueca canto y baile Peru," www.youtube.com/watch?v=t7azgIXp6kQ&ab_channel=JaimeCasquero

Bibliography

Aguirre, Carlos. 2005. *Breve historia de la esclavitud en el Perú: una herida que no deja de sangrar.* Lima: Fondo Editorial del Congreso del Perú.

Arrelucea Barrantes, Maribel. 2009. *Replanteando la esclavitud: estudios de etnicidad y género en Lima borbónica / Maribel Arrelucea Barrantes.* 1st ed. Lima: CEDET, Centro de Desarrollo Étnico.

Bonnaffé, A.A. 1857. *Recuerdos de Lima: album tipos, trajes, y costumbres dibujado y publicado por A.A. Bonnaffé en Lima, 1857.* Lima: A.A. Bonnaffé.

Cadena, Marisol de la. 2000. *Indigenous mestizos: The Politics of Race and Culture in Cuzco, Peru, 1919-1991.* Durham, NC: Duke University Press.

Cisneros Sanchez, Manuel. 1975. *Pancho Fierro y la Lima del 800.* Lima: Importadora, Exportadora, y Librería Garcia Ribeyros, S.C.R.L.

Cozart, Daniel S. 2017. "Afro-Peruvian Creoles: A Social and Political History of Afro-Descended Peruvians in an Era of Nationalism and Scientific Racism," Ph.D. diss., University of New Mexico.

Graubart, Karen. 2007. *With Our Labor and Sweat: Indigenous Women and the Formation of Colonial Society in Peru, 1550–1700.* Stanford, CA: Stanford University Press.

Karush, Matthew B. 2012. "Blackness in Argentina: Jazz, Tango and Race Before Peron." *Past & Present* 216 (1): 215–245.

León y León Duran, Gustavo. 2004. *Apuntes histórico-genealógicos de Francisco Fierro: Pancho Fierro*. Lima: Biblioteca Nacional del Perú, Fondo Editorial.

Moore, Robin D. 1997. *Nationalizing Blackness: Afrocubanismo and Artistic Revolution in Havana, 1920–1940 / Robin Moore*. Pittsburgh, PA: University of Pittsburgh Press.

Palma, Angelica. 1935 (1975). *Pancho Fierro: Acuarelista Limeño*. Lima: San Martín y CIA, S.A.

Parker, David S. 1992. "White-Collar Lima, 1910–1929: Commercial Employees and the Rise of the Peruvian Middle Class." *The Hispanic American Historical Review* 72 (1): 47–72.

Pérez, Louis A. 1999. *On Becoming Cuban: Identity, Nationality and Culture / Louis A. Pérez, Jr.* Chapel Hill: University of North Carolina Press.

Radcliffe, Sarah A. 1990. "Between Hearth and Labor Market: The Recruitment of Peasant Women in the Andes." *The International Migration Review* 24 (2): 229–249.

Romero, Fernando. 1988. *Quimba, fa, malambo, ñeque: afronegrismos en el Perú / Fernando Romero*. Lima: Instituto de Estudios Peruanos.

Sanchez, Robert L. 2008. "Black Mosaic: The Assimilation and Marginalization of Afro-Peruvians in Post-Abolition Peru, 1854–1930." ProQuest Dissertations Publishing.

Walker, Tamara J. 2020. "María Hipolíta Lozano, Eighteenth-Century Lima (Peru)." In *As if She Were Free: A Collective Biography of Women and Emancipation in the Americas*, 236–252, edited by Terri L. Snyder, Tatiana Seijas and Erica L. Ball. Cambridge: Cambridge University Press.

8

"Are Feminists Elegant?": Shaping Gender and Literary Style Through Fashion

Alba F. Aragón

Shortly after the first issue of the fashion magazine *Elegancias* [Elegances] was published, Guatemalan writer Ernesto Gómez Carrillo wrote to its literary editor: "Everyone who speaks to me about [it] tells me, What a pity, a thing so pretty and so badly written, so badly, so badly. . ." (Gómez Carrillo 1911).[1] The same outlook prevailed for a century among scholars, who disregarded the publication entirely though its literary editor was Nicaraguan poet Rubén Darío, head figure of Spanish American *modernismo*[2] and one of the most important writers of the Spanish language. The present work reconsiders the significance of *Elegancias*, which was published in Paris for a Latin American readership from 1911 to 1914, along with its better-known sister publication *Mundial Magazine* [Worldwide Magazine]. This chapter begins with some archival considerations, to then focus on how the interplay of literature and commodity culture in *Elegancias* underscores Latin American women's participation in shaping literary style as readers and consumers of fashion during a time in which periodicals were key to the diffusion of Latin American literature and to women's participation in public discourse. Second, I analyze how the magazine's discourse on fashion, femininity, and feminism illustrates the tensions generated by women's growing presence in the public sphere, revealing a paradoxical attitude of its time: while the magazine champions modernist literature as a hallmark of cosmopolitan, modern life, it treats both fashion and feminism as dangerous practices, reinforcing traditional gender roles through the subterfuge of the "good taste" proclaimed in its title.[3]

In "The Power of the Archive and Its Limits," historian Achille Mbembe reflects on how the term "archives" originally refers to "a building, a symbol of a public institution," and thus derives its power "from this entanglement of building and documents" (2002, 19). When I began researching *Elegancias* in

2010, it was only available in print form at the National Library of France, a site inaccessible to me as a graduate student at the time. I was uncertain as to whether the material warranted a costly research trip, so I worked with microfilm reproductions available from the University of Illinois.[4] I effectively created my own *Elegancias* archive by reviewing microfilm images and digitizing them one by one, then printing and manually binding each issue. While these reproductions lacked the color, clarity, and texture of the originals, they helped me approximate the original readers' tactile experience of the magazine. A researcher equipped with better resources might wonder how, or why, go through such a process. The devalued status of *Elegancias* seemed intriguing. Despite its connection to Rubén Darío, scholarly references to the magazine were rare, inaccurate, or disparaging. There was inconsistent information on its duration and the number of issues published.[5] Rubén Darío's name was attached to it, but his involvement appears to have been brief. He reneged of it in a personal letter, calling it "this thing. . . for which, no doubt, I will earn something to live on, but over which my good taste sweats and my dignity slumps" (Carilla 1967, 286). Such omissions and disavowals flashed out as potentially productive, especially in light of Foucault's insight that "archives are often both documents of exclusion and monuments to particular configurations of power" (quoted in Hamilton et al. 2002, 9). Indeed, previous scholarly references to *Elegancias* seemed to assume that "feminine" pursuits such as fashion and shopping were unworthy of scholarly attention, perhaps reflecting the misogyny of many *modernista* texts (Molloy 1984, 21). At times, they seemed to echo the ambivalence of *modernista* writers towards bourgeois consumerism and the literary marketplace.[6] Having wrested the *Elegancias* archive from the building (in a sense), I understood that to learn what *Elegancias* had to say to contemporary scholarship, I would have to view it on new terms: not as a curiosity in Darío's biography, but as an indicator of *modernismo's* complex relationship with gender and modernity, and in the context of Latin American periodicals at large.

Fashion can serve as a prism with which to better understand the relationship between print culture, power, and politics, which is a key theme in Latin America and throughout the globe. Víctor Goldgel (2013) has shed light on how periodicals and fashion, viewed as "a social mechanism that sets in motion a constant renewal of objects and practices," helped to establish "newness" or "the new" as a central value in Latin American culture, helping to spark the movements for independence in Cuba, Argentina, and Chile. Similarly, Regina A, Root's *Couture and Consensus: Fashion and Politics in Postcolonial Argentina* (2010) shows how dress served as a critical expression of political agency and citizenship, with particular attention to fashion writing and women's participation in the public sphere. These critical interventions call into question an outdated dichotomy in fashion studies between "fashion" as an exclusively European phenomenon characterized by change versus the supposedly static "dress" practices of other parts of the world, while also underscoring the centrality of modernity, through fashion, to cultural identities in Latin America. *Elegancias*, published between 1911 and 1914, belongs to a later moment in the history of Latin American periodicals, marked by the cosmopolitan character of *modernismo*, the professionalization of Spanish American writers, the exponential growth of serialized printing, and women's increasing engagement with consumerism and print culture. As I aim to show below, *Elegancias* illuminates Latin American women's participation in the literary marketplace and the complex mechanisms by which *modernistas* (almost always male) created and sustained demand for their work among their female readership, which was "possibly its majority audience" (Martínez 2001, 15).

The literary movement known as *modernismo*, which originated in the 1880s in Spanish America, is credited with reinvigorating Spanish-language literature through the pursuit of formal perfection and innovation. Early detractors considered it escapist because of its exuberant themes, cosmopolitanism, and apparent attitude of art for art's sake. Since the 1960s, Uruguayan critic Ángel Rama and others have established that, quite on the contrary, Spanish American *modernistas* were remarkably in tune with their sociohistorical circumstances, becoming professionals of the written word as the traditional Spanish American prototype of the writer-statesman who enjoyed state patronage faded (Rama 1970; Ramos 1989). Today, the aesthetic innovations of Spanish American modernism are understood as part of the movement's ongoing engagement with issues related to modernization. One of these issues was the perceived marginality of Spanish American culture to Western modernity.[7] *Modernistas* responded to this concern by appealing to cosmopolitanism in a bid to gain equal status with the great centers of Western modernity. *Elegancias*, along with its sister publication *Mundial Magazine*, is best understood as part of this effort. Edited and printed in Paris for distribution in Latin America from 1911–1914, both publications aimed to be purveyors of the latest developments in literature, science, art, society, and fashion to an elite Latin American readership. Their use of color, embossing, photography, and ornate graphics represented the latest in print technology at the time. The magazines' manufacture in Paris added to their cachet as luxury commodities. As Jaime Hanneken put it, "The narrative that *Mundial* tells its readers about the latest feats of print culture is inscribed in an epic of import and export whereby local culture travels to Paris, is magically transmuted by modern machinery, and is shipped back to readers on glossy pages, shimmering with a metropolitan aura" (2010, 140–141). *Mundial* was addressed to a male audience and billed itself as "the first Spanish American magazine" (Merello and Guido 1911, 1). It is an ambitious claim considering that the magazine format so familiar, with its emphasis on current events and visual content, was a true technological novelty in the early twentieth century. In addition to using the latest technologies, *Mundial Magazine* and *Elegancias* also claimed a literal space for Hispanic culture in the center of modernity by having offices and a reading room in Paris, which readers were invited to visit. To my knowledge, no records remain indicating the number of subscribers to these magazines, but they circulated in Latin America, London, Paris, and Madrid, making them part of the prolific transatlantic print network that characterized *modernismo*.

Mundial and *Elegancias* also provided a forum in which Latin Americans could represent themselves as modern, "rather than being relegated to mere objects in the discourses of metropolitan modernity" (Mejías López 2006, 149). In *Mundial*, this aspiration is evident in a series of expository essays by Rubén Darío, each devoted to a Latin American nation. Critic Beatriz Colombi has characterized the series, which constructs a sort of catalog of the region, as "an effort to inform" imbued with the "markedly advertising tone" of an increasingly stylized discourse of *latinoamericanismo* or Latin American identity which arose in the early twentieth century (2005, 237). According to critic Beatriz González-Stephan, the first universal expositions, in which Latin American nations represented themselves through raw materials (such as meat, coffee, or copper), inspired the publication of catalogs and illustrated literary histories intended to demonstrate the existence of social and cultural heritage in Latin America (2003, 230–231). Remnants of this spirit can be seen in *Elegancias*, in a series featuring photographs of Latin American women dressed in European fashions who are showcased as representative of specific Latin American nations with captions such as "Bellezas chilenas" (Chilean Beauties) or "La mujer argentina" (The Argentinian Woman). At times, the photos are accompanied by an essay on the characteristic attributes of women from the featured nation. The series deploys the familiar metaphor of the female body as territory, constructing a catalog of Latin America in the form of ideally fashioned female bodies that illustrate both the region's particularity as well as its compliance with the visual culture of modernity. These fashionable bodies convey the elites' access to modernity in images meant to elicit identification as well as desire through the allure of fashion.

While *Mundial* was aimed at a male readership purportedly more concerned with information and content, *Elegancias* addressed a female readership assumed to be more interested in aesthetic forms. There is plenty of overlap among the publications, chiefly their link to commodity culture, as aptly expressed by the French word *magasin*, which denotes both this kind of publication and a store. In the magazines, literary texts and the experience of reading are presented as desirable commodities. For instance, an advertisement for the fragrance "Le parfum de la Dame en noir" (The perfume of the lady in Black), which was named after a 1908 novel by Gaston Leroux, claims to capture the protagonist's seductive fragrance, which "the great novelist has been able to describe with his great power of expression" ("Perfumes de Lenthéric . . ." 1911, 31). According to the advertiser's copy, the novel's "lovely atmosphere of bewilderment has been captured for our embellishment . . . Women have embraced it with the same enthusiasm as they did the novel" (ibid.). Thus, a novel's mood or "atmosphere" is offered as perfume, a fashionable bodily adornment that the reader/consumer can wear.

In the pages devoted to poems in *Elegancias*, the literary work is similarly treated like an object, as in the page displaying Rubén Darío's poem "Balada sobre la sencillez de las rosas perfectas" (Ballad on the simplicity of perfect roses) published in January 1912. The actual text of the poem nearly takes second place to its elaborate visual presentation, which resorts to a variety of artistic resources – drawing, painting, calligraphy – to resemble a decorative trinket. In the poem, the speaker asks himself rhetorically whether he has seen the poem's beautiful addressee in an "illuminated medieval poem" ("¿La he visto yo . . . / en medioeval poema iluminado?" l. 3–6). The graphic composition of the page interacts with this question by reproducing the poetic text in calligraphic lettering with the illustration of a scroll as a frame, as if Darío's text itself were the medieval poem it references. Above the scroll, an oval inset features a reproduction of a classically painted portrait, probably of the addressee named below the poem's title (Carmen de S. Concha), whom the poem describes as possessing "the simplicity of perfect roses." Accordingly, the portrait is flanked by illustrated rose stems and flowers, giving it the appearance of a fashion accessory – a cameo brooch. All of these features constitute a purposeful "dressing up" of the literary text to appeal to its intended readership. Like the advertising copy for "Le parfum de la Dame en noir," which offers the atmosphere of the eponymous novel in the form of perfume, Darío's poem is offered to the reader as a multisensory experience she can possess.

Figure 8.1 "Balada sobre la sencillez de las rosas perfectas" (Ballad on the Simplicity of Perfect Roses) by Rubén Darío, in *Elegancias,* January 1, 1912. Image in the public domain.

Critic José María Martínez's work proves illuminating in this regard (2001, 2004). Martínez has explored how certain literary texts by *modernistas* Manuel Gutiérrez Nájera and Amado Nervo dialogue with a reading public accustomed to switching between browsing and reading, addressing a figurative or historical female reader who is envisioned as more drawn to the sensory than to the abstract or intellectual aspects of reading (2001, 24). Martínez also notes the frequent "objetualización" (objectification) of books in fictional scenes that portray them as yet another trinket in a bourgeois interior, or as yet another accessory of feminine attire. Similar dynamics are at play in the examples from *Elegancias* discussed above, in which literary texts are offered to the reader as consumable objects of fashion.

In appealing to readers who are envisioned as more drawn to the sensory, *Elegancias* activates one of *modernismo*'s primary motifs: the *reino interior* or interior realm. The "reino interior" refers to an idealized interior space in which writers can achieve artistic self-realization away from the perceived vulgarity of bourgeois consumerism. Critic Gerald Aching has characterized this trope as "exemplifying an ambiguous resistance to the marketplace," since "the *modernistas*' idealization of these exclusive sanctuaries also . . . captured the aspirations of the monied classes to cultivate the art of leisure away from the 'debasing' commercial and industrial labor upon which they depended for their own economic welfare" (1997, 28). In other words, in spite of their disavowal of the "mundanities" of economic life, the imagined sanctuaries of *modernistas* provided their "bourgeois and well-to-do readers with a social imaginary grounded in class exclusivity" (1997, 27).

Modernist disavowal of bourgeois consumerism edges into complicity when, for example, the readers of *Elegancias* are invited to inhabit the space of poetic creation in an advertisement for Poema Parfum featuring a line drawing of a female figure in a secluded garden. She is wearing various symbols of poetic creation: a Hellenic robe, a crown of laurels on her head, a lyre in one hand and a book in the other. Another evocation of the *reino interior* appears in *Elegancias* in March 1913 under the section "El arte de la dueña de la casa" (The art of the lady of the house): "There is a corner in the bedroom, apartment or house, which suits the spirit of the lady of the house better than any other: the dressing room, which these days is called in France *petit salon*, and which for many working or intellectual women has become 'the office.' It is where the lady of the house enjoys tea with her best friend. . . or her husband. There, she dreams, writes, settles her accounts, reads the latest novel, embroiders wonderful fabrics. . ." (Bertin 1913, 422). This private space, where everything is "delicate, fresh, in perfect harmony" is where books are arranged, in the "small rotating bookcases we are all familiar with" or in "wooden bookcases sculpted or engraved in bronze" (ibid.). Despite alluding to intellectual activity, the description of this private realm turns to the sensory – to how the room looks and feels, to the colors and textures of bookcases. Here, as in previous examples, literary texts and even the private spaces of reading and writing are treated as collectable objects made desirable by their association with France ("*le petit salon*"), thus functioning as symbols of cosmopolitan modernity. In this context, the advertisements which appear in multiple issues of *Elegancias* about a book series on Spanish American authors including the Guatemalan modernists Ernesto Gómez Carrillo and the Colombian José Asunción Silva serve double duty: they cast the work of these Latin American writers as part of an assortment of desirable, cosmopolitan cultural goods, while also reaching an elite female readership in Latin America that is able to acquire them.

Like the *grand magasins* or department stores which emerged in nineteenth-century France, *Elegancias* offers a symbolic interior that engages readers through the senses, a "browsing" space in which art and literature appear as another kind of merchandise. As such, *Elegancias* is a place of reverie and plenitude, but also one of exclusivity and control. As Ellen Gruber Garvey has said about US women's magazines in the late nineteenth century:

> Both magazines and department stores were considered respectable spaces in which middle-class women could wander; unlike a city street, the department store was an enclosed and monitored space. A visit there would not excite comment, and once inside the shopper was allowed seemingly limited choices. The magazine, too, was monitored space, from which questionable, risqué, or politically incendiary matter was excluded; within it the reader could wander seemingly at will, choosing among articles, stories, poems, and ads.
>
> (1996, 15)

Paradoxically, *Elegancias* does not simply celebrate fashion for its own sake. Issue after issue, and in different ways, the magazine elaborates a discourse about social distinction as a more desirable trait than sheer novelty, as the title's allusion to elegance suggests. For instance, one opinion essay claims that elegance "is an art because it depends on aptitudes granted only by nature... An elegant person is born, not made" (Ricart 1911, 206). Another states, "Elegance is a seal of personal distinction... belonging to people who are well bred and educated" (Badaracco 1911, 328). Yet another complains of the "crisis of good taste" caused by people readily accepting new trends, and posits that "it is women's job... to acquire good taste... and fix our democracy, which tends to become too vulgar" (J.S. 1912, 312). *Elegancias'* main section, the fashion column entitled "Gran Moda" (Grand Fashion), reports on the popularity of certain styles with suspicion: "What will be in fashion this winter?... Nothing too good. Too many styles have been put together to say that anything is in perfectly good taste" (Magda 1911, 376). The same chronicle informs readers of the availability of plaid in upcoming fashion collections, urging them to take advantage of it "for it will be quickly taken over by novelty, and then it will lose all its chic" (ibid.). Like Spanish American modernism, whose luxurious themes and verbal embellishments have been interpreted as "an effort to erect and enforce an imaginary of social distinction based on class and certain cultural competencies" (Aching 1997, 3, 21–22), the discourse of fashion in *Elegancias* has an aristocratic outlook. The idea that a fashion item will "lose all its chic" when novelty takes it over highlights the difference between fashion and distinction or elegance. While in the language of fashion the new is an absolute value, *Elegancias* seeks to educate readers on how to discriminate among all that is new.

And so, maybe surprisingly, *Elegancias* treats fashion like a dangerous practice. The magazine's fashion spreads conjure up ideal visions of metropolitan beauty, but its contents warn readers against dangerous breaches of traditional femininity. An interesting example is the discussion, over the course of several issues, of two fashion items launched in 1911 by renowned designer Paul Poiret: the *style sultane* or sultana skirt (a long skirt cinched at the ankles, which caused the wearer to walk with difficulty) and the *jupe-culotte* (a "harem" pantskirt of orientalist inspiration that some in France rejected due to its perceived exoticism). Both styles enjoyed great success, initially circulating as unique designer pieces ordered by affluent clients, and later as adapted by a larger audience into, on the one hand, extremely restrictive skirts known as *entravée*, and on the other, practical pantskirts that allowed the wearer to easily walk, get into and out of cars, or ride bicycles. In a chronicle about the Bois de Boulogne, Argentinean writer Fernán Félix de Amador reports seeing both "women dressed in the Turkish style, with the scandalous *jupe-culotte*" as well as others "walking more *entravée* [restricted] than ever" (1911, 66). A sonnet by Uruguayan Adolfo Montiel Ballesteros printed in *Elegancias* that same year, partially quoted below, indicates which of the two styles the magazine might recommend to its readers:

L'entravée renders her finer:
her step is softer and lighter
underneath the satin skirt

> when flirtatiously she walks.
> Her claylike forms
> are accentuated to the point
> that one fears a swat
> towards the feline curves.[8]

In these lines, it is clear that the woman's immobility is exciting to the poetic speaker/spectator, who compares her to a malleable thing (clay) and an animal (feline), remarking on the tension between the control exercised by the skirt over the female body and the self-control he "fears" might be lost as she walks by. An essay published in January 1912 discusses the *entravée* and the *jupe-culotte* as the two most salient fashion items of the previous year, with the following commentary:

> [The *jupe-culotte*] had an ephemeral life... Precisely at this time, when feminism is fighting tenaciously for its claims, it would have been a mistake to abandon one of its most important attributes, the skirt, in order to adopt the greatest symbol of masculinity, trousers. Fortunately, beautiful women soon realized that skirts held the greatest charm, and contritely returned to honor it... The skirt is a sacred and irreplaceable thing, and if women had consulted men before discarding it, I am sure men would have declared in unison that it is preferable to trousers.
>
> J.B. 1912, 113

Despite alluding to a "feminist fight," the author seems more invested in women's compliance to men's preferences. The language used to speak about skirts is moralizing ("contrite," "sacred"). And, although jupe-culottes are described as ephemeral, both Poiret's orientalist styles and feminism continued to elicit commentary in *Elegancias* until it went out of print in 1914.

Indeed, feminism is portrayed by *Elegancias* as a metropolitan fad that the magazine must register and mediate for its Latin American readership. The increasing visibility of women in the public sphere is presented as a sign of both modern progress and its dangers. The opinions expressed in the magazine with regards to women's status and their ideal place in society are varied, but they concur on drawing the line at suffrage and state politics. An interesting issue in this regard is the news, discussed in several issues of *Elegancias* in 1914, of the exclusion of renowned Spanish writer Emilia Pardo Bazán from the Spanish Royal Academy. Guatemalan writer Ernesto Gómez Carrillo expresses the view that she is deserving of a seat in the Academy, conceding that there have always been female writers as deserving as their masculine counterparts. Besides, he argues, "Isn't art a feminine matter by excellence? I do not see a difference between using words to make an embroidery of rhythms, and using a needle to make an embroidery of thread" (1914a, 82). However, when it comes to using words for political purposes, Gómez Carrillo does not so easily accept women's participation. Regarding the opening of a school of public speaking for women in Paris, he writes: "What is the purpose of these innovators? Do they wish to contribute to suffragism, providing . . . new weapons for political struggle? Or do they think, perhaps, that by inviting ladies to simulations of parliamentarism, it will be easier to make them understand how unpleasant and inadequate to grace the whole thing is?" (1914b, 6). The commentary is accompanied by caricatures of a parrot, an overweight drunk woman gesticulating with an open, toothless mouth, and lastly, a woman fashionably dressed in a *jupe-culotte* who seems foolishly enraptured reciting a speech to her small dog. While feminists may or may not be fashionable, the magazine's clear answer to the question, "Are feminists elegant?" is a resounding "no." In the cheeky-toned chronicle from 1914 whose title I borrow for this essay, the writer reports on a feminist protest in Montmartre and answers their own rhetorical question as follows: "There is not much to say about the elegance of feminists, because they are a living collection of the fashions of all time" (Ysis 1914). Clearly disparaged in the chronicle and accompanying caricature, feminists are portrayed as lacking the discernment or "good taste" that *Elegancias* aims to teach.

Thus, *Elegancias* uses fashion to draw and enforce gendered lines in a project with multiple aims: imagining a Latin American identity anchored in the center of the modern metropolis; promoting *modernista* literature as a hallmark of a cosmopolitan, modern lifestyle; and mediating modern fashions for the Latin American reader, including what it considers to be "trendy" metropolitan ideas regarding women's rights and participation in state politics. In its presentation of ideal feminine norms of appearance and behavior, the magazine is like a shop window in which the idealized woman-object of *modernista* poetry sparkles next to its enthralled, desired reader. *Elegancias* brings into focus women's participation in the literary marketplace, a crucial factor in the stance of Latin American writers towards their craft at the start of the twentieth century. It also exhibits the tension between the desire of male *modernistas* to satisfy the demands of an emerging female readership, and their ambivalence towards social changes brought about by modernity. *Elegancias* suggests a complex relationship between literary modernism and fashion, as well as the need to examine more closely the ways in which the literary marketplace mediated women's social roles and participation in the public sphere.

"Are Feminists Elegant?" 131

Figure 8.2 Illustration accompanying the chronicle "¿Las feministas son elegantes?" (Are Feminists Elegant) by Ysis in *Elegancias* May 1, 1914. Image in the public domain.

Notes

1 The original reads, "Cada persona que me habla de 'Elegancia' [sic] me dice que es una lástima una cosa tan bonita y tan mal escrita, tan mal, tan mal . . ." All translations in this chapter are mine, unless otherwise noted.

2 *Modernismo* designates a Spanish American literary movement lasting roughly from the 1880s to the 1920s. The term is also used to refer to a Brazilian literary movement launched with the Modern Art Week festival in 1922 whose principal figures include poet Oswald de Andrade and painter Tarsila do Amaral. The reader might find the following definitions from Rita Felski's *The Gender of Modernity* useful: "*Modernism* ... [is] an umbrella term for a mélange of artistic schools and styles which first arose in late nineteenth-century Europe and America. Characterized by such features as aesthetic self-consciousness, stylistic fragmentation, and a questioning of representation, modernist texts bore a highly ambivalent and often critical relationship to processes of modernization. The French term *modernité*, while also concerned with a distinctively modern sense of dislocation and ambiguity, locates it in the more general experience of the aestheticization of everyday life, as exemplified by the ephemeral and transitory qualities of an urban culture shaped by the imperatives of fashion, consumerism, and constant innovation. Finally, *modernity* is often used as an overarching periodizing term to denote a historical era which may encompass any or all of the above features" (1995, 12–13).

3 I have discussed other important aspects of this magazine in previous publications. "Huellas y textos inéditos de Rubén Darío en la revista *Elegancias* (1911–1914)" (Unpublished Texts and Traces of Rubén Darío in *Elegancias* Magazine, 1911–1914, 2016) represents the first thorough study of the magazine; it establishes basic facts about the publication and Rubén Darío's role in it; analyzes four texts of Darío's that had not been re-published since their first appearance in *Elegancias;* and provides a complete list of Darío's contributions to the fashion magazine. "Modas peligrosas: Darío y disonancias del género en la revista *Elegancias*" ("Dangerous Fashions: Rubén Darío and Dissonant Genders in *Elegancias* Magazine") is the text of a presentation delivered at the Congreso Internacional Rubén Darío (Buenos Aires, 2016), which discusses how Darío's literary contributions to *Elegancias* support the magazine's efforts to mold and appeal to the magazine's female readership. It also analyzes Darío's ambiguous attitude towards lettered women, whom he characterizes as "monstrous" in opposition to idealized feminine types praised in *Elegancias.*

4 For my initial review of *Elegancias*, I consulted microfilm reels available through the University of Illinois at Urbana-Champaign. Today, readers can freely access the complete collections of *Mundial Magazine* and *Elegancias* through the digital repository Archivo Rubén Darío Ordenado y Centralizado (Universidad Nacional de Tres de Febrero) at <https://archivoiiac.untref.edu.ar/ar-doc>

5 My research established that a total of forty-six issues of *Elegancias* were published from May 1, 1911 to August 1, 1914. Ten of them were biweekly issues published from May 1 to October 15, 1911; thirty-six were monthly issues published from

November 1, 1911, to August 1, 1914. See Aragón 2016 for additional facts about the magazine and Rubén Darío's role in it.

6 Though it was not the case with Darío, as Stephen Hart put it, "The typical modernista was the scion of a wealthy, often patrician, family who earned his daily bread and butter by writing journalism and who dreamed of being just a poet" (1998, 169).

7 Modernity is a complex term deserving a few words here. As Rita Felski put it in *The Gender of Modernity,* a political theorist may believe that modernity originates in the seventeenth century while a literary critic might place it in the mid or late nineteenth century; indeed modernity "is not a homogenous Zeitgeist which was born at a particular moment in history, but rather . . . comprises a collection of interlocking institutional, cultural, and philosophical strands which emerge and develop at different times" (1995, 12). There is a rich body of work on Latin American critical approaches to modernity, including Garcia Canclini (2005), Ramos (2001), Alonso (1998), to name a few.

8 The original reads: "L'entravée le hace más fina: / más suave y leve es su paso / bajo la falda de raso / cuando coqueta camina. / Sus formas de figulina / se acentúan hasta el caso / de que se teme el zarpazo / ante la curva felina."

Bibliography

Aching, Gerard. 1997. *The Politics of Spanish American Modernism: By Exquisite Design.* New York: Cambridge University Press.

Amador, Fernán Félix. 1911. "Crónica: El Bois de Boulogne." *Elegancias.* June 1, 1911: 66–68.

Aragón, Alba. 2019. "Modas peligrosas: Darío y disonancias del género en la revista *Elegancias*" ("Dangerous Fashions: Rubén Darío and Dissonant Genders in *Elegancias* Magazine"). *Actas del Congreso Internacional Rubén Darío "La sutura de los mundos,"* edited by Bartalini Carolina and Rodrigo Caserani. Sáenz Peña: Universidad Nacional de Tres de Febrero.

Aragón, Alba. 2016. "Huellas y textos inéditos de Rubén Darío en la revista *Elegancias* (1911-1914)" ("Unpublished Texts and Traces of Rubén Darío in *Elegancias* Magazine, 1911-1914"). *Revista de Crítica Literaria Latinoamericana.* XLII.83: 145–178.

Alonso, Carlos. 1998. *The Burden of Modernity: The Rhetoric of Cultural Discourse in Spanish America.* New York: Oxford University Press.

Badaracco, Marco-Tulio. 1911. "La elegancia." *Elegancias.* October 1, 1911: 328.

Ballesteros Montiel, Adolfo. 1911. "L'entravée." *Elegancias.* September 1, 1911: 265.

Becón, Juan de. 1913. "Cosas de París." *Elegancias.* February 1, 1913: 387.

Bertin, Marie. 1913. "El gusto y la elegancia en la intimidad. El tocador." *Elegancias.* March 1, 1913: 422–423.

Canclini, Néstor Garcia. 2005. *Hybrid Cultures: Strategies for Entering and Leaving Modernity.* Minneapolis: University of Minnesota Press.

Carilla, Emilio. 1967. "Las revistas de Rubén Darío." *Atenea* 415: 279–292.

Carter, Boyd G. 1959. *Las revistas literarias de Hispanoamérica: Breve historia y contenido.* Mexico D.F.: Ediciones de Andrea.

Colombi, Beatriz. 2005. "*Mundial* Magazine o el álbum de familia." *Sesgos, cesuras, métodos. Literatura latinoamericana*, edited by Noé Jitrik. Buenos Aires: Eudeba. 233–239.

Darío, Rubén. 1912. "Balada sobre la sencillez de las rosas perfectas." *Elegancias.* January 1, 1912: 101.

Felski, Rita. 2009. *The Gender of Modernity.* Cambridge: Harvard University Press.

Goldgel, Víctor. 2013. *Cuando lo nuevo conquistó América: prensa, moda y literatura en el siglo XIX.* Buenos Aires: Siglo Veintiuno Editores.

Gómez Carrillo, Ernesto. 1914a. "La escuela de oradoras." *Elegancias.* May 1, 1914: 4–6.

Gómez Carrillo, Ernesto 1914 b. "Las gentiles candidatas." *Elegancias.* January 1, 1914: 82–84.

Gómez Carrillo, Ernesto. 1911. Carta a Rubén Darío. Junio 1911. Archivo Rubén Darío, Documento 1106. Universidad Complutense, Madrid.

González-Stephan, Beatriz. 2003. "Showcases of Consumption: Historical Panoramas and Universal Expositions." *Beyond Imagined Communities: Reading and Writing the Nation in Nineteenth-century Latin America.* Eds Sara Castro-Klarén and John C. Chasteen. Baltimore: Johns Hopkins University Press.

Greenberg, Janet. 1990. "Toward a History of Women's Periodicals in Latin America: Introduction." *Women, Culture, and Politics in Latin America.* Seminar on Feminism & Culture in Latin America. Berkeley: University of California Press. http://ark.cdlib.org/ark:/13030/ft7c600832/

Gruber Garvey, Ellen. 1996. *The Adman in the Parlor: Magazines and the Gendering of Consumer Culture, 1880s to 1910s.* New York: Oxford University Press.

Hamilton, Carolyn, Verne Harris, and Graeme Reid. 2002. "Introduction." *Refiguring the Archive*, edited by Carolyn Hamilton et al. Dordrecht/Boston/London: Kluwer Academic Publishers.

Hanneken, Jaime. 2010. "Going Mundial: What It Really Means to Desire Paris." *Modern Language Quarterly* 71 (2) (June): 129–152.

Hart, Stephen. 1998. "Some Notes on Literary Print Culture in Spanish America: 1880–1920." *Anales de la literatura española contemporánea* 23 (1/2): 165–180.

J. S. 1912. "La crisis del gusto." *Elegancias.* November 1, 1912: 312.

J.B. 1912. "La Moda en 1911." *Elegancias.* January 1, 1912: 113.

Jitrik, Noé. 1978. *Las contradicciones del modernismo.* México: El Colegio de México, 1978.

"Los perfumes de Lenthéric. El perfume de 'La Dame en noir.'" *Elegancias*. May 1, 1911: 31.

Magda. 1911. "Gran Moda: El otoño avanza. . ." *Elegancias*. October 1, 1911: 376–377.

Martínez, José María. 2001. "El público femenino del modernismo: De la lectora figurada a la lectora histórica en las prosas de Gutiérrez Nájera." *Revista Iberoamericana* LXVII (194–195): 15–29.

Martínez, José María. 2004. "El público femenino del modernismo: las lectoras pretendidas de Amado Nervo." *Actas del XIV Congreso de la Asociación Internacional de Hispanistas: New York, 16-21 de julio de 2001*, edited by Isaías Lerner, Robert Nival, Alejandro Donoso , 389–396. Newark, Delaware: Juan de la Cuesta.

Mbembe, Achille. 2002. "The Power of the Archive and Its Limits." *Refiguring the Archive*, edited by Hamilton, Carolyn et. al. Dordrecht/Boston/London: Kluwer Academic Publishers.

Mejías López, Alejandro. 2006. "'Conocer y ser conocido': Identidad cultural, mercado y discursos globales en tres revistas latinoamericanas de entre siglos." *Revista Iberoamericana* LXXII (214): 139–153.

Merelo, Leo, Alfredo Guido, and Armando Guido. 1911. "Al público en general." *Elegancias*. May 1, 1911: 1.

Molloy, Silvia. 1984. "Lecturas de descubrimiento: La otra cara del fin de siglo." *Actas del XI Congreso de la Asociación Internacional de Hispanistas: Irvine, 24–29 de agosto de 1992. Volumen I. De historia, lingüísticas, retóricas y poéticas: De historia y poéticas. (Sesiones plenarias)*. Irvine, Universidad de California: 17–28

Rama, Ángel. 1970. *Rubén Darío y el modernismo (circunstancia socioeconómica de un arte americano)*. Caracas: Ediciones de la Biblioteca de la Universidad Central de Venezuela.

Ramos, Julio. 1989. *Desencuentros de la modernidad en América Latina: Literatura y política en el siglo XIX*. México: Fondo de Cultura Económica.

Ricart, Camilo. 1911. "La elegancia." *Elegancias*. August 1, 1911: 206–207.

Root, Regina A. 2010. *Couture and Consensus: Fashion and Politics in Postcolonial Argentina*. Minneapolis: University of Minnesota Press.

Seminar on Feminism & Culture in Latin America. 1990. *Women, Culture, and Politics in Latin America*. Berkeley: University of California Press. http://ark.cdlib.org/ark:/13030/ft7c600832/

Ysis. 1914. "¿Las feministas son elegantes?" *Elegancias*. May 1, 1914: 14.

9

Imagining through Images: Clothes and Family Memories in Afro-Brazilian Identities

Hanayrá Negreiros

Upon finding a box of old photographs at my mother's house, I realized there were significant family fragments involving attire and identity. My grandmother worked as a seamstress in the 1950s, and I already held fond memories of her old sewing machine. I was even more amazed when I realized the importance of these historical records of my family, with a particular interest in the clothes my ancestors wore and the stories behind the garments. This chapter delves into sartorial studies, utilizing photography and personal archives as the launchpad for a discourse on attire and Black heritage. Furthermore, it contemplates preliminary and exploratory facets of autoethnography as a research methodology, while also providing an introductory exploration of critical race theories, elucidating the manifestation of racism from centuries past to the contemporary moment in Brazil, the last territory in the Americas to abolish slavery, belatedly in 1888.

The memories of many Afro-Brazilian families marked by slavery processes are, in great part, shattered. It is, furthermore, quite rare to find Black family units that can track the names of their ancestors, their places of birth, their occupations, and life stories. Some people have no photographs of their ancestors. Part of the ominous plan of Afro-Atlantic slavery was the devastation of memory and consecutive attempts to annihilate signs of African cultures as its people were forced to work in many sectors, such as sugar cane and coffee farming and the mining system of precious rocks and metals such as diamond and gold, for over three consecutive centuries.

I consider myself fortunate to be part of a Black family who has a considerable number of pictures that keep record of some important moments of our history, especially on my mother's side. In fact, my mother kept and shared these memories in a personal archive. To embark on this endeavor of documenting my family's past, I have drawn from Saidiya Hartman, whose reflections on colonial archives reveal the centrality of intimate narrative styles and storytelling techniques to piece together what can only be fragmented memories (2020, 11). Hartman explains, "Every historian of the multitude, the dispossessed, the subaltern, and the enslaved is forced to grapple with the power and authority of the archive and the limits it sets on what can be known, whose perspective matters, and who is endowed with the gravity and authority of historical actor (2020, 06). Within this larger framework, my narrative is grounded in personal experiences and is told from within the circle.

What might be the significance of studies that address Black personal collections? And how does this relate to Afro-Brazilian histories and identities overall? Choosing to delve into such an intimately intertwined subject challenges the traditional academic perspective. This is my own personal history. While it might appear ostensibly simpler to observe other individuals at a distance, the emotional resonance of these stories and memories I uncovered facilitated a more profound and inward-looking analysis. In the discourse surrounding Black narratives in diaspora, characterized by centuries of attempted erasure, I deem this viewpoint of amplifying the voices of these experiences as invaluable. Such work would seem to serve as fertile ground for those untold stories calling into question the violent silence of colonial processes.

In my collection there are approximately thirty photographs. Two in particular reveal how clothes evoke the memories of the ancestors who wore them, allowing for a reimagining of the possibilities for creating more complete Brazilian fashion histories to include those that share Black perspectives. Clothes stand out in important ways. In one of my favorite photographs (Figure 9.1), a part of my family appears to celebrate a special moment. While my grandparents are present, the focal point is occupied by my great-grandfather, Zeferino Negreiros. Seated in the center of the photo, he wears a light shirt surrounded by his children, sons-in-law, and grandchildren. In the foreground, a table full of bottles and food; in the background, family. The girls wear their most outstanding clothes, seemingly simple dresses, while the women mainly have fitted dresses. The younger men wear open shirts while my great-grandfather dons a shirt buttoned up to his neck. In the second photograph I share from this album (Figure 9.2), my younger grandfather wears a tailcoat and shiny shoes at a gala night in São Paulo, Brazil. Holding what appears to be a pocket watch, he poses for the photograph. Even if the images are very different, they portray reminders of personal taste and layers of history.

Images chosen from a personal collection reveal more than family matters, as they can transcend the memories of that nucleus. Analyzing personal archives can be a way to understand how those represented in an image represent larger communities. And with this album in particular, representations of Afro-Brazilian families also mean thinking through the social and racial contexts that involve their stories in the greater Latin America, a territory with deep ties to slavery and the enslaved, and racism sophisticated enough to limit Black and Indigenous peoples to subordinate segments of society through the ideology of whitening (Gonzalez 2020, 143). To counteract the erasure of memories and Afro-Brazilian identities, these photographs and personal collections become a form of "sewing" and historical reconstruction.

Tina M. Campt emphasizes the centrality of personal archives, pictures, and clothes to the elaboration of studies about the African diaspora. *On Family Tales and Photographic Records* details how Campt's research emerged from family archives, photographs, and one special conversation with her aunt Joanne from her mother's side.

> Our conversations helped me understand how photographs reflect shared cultural practices in different Black communities and how photography offers individuals in those communities a medium through which to create a vision of themselves that does not always square with how they are popularly perceived or with what we associate with those contexts in the present. Time and again, our conversations returned to the same point: that images matter to Black folks.
>
> Campt 2012, 5

Family photographs, Campt writes, serve as "valuable historical sources" and as "crucial forms of historical documentation of the events, individuals, and contexts [. . .]" (6). The "traces" of memory witness history (Campt 6), unspoken yet understood.

In *Picturing Us*, Deborah Willis (1994) reflects on the personal and its culmination in the collective to understand the role of dressing and visibility among African Americans in the United States. Some of this relationship between the personal and the collective also seems relevant to the Afro-Brazilian context. How might the choice of images potentially alter the interpretation of a collection? For my own box of photographs, the first reading was affective and the next social. The selection of images at large would, in itself, start from the definition of the guiding questions and final objectives, such as a personal collection, research into a topic, and perhaps an exhibition. Categories that arise within an exhibit emerge from both hypotheses and interpretations reveal a kind of panorama consisting of order and its contestations, the ordinary and the counter-historical, the variability and agency of those represented.

The affective readings have the potential to generate anti-racist healing and empowerment, which can in turn impact the curator, researcher, or spectator in deeply personal ways. Family and community ties may potentially strengthen from conversation with elders regarding their memories and understandings. Images can signal unique moments during which to stimulate the historical imagination, with the power to fill in gaps imposed by inequality.

The social reading expands the relevance of the images. What was left out of the framing process may be central to the understanding of an image. The hierarchy of the composition may reveal hidden truths. At the beginning of the COVID-19 pandemic, I began working as an online columnist for *ELLE Brazil*. In "Negras Maneiras" (Black Ways), I shared with readers my feelings of nostalgia for family life at a moment of isolation and lockdowns. With some time on my hands, I was able to organize some documents and pictures, realizing the great opportunity I had to understand my family tree. After the article had been published, many readers and especially Black readers, told me that they, too, had opened up old boxes with photographs yellowed by time. Others shared their frustration of not having a personal image archive. Yet others told me how they appreciated clothes that had appeared in family photographs, realizing that some had been passed along as heirlooms. Reading these comments, I realized that I wasn't alone and that the family images, along with the clothes represented therein, had great symbolic value, and promised to reconstruct the fragments in some powerful way.

I grew up surrounded by stories of clothing, as I come from a family of seamstresses, laundresses, and tailors, or people who had as their occupation the making and caring for clothes. These occupations were considered subordinate roles in Brazil and mainly performed by Afro-Brazilians. During the early 1950s, my paternal grandfather was a tailor, specializing in men's shirts and suits. His wife, my grandmother, was a laundress in charge of cleaning and starching pieces of clothes of wealthy white families from an early age.

My maternal grandmother was a seamstress, information I uncovered only because I spent countless hours researching the documents stored in some old boxes in my childhood home. The dresses she made, her sewing machine, and the advantages of having a seamstress for a mother were the subject of affectionate family stories. The possibility of work and emancipation in the twentieth century took on unique meanings for seamstresses. Stephanie N. Saunders (2021) reflects on the stereotypes and negative representations of seamstresses in Spanish and Latin American literature, which several works ultimately challenged.

Although a seamstress might have brought more economic autonomy to a home, my grandmother's story was a very different one. Because my grandfather was financially successful, he forbade my grandmother to work after marriage. This situation likely differs from the experiences of most Afro-Brazilian women at that time who kept sewing for clients in order to help with household bills. My grandmother worked only at home for our family; sewing was a creative act. I grew up in the house built at the time of her wedding, one of the oldest in the neighborhood, in which she also raised her four children. I remember her yellow silk shirt and her sewing machine from the 1960s as if I had only been around them yesterday.

From my mother, I know that my grandmother was a discreet woman who enjoyed dressing up, who liked flowered patterns to match with her one pair of jeans. She enjoyed taking care of her appearance, taking pleasure in the care of her hair and jewelry, like a pearl necklace and some diamonds which were lost with time. Since I never met her personally, it was through these old photographs that I continued to learn more about her and other ancestors.

Accessing photographs and personal files are ways of (re)building Black identities. From memories printed on images, we can create the positive values related to stories of Afro-Brazilian families. This is an important social affective consequence, since this process of diving into a personal archive allows for an identification of the subjects remembered and a way to imagine how they lived, what they wore, and what might have been important to them. bell hooks (1992) rethinks the terms of race and representation "to break with the hegemonic models of seeing, thinking, and being that block our capacity to see ourselves oppositionally, to imagine, describe and invent ourselves in ways that are liberatory" (2). As a strategy to rebuild Black memories, in my experience as a diasporic Afro-Brazilian woman, photographs and family objects are the bridges to the memories of Brazil's racist and violent past.

I return to my box of family photographs. One of my favorites represents a celebration at my great-grandfather Zeferino's house. Present in the photograph are my grandparents, some children, and my great-aunts on the right. At the center, my great-grandfather stands with his shirt fully buttoned. One aunt wears a patterned dress, a dark leather belt, and a scarf on her head. She wears a matching striped blouse and waisted skirt, an off-the-shoulder neckline fashionable in the 1950s. Because everyone is in light-colored clothes, which in Brazil would be used to celebrate a new year, was this perhaps a New Year's Eve gathering?

Imagining through Images 141

Figure 9.1 Party at my great-grandfather's house (center) in the 1950s. São Paulo, Brazil. Personal archive.

Carol Tulloch writes that the personal stories of diasporic Black people are also pathways to think about fashion and style. Tulloch, who is British and whose family has Jamaican origins, details her father's exacting relationship with his clothes and grooming habits. She remembers him tying knots and ordering tailor-made suits made of high-quality fabrics. Style, Tulloch argues, is agency, a "[. . .] construction of self through the assemblage of garments and accessories, hairstyles and beauty regimes that may, or may not, be 'in fashion' at the time of use" (Tulloch 2016, 4). This insightful analysis provided me with a way to interpret my own story, in particular, my great-grandfather's donning of formal attire in every family photograph.

My mom often recounted her father's elegance and his love of tailored suits and shined shoes, regardless the occasion. Much to my uncles' chagrin, they were charged with keeping their father's shoes with a perfect polish, and in this way, playing a participatory role. In one photograph, my maternal grandfather wears a dark tailcoat, with a flower in his lapel, a pocket watch, and his signature shoes at an evening formal.

Well-tailored shirts, vests, jackets, pants. . . perfectly designed creases. . . sleek shoes along with hats, rings, and watches. . . These are the symbols of elegance

Figure 9.2 My grandfather wearing a tailcoat and shoes in the 1950s. São Paulo, Brazil. Personal archive.

and the topics of stories and social codes. It could be argued that the orientation to European dress in Afro-Brazilian fashion emulates the styles of white elites. The concept of "dressing up," however, acquires a different meaning for Black male bodies, as these can also represent social respect, financial power, and resistance against colonial power. Historians still search for documents like decrees to understand this phenomenon. Even the act of wearing shiny shoes carries meaning, especially since enslaved Black people often could not wear shoes in Brazil. Enslaved individuals who were granted their freedom might have been distinguished through their attire. The records of travelers, mostly European observers from the eighteenth and nineteenth centuries, depict barefoot Black people. With emancipation at the end of the nineteenth century, shoes became a very special possession for Black men and women, as if somehow the symbol of freedom.

Elegant suits were also a part of my grandfather's wardrobe, since he loved going to dances in which Black people could socialize together. As well as in other parts of the world inhabited by the African diaspora, Black people created their own safe spaces. The social clubs for more affluent Afro-Brazilians were also places to strengthen business ties. These clubs also sponsored special events like weddings, birthday parties, balls, and contests. As Gilda de Mello e Souza (1987) writes, clothing in Brazil is a coded language and the use of expensive and elaborate clothes was a way for my grandfather and so many others, through appearance and style, to circumvent the colonial remnants that were still ingrained in his condition as a Black Brazilian man, born less than half a century after the abolition of slavery. To speak of fashion and memory in Brazil is also to speak of Black heritage.

Delving deeper into photographic images within our own imagination may connect us to the study of photography itself. Sewing the stories together, as perhaps my grandmother might have done. Afro-Brazilian fashion and dress might always have been sophisticated aesthetic codes, ones which developed themselves alongside the diaspora, writes Catherine McKinley, and which were sometimes celebrated and displayed (McKinley 2021, 4). She writes that family histories were often "encoded in the clothes." She continues, "Cultural capital was encoded as well. The art of dress was exacting. Cloth served as a literal commentary on family and social events, a prestige record, a communication with the ancestors" (McKinley 2021, 5). Thinking about Afro-Brazilian images throughout time is to challenge cultural erasure, as the lives of individuals and communities celebrate living, loving, and the formation of social bonds. For a long time, some believed that Black families didn't even exist. The images we keep inside drawers, on the walls and in personal albums serve to materialize and remember what is itself, sewing. As the history of fashion aligns with decolonial perspectives that seem committed to ending racism and its archaic stereotypes, the images of Black families and their sartorial choices open new ways to imagine affective perspectives past and present. While we heal our wounds, revisiting these memories, faces, fabrics, colors, and the love for people who existed and helped shape the Brazilian and many other Latin American nations, we can use the words of Tanisha Ford (2019) to describe this intense process: "Our garments are archives of memories—individual and collective, material and emotional—that tell these rich, textured stories of our lives" (3). Photography allows the reimagining of family narratives—complete with clothes and identities—in Afro-Brazilian culture, resulting in a mindful practice for freedom and healing.

Acknowledgements

I would like to thank Mariana Souza for the first translation of this text and Felipe Torres for his rich contributions, ideas, and help in the editing and final translation of the chapter.

Bibliography

Campt, Tina. 2012. *Image Matters: Archive, Photography, and the African Diaspora in Europe*, Durham, NC: Duke University Press.

Ford, Tanisha. 2019. *Dressed in Dreams: A Black Girl's Love Letter to the Power of Fashion*, New York: St. Martin's Press.

Gonzalez, Lélia. 2020. *Por um feminismo afro-latino-americano: ensaios, intervenções e diálogos*. Orgs. Rios, Flavia, Lima, Márcia, Rio de Janeiro: Zahar.

Hartman, Saidiya. 2020. *Wayward Lives, Beautiful Experiments: Intimate Histories of Riotous Black Girls, Troublesome Women, and Queer Radicals*. New York: W. W. Norton & Co.

hooks, bell. 1992. *Black Looks: Race and Representation*. Boston: South End Press.

McKinley, Catherine. 2021. *The African Lookbook: A Visual History of 100 years of African Women*. New York: Bloomsbury.

Mello e Souza, Gilda de. 1987. *O espírito das roupas: a moda no século dezenove*. São Paulo: Companhia das Letras.

Saunders, Stephanie. 2021. *Fashion, Gender and Agency in Latin American and Spanish Literature*. Woodbridge: Tamesis Books.

Tulloch, Carol. 2016. *The Birth of Cool: Style Narratives of the African Diaspora*. London: Bloomsbury Academic.

Willis, Deborah. 1994. *Picturing Us: African American Identity in Photography*. New York: The New Press.

Part 3

Social Unrest and Resistance

10

Skirting the Colonial Gaze: Indigenous Reconfigurations of Feminine Identity

María Claudia Andre

Shifts and challenges in contemporary feminist theory have brought new perspectives to the fore, generating not only alternative ways to think about the complexities and nuances of gender experiences, but also more accurate approaches to examine the diverse tapestry of cultural, racial, and sexual identities of women and minorities worldwide. While the evolution of feminism, both as a movement and an ideology, is a step in the right direction, contemporary epistemologies on feminine diversity and self-expression remain circumscribed to Western gender identity politics and filtered through Anglo-American interpretations of culture and society. Addressing the urgency to debunk monolithic and arbitrary constructs of femininity, contemporary social scientists and academics are beginning to visualize the potential of femme studies to gain further insights into how alternative and queer femininities are constructed and performed across nations, races, classes, and sexualities.

Through the lens of femme theory, transnational, queer, and fashion studies, this chapter examines the ways in which Bolivian Quechuan and Aymara women—identified as *cholas* or *cholitas*[1]—challenge normative constructs of femininity by making their Indigenous skirts a symbol of womanhood and feminine empowerment, while fully occupying social and political spaces traditionally assigned to men. Ascribing to Judith Halberstam's theory of queer failure, this chapter explores how, in failing to subject to traditional categorizations based on class and gender systems, *cholitas* are rewriting their own gender script and, in so doing, they are reaffirming their racialized femininity, but also their own interpretations of beauty, fashion, and identity.

Recently, *cholitas*' unique stylization of social and gender identity has caught the attention of fashion, media, and pop culture; nonetheless, as the chapter examines, while such recognition has facilitated their assimilation into mainstream society, it has also overlooked the multifaceted dimensions of Indigenous practices and traditions, homogenizing the myriad expressions of femininity.

To conceptualize theorizations over femme identities, the essay draws on Rhea A. Hoskin's definition of femme as "sassy queer men; unapologetically straight women; transwomen; crip bodied femmes who refuse to be desexualized or degendered, and femmes of color who refuse to approximate white beauty norms" (2017, 99). Contrary to patriarchal femininity sustained and reinforced through essentialism, the femme is a boundary-dweller who evades fixed definitions of gender and regulatory standards of feminine beauty or behavior. Femme identities advance different approaches to socially instituted categories of gender complementarity, thereby challenging the perception that femaleness means being submissive, sexually available, and physically attractive to men.

Whereas theoretical and fictional collections authored by femme writers continue to envision alternative ways of looking and reframing current heteronormative paradigms of femininity, there still is a gap in the theorization of femmeness as a political form of resistance across the different ethnicities, countries, and communities. Legitimizing unconventional femmebodiments[2] and gaining a deeper understanding of the multiple expressions of gender performance through the study of non-Western cultures, is a significant move towards reducing femmephobia, gender discrimination, and other forms of sexual oppression. Indigenous people—in particular, women—are among the many social groups who are often subjected to racial preconceptions and arbitrary representations as ahistorical subjects, devoid of agency, and irrevocably tied to variant degrees of failure. As a result, the constitutive complexities which characterize their lives and cultures, including their potential for reshaping the material conditions that perpetuate colonial structures of oppression and discrimination, are often ignored.

In *The Queer Art of Failure*, Jack Halberstam uses low theory and popular knowledge to build an argument in favor of queerness, dysfunctionality, and passivity as strategies to contest and negotiate normative discourses of gender and sexuality designed to suppress non-conforming expressions of femininity. According to Halberstam, failure might become a new rationale for ordering or disordering canonical structures of power as well as a breeding ground to produce counter-hegemonic forms of theorizing (2011, 18). For instance, seeing that feminine success is always measured by male standards, Halberstam proposes failing at womanhood as an alternative strategy to break away from the pressures of accomplishing unrealistic ideals of beauty and femininity (2011, 4). As an example of oppositional tools to fight against economic determinism, Halberstam notes the utility of James C. Scott's concept "weapons of the weak," a tactic devised by the slaves to resist dominant powers, and which consisted in feigning incompetence to stall the business of the ruling class and override its control.[3] For failure as a practice, according to Halberstam, "recognizes that alternatives are embedded already in the dominant and that power is never total or consistent" (2011, 88). Throughout history, Indigenous communities in the Americas have employed a variety of resistance tactics to challenge or stall colonization, from feigning stupidity to abortion or suicide, as passive acts of failure by way of non-compliance to the ruling powers. Halberstam interprets such radical forms of "masochistic passivity" as an incisive critique of the organizing logic behind agency and subjectivity. By disengaging from the colonizer in colonized dialectics, subaltern groups refused "to become part of the colonial story" (2011, 131), thus liberating themselves from the cycle of oppression and exploitation.

Manuela M. Picq and Josi Tikuna argue that, although Indigenous gendered identities and sexualities are rarely "considered as a locus of sexual diversity"—because sexual freedom is associated with the secular modernity of the West—fluid understandings of gender existed before the formulation of queer and LGBTQI+ frameworks (2019). The multifarious nature of Indigenous identities cannot be reduced to Western gender and sexuality notions given that most terminologies are either misinterpreted or lost in translation. "The meanings of gender roles and sexual practices are cultural constructions that inevitably get lost when they are decontextualized in cultural (and linguistic) translation" (Picq and Tikuna 2019). For this reason, Indigenous notions of sex and gender "are better approached from queer understandings of sexuality as fluid" (Picq and Tikuna 2019). Therefore, a critical overview on how Bolivian *cholitas* contest hegemonic discourses on gender and sexuality may bring to light not only alternate ways of theorizing femme identities, but also of conceptualizing resistance strategies to curtail essentialist definitions of femininity.

Rigid social signifiers perpetuate Bolivia's highly polarized and stratified caste system in terms of gender, ethnicity, and race, placing whites at the top of the social stratum, *mestizos/mestizas* (mix European and Indian) in the middle, and Indigenous, *cholos/cholas* (urban Indians), and Blacks at the bottom.[4] Socioeconomic differences are materialized in the distinction of intelligible categorizations in terms of class, lifestyle, and occupation. The lives of upper-class women revolve around the family and the realm of the domestic; in contrast, *cholitas* resist patriarchal paradigms of femininity by having children out of wedlock with multiple partners, living independently, engaging in business and politics, and performing masculine sports and jobs (Murillo 2020, 137).[5] Dress and clothing items are additional indicators of economic and cultural identity since fashion, as Leslie Gill reminds us, constitutes an important arena in which dominant and subordinate notions of femininity are contested and transformed (1993, 73). Unlike white and middle-class mestiza women who mostly adopt cosmopolitan fashion trends, *cholitas* wear a traditional outfit consisting of a felt bowler hat, a shawl over the back (*llikllas*), several *polleras* (full-pleated skirts), a sweater or cardigan. Urban *cholitas* wear flat shoes embroidered or ornamented with fake stones, whereas those in the rural areas opt for different styles of sandals from retreaded tires.[6] Hats and the length of a woman's pollera, as Anna M. Babel notes, also index distinct regional variants; for instance, *cholitas paceñas* (*cholitas* from La Paz city) top their outfits with a Black Italian Borsalino (bowler hat) and shin-length polleras, *cholitas* in the Cochabamba valley wear a straw hat tied with a colorful ribbon and polleras just above the knee, and *cholitas* in the Santa Cruz de la Sierra region wear polleras just below the knee and Black fedora (2018, 183). Originally, the pollera was introduced to South America from Spain in the late nineteenth and early twentieth centuries, and contrary to today's perception, it was not an indicator of indigeneity but "a sign of integration in the mestizo culture and a rejection of Indigenous values, an orientation toward European fashion and morality" (Babel 2018, 180). In time, polleras were adopted by Indigenous Bolivian women and distinctively readapted by the different ethnic groups and regions. The prevalent pollera fabric is hand-spun llama, alpaca, or sheep yarn with colorful embroidered designs on a solid background. Polleras for everyday use are made of a rough durable fabric in darker colors to hide stains and often covered by an apron (Babel 2018, 181). For most Indigenous women, however, wearing a pollera is not a fashion choice but an identity category as every article of the cholita's attire is a marker of her region of origin, her social class, and fashion sense (Babel 2018, 193).[7] Commenting on the hairstyles, Babel adds that most Indigenous women wear long braids, augmenting their volume and length with hair extensions in matching shades of Black and brown. Extensions are fastened with laces and braided into the woman's long natural hair. Some women wear laces and beaded tassels that "create the illusion of length and lushness of a wearer's hair" (2018, 182).

Increased earning power and outmigration opportunities have granted *cholitas* not only the financial freedom to live more independently than upper-class women but also a wider access to consumer goods, thereby allowing them to develop their own sense of urban sophistication. Their fashion sense and their disregard for societal conventions, though, "has disquieted members of the newly emerging middle strata and upper class, who employ them, and threatened the relative social and economic gains of a small group of more prosperous Aymara women" (Gill 1993, 73). Thus, to display their privilege to class positions and distinguish and distance themselves from Aymara immigrants, white employers, and affluent urban Aymara women, selectively manipulate aspects of gender and ethnicity through more exaggerated and ostentatious fashion styles. They may exhibit their wealth by using higher-quality textiles in their polleras along with an array of Italian-style Borsalino derbies and vicuña shawls, or wear nylon stockings with back seams, and dangling earrings made with precious stones and pearls (Gill 1993, 79).

Every year, new pollera fashions replace outdated looks. These trendy polleras, the newest and the most expensive, are used mainly on special occasions, like holidays, social gatherings, and ceremonies (Babel 2018, 181). Elaine Zorn notes that a handmade cholita outfit in the latest fashion style usually costs far more than cosmopolitan factory-made or second hand-clothing worn by mestizo or white Bolivian women as they are labor-intensive, requiring several yards of fabric and specialized tailoring (2005, 126; Babel 2018, 184).[8]

Displays of fashion, consumer consumption, and ritual prowess throughout Bolivia take place during Carnival, one of the country's most important celebrations. And, as Krista Van Vleet argues, it is also a time when working *cholitas* return to their rural communities from jobs in urbanized areas bringing an array of fashionable polleras and specialized clothing which they use when they participate in singing and dancing in the local festivities: "By wearing their new clothes, the *cholitas* are also displaying their success, their ability to consume commodities, attain a higher standard of living, speak Spanish, and become more educated" (2005, 117). Yet, despite *cholitas*' increased social and political clout and earning power, they remain systematically discriminated against and their expressions of femininity looked down upon. Marcela Murillo's study on the monstrous portrayal of the maternal chola in contemporary Bolivian comics examines that, still today, "Chola femininity is framed as monstrous under the *mestizaje* gaze"[9] (2020, 149) and used as a trope aimed to warn *cholas*' children against crossing social conventions and resistance to assimilate to the Europeanizing model of modernity (Murillo 2020, 138).[10]

In recent decades, however, *cholitas*' undomesticated femininity has caught the attention of the media for their increasing participation in masculine sports, such as mountain climbing, soccer, and freestyle wrestling. Physical activities they perform with great ability and success donning their colorful polleras. In particular, the underlying transgressive text to the ritual of wrestling—where the wrestlers act out a representative rebellion against the imposition of social order outside the arena– is symbolic of the discrimination and marginalization that *cholitas* face daily. Wrestling may also be interpreted as a parody of machismo and an affirmation of Indigenous women's empowerment or, as Ken Lehman posits, could be read as a different manifestation of femininity and eroticism since along with the violence, "there is a suggestion of sex; the swirl of the skirts, the glimpse of undergarments, and the sense that at any moment rules may no longer apply, and chaos may reign" (2015, 42). Contributing to this spectacle is the myth that *cholitas* do not use underwear under their bulky polleras.

For their bravado and unique sense of style, *cholitas* have been featured in a variety of international and national publications, documentaries, and fashion magazines; attention that has mostly centered on *cholitas*' empowerment through their performance in male sports and their newly gained agency in the realm of politics and economic development under the presidency of Evo Morales.[11] Examining the implications of gender essentialization of the fighting *cholitas* as a pop culture attraction, Nell Haynes observes that, while wrestling has provided a form of empowerment to the wrestlers by granting them local fame and international mobility, the exoticization of their performance as Indigenous women is usually the focus of the show (2015, 3). Haynes further notes that chola wrestling, rather than elevating the status of the *cholitas* as a group, reinforces the image of Indigenous women as violent and unruly, thereby reproducing ideologies of the elites; or conversely, depending on the viewer, it may advance the *cholitas*' social capital, thereby empowering their Indigenous communities (2015, 15). Chola wrestlers, nonetheless, seem to have adopted a femme-inist positionality, embracing not only their unique perceptions about feminine agency but also implementing their own "weapons of the weak" to resist colonial systems of oppression and Western configurations of femininity. Addressing gender conflict, Carmen Rosa, a wrestler, and survivor of domestic violence, examines: "Men used to mock us, but we have shown them that we have come further than male fighters" (qtd. in Lehman 2015, 47). Likewise, Juanita la Cariñosa examines that their performance contributes to change the old-fashioned and conservative ways that still prevail in the rural area due to lack of resources and illiteracy, but "that's going to change, it's going to change soon. We are actually an example of that change. We are role models" (quoted. in Haynes 2015, 16).

In a similar fashion to American wrestling divas whose revealing outfits and sex appeal attract audiences to their matches, wrestling *cholitas* make their uncouth, feisty, and unruly image the focus of their performance to gain public acclaim. Their failure to yield to Western constructs of femininity, beauty, and "civilized" behavior underscores the hidden potential of femme identities and the significance of gender performance as unique sources to challenge binary discourses and promote alternative femme-inine discourses. Haynes is correct in her appreciation that the wrestling *cholitas*' ethnicity adds to the singularity of their performance, however, their appeal to tourists and locals alike does not solely rely on race, but also in the fact that the wrestlers are women. In other words, if the wrestlers were Indian men, the gender discourse behind performances would center on their skills and strength, drawing a different kind of crowd and media attention.

Then again, we cannot ignore the dangers of the essentialization and exoticization of *cholitas*' racially marked femininity as noted by Haynes, since essentialism and exoticism tend to rely on cultural discourses that value Indigenous cultures for their display of stereotyped and easily recognizable symbols of indigeneity while ignoring institutionalized ideologies that have historically displaced them to the margins of society. Iconizing and exoticizing Indigenous women, as Haynes reminds us, may diminish their political power of protest, reducing their plight for recognition and agency to apolitical performance (2015, 6). Similarly to femme, queer, and women of color, Indigenous women's identities are frequently the product of the interconnected nature of social categorizations—such as racism, ableism, gender, and sexism, among others—creating juxtaposing mechanisms of oppression and discrimination; therefore, to understand how gender identities in Indigenous communities are negotiated, contested, and recreated, we must pay attention to the interplay of identity categorizations within individuals and their respective communities.

The commodification and consumption of gender and ethnicity become problematic as, in developing countries, it is frequently the result of postcolonial and capitalist power relations built over distinctions of class and race, where the ruling elite profits from the cultural capital of the colonized. Such dynamics work similarly as heteronormative consumer-oriented policies that, on one hand, discriminate against LGTBQ+ individuals over the basis of gender and sexuality, while on the other, use them frequently as exotic and colorful tokens in advertising and social media.

Employing the "weapons of the weak" as a political strategy, the *cholitas* appropriated several of the symbols traditionally used to oppress and mock their cultural signifiers, like the bowler hat and the *pollera*, and turned them into symbols of resistance (Stephenson 1977, 19). As Mary Weismantel posits, "We might liken the chola's clothing to a drag performance. To attempt to pass as white would be to admit to white racial superiority; to fail at the attempt would inadvertently admit racial inferiority. But to intentionally occupy a position in between is a brazen disruption of the binary categories themselves" (2001, 91). Through failure to compromise their ethnic and femme identities to Westernized patriarchal gender codes, Indigenous women are subverting both race and gender configurations, but they are also exposing the systemic erasure of native cultures and ethnicities—particularly, those that stray from the patriarchal heteronormative ideal. Moreover, by embracing their Indigenous roots, *cholitas* are combating a long history of colonization while helping to redefine what it means to be an urban Indigenous female in the rapidly changing society. Their racially marked femme-ininity, therefore, is no longer a signifier of shame, passivity, and inferiority, but a source of empowerment with which to decolonize gender and sexuality in their own terms and according to their own beliefs and traditions. Nowadays, *mujeres de pollera* (pollera women) are athletes, truck or taxi drivers, university graduates, and construction workers. They also occupy political positions in the House of Deputies, presiding over courts of law or serving as officials in city councils, like Remedios Loza, an elective representative in La Paz; Cristina Mamani, head of the Magistrates Council; and Silvia Lazarte, president of the Constitutional Assembly (Murillo 2020, 138; Zorn 2005, 123; Babel 2018, 186; Lehman 2015, 57).

Indigenous queer and femme studies offer counter-discourse strategies to contest and challenge Eurocentric notions of beauty, gender, and sexuality, turning what Western culture considers negative into a positive. Despite centuries of oppression and marginalization, *cholitas* continue to deliberately disengage from hegemonic constructs of femininity and maintain their own distinct identities, aesthetics, values, languages, and traditions alive. Decolonizing the native body through the affirmation of diversity is at the core of their struggle against femmephobia, racism, and the heteropatriarchal logic that makes social and ethnic hierarchies seem natural. Rhea A. Hoskin and Allison Taylor, who have written about the discursive use of racism and cultural shame to police the borders that divide subjects, argue in favor of shame's productive potential as another resistance strategy to dislodge the underpinnings of normative systems of oppression and "bring subjects together by emphasizing mutual experiences of abjection and rejection [. . .] the failure or refusal to be shamed *opens up* sites of resistance" (2019, 6). *Cholitas*, by refusing to be shamed or complicit in reproducing a disciplined feminized body according to society's mandate and to the latest consumer trends, are denaturalizing not only normative assumptions of gender, sex, and sexuality—as well as the relations between them—but also the regulatory powers and gender policies in place that curtail women's political empowerment and economic advancement.

Body and fashion expressions require a broader transcultural theorization of gender and sexuality since not all cultures tend to rely on binary constructs or identity categorizations. Bolivian *cholitas*, as herein examined, place less emphasis on sexuality and more on the customs, languages, and worldviews of the communities to which they belong. They express their agency through their "failure" to reproduce traditional conceptions of modesty and femininity and through their capacity to navigate social, racial, and economic restraints among various interlocutors and social groups. Although Indigenous queer and femme practices may not be adaptable to the specificities of Western models, they may contribute to the diversification of ways of knowing and offer innovative ways of thinking about gender and corporeal expression, thus expanding the current landscape of identity narratives and discursive possibilities.

Notes

1 *Cholita* is a signifier for a young woman who wears pollera, while *señoritas* are young women (usually unmarried) who wear skirts, pants, or cosmopolitan clothing. Older women who wear polleras or skirts are *señoras*. Pollera wearing women are also referred to as "*de pollera.*" The word *cholita* derives from *cholo,* an urban Indigenous male who adopted Western clothing style; but, without the diminutive, the term *chola* is considered derogatory (Babel 2018, 177; Van Vleet 2005, 112).

2 Femmebodiment is a term coined by Ulrika Dahl to define "a queerly feminine corporeality or embodiment." Dahl proposes that skin "is a surface boundary, a border and a canvas for femme-inine expression and the body's largest sensory organ, that in its nakedness (beneath the shield) both undoes and empowers figuration" (2017, 37).

3 See James C. Scott, *Weapons of the Weak: Everyday Forms of Peasant Resistance* (1987) by (New Haven and London: Yale University Press).

4 According to Elaine Zorn, the term *mestizo/mestiza* is a way to depoliticize class identity, and although most mestizos identify themselves as Bolivians, society remains racially polarized (2005, 117; Van Vleet 2005, 111).

5 Discrimination, as Murillo notes, was often institutionalized. From 1925 to 1950, Indigenous people were prohibited to enter public squares and, in 1935, *cholitas* were restricted from using the trams "to prevent middle- and upper-class passengers from having to smell the *cholas*' body odor." (2020, 137). Domestic workers were also required to have a medical examination and get a sanitary card for which *cholas* had to undress completely. The same accreditation was required for prostitutes, discriminatory measures that also dehumanized *cholas* and "established a sordid connection between Indigenous women and sex workers" (Murillo 2020, 138).

6 Most women wear tire sandals with thinner soles and straps which are more feminine than the thick-soled ones worn by men. Canvas shoes are also an option for women and girls who identify with more contemporary trends (Van Vleet 2005, 112; Weismantel 2001, 188–890).
7 Although *cholitas* wear polleras or some style of ethnic dress daily, according to Zorn, every year, this becomes less common as Indigenous women hope that, by changing from ethnic to cosmopolitan dress, they will face less discrimination and thus enhance their lives (2005, 117).
8 Depending on the fabric and tailoring, a single pollera may cost up to 150 dollars. According to Van Vleet, women often go into debt to buy or borrow polleras to participate in carnival or communal festivities (2005, 117). Second-hand clothes are mostly imported from the US and arrive as donations, which are later sold in batches at local markets, like "El Gran Poder," at very low prices (Babel 2018, 184; Gill 1993, 99).
9 *Mestizaje* was a national building project developed in the 1920s that sought to modernize the country through the adoption of European social customs and values. As Murillo sustains, *cholas*' monstrosity is shaped by rejection of social norms and "of the national identity project of the twentieth century: mestizaje" (2020, 148).
10 To protect *cholas* and Indigenous people from discrimination, in 2013 the cholita figure was declared a national intangible cultural heritage by the municipal law of La Paz (Murillo 2020, 138).
11 *Cholitas* have been featured in *The New York Times, National Geographic,* and *Vogue* magazine, and some flew to Miami for an in-studio interview with talk-show host Cristina Saralegui (*Show de Cristina*). Additionally, films and documentaries such as *The Fighting Cholitas, Mamachas del Ring,* and *Cholita Libre* focus on the *cholitas*' plight for recognition and social equality (Lehman 2015, 47–51).

Bibliography

Babel, Anna M. 2018. *Between the Andes and the Amazon: Language and Social Meaning in Bolivia.* Arizona: University of Arizona Press.

Baule, Christine D. 2018. "Indigenous Clothing Changes in the Andean Highlands under Spanish Colonialism." *Estudios Atacameños* 59: 7–26.

Dahl, Ulrika. 2017. "Femmebodiment: Notes on Queer Feminine Shapes of Vulnerability." *Feminist Theory* 18 (1): 35–53.

Gill, Lesley. 1993. "'Proper Women' and City Pleasures: Gender, Class, and Contested Meanings in La Paz." *American Ethnologist* 20 (1): 72–88.

Halberstam, Jack. 2011. *The Queer Art of Failure.* Durham and London: Duke University Press.

Haynes, Nell. 2015. "UnBoliviable Bouts: Gender and Essentialization of Bolivia's *cholitas* Luchadoras." In *Global Perspectives on Women in Combat Sports: Women Warriors around the World*, edited by Christopher R. Matthews and Alex Channon, 267–283. London: Palgrave Macmillan.

Hoskin, Rhea A. 2017. "Femme theory: Refocusing the Intersectional Lens." *Atlantis: Critical Studies in Gender, Culture and Social Justice: What Is Intersectional about Intersectionality Now?* 38 (1): 95–99.

Hoskin, Rhea A. and Allison Taylor. 2019. "Femme Resistance: the Fem(me)inine Art of Failure." *Psychology and Sexuality* 10 (4): 281–300.

Lehman, Ken. 2015. "Fighting on the Edge: *Cholitas* Luchadoras in Bolivia's Cholo Revolution." In *Sports Culture in Latin American History*, edited by David M. K. Sheinin, 39–60. Pittsburgh: University of Pittsburgh Press.

Murillo, Marcela. 2020. "The Monstrous Portrayal of the Maternal Bolivian Chola in Contemporary Comics." *Monstrous Women in Comics: Horror and Monstrosity Study Series*, edited by Samantha Landsdale and Elizabeth Rae Coody, 135–151. Jackson: University Press of Mississippi.

Picq Manuela L. and Josi Tikuna. 2019. "Indigenous Sexualities: Resisting Conquest and Translation." *E-International Relations*. Accessed May 5, 2022. https://cholitas.e-ir.info/2019/08/20/indigenous-sexualities-resisting-conquest-and-translation.

Pullen, Christopher. 2012. *LGBT Transnational Identity and the Media*. New York: Palgrave Macmillan.

Stephenson, Marcia C. 1977. "Faldas *cholitas* polleras: Las ideologías de feminidad *cholitas* la conquista de nuevos espacios públicos en Bolivia (1920–1950)." *Chasqui* 26 (1): 17–33.

Van Vleet, Krista. 2005. "Dancing on the Borderlands: Girls (Re)Fashioning National Belonging in the Andes." In *Natives Making Nation: Gender, Indigeneity, and the State in the Andes*, edited by Andrew Canesa, 108–129. Phoenix: University of Arizona Press.

Weismantel, Mary. 2001. *Cholas and Pishtacos: Stories of Race and Sex in the Andes*. Chicago: University of Chicago Press.

Zorn, Elaine. 2005. "Dressed to Kill: The Embroidered Fashion Industry of the Sakaka Highland Bolivia." In *The Latin American Fashion Reader*, edited by Regina A. Root, 114–141. New York, Oxford: Berg.

11

Fashion, Performance, and Resistance in Trans Representation

Stephanie N. Saunders

In 2011, I approached Pedro Lemebel's apartment door, as he waited energetically. It was the second time I had been in Pedro's home. The first had been four years earlier. "No interviews" he requested and seated me with tea and toast. In Pedro's apartment, I felt enchanted, like a child peeking into my mother's makeup drawer. Artwork greeted visitors—most notably the large portrait of Pedro visible upon entering—and cosmetics and accessories scattered across the bathroom sink. It was my birthday, and Pedro made a day out of it, insisting we go to a photography exhibit that displayed his performance days, those politically charged years that changed the course of Chilean history. For the occasion, Pedro dressed comfortably, with a cotton black tunic, a brown cotton turban, and a plum and silver-threaded scarf, the type one might purchase from a street vendor in Santiago. His carefully applied foundation, hint of blush, and eyeliner, exuded the "no-makeup look," with ease. We arrived at Los Heroes subway stop but never found the exhibition. Irritated, Pedro yelled obscenities at every policeman we encountered. My heart pounded as the officials stood solemnly in their infamously austere garb while he provoked without response. I looked up at Pedro's flawlessly powdered complexion, wanting to ask if he was disappointed. Did he miss those resistance-filled days? Was he hanging on to his performance mode, or were these screams resulting from a lack of reconciliation? I didn't get up the nerve to pry into the past and instead enjoyed the crook of my arm nestled in his, linked against the imminent winter's warning chill.

Pedro Lemebel, a cross-dressing queen, as he liked to identify himself, railed against the atrocities of Chile's seventeen-year dictatorship (1973–1988). His writings and provocative performance art jolted the country like the earthquakes that often make Chile crumble and dance. Despite the tyrannical dictatorship and the cultural oppression that loomed over the slinky country like thick smog ensconcing the Andes, Lemebel and teams of writers and artists pushed onward and changes plunged forward. During the transition to democracy, divorce was legalized, LGBTQIA+ identity decriminalized, and AIDS education prospered. Humanists had made a difference. Collaboration among economists, politicians, and scientists flourished. Change was possible. When Lemebel passed away in 2015, Santiago's streets were lined with mourners from all socio-economic positions. In a land where he had once been ridiculed, beaten, and imprisoned, watching his loved ones "disappear" and endure disturbingly creative torture tactics, such mutual respect from divisive groups reminded us, change is possible.

Yet, resistance to trans rights has continued to shake the country. Trans communities have been impacted disproportionately by violence, as well as inadequate professional opportunities forcing many to enter unprotected positions as sex workers. During the early months of the COVID-19 pandemic, transgender people in Peru and Colombia suffered from governmental attempts to control the virus through limiting days in which individuals could be in public according to a person's gender. In many ways, the COVID-19 pandemic increased visibility of trans communities' plights for increased understanding throughout Latin America. According to Julia Symmes Cobb (2020), "From Panama to Peru, transgender people say gender-based quarantine restrictions have exposed them to discrimination and violence from people questioning their right to be out" (*Rueters*). These limitations have resulted in a cascading effect of mental and physical health challenges from economically precarious situations. Fabricio Forastelli (2005) notes, "The body Trans is one who has lost its material support. It is, first of all, an unemployed body or a body engaged in some sort of slightly illegal activity. And second, it is slightly illegal not only because nobody knows for sure where legality starts, but also because without material support the body becomes illegal in itself. It is a void" (286). In the face of such uncertainty, fashion, however, has presented communities with prospects for creativity, self-expression, political resistance, and economic livelihood. In the nineties and early aughts, Pedro Lemebel, reappropriated fashion to communicate the gravities of the AIDS pandemic within LGBTQIA+ communities. Beginning with the writer's urban chronicles, this chapter traces fashion's role in providing a dialectical outlet for trans communities.

Before continuing, it is imperative to recognize changes in terminology regarding gender and sexual identity in the early nineties versus today. Although some identity labels have gone out of fashion and may be deemed offensive in English-speaking contexts, they are embraced within Latin American communities. Differences in identity referencing and the limitation of translations must also be considered. In

Translocas: The Politics of Puerto Rican Drag and Trans Performance (2021), Lawrence La Fountain Stokes acknowledges lengthy lists of Spanish, Spanglish, Portuguese, Latin American, and Latinx vernacular categories for referring to sexual and gender identities before questioning: "How are all of these terms *translated*, if this is even possible? What are the limits and potentialities of cultural and linguistic translation? And how do artists, activists, and scholars fail or succeed?" (8). This chapter does not attempt to place labels on linguistic and cultural shifts, rather, out of respect for LGBTQIA+ communities, the word "trans" will be implemented, with a conscious understanding of the fluidity of sexual and gender identity.

In the Chilean context, the Society "Organizing Trans Diversities," also known as OTD Chile, provides a glossary to facilitate respectful discourse. In addition to "transfeminine," "transmasculine," and "trans nonbinary," the organization defines "las trasvestis" or transvestites—a term that has fallen out of usage in English-speaking communities—as "people assigned to the male gender at birth and who move towards the female gender. Transvestites claim their right to be transvestites, they do not necessarily want to be women. It is one of the first trans identities to emerge in the Western world and that still remains, especially in more vulnerable social classes."[1] The vulnerability and also performativity of *loca* identity is one of Pedro Lemebel's lasting contributions due to his questioning of intragroup and intergroup norms:

> Pedro Lemebel, a Chilean author and performance artist who identifies as a *loca*, has become famous for making perspicacious and scathing critiques of the contemporary, homonormative forms of gayness that cast nonnormative femininity as shameful. Lemebel's usage of the term *loca* describes homosexual people whose femininity crosses the boundaries of their assigned male gender because they wear makeup and/or accessories traditionally reserved for women—such as shawls and heels—and interchangeably use both masculine and feminine pronouns.
>
> González 2014

Lemebel's self-identification and prolongation of the term "loca" was steeped deeply in his conviction to signal different access to economic resources. Fashion became one of Lemebel's most prevalent mediums for calling attention to this divide. In Lemebel's chronicles, access to fashion—or a lack thereof—among his vibrant *loca* characters, highlights the socioeconomic layers involved in *loca* survival and identity.

In *The Handbook of Fashion Studies* (2013), Joanne Entwistle reflects on what the critic notes would first appear as an overtreatment of identity and fashion, resulting, in part, from decades of fashion studies research and interpretation on their interplay (cf. 97). Despite the study of identity's long-standing hold within fashion studies, one must recognize that "[. . .] identities are themselves *performed through* the forms of dress adopted" (Entwistle 2013, 97). In particular, Entwistle stresses the importance of class, gender, and sexuality as intersections of identity, and concludes, "If gender has long been theorized in terms of fashion, sexual identities have not been attended to until relatively recently, although particular styles of dress have long enjoyed associations with lesbian identity" (2013, 99). Entwistle goes on to point out that societal changes influence perceptions of gender and sexuality, and in turn, lead to more fluidity and fewer style confinements: "Alongside this, recognition of gender as drag further challenged our notions of stable sexual identities" (Entwistle 2013, 100). In the context of Latin America, Forastelli characterizes trans fashion as "[. . .] a process that mimics and improves upon the contours of the female, a "creole" mixture of street fashion and hopelessness" (2005, 286). Forastelli's categorization adds race and ethnicity as important components for consideration. Likewise, Lemebel's writings and performance art present a unique showcasing of the intersections of gender, sexuality, ethnicity, and class, all within the dynamic fashioning of the *loca* community.

Unstitching the oppressive seams of Pinochet's military regime, Pedro Lemebel published his third book, *Loco afán* (1996) in the midst of Chile's transition to democracy.[2] It titillates the reader's interest with humorous images, weaving them not so subtly with the—at the time—debilitating reality of AIDS. These darkly humoristic vignette-of-sorts—in Lemebel's case—are known as urban chronicles, described by Viviane Mathieux (2011) as, "A somewhat unstructured genre that combines literary aestheticism with journalistic form [. . .]" (1). The critic recognizes this literary genre's importance, particularly at the turn of the twenty-first century, due to "[. . .] its inherent ability to capture urban life in all of its chaotic, fragmented, and often dysfunctional grandeur" (2011, 1). With rich neologisms and a reclaiming of slurs historically directed at LGBTQIA+ individuals, Lemebel's chronicles portray the vibrant streets of Santiago, especially the underrepresented trans community—at the time—confronting grief and loss resulting from the AIDS epidemic.

Lemebel's work requires readers to take notice of the injustices and oppression that coupled with the destruction of AIDS within his community. In *Loco Afán*, physical appearances indicate not only the health of the characters, but also provide a metaphor for the current and future state of the country. The importance of fashion, treated in meticulous detail, exonerates the growing power of the neoliberal market and globalization in terms of national identity. From the opening chronicle, "La noche de los visones," fashion takes center stage as a key player. In particular, we see the intimate and layered depiction of different classes within the Trans community through their rich contrasts of fashion: the "rotas" ("the broken ones," those of a lower class) and the "regias" ("the regal ones," those of a higher class). Throughout Lemebel's work, nicknames and self-selected monikers weave a continual thread.[3] The *regias* have the luxury of fashion choices and name drop designer brands such as Saint Tropez and impractical footwear such as clogs with mink-covered tops (Lemebel 1996, 12). They revel in a successful fashion debut: "The neighborhood came out to see them. They were as sophisticated as movie stars, as models from *Paula* magazine" (Lemebel 1996, 13).[4] *Paula* has a long history in Chile since its beginnings in 1967. Recently, it merged with Copesca in 2018 and became a Sunday circular with the newspaper *La Tercera*. *Paula's* dedication to fashion has become more visible over the years, with a special sub-edition *Moda Paula*, as well as the international fashion fair, Ropero Paula in the posh area of Parque Araucano.[5] Lemebel's reference to *Paula* contains the haute couture-performance of the *regias* within a national stage. As we shall see, this contrasts directly with the fashion references denoting global expansion in later chronicles of the collection. Unlike those fashion divas, *las rotas*, on the other hand, are starving, devouring no fewer than twenty turkeys: "[. . .] As if they were coming from a war" (Lemebel 1996, 13).[6] These "malnourished mirrors of our queens" (Lemebel 1996, 22) contrast with the imported stereotype of "mister gay," according to Lemebel, defined by exaggerated muscles and a first-world diet, a physical representation of class.

With the pile of turkey bones, the *rotas* construct a monument and cover it with the Chilean flag. This macabre scene forecasts the image of the body debilitated by AIDS, as globalized fashion simultaneously required unrealistic bodily demands. In the chronicle, Lemebel likens Pilola Alessandri's contraction of AIDS to obtaining the latest fashion: "She bought the epidemic in New York, it was the first that she brought exclusively, the most authentic, the newly released gay fashion to die for. The latest funeral fad that slimmed her down like no diet ever had" (Lemebel 1996, 16). She is compared to a chic, *Vogue* model.[7] Not only are the fashion industry's bodily standards for extreme thinness highlighted, but in this chronicle, we note the displacement from the national magazine *Paula* to the international presence of *Vogue*. This parallel reflects the increasing splinters of globalization and a broadening of the neoliberal market that psychologically invaded the Chilean collective consciousness, just like, according to the author, the physical invasion of the AIDS epidemic.

Lemebel further depicts the perils of outside influences through representations of used clothing, known in Chile as *ropa americana* or "American clothing." According to Mélissa Gauthier (2005), used clothing importations to Latin America have been on a steady incline, with Chile the number three importer in the region, a phenomenon that has created a culture of smuggling to neighboring countries such as Bolivia that have outlawed secondhand clothing (72–73). According to Chilean cultural critic Nelly Richard in *Cultural Residues* (2004a), "The peripheral transvestite finds in the bazaar of US clothing her own code of impropriety and of counterappropriations that degrade the correct rules of dressing well exhibited by bourgeois femininity, with coarse, carnivalesque exaggerations and maskings" (2004a, 80). Richard exposes the result of this imported phenomenon as an identity collage without style coherence or vocabulary (2004a, 111–112). Without advertisements or the non-verbal codes of shop displays, secondhand clothing bins and racks create endless possibilities for expression of identity. For Lemebel, these spaces exude "[…] a post-mortis wardrobe of fabrics and clothes with little use, recycled as evidence of the plague permeated through fashion" (Lemebel 1996, 93).[8] In Lemebel's chronicles, used clothing presents opportunities for creativity and resistance to outside influences. By transferring his axis of the disease from Latin America to the United States, Diana Palaversich (2010) acknowledges this powerful displacement: "By attributing the origin of the disease to the United States, Lemebel inverts the narrative of American AIDS, which attributes the contamination to an external agent, African and Haitian. Lemebel places the center of infection in the most powerful country in the first world, where this disease becomes a powerful symbol of the decline of capitalist society" (261).[9] The setting of New York for the NAMES project AIDS quilt at the 1987 March on Washington permits an exploration of, as the subtitle suggests, "a sentimental map" of the former clothing of victims of the AIDS epidemic.[10] As Lemebel identifies, this map, crosses ethnic and cultural borders and forms,

> Cross-cultural crosses that are found in the rubbing of sandpaper that unites these offerings. Glittering names in gold threads such as Foucault, Hudson, Liberace, Nureyev, greet each other with the anonymous "LOUIS, LAST NIGHT IT DIDN'T SEEM LIKE IT WAS GOING TO RAIN ," "MICHAEL, I DIDN'T GET TO TELL YOU," "CARLOS, THE TIME PASSED, WHAT A TIME IT WAS."
> Lemebel 1996, 92[11]

Since the publication of this chronicle, the new linguistic registry that technology has provided us adds a new layer to this passage. In a world filled with text messages and "character" limits, Lemebel's use of all caps metaphorically yells at the reader to take notice of the private conversations of the deceased.[12] The use of names is a timely protest, a bold contrast with the use of nicknames throughout the chronicles. Likewise, the reappropriation of clothing carries a loud message separated from the deceased body. The quilt, a folk art perhaps reminiscent of *arpilleras*, visually comes together to craft the annihilation of the AIDS epidemic. The *arpilleras*, patchwork tapestries created during the dictatorship—first through government-sponsored workshops, and later through individual and community initiates seeking to provide a more revealing and critical message concerning the dictatorship—garnered international attention for their technique and beauty. The NAMES quilt and *arpilleras* alike employed textile arts to denounce the disappearance of their loved ones, respectively through the AIDS epidemic and the human rights abuses of the dictatorship.

The other means of employing used clothing involves rediscovery and refashioning. Lemebel's protagonists celebrate the creative possibilities of secondhand clothing and accessories as a way to increase their access to fashion choices, especially in the face of limited economic resources. Throughout this chronicle, as well as others such as "Lycra Bootie, Disco Sodom," Lemebel uses the Anglicism "look" to refer to the importance of a personal style accessible through the pluralities of fashion seasons available in used clothing. At the same time, he requires consumers to remember the daily lives of those who inhabited the previously owned garments: "The Oscar de la Renta suit that the family bought for him. The patient would die in uniform, so that in the last goodbye he would look like a man, hanged by the Italian tie" (Lemebel 1996, 93).[13] In *Fashion on the Edge: Spectacle, Modernity and Deathliness* (2003) Caroline Evans applies Marxist theories of merchandise—"the value of a commodity represents nothing but the quantity of labor embodied in it"—to the practice of designers of aging new fabrics to make them look used (261). The author recognizes the paradox in the convergence of haute couture that tends to distance itself from mass production with the image that "[. . .] remains locked, like the foraging of the nineteenth-century rag picker, into the very capitalist system whose cycles of production and consumption it might be seen to be criticizing" (2003, 262). In the same way, these Lemebelian consumers become "ragpickers" when they economically buy in the "post-death" market, and with a morbid twist of the implementation of upcycling or recycling, they must, at the same time, remain aware of the daily events that these clothes suffered, both due to bodily and sexual limits. Lemebel reminds the consumer of the phantasmagorical nature of the garments of the deceased, "Ghost clothes, hiding, floating, playing camouflage in the closet alongside the clothes of the living" (Lemebel 1996, 94). Above all else, the author fosters a sense of reverence and consciousness among his readers for the multiple lives behind each fashion selection.

One of the most well-known of Lemebel's chronicles, "The Death of Madonna," intertwines the creativity of styling "looks"—made available through importation of used clothing—with the dire warning of the Global North's hold on national identity. Although the author recounts a series of Latin American figures throughout his chronicles, including María Félix, Violeta Parra, and Eva Perón— to name a few—Chile's importation of popular culture from the United States appears most notably through the ubiquitous figures of Elizabeth Taylor and Madonna. As Vicki Karaminas (2013) notes, "Madonna, the quintessential female fashion and gay icon of the 1980s, reinforced gender ambiguity in her performances by traversing the space between the sexual mainstream and the sexual fringes of culture" (145). The critic recognizes Madonna's constant fashion reinvention in terms of style and identity (2013, 146). This pop star became an obsession of one devoted fan in Lemebel's depiction of the trans community. Having dabbled heavily with peroxide to recreate Madonna's infamous blond strands, "the Mapuche Madonna"—as the chronicle quips—refuses to wear a wig (Lemebel 1996, 34). Instead, the protagonist's bald head presents the reader with a blank canvas ready for a stylish identity makeover: "And she imitated Madonna with a piece of a skirt, a turtleneck sweater too long for her. A wool vest with lamé, the kind they sell in the used clothing shops. She cinched it in with a belt to make a fabulous miniskirt. *La cola* was so creative, from any cloth she would invent a dress" (Lemebel 1996, 34).[14] For Richard, such thrifty fashionable creations result in a carnivalesque effect: "Leftover and scraps are part of the Latin American carnival through which the poor Chilean transvestite assaults the cosmetic façade of imported femininity with the grimace of an outré personality who can't be made fit in" (2004a, 81). These carnival-infused elements set the stage for fashionable performances, but the author also leaves us with a stark contrast. While the protagonist's style is innovative, her artistic performance is imitation: "She repeated the phrases in English like a parrot, adding charm to her illiterate harvest" (Lemebel 1996, 34).[15] Through this character, Lemebel exposes the danger of simply repeating outside influences or internalizing them. Instead, he calls for active confrontation with cultural values that too often are victim to the influence of outsiders.

In addition to his urban chronicles, Pedro Lemebel's performance art often reconstructed well-done art and iconography such as Frida Kahlo's *Dos Fridas*, a piece that he and Francisco Casas revisited in their recreation *The Two Fridas*.[16]

The legacy of performance art among trans communities is a phenomenon that transposes the stage or catwalk. In *Performing Queer Latinidad: Dance, Sexuality, Politics* (2012), Ramón Rivera-Servera explores the uniting power of public performance. Within the context of the United States, the author finds a "coming together" of LGBTQIA+ peoples of Latin American descent, despite differences in culture, history and living conditions, and in the process "[...] build(s) social, cultural, and political bonds" (6). Performance and resistance of trans communities have expanded their audiences and fans through various social media platforms. In April of 2021, dancers Piisciis (Akhil Canizales who identifies as nonbinary), Nova (Felipe Velandia who identifies as nonbinary) and Axid (Andrés Ramos who is trans) vogued their way to becoming a viral sensation in the months of social unrest. Piisciis created a guaracha song "Por Colombia hasta el Fin." ("For Colombia Until the End"), an energizing backdrop as the trio danced up the steps of the Plaza Bolívar in the nation's capital, weaving their provocative moves between police officers dressed in riot attire. The dancers had fashioned tube tops out of caution tape, and at times grabbed Colombia flags from the audience as props. Nova's ski mask and well-worn Doc Martens sent a revolutionary fashion vibe while Axid and Piisciis donned stilletto-heeled boots and whipped their free-flowing hair in dramatic poses. Axid's long-flowing blond wig stood out, as did Piisciis's confident smile. The historical underpinnings of vogueing is a powerful message in itself. As Garcia points out, the drag ballroom tradition that first began in Harlem in the 1970s were spaces that provided "a sanctuary for L.G.B.T.Q. Black and Latino people who had been ostracized from mainstream white society" (2021b).[17] Axis's platinum wig could be read as a nod to the pop icon. In addition to the thousands of screaming and whistling voices cheering the dancers' nimble moves, messages from social media platforms fluttered with support. This performance added even more visibility to the long-standing denunciations about human rights violations in Colombia, which have been previously shown by ONGs and organizations such as Human Rights Watch, among others.

Although Lemebel's fashionable protagonists could only aspire to imitate *Vogue*'s glossy pages, recent *Vogue México* articles place trans models in the spotlight. As Melissa R. Michelson and Brian F. Harrison highlight in *Transforming Prejudice* (2020), "The power of parasocial contact is limited by the available supply of trans-gender celebrities and public figures who are well known and liked by the mass public, and by the availability of positively portrayed transgender characters in film and television shows" (18). Celebratory non-binary representations of gender are catalysts for educating societal perceptions.

Vogue México is making tangible commitments towards inclusivity. In August–September 2020, for the first time in the 128 years of *Vogue's* history, twenty-six editorial directors committed to sharing images and stories of hope.[18] *Vogue México* elaborates on the intertwined message of the fashion world and beyond to address some of the world's most pressing issues: "Featuring letters of hope from celebrities, designers, models, and activists, thought-provoking fashion, and enlightening essays on diversity and inclusion, the climate crisis, LGBTQIA+ rights, and other topics. Each *Vogue* publication casts a particular eye on the biggest issues facing the ones we face today, in a testament to the power of photography, art and reporting."[19] Dominican-Colombian rapper, Rosa Isabel Rayos, known as Mrs. Boogie, centers her work on "spreading that 'femme queen joy [by] provid[ing] an inspirational message clad in haute couture.[20]'" The rapper and artist has a powerful way of connecting us all and calling to action: "The message I would like to share today is for my fellow creators. Make room for realities outside your own. We are all vessels of communication, so we all have a responsibility to share each other's stories in any way we can. Either through your art or casual interactions. Let's normalize by telling the stories of others" (*Vogue México* 2020).[21] In a piece "Libertad de Ser," a tribute to the Afro-Transgender community, Rayos took center stage with vintage Chanel in Brooklyn Bleu earrings and a vibrant emerald green evening wear gown with feathers trimming the shoulders and cuffs by Danielle Guizio.[22] The photo exudes a celestial quality as we are only privy to the mode's upper torso. Rayo's peaceful pose turns upward to the blue sky encompassing her background. This photo by Juan Veloz cultivates an aura of old Hollywood glamor, thus, retouching the cinematic realm to which many Black artists and trans individuals were excluded historically. At the same time, the rapper flashes her long-sparkly nails, adding a contemporary touch, and staying true to her own personal style and identity.

Through fashion's reach of diverse audiences, Pedro Lemebel addressed the silent reality of AIDS. In the author's playful chronicles, trans characters achieve an ephemeral beauty, a style comparable to that of movie stars and magazine covers. Fashion allowed Lemebel to question the consumer's own participation in the tireless search to achieve a look, which often does not take into account where or how a garment is obtained in a globalized and distanced market from the source of production itself. In recent years, trans creativity shines on a catwalk that celebrates design, possibilities, and sources of bodily empowerment. May performance, art, social media, fashion design, and media—to name a few sources—continue to increase trans presence and opportunities.

Notes

1 Throughout this chapter, all translations are mine unless noted in the bibliography.
2 Part of this chapter, specifically pp. 3–9, was previously published in Spanish as the article: "Recrear una conciencia social: Reciclar/reapropiar la moda en *Loco afán: crónicas de sidario* de Pedro Lemebel" (2013). *Taller de Letras*: 99–108. Many thanks to *Taller de Letras* for permission to translate and reimagine this section.
3 See Saunders's *Fashion, Gender and Agency in Latin American and Spanish Literature* for more information regarding the importance of nicknames within the LGBTQIA+ community in Chile (2021, 113–114).
4 "El barrio se despobló para verlas, a ellas tan sofisticadas como estrellas de cine, como modelos de la revista *Paula*" (Lemebel 1996, 13).
5 Ropero Paula began in 2011. Since 2020, the event has been moved online.
6 "Como si viniera una guerra" (Lemebel 1996, 13).
7 "Ella se compró la epidemia en Nueva York, fue la primera que la trajo en exclusiva, la más auténtica, la recién estrenada moda gay para morir. La última moda fúnebre que la adelgazó como ninguna dieta lo había conseguido." (Lemebel 1996, 16).
8 "Así fuera un gran supermarket, un vestuario posmortis de telas y ropas con poco uso, reciclada como evidencia de la plaga permeada a través de la moda" (Lemebel 1996, 93).
9 Translation mine.
10 For more information about the history of names, as well as sample quilt blocks, please see Rice University's Woodson Research Center Houston LGBTQIA+ Exhibts: https://digitalprojects.rice.edu/wrc/Houston-LGBTQ/exhibits/show/names-project/names-project-foundation
11 "Cruces transculturales que se encuentran en el roce de la lija que une estos ajuares. Nombres rutilantes en hilos de oro como Foucault, Hudson, Liberace, Nureyev, se saludan con el anónimo 'LOUIS, ANOCHE NO PARECÍA QUE IBA A LLOVER', 'MICHAEL, NO ALCANCÉ A DECÍRTELO', 'CARLOS, EL TIEMPO FUE, FUE UN TIEMPO'" (Lemebel 1996, 92).
12 The inclusion of first names is reminiscent of protests that swept the world following instances of police brutality. In 2020 and 2021, while "Say Their Name" became a proverbial rally cry in Black Lives Matter Movements in the United States and around the globe, in Colombia, the death of Nicolas Guerrero, sparked outcry at the loss of "Nico" at the hands of the police. See www.bbc.com/mundo/noticias-america-latina-56910572.
13 "El terno Oscar de la Renta que le compró la familia para que el enfermo muriera uniformado, para que en el último adiós pareciera hombre, ahorcado por la corbata italiana" (Lemebel 1996, 93).
14 "Y ella imitando a la Madonna con el pedazo de falda, que era un chaleco beatle que le quedaba largo. Un chaleco canutón, de lana con lamé, de esos que venden en la

ropa americana. Ella lo arremangaba con un cinturón y le quedaba una regia minifalda. Tan creativa la cola, de cualquier trapo inventaba un vestido" (Lemebel 1996, 34). The term "cola" is a derogatory term that refers to a gay male.

15 "Repetía como lora las frases en inglés, poniéndole el encanto de su cosecha analfabeta" (Lemebel 1996, 34).

16 Richard, in *Masculine/Feminine*, explores the signals of gender and how "[. . .] during and after the dictatorship, the figure of the transvestite deconstructs these discrepancies through an explosion of creative manifestations such as art, photography, video, literature and theater" (2004 b, 52).

17 Karaminas explores Madonna's 1990 music video as a celebration and tribute to this formerly underground dance (2013, 146).

18 Although the COVID-19 pandemic appears to have motivated *Vogue*'s focus on expanding its diverse representations of gender, Mrs. Boogie's debut in 2020 was not the first historic cover in this regard. In December of 2019, Estrella Vazquez made international headlines as the first *muxe* model to appear in *Vogue México* and *British Vogue*'s cover. *Muxes* (also known as *muxhes*) have lived in Juchitán de Zaragoza, Oaxaca since pre-colonial times, representing a third gender. The community is known for exquisite embroidery, and vibrant, traditional attire. The magazine's celebration of *muxes* dives into the slow fashion involved in making the now iconic huipiles and highlights the generations-old techniques, coupled with spiritual reverence as found in the religious festivals celebrating the *muxes*' work. This integration into the fiber of their region has not, however, spared the *muxe* community from bullying, hate crimes, and the AIDS epidemic—challenges that have united the Jachitán community as a whole.

19 "Presentando cartas de esperanza de celebridades, diseñadores, modelos y activistas, moda estimulante y ensayos esclarecedores acerca de la diversidad y la inclusión, la crisis climática, los derechos LGBTQIA+ y otros temas, cada publicación de *Vogue* arroja su mirada particular sobre los mayores problemas a los que nos enfrentamos hoy día, en un testamento sobre el poder de la fotografía, el arte y el reportaje" (*Vogue*, 2020, vogue.mx).

20 Under #voguehope, the featured models answered four questions concerning what it means to be someone of Afro-Transgender identity in 2020, what are some of the challenges, how has the Black Lives Matter movement entered in their daily way of speaking, how young generations should be educated about gender identity, and what message of hope one would like to share.

21 "El mensaje que me gustaría compartir hoy es para mis compañeros creadores. Haz espacio para realidades ajenas a la tuya. Todos somos vasos de comunicación, por lo que todos tenemos la responsabilidad de compartir las historias de los demás de cualquier manera que podamos. Ya sea a través de su arte o interacciones casuales. Normalicemos contando las historias de otros" (*Vogue México*, 2020).

22 Other Afro-Latinx models included in this edition include Sebastián J. Flowers (Belician author, actor, and model), MJ Rodríguez (US-Puerto Rican actor), Leiomy Maldonado (Puerto Rican, choreographer, dancer, actress, model, and activist), Allen Ruiz (Honduran graphic designer and YouTuber), Marizol Leyva (Dominican-Puerto Rican-Cuban model activist and coauthor), Marquise Vilson (Cuban-American actor), Aneiry Zapata (Honduran, Defender of Human Rights for Black LGBTQ+Migrant Project), Jensy Lacayo (Honduran, Operations Manager), Martha Zrzú (Honduran Specialist in Quality assurance and law student).

Bibliography

Entwistle, Joanne. 2013. "Fashion, Identity, and Difference: Introduction." *The Handbook of Fashion Studies*, ed. by Black, Sandy, Amy De La Haye, Joanne Entwistle, Agnès Rocamora, Regina A. Root, and Helen Thomas, 97–101. London: Bloomsbury.

Evans, Caroline. 2003. *Fashion on the Edge: Spectacle, Modernity and Deathliness*. New Haven: Yale University Press.

Forastelli, Fabricio. 2005. "Scattered Bodies, Unfashionable Flesh." *The Latin American Fashion Reader*, edited by Regina A. Root, 283–289. Oxford: Berg.

Garcia, Sandra E. 2020a. "Living and Performing 'Femme Queen Joy,'" *New York Times*, November 20, 2020. www.nytimes.com/2020/11/30/style/Ms-Boogie-Rapper-Trans-Woman.html

Garcia, Sandra E. 2021b. "The Vogueing Protesters of Bogotá." *New York Times*, May 31, 2021. www.nytimes.com/2021/05/31/style/colombia-protests-bogota-dancers.html

Gauthier, Mélissa. 2005. "Used Clothing." In *Berg Encyclopedia of World Dress and Fashion: Latin America and the Caribbean*, edited by Margot Blum Schevill, 72–78. Oxford: Bloomsbury Academic. http://dx.doi.org/10.2752/BEWDF/EDch2011.

González, Melissa M. 2014. "La Loca." *TSQ (Transgender Studies Quarterly)* 1 (1–2): 123–125. May 1, 2014. doi: https://doi.org/10.1215/23289252-2399794

González Ulloa, Karina. 2019. "Muxes: el tercer género que vive en México desde tiempo inmemoriales," *Vogue México*. November 18, 2019. www.vogue.mx/estilo-de-vida/articulo/muxes-en-oaxaca-fotografiados-por-tim-walker

Karaminas, Vicki. 2013. "Lesbian Style." *The Handbook of Fashion Studies*, ed. by Black, Sandy, Amy De La Haye, Joanne Entwistle, Agnès Rocamora, Regina A. Root, and Helen Thomas, 137–156. London: Bloomsbury.

La Fountain-Stokes, Lawrence. 2021. *Translocas: The Politics of Puerto Rican Drag and Trans Performance*. Ann Arbor: University of Michigan Press.

Lemebel, Pedro. 1996. *Loco afán: crónicas de sidario*. Santiago: LOM.

Mahieux, Viviane. 2011. *Urban Chroniclers in Modern Latin America: The Shared Intimacy of Everyday Life*. Austin: University of Texas.

Michelson, Melissa R. and Brian F. Harrison. 2020. *Transforming Prejudice: Identity, Fear, and Transgender Rights*. New York: Oxford UP.

Morales de la Cruz, Atenea. 2020. "Mrs. Boogie: 'Normalicemos contando historias de otros,'" September 10, 2020. www.vogue.mx/estilo-de-vida/articulo/mrs-boogie-quien-es-la-rapera-afro-latina

Organizando Trans Diversidades. "Glosario." https://otdchile.org/recursos/glosario-otd/

Palaversich, Diana. 2010. "El cuerpo agredido de la homosexualidad proletaria y *Loco afán* de Pedro Lemebel." *Desdén al infortunio: sujeto, comunicación y público en la narrativa de Pedro Lemebel*, edited by Blanco, Fernando A. and Juan Poblete, 243–265. Santiago: Editorial Cuarto Propio.

"Protestas en Colombia: las imágenes que dejan los violentos enfrentamientos entre manifestantes y policía." *Editorial*, May 4, 2021. www.bbc.com/mundo/noticias-america-latina-56910572

Richard, Nelly. 2004a. *Cultural Residues: Chile in Transition*. Translated by Alan West Durán and Theodore Quester. Minnesota: University of Minnesota P.

Richard, Nelly 2004b. *Masculine/Feminine: Practices of Difference(s)*. 2004. Translated by Silvia Tandeciarz and Alice A. Nelson. Durham: Duke University Press.

Rivera-Servera, Ramón H. 2012. *Performing, Queer Latinidad: Dance, Sexuality, Politics*. The Ann Arbor: University of Michigan Press.

Saunders, Stephanie N. 2021. *Fashion, Gender and Agency in Latin American and Spanish Literature*. United Kingdom: Tamesis.

Symmes Cobb, Julia. 2020. "Transgender People Face Discrimination, Violence amid Latin American Quarantines." *Reuters*, May 5, 2020. www.reuters.com/article/us-health-coronavirus-latam-lgbt/transgender-people-face-discrimination-violence-amid-latin-american-quarantines-idUSKBN22H2PT/

Veloz, Juan. 2020. "Libertad de Ser," *Vogue México*, August–September 2020, 128–137. www.juanveloz.com/vogue-mexico-sept-issue/

Vogue México. 2020, August 3 "La edición Hope de *Vogue*: Todo lo que tienes que saber." August 3, 2020. www.vogue.mx/estilo-de-vida/articulo/edicion-hope-de-vogue.

12

Politics of the Clothed Body During the Social Outburst, Chile 2019

Pía Montalva

It's not about 30 pesos, it's about 30 years.[1]

On October 18, 2019, the Santiago Metro System raised its fare, and resistance ensued for people to not pay. This triggered a series of public protests that lasted about four months and took many different forms: chants and banging of pots, barricades, violent struggles with the police and special forces, burning of buses and public businesses, attacks on military and police quarters, lootings in warehouses, supermarkets and drugstores, fast food restaurants, and shops in general. From October 21, 2019, onwards, people began gathering in Plaza Italia, renamed "Plaza Dignidad" (Dignity Square). This Square is the frontier between various suburbs and numerous metro lines; it is also the singular spot for people in Santiago to celebrate sporting feats and elections. On Friday October 25, 2019, 1.2 million people gathered in this spot to protest and convey rejection *en-masse* of the current economic model, demanding reforms, and an end to inequality (Villaroel and Flores, 2019). The demands were broad,[2] but there was a feeling of common ground against systematic abuse, over many years, by the private sector, various governments, and politicians, who, since the end of the dictatorship in 1990, have collectively failed to make changes and push for reforms that steer towards a fairer, more equal distribution of wealth.[3]

In contrast to what happened years before—when protests and rallies were summoned by students and specific civil society groups[4]—these rallies displayed a break from traditional protests, political slogans, and how demonstrators' demands were communicated. Its inorganic and spontaneous nature made the collective production of banners incongruent, making individual action, on its own, autonomous. The intervened and covered body became the perfect instrument to activate protest, and to spontaneously recognize those who share similar complaints on site. Each participant chose an identity of resistance to come forward and present themselves in this public sphere, where urban heterogenous microcultures come together, many of whom were only meeting and recognizing each other for the first time. In the process, the use of face covers and masks was an absolute must. Yet, men and women approached mask-wearing in radically different ways. While men prioritized anonymity, based on the uniformity that a limited local sports gear market provided in terms of variety and types of face coverings, women tended to explore the creative potential of the face mask and hand craft and decorate it individually to make it their own. This chapter seeks to explore clothing and dressing practices during the social unrest that exploded in Chile in October 2019, and account for the body politics that inflame it, as well the gender expressions and socio-cultural links that arose.

Even though the expressions through clothing[5] and the politics of the body[6] are fragmented, multiple, and diverse, there are common elements mediated by the contingency. The need for face covering plays an important role for two reasons: firstly, to protect their identity when they are acting as resistance players, out for fear of being identified through surveillance cameras when they are common citizens; secondly, as a guard against the increasingly toxic tear gas and various liquids hurled from armored vehicles to disperse the crowds. Both purposes are relevant for fighters on the frontline.

This territorial formation divided into clans, without hierarchy or leadership, and defined itself as a self-organized movement. They were made up of *capuchas* (hooded and face-covered protesters), *barras bravas* (extremist, violent football hooligans), professional anarchists, drug traffickers, university and highschool students, youth who had escaped from the social housing institutions for vulnerable minors, among others (Joignant 2020). The *capuchas* mission was to "dispute the power enforced by the authorities imposing order" so that skirmishes are focused in one spot, while the general protests by citizens who are further behind, can continue its course without problems (Claude 2019). The *capucha* has been used over the past ten years and coincides with the emergency of the first mass manifestations against the economic and political model implemented post dictatorship. Due to its versatility, these face coverings have been mass produced from 2011 onwards, in the context of the numerous student protests that took place that year. Made from t-shirts or sweatshirts, they are wrapped around the face through the neck hole, while covering the rest of the head with the rest of the garment and tying the sleeves below the chin. They are ephemeral and inorganic in nature, lacking any pretense of uniformity, except for the homogeneity of the clothing used. They serve as a coherent garment that is used during clashes and violent skirmishes, and when the peaceful protest resumes or dissipates, they can camouflage among the crowd by using the garment in its intended way, thus dodging being a suspect. *Encapuchados* are described by intelligence organizations as people who have been trained by ex-members of insurgent forces that were broken up in the early nineties (Giordano 2011). The media highlight their violent strategies, which go against the majority who want to protest peacefully, and whose methods tend toward artistic expression and carnival-like behavior (Giordano 2011).

However, the balaclavas or traditional ski-masks were still heavily used in 2019, echoing the techniques used by clandestine subversive groups who operated in Chile in the eighties, during the dictatorship, and particularly, the Frente Patriótico Manuel Rodríguez. They are woolen, hand-knitted hoods worn by rural folk to guard against the rain and cold. In 1984, clandestine press recorded an interview where Raul y Tamara, who later disappeared, registered the use of these masks for French television (TamaraTVchile, 2015).[7]

During the social unrest of 2019, as the fight became permanent and systematic—and lasted for hours—protection made of textiles, whether they be balaclavas or sweatshirts or *capuchas*, became insufficient. Moreover, violence stemming from Special Police Forces' treatment of protesters, forced individuals to quickly rethink their outfits and take different precautions. On Monday, October 21, 2019, a national newspaper reported on a significant increase in eye lesions due to the use of anti-protest rifles with supposedly rubber bullets, used against the crowds, especially aiming at their eyes. They mention seventeen people affected over three days (Miranda, Albert and Sepúlveda 2019). Protesters quickly reacted and added protective eye gear to their face masks, with relative effectiveness. They used swimming, skiing and deep diving goggles, protective eyewear for tradespeople, and facial masks that had been approved by the Chilean Ministry of Health in 2012 (2013). During the 2019 protests, the quality of protective gear depended on the resources available to the protesters, many of whom used imitations that could be purchased on the streets by local street merchants (Labs 2019).

The accessories implemented were not solely to protect the face. Protesters began using security helmets and bike helmets which people embellished with symbols, such as, for example, a red cross on the front, to signal they were part of the health and safety brigade that would assist the injured and administer first aid when necessary. There was also abundant use of helmets among the protesters who were referred to as *miners*; they removed cobble stones from the road and sidewalks, turned them into smaller rocks and carried them in backpacks on foot or bikes, to the battle zone (Claude 2020). Industrial gloves were used by the "anti-gassers" to guard against possible burns from grabbing the tear gas canisters and dipping them into water with bicarbonate before they exploded or picking them up and throwing them back to the police and special forces, so they would be unable to disperse the crowds (Claude 2020). Disposable rubber gloves were also used by protesters who were assisting the injured.

Industrial grade gas masks and reusable respirators used for safety in the workplace were fundamental for some protesters. Made of silicone, they have interchangeable filters that work against certain particles, vapors, and poisonous gases. Those with no access to these masks, covered their mouth and nose with their *capucha* or a triangular, usually black or red bandanas, printed either with traditional paisley or with protest calls printed on them. This last piece is common among all young independent protesters, regardless of position in the protest, gender, or specific cause. These are associated with adventure, cowboy movies, rap, and biker subculture; they provide a color code that allows everyone to choose the one which represents them the most.

The growing deployment of accessories worn by the fighters worked as a mirror to the infrastructure displayed and used by the forces of order. Just as it is described by a member of the ACAB (All Cops Are Bastards) clan, "(the attire) arose out of the need to protect ourselves against police violence. All of it arises out of a need: the key word here is necessity. From the tools we use to defend ourselves to the ones we use to attack . . ." (Claude 2020). Aside from helmets, masks, and goggles, they added knee pads and even vests used for mountain biking. This vest was used as the first protective layer, a shield. For the police, it is transparent and unbreakable, whereas for the protesters, it's usually made of recycled materials and crafted at home. The shield/armor bearer used round satellite antennas, barrels split in half, road signs, wooden planks, roofing materials and pretty much anything they could get their hands from nearby buildings (Claude 2020).

The social demands that came to the forefront in October 2019, had been brewing for some time and exploded a year earlier.[8] From 2018, in the context of the global phenomena "Me Too," female Chilean university students denounced and gave visibility to the sexist violence and harassment they have been subjected to, from both peers and academics, on various campuses. On April 17, feminist female students took control of Universidad Austral de Chile, in the southern city of Valdivia. A month later there were more than thirty faculties in more than fifteen universities under the control of their female student bodies. In parallel to the actions led by the Coordinadora Feminista Universitaria (Cofeu) (Feminist

University Coordinator) as well as independently, young women mobilized for changes to education, under the motto "the revolution will be feminist, or it will not be."

In 2018, to call yourself a feminist assumed you adhered to "antipatriarchal and anti-capitalist concepts, with an autonomous focus, assembly-oriented and non-hierarchical" (Alfaro-Álvarez and De Armas Pedraza 2019). These diverse leaderships, voices, and vertical organizations—which were very different to the traditional models usually hegemonized by men—become evident when dressing bodies to encourage individual expressions and that of belonging to small collectives, signifying a new way of power distribution in matters related to leaderships.

During that wave of feminist uproar which lasted nearly three months, the women used their bodies as an instrument for battle (the word "body" in Spanish is gendered masculine; they began to use it as gendered feminine.) They also recognize the material dimensions and corporal performance practices, as well as its political and transformative potential, while parodying original female roles, such as maternity, breastfeeding, sexualization of female bodies, heteronormative behaviors, the male gaze, and desire.[9] One of the emblematic expressions in these protests is the simultaneous naked torso and *capucha* (face covering). It emerges during one of the mass marches down the main artery of Santiago. The act is photographed and widely published and commented on in the press and social networks. The half-dressed body and the act of exhibiting in public becomes the center of the debate. According to the Plaza Pública CADEM poll N°228, during the fourth and last week in May, 71 percent of Chileans believed it inappropriate that women march topless down the Alameda Avenue, although support for mobilizing was at 68 percent and support for marches was at 69 percent (*Plaza Pública* 2018). However, no public mentions were made regarding the never-before-seen appropriation and resignifying of the *capucha* by these women, nor the political strategies undertaken. Both aspects would evidently be addressed within the context of the social uprising a year later.

The *capuchas* of the feminist wave of 2018 are either red or burgundy, "because of its poetic level of symbolism." Generally, it is a balaclava in a stretchy knit that leaves the eyes and mouth clear. It is reminiscent of the Russian collective punk-rock Pussy Riot. According to Laura Ibáñez, they are inspired by Mexican wrestling and the Zapatista movement. Its function was to uniform the protesters (Montes 2020). However, from the outset they incorporated subtle accessories that did not disturb the collective look: sequins around the eyes, simulating eyelashes or eyebrows, as well as holes cut out to allow for a braid or a ponytail.

On the contrary, in the context of the 2019 protests, and in a much more menacing urban environment, the protesters share their space with fighters and police force, and sometimes, even participate in some of the skirmishes, where the feminist balaclavas paradoxically turn even more anonymous and more individualized, standing out from the masculine wrappings. Andrea, part of the Colectivo Complejo Conejo, who fashion with textile art, explains:

> Many feminists are appropriating the *capucha* as a symbol. The *capucha* was seen as a masculine symbol, of men fighting in the front line, with a black t-shirt tied around their head, much more improvised. Feminism has taken it into a different aesthetic, a new identity, without fearing that if you embellish it and bling it up, it stops being a subversive garment. The gender roles are completely fractured, diversifying the fight. [. . .] the *capucha* stopped being a specific and patriarchal element.
>
> Di Girolamo 2019

That is to say, aesthetic cult dimensions were associated with an evident expression of the subjectivity that distinguishes a women with balaclava, aside from her affiliations, and resists total invisibility. This is possibly because her historical battles are intrinsically linked to her legitimate presence in the public sphere.

Aside from the versatility to incarnate a multiplicity of social functions, the 2019 *capucha* dominates as the central element in the autobiographical narrative that their wearer materializes and exhibits through the garment.[10] Each woman recreates it according to her life experiences, political agenda, and gender. For Di Girolamo, to wear a balaclava means:

> to wear my disposition to protest, to fight. It's to carry upon my shoulders, all of my political convictions, to find strength and to wear my collective emotions on my sleeve. I have screamed, cried, danced wearing a *capucha*. When I put it on, I feel unique, but at the same time, also part of an enormous body of people pushing the same causes.
>
> (2021)

In another sense, only the anonymity and identity protection provided by the *capucha* allow for the exploration and pushing of boundaries when exhibiting the naked body in a public space: "Only wearing a *capucha* have I had the courage to march baring my tits" (Di Girolamo 2021).

The first step when creating the *capucha* is figuring out the supporting structure, starting with the common base, which can be an already existing piece (a beanie, a scarf, a tube scarf, or a snood) adapted to the head, or a new piece made from stretchy fabric. It is here we first see the variations. Although many prefer red or purple to symbolize the battle for women's rights, or green which is associated with the legalization of abortion movement, the majority add new symbols: designs, animal prints, velvet, lace, beading, sequins, metallic lycra, and glam star stamps. The decorations are even more diverse and combine native references with traditional crafts and fashion trends: pompoms, woolen plaits, scrunchies, multicolored ribbons, fabric blooms and flowers, gemstones, sequins, beads, pearls, mirrors, coins, feathers, broches, appliqués made with fabric remnants, décor from Andean carnivals, and slogans such as "No estamos solas" (we are not alone) or "Ni una menos" (not one less), flowers and endless embroidered motifs.

One of the fundamental tools for propagating *capuchas* are the organized workshops that teach how to make them. Free or cheap workshops emerged after the feminist wave of 2018, which grew after the social unrest of 2019. Convened through social media networks by various groups throughout the country, their dynamic is quite simple. The women in charge hand out patterns made of newspaper. These are transferred onto fabric; then, they are cut and sewn together. The other participants of the workshop help with the orifices for the eyes and mouth (Di Girolamo 2019). They then proceed to decorate them: "everyone puts their own seal on them. Some of the *capuchas* have a hippie feel, others more metal rock" (Alison in Montes 2020). During the making of the *capucha*, there are textile elements that are linked to the life stories of their owner/maker: "From the materials available, I used a stretchy plush burgundy fabric as the base, sequins, needle, and thread. I brought some red lace underwear, the charm in the middle and my grandmother's boa that I used as a Mohawk" (Di Girolamo 2021). Javiera, 25 years old, highlights the value of the artisanal process and how, through these characteristics, the identity of both the individual and the group can be revealed:

> Little by little I start to find meaning in the things that I put on it; you find meanings. The feminist *capucha* doesn't just have eyes and a mouth. It has other things: braids, outlined eyes, pompoms. They have more meaning than the male ones, which are basically to hide behind. Ours have more color, shapes, and I like that because it provides a contrast to the others. We not only want to hide our faces, but we are protesting, and we want them to see us and listen to what we are expressing.
>
> in Di Girolamo 2019

However, the decorative interventions go beyond the merely aesthetic. Its nature is principally testimonial because each *capucha* is also a visual and material story of the experiences that have spurred their owners to mobilize.

The Colectivo Las Tesis, in which they replaced the colorful *capucha* with a black blindfold, made the former less visible, especially as the performances increased media coverage. On November 19, 2019, the group staged the first choreography of "Un violador en tu camino" (A rapist in your path) in Plaza Aníbal Pinto in Valparaíso. From that day forth, the choreography was performed almost on a daily basis by various groups of women throughout the country. According to Dafne Valdés, a member of the collective, the premise was to "try to turn feminist theories into a performance in a simple, easy format that sticks, so that the message from different feminist theorists could reach people who maybe had not had the opportunity to read or analyze it" (*Interferencia* 2019). Their main references come from the work by Argentinean anthropologist, Rita Segato, for whom rape is not about some out of control male libido. It is an act of power and even a political act that constructs masculinity upon the domination of women.

The black blindfolds, strategically placed over the eyes, allowed a visual unification of the participants, all dressed very differently, and immersed in the daily hustle of a city where they coexisted with multiple manifestations of protest.[11] This twist allowed the collective to have their own emblem, clearly profiling them within the context of the demonstrations. Moreover, the visual effect of the austere black blindfold contrasted with attractive, colorful attire and contributed to the questioning of the traditional link between non-demure feminine clothing worn in public, and sexual aggression. Such a triad allowed the construction of broadly known and used arguments that place blame on the woman who suffers abuse, by associating her with a prostitute: "and the fault wasn't mine, nor where I was, nor what I wore" (Las Tesis 2019). This explains why, in some of the gatherings, the collective encourages wearing glamorous, evening clothing—leggings, crop tops, lacy bras, velvet hotpants, shorts, lycra or leather miniskirts, black mesh stockings, tight little black dresses, see-through clothing, deep plunging necklines, sequins—all of these items revendicated the right to multiple expressions of sensuality and erotica, embodied in the clothed–unclothed body, as a strategy to annul the protective decoration system/outline.[12]

The blindfolds that come with the Las Tesis performance resignified an emblematic piece in the enforcement of political violence in the context of human rights violations that occurred during the military dictatorship in Chile.[13] During this time, blindfolds were so significant and so widely used in these clandestine detention centers that female survivors of violence and sexual torture to this day refer to them as *vendas* (blindfolds). The blindfolds of the dictatorship were varied. Tape blindfolds were used only to control the detainees when they were captured. More permanent ones were manufactured from recycled materials obtained from the clothing of the detainees; clothing collected during raids of the homes of suspects, or from garments removed or torn during torture (for example, shirt sleeves). On the contrary, the blindfolds used during the Las Tesis performances were voluntarily adopted by the women. As with the *capucha*, each woman chose which blindfold represented her and felt comfortable. The dominance of the color black reinforces the pain associated with the experience of abuse in everyday life, as well as complicity among the authorities, and a shared demand for justice.

Figure 12.1 Greta di Girolamo covered with a hood she made herself from a lace panty and a stole inherited from her grandmother, at a protest in Plaza Italia, Santiago, Chile, 2019. Photographer: Roque Rodríguez.

However, the emergence of the blindfolds was not the only explanation for the demise of the feminist *capucha*. Political and institutional factors altered the priorities in choosing a garment. Among them, the presidential initiative to discuss, with urgency, an anti-*encapuchados* law, which sought to sanction with jail time (from 541 days to 3 years) anyone who intentionally covered their face to hide their identity by means of wearing *capuchas* (balaclavas), scarves, or similar elements (T13, 2019) while taking part in disturbances of the peace. Although there was thoughtful debate in both chambers of congress around this possible legislation, by the end of December, the debate was halted. With the arrival of Christmas, the onslaught of high summer temperatures during the month of January, and the mass departure from Santiago for holiday goers

Figure 12.2 Hooded man wears a t-shirt with the image of Argentine *guerrillero* Che Guevara to cover his mouth area and protect himself from the gas thrown by security forces cars, Plaza Italia, Santiago de Chile, 2019. Photographer: Diego Urbina.

in February meant that protest numbers had dwindled to small groups who still gathered at the "Plaza Dignidad" and still faced off in skirmishes with the police. During the days before Sunday, March 8, when mass crowds were expected to celebrate International Woman's Day, the production of feminist *capuchas*, in red or purple, increased exponentially, in order to be used during the many performances organized by the various collectives (Montes 2020). On Sunday, March 8, two million women gathered at the "Plaza de la Dignidad" (CNN Chile, 2020). This was to be the last mass march for this period, and marked the reappearance, however fleeting, of the feminist *capucha*.

On March 3, 2020, the first case of Coronavirus SARS-Cov-2 was detected in the country. On March 14, the first restrictions were implemented in order to reduce the number of people able to gather for public events, and four days later, a State of Emergency/State of Exception was decreed. By the end of the month, borders were closed, there was a curfew in place, and the suburbs where most protests took place, Santiago and Providencia, were under quarantine. The *capucha* was replaced with surgical masks and cloth masks made at home. Those referred to as "front-line" fighters were no longer the protesters, but health workers in hospitals and clinics, looking after the sick and fighting the new virus. Both health workers and subversives shared the exposure to harm, the heroic nature of their acts, the need to organize and the sense of sacrifice (Chermin and Radovic, 2021). Thus, a divisive line was established between the space where a deadly battle against Covid-19 was being fought, while on another, a masked daily life transpired; a life that oscillated between lockdown and relative normality.

Notes

1 Chant that arose during the Social Outburst of 2019 in Chile. Refers to a general unrest that was triggered by the 30 pesos price hike in the Metro/public transport system, equated with the general malaise of 30 years of democratic governments that reinforced the neoliberal economic model inherited from the military dictatorship, which deepened inequities and social injustices.

2 Such as access to healthcare, education, housing, basic services, minimum wage increases, fair retirement pensions, gender equality, an end to sexual discrimination,

an end to discrimination against Indigenous population, environmental justice, among many others.

3 For further analysis of the Chilean situation, see: Alberto Mayol, 2019, *Bing Bang. Estallido social 2019* (Santiago: Catalonia); Alberto Mayol, 2021, *El derrumbe de modelo* (Santiago: LOM); Pablo Artaza, et al., 2019, *Chile despertó: lecturas de la historia del estallido social de octubre* (Santiago: Universidad de Chile); Carlos Ruiz Encina, 2020, *Octubre chileno. La irrupción de un nuevo pueblo* (Santiago: Taurus); Oscar Contardo, 2020, *Antes de que fuera octubre* (Santiago: Planeta); Kathya Araujo, (ed.), 2019, *Hilos tensados. Para leer el octubre* (Santiago: Editorial Universidad de Santiago de Chile).

4 Since the post-dictatorship years in 1990, there have been many mass marches against the economic model, and they were often evoked by student groups: The Coordinating Assembly for Secondary Students (2006); and the National Coordinator for Secondary Students of the Chilean Student Confederate (2011), among others.

5 The term "clothing" in this context refers to dress, clothing, and accessories that by covering the body, whether fully or partially, inscribe it to a determined space and time, and that the relationship to that body plays a role in the identity of the subject and its autobiography. It considers three-dimensional elements which have been designed to fit in or wrap around a body part; bidimensional elements that lack any predetermined configuration, and the appearance of it will depend on the way they are placed on or attached to the body; and others which, when covering the skin, and by default, the body, function as bi- and tridimensional elements at the same time.

6 Politics of the body, shaped by social relations, has become a key terrain of contemporary political struggle, particularly where material and discursive dimensions intersect. It involves both individual and collective bodies, shaped by discipline or resistance (Foucault 1992). For how these dynamics manifest through clothing and style, see Djurdja Bartlett's *Fashion and Politics* (2019) on the relationship between politics and clothed bodies (2019). Carol Tulloch's notion of style activism in relation to the Black Panther Party as well as Jane Tynan's analysis of the resignification of the keffiyeh are also insightful. The global politicization of fashion is also addressed in Elke Gaugele and Monica Titton's editorial (2019). See in particular Titton's work on the dialectical relationship between fashion and feminism and the style codes of contemporary feminists in this same issue (2019). The case I have discussed here differs significantly due to the small size of the Chilean fashion system and the presence of artisanal interventions that make up the clothing of several feminist activists who also make it challenging for practices to become fashion trends.

7 Another significant reference associated with the balaclava, is the image of Subcomandante Marcos, Mexican leader of the National Zapatista Liberation Army, an Indigenous movement that operates in the Chiapas region. Wearing a black balaclava "so that they can see us, we covered our faces" (Marcos 1995) embodies a contemporary warrior that combines a clandestine life and media presence. For how face coverings from the nineties are used by present-day university protesters to commemorate recent, painful national history, see Grau in Richard, 2000.

8 Chilean feminism can be traced back to the nineteenth century with the first groups of women laborers. At the beginning of the twentieth century, through women's reading groups and book clubs, gatherings were specific to the social classes. Several associations were formed with the focus on obtaining political and civil rights. The women's suffrage movement succeeded in obtaining the vote in 1949 and, thereafter, experienced a slight decline in popular gatherings. From 1973 on, groups resurfaced during the struggle against authoritarianism. Upon the return of democracy, feminism dispersed, and in 2000, demands for reproductive rights and the right to dissent activated a more fragmented form of social movement. See Kirkwood (1986) on feminist theory in Chile; Gaviola, Largo, and Palestra (1994) for a historical overview of women from 1973 to 1990; and Richard (2001) on the challenges feminism faced during Chile's post-dictatorship transition.

9 Judith Butler's (1990) concepts have been widely adopted across Chile, from academic settings to grassroots feminist and queer collectives. See also Grau's essay "Un cardo en la mano," a powerful analysis of embodiment during the 2018 Chilean Feminist May, in Zerán (2018).

10 The concept of autobiographical narrative alludes to the concept that each subject constructs and structures their life with the objective of creating identity, and through the act of dressing and undressing, configuring, through this process, a unique materiality that we have denominated body-dressing (Montalva 2013).

11 Another distinctive accessory used by Las Tesis, which serves to unify the protesters in much the same way as the black blindfold, is the bandana tied around the wrist or around their neck either in purple or green (symbols of feminist causes and abortion rights).

12 Protection that is understood beyond physical phenomena, and incorporates a moral dimension, relative to the exhibition of the body, and thus connected to notions of decorum (Flügel 2015).

13 Materials, use and meaning of the blindfold during the military dictatorship in Chile have been covered in detail in Montalva, Pía. 2013. *Tejidos blandos. Indumentaria y violencia política en Chile, 1973–1990*. Santiago: Fondo de Cultura Económica.

Bibliography

Alfaro-Álvarez, Jessica and Tania de Armas Pedraza. 2019. "Estudiantes universitarias chilenas: discursos y prácticas contra la violencia sexista." *Nómadas* 51: 31–47. https://doi.org/10.30578/nomadas.n51a2

Araujo, Kathya. 2019. *Hilos tensados. Para leer el octubre chileno*. Santiago: Editorial Universidad de Santiago de Chile.

Artaza, Pablo, et al. 2019. *Chile despertó: lecturas de la historia del estallido social de octubre*. Santiago: Universidad de Chile.

Bartlett, Djurdja. 2019. *Fashion and Politics*. New Haven and London: Yale University Press.

Butler, Judith. 2001. *El género en disputa: feminismo y subversión de la identidad*. Barcelona: Paidós.

Butler, Judith. 1990. *Gender Trouble: Feminism and the Subversion of Identity*. New York: Routledge.

Cisternas, Pablo Andrés, Paula Loncón, and Juan Pablo Klenner. 2020. *De-Manifiesto. Expresiones ciudadanas a un año del estallido*. Puerto Varas: Editorial Oso libre.

Claude, Magdalena. 2020. "Retrato de un clan de Primera Línea." *Ciper Chile*. Accessed January 6, 2020. www.ciperchile.cl/2020/01/06/retrato-de-un-clan-de-la-primera-linea/

CNN Chile. 2020. "Día de la Mujer: Coordinadora 8M cifra en más de 2 millones las asistentes a la marcha y Carabineros en 150 mil." www.cnnchile.com/8m/dia-mujer-coordinadora-8m-cifra-asistentes-marcha-carabineros_20200308/

Contardo, Oscar. 2020. *Antes de que fuera octubre*. Santiago: Planeta.

Chermin, Andrew and Paz Radovic. 2021. "Diccionario de las nuevas palabras de la política chilena." *La Tercera*. www.latercera.com/la-tercera-domingo/noticia/diccionario-de-las-nuevas-palabras-de-la-politica-chilena/3P52ODXOQFBHRFD3BB5JTOYA5I/

Di Girolamo, Greta. 2019. "Capuchas feministas a la chilena." *Vice*. www.vice.com/en/article/5dmmn8/30-wild-photos-of-chiles-masked-feminists

Di Girolamo, Greta. 2021. Interview by Pía Montalva.

Flügel, John Carl. 2015. *Psicología del vestido*. España: Melusina.

Foucault, Michel. 1992. *Microfísica del poder*. Madrid: La Piqueta.

Gaugele, Elke and Monica Titton. 2019. "Letter from the Editors: Fashion as Politics: Dressing Dissent." *Fashion Theory* 23 (6): 615–618.

Gaviola, Edda, Eliana Largo, and Sandra Palestra. 1994. *Una historia necesaria: mujeres en Chile: 1973–1990*. Santiago: s. e.

Giordano, Franco. 2011. "Autogestión y violencia, en el movimiento estudiantil secundario ¿Respuesta o propuestas de autonomía?" Ph.D. dissertation, Universidad de Chile. http://repositorio.uchile.cl/bitstream/handle/2250/143643/Autogestion-y-violencia-en-el-movimiento-estudiantil-secundario.pdf?sequence=1andisAllowed=y

Grau, Olga. 2000. "El encapuchamiento de la memoria." In *Políticas y estéticas de la memoria*, edited by Nelly Richard. Santiago: Cuarto Propio.

Grau, Olga. 2018. "Un cardo en la mano." In *Mayo feminista: la rebelión contra el patriarcado*, edited by Faride Zerán, 91–98. Santiago: LOM.
Joignant, Alfredo. 2020. "La primera línea: radicalización y efectos de trayectoria." *El Mercurio*.
Kikwood, Julieta. 1986. *Ser política en Chile. Los nudos de la sabiduría feminista*. Santiago: Cuarto Propio.
Las Tesis. 2019. "Un violador en tu camino." https://nacla.org/news/2019/12/27/un-violador-en-tu-camino-virality-feminist-protest
Mayol, Alberto. 2019 *Bing Bang. Estallido social 2019*. Santiago: Catalonia.
Mayol, Alberto. 2021. *El derrumbe de modelo*. Santiago: LOM.
Ministerio de Salud, Subsecretaría de Salud Pública. 2013. "Resolución 3.457 exenta." In Ley Chile, BCN. Santiago. http://bcn.cl/2etjb
Ministerio de Salud, Subsecretaría de Salud Pública. 2020. "Resolución N° 591 exenta." In Ley Chile, BCN. Santiago. http://bcn.cl/2opg7
Miranda, Benjamín, Catalina Albert and Nicolás Sepúlveda. 2019. "Lesiones oculares: advertencias ignoradas por 20 días podrían ser clave en querella contra Piñera." *Ciper Chile*. www.ciperchile.cl/2019/11/11/lesiones-oculares-advertencias-ignoradas-durante-20-dias-podrian-ser-clave-en-proceso-penal-contra-pinera/
Miranda, Rodrigo. 2019. "Entrevista a una capucha: 'En la primera línea damos la cara contra la yuta." *El Desconcierto*. www.eldesconcierto.cl/tipos-moviles/2019/12/07/entrevista-a-un-capucha-en-la-primera-linea-damos-la-cara-contra-la-yuta.html
Montalva, Pía. 2013. *Tejidos Blandos. Indumentaria y violencia política en Chile, 1973–1990*. Santiago: Fondo de Cultura Económica.
Montes, Rocío. 2020. "Cubrirse el rostro para ser legión: el icono de la lucha feminista en Chile." *El País*. https://elpais.com/sociedad/2020-03-07/cubrirse-el-rostro-para-ser-legion-el-icono-de-la-lucha-feminista-en-chile.html
Pichel, Mar. 2019. "Rita Segato, la feminista cuyas tesis inspiraron 'Un violador en tu camino': 'La violación no es un acto sexual, es un acto de poder, de dominación, es un acto político." *BBC*. www.bbc.com/mundo/noticias-50735010
Plaza Pública. 2018. "Encuesta Plaza Pública-Cadem, N° 228." *Plaza Pública*.
Richard, Nelly. 2001. "La problemática del Feminismo en los años de la transición en Chile." In *Cultura y transformaciones sociales en tiempos de globalización*, edited by Daniel Mato, 185–200. Buenos Aires: CLACSO, 2001.
Ruiz Encina, Carlos. 1995. *Octubre chileno. La irrupción de un nuevo pueblo*. Santiago: Taurus.
Subcomandante Marcos. 1995. "La flor prometida." *El País*. March 8, 1995. https://elpais.com/diario/1995/03/29/internacional/796428018_850215.html
T13. 2019. "Ley Antiencapuchados: Qué situaciones serán agravadas y qué penas tendrán." *T13*. www.t13.cl/noticia/nacional/que-es-ley-antiencapuchados-penas-28-11-2019
TamaraTVchile. 2015. "Raúl y Tamara entrevista 1984." TamaraTVchile. www.youtube.com/watch?v=hBC2q7IqMUQ

Villaroel, María José and Jonathan Flores. 2019. "Plaza Italia reúne a 1,2 millones de personas y se convierte en la mayor marcha en 30 años." *Biobio Chile*. www.biobiochile.cl/noticias/nacional/regionmetropolitana/2019/10/25/comienzan-a-concentrarse-manifestantes-en-plaza-italia-para-la-marcha-mas-grande-de-chile.shtml

13

Fashion in Distress: Cultural Fragments and Recycled Identities in Contemporary Argentina

Regina A. Root

"Ancient Myths, New Masks" is about to begin, a collective design workshop led by the designers of 12-na who have flown from Chile to take part in the Argentine creative industries marketplace at 4 p.m. in the Design Sector of Tecnópolis.[1] It is raining outside, and the brisk autumn has us all bundled up inside. Despite floods in many parts of the city, including Villa Martelli where Tecnópolis was erected as an open cultural center to the dismay of an active military base, several participants are ready to open the conversation and share ideas.

In the conference salon, a large open space without walls, there are chairs and tables with sewing machines and tools. A pink poster announces the title "Clothing and Textiles," indicating that designers, weavers, and textile illustrators will meet here. Furthermore, the goals are to create collective textile interventions, interventions in public space, and "multiple expressive formats in projects that incorporate costumes, installations, films . . ."

On a large metal table, there are heaps of clothes in blue plastic bags. Six young designers begin to dig through the piles, hunting for useful fragments. The bags contain faux and real fur, vinyl jackets, course cloth with diamond dots, red tulle, sweaters in well-worn grays and dark blues, multi-colored threads, fragments of knitwear (one in coral, shredded with scissors), a natural woven vest . . . Ten other young designers join the search. Mariano Breccia, who leads this workshop with Mechi Martínez, explains to me that those present are designers, artisans, and seamstresses, and will work in groups of two or three, to assess textiles collaboratively and bring together their selected fragments to create twelve masks based on twelve regional Indigenous myths.

During the creation process, no one seems to think through the origin or texture of the textiles. Everything used is textile waste, but with a future to narrate. According to the preferences of each group, the collaborative designers sew together and elaborate new features for these recycled textiles. At 4:20 p.m., there are more than twenty people working on these recycled textile masks. Each myth emerges from this shared collaboration, each member generating ideas on how to interpret its meanings through design and then carrying out a specific role in the creation process. They negotiate how to use each garment or textile fragment to solve the more predictable problems: If the fur gets used, will the final product make the wearer feel itchy? If plastics get introduced, will they feel too rigid for the wearer? Three hours later, with the fragments sewn together to form the masks, they are presented as ready to wear and facilitate interaction.

Upon choosing fragments of textiles to create new pieces, the youth of 12-na, a concept of the textile artists Mariano Breccia and Mechi Martínez, Argentines who live in Chile, began a social process that imagines collective interventions in the public space using the remains of garments discarded by others. Inside the sphere of global capitalism, clothes cross boundaries and travel the world during their creation, production, consumption, and in this case, reconstruction. For Argentina, a country that at that particular moment of the cultural workshop had commemorated three decades of democracy, one might position the question: what does such a narrative of design and consumption potentially mean?

The stories emerging from Argentinian design pose their own ritualized order within democracy. Through regional and national landscapes and designs rooted in cultural heritage, fashion evokes dignity, humanity, and equality. These connections became especially significant after the 2001 economic crisis and, some years later, with the bicentennial of Argentinian independence. At the latter milestone of national history, design retrospectives renewed the idea of fashion as "historical testimony" and a "key factor in the formation of our identity," expressions used by the "Pasado de Moda, 1810–2010" campaign initiated by the government of the City of Buenos Aires. Designs have been in various stages of deconstruction and reconstruction—literally and actively—emerging from fragments of local significance and shared knowledge. Some current proposals blur the individual limits to instill in their place a sentiment of solidarity. This chapter analyzes the cultural fragments and new rituals that have nourished various imaginative acts and cultural innovations in Argentina since dictatorship. Cultural policies during and following the bicentennial of 2010, which commemorated the creation of a first Argentine government following the overthrow of the Spanish viceregal regime, highlight how aesthetic independence initiated an unfolding creative process to inspire active collective roles (Root 2013, 391–407). Using recycled materials, local design workshops, collaborations between regional designers, and a focus on the inclusivity within the national scope, design experiments focused on new ways of creation and production within a more sustainable fashion system. The creative industries focused on the future of recovery and repair, from social connections to the ethics of consumption, the primary objective being to summon new ways of thinking, creating, and even buying. Beyond these proposals, it has also become about recovering all that one could not find because it was no longer there. With these small acts of taking forgotten fragments to make something new, collaborations seemed to restore and repurpose the traces of memory.

Secondhand clothing can involve reckoning with the mystery of previous human experience. Wearing something used today can signify questioning the relationship between the individual, consumption, and society, a link forged within the framework of advanced capitalism and globalization. The use of these garments, however, may correspond to an empathy for present situations and, at the same time, a return to past styles, which in Argentina would carry a particular symbolic charge. One would only need to think, for example, of the campaigns for recycled merchandise sold by Señor Amor (the Salvation Army). This brand proposed to incentivize a public unused to thinking about secondhand clothing, to reutilize textile fragments as a type of *coolhunting*, not without ceasing to understand recycling as an act of charity and solidarity. Señor Amor, bringing together several designers celebrated for their urban edge, created new pieces from used garments and sold them from a festive catwalk, thus posing a reflection of consumption and its political and economic logics. Given the commercialization of garments from previous decades, especially used clothing from the 1970s and 1980s, it seems prudent to return to the past to understand fully the emotional weight of recycled fashion and the vocabulary its history evokes.

If cultural memory is a practice, we have an interesting opportunity to unravel each of the historical layers of a garment. Several contemporary design proposals cite cultural fragments of moments past, as in the use of geometric elements inspired by the iconic headscarves of the Mothers of the Plaza de Mayo.[2] Some proposals have even incorporated scenes of violence and torture that refer to the "Dirty War," a concept to be unpacked later in this chapter. Whether or not the aspiration, these proposals often appear to degrade the idea of memory rather than create a sense of participatory empathy that has been reconstructed in democracy. As Jill Bennett points out, the politics of a traumatic experience registers and embodies conscious and subjective affections or emotions and approximates trauma "in a way that respects and contributes to its politics." It cannot end in appropriation, reduction, or imitation (Bennett 2005, 6). It is not entirely clear if fashion, new or used, is an adequate tool with which to explore the issues of cultural memory, although it is certain that the creation of new pieces from used clothing do appear to connect style and the material objects of identity with the idea of "solidarity." Unfortunately, histories of Argentinian fashion offer few elaborations or respective ideas, even when the design archive and interventions contrast the new with the old, consumption with democracy, the individual with the collective, in a constant struggle against the limits of representation.

During the Dirty War (1976–1983), it is estimated that 30,000 people were "disappeared," or kidnapped, tortured and killed by a bureaucratic authoritarian regime. The official culture projected a control over the physical body and a particular disdain towards the feminine (Taylor 1997, 93; Forastelli 2005, 284). With the population under scrutiny of a joint military, the terms of representation were controlled, and a collective "perceptecide"—understood as the murder of all senses—stimulated a type of "displacement and disappearance" of social problems such as exploitation (Taylor 2003, 28). "People no longer identified with the space they inhabited. They felt like strangers in their country, in their city, in their own homes," writes Taylor (1997, 98). Those citizens "in fashion" did not want to be recognized that way, and the bold were harshly attacked, as in the case of queer icon Federico Jorge Klemm (99, 104). Magazines such as *Para Ti* warned women to be attentive to "revolutionary words" that their children might use, like *dialogue, bourgeoisie, Latin America* (ibid.). With the reorganization of society, appearances and particular behaviors for the youth were prescribed, and in this way, rearranged the semantics and "physical semiology" (ibid.) of society. To reactivate this past was and remains an extremely difficult task and—for good reason—filled with concerns and controversies, since representations resurrect a collective trauma.

Clothing that is "anonymous" and "transferred" frames people in profound ways. *Couture and Consensus* describes the early moments in the life of the Republic, when recycled clothing could represent a *mudanza de traje*, or a shift in dress perceived as a particularly suspicious act in the context of a repressive regime (Root 2010, 37–82). At the end of the twentieth century, used clothing could evoke and honor the memory of a loved one, at times resisting the injustices. These possessions, after all, embodied something because they had *belonged* to someone. They represented memories, experiences, and lives like the buttons in the box of a grandmother described by Hebe de Bonafini,³ or the white handkerchiefs that were utilized by the Mothers of the Plaza de Mayo to be able to identify one another as they took the places of their disappeared children during a youth pilgrimage to Luján, a city just beyond Buenos Aires.⁴ In a collective text titled *El corazón en la escritura* [*The Heart of Writing*], the Mothers overtake the Plaza de Mayo, with its monument to independence, and say, "With our white handkerchiefs / we march together, *compañeras* / justice is in the plaza / 30,000 children wait."⁵ The shared experience gave these possessions a fetish-like status that would not allow them to be discarded or gifted.

In memoirs, garments appear "eternized" in the wardrobe (Mercado 1990, 35), symbols of the emotional toll of violence and repression. In *States of Memory*, Tununa Mercado represents second-hand clothing and furniture as if the author were not able to "exercise the privileges of individualism" (Franco 2001, xviii). In the chapter titled "Poor Person's Body," Mercado details how wearing used clothing during exile felt like the equivalent of taking the same person who had worn them in their lifetime with her, an act of comfort, as if "by some sort of ingenious transmigration of the soul, they had left part of themselves in one of the sleeves, in the waistband, or in one of the cuffs" (Mercado 1990 (2001), 37). Whoever adopts such a garment does not imagine "the space that these clothes of the absent owner can occupy: hanging helplessly from the hangers, taking the form of the hook and acquiring the marks of definitive drops ..." (idem.). Mercado reflects on this state of memory:

> Clothing begins to wear out of its own accord, its flanks droop and disintegrate, exhausted; although this happens to everyone and everything in unequal measure, they all succumb over time. Few people perceive the fatigue of their fabrics because they usually abandon them before this occurs; it is a rare coat indeed that survives the social pressures that define it as being out of fashion, and it requires a strong ethic to accompany a coat through its fall from grace. I have lived my life dependent on my clothing, on the clothing of others that has become mine, the clothing of my dead friends, the clothing that others have given me through capricious benevolence or so as not to condemn it to oblivion; and this destiny, to go around wearing clothing at the tail end of its life cycle, to be one and the same as your clothing and at the same time to feel the horror of this relationship, is a misfortune whose significance is fair game for analysis.
>
> (1990 (2001), 39)

It is with the spirit of the material and the traces of presence that the trauma of state terror and exile unravels. Recording loss, it becomes possible to contemplate the politics behind traumatic experiences. As an everyday symbol that circulates between all, the garments of the past reveal individual states and collective wounds… fragments as emotional as they are material.

The newspaper columns dedicated to fashion of the dictatorship period evoked the vocabulary of terror to emphasize key points. In some cases, trends were associated with fashion's "past" as a strategy not unlike the one used by the founders of the Republic, which utilized the discourse of fashion to criticize the regime of Juan Manuel de Rosas (1829–1852). "Autumn Threatens With Its Pointed Shoes," Norbert Bensaid explains: "Starting a few years ago, indeed, fashion-induced terrorism was more calm. By being thin and not overly poor, anybody could dress according to their own taste." "Sadistic fashions," like the pointed shoes then in vogue, were sure to lose their reign of "terror" only when those in style renounced them as old models. "Fashion, by definition, should change," he concluded (*La Opinión* 1:16, 18 to the 24 of October of 1976, 50). Such sentiments of resistance appeared in various editions of magazines during this time; it was also very much in vogue to wear used clothing, as donned by the wealthy women of Rio de Janeiro or the models of Kenzo in international catwalks. One cover of the magazine *La Opinión* published the heading of "Human Rights in Argentina" and, underneath, larger font that followed with "What is going on with fashion?," as if to emphasize the lack of attention granted by the previous headline. Another edition of the same periodical, with a title referring to "Feminine Fashion: What is Autumn?" also pondered "The Question of Human Rights" (Figure 13.2). "The Youth Revolution," an article written by Miguel Grinberg, suggested the possibility of "reaching the equilibrium between tolerance and authority." "Every trunk needs new sap," Grinberg writes: "Any society that closes the floodgates of expansion to its children runs the risk of manufacturing the same monsters time and again. The evolution of Humanity has occurred—to a great extent—thanks to those who did not conform" (*La Opinión* 1:15, 2 to the 3 of August 1976, p. 59). This tension between homegrown fashions that resisted the status quo with an air of edge and resistance—and risked life itself—and the marketing of an idea of access to international brands were indeed evident in department store advertisement campaigns by Harrod's of Buenos Aires, newspaper columns, and fashion magazines.

The historiography of fashion in Argentina inherited this vocabulary. "Can one eventually think of the disappearance and death of fashion?" Susana Saulquin asks (2010, 17). For the sociologist known for writing one of Argentina's

Figure 13.1 Fashion confronts politics in peculiar ways during the period of State Terrorism. Photograph of the cover of *La Opinión* (20–26 February, 1977).

first national fashion history books, however, those notions were ultimately constructed globally, with "the dictatorship of [Charles Frederick] Worth," "the dictatorship of the image" (ibid., 83, 88), modern-day fashion as "an essential drug that relieved, in authoritative ways, the anguishes of liberty in the forms of dressing," the "disappeared" obstacles, or the "social dictatorships" that make up what she perceives somehow as an "autistic and dictatorial fashion system" (ibid., 105, 138, 142, 152). Her work mentions a "body that has been denied," "utilized and buried for communal interests" that transformed this body into "a perfectly empty shell…" (ibid., 105), but which in another context would have been whole.

The scant mention of the 1970s in Argentine fashion allows for the most basic understanding of a "textile and fashion industry in crisis" and a "new fashion order" whose "perfect products…., empty and stripped of content" are characterized by "a lack of the logic of consumption" and "the disappearance of the system of signs" (ibid., 156, 159). At this time, however, European styles were contrasted with Argentinian ones in very interesting ways, with essays attentive to Parisian fashion that spoke to "soft lines, without aggression" that "did not surprise anybody in Buenos Aires," and the eagerness for national consumption. One article of the period, for example, describes Harrod's new international boutiques within its Buenos Aires department store, the headline observing: "The Public Went for Imported Merchandise but Opted for the National." In between bodies that were "democratized" and "fragmented" (Saulquin, 2010, 198), and "bodies as punished as they were submissive" (ibid., 182), the vocabulary of Argentine fashion history would not appear to acknowledge or even value wholeheartedly its own path within global fashion history.

With the transition to democracy in 1983, amidst hyperinflation (12,000 percent in 1989) and outlandish neoliberal consumption practices, alternative designers known as the "poor geniuses" responded harshly to exuberant lifestyles with their version of fashion in distress. Even so, used clothes and textiles were uncommon. Designer Sergio de Loof, who wrote poetry about his designs and posted them on single sheets of paper he displayed in Buenos Aires coffee shops, wrote, "My suit is poor—my suit is / almost forgotten, abandoned." Designers and performance artists began to work with concepts related to memory and the limits between the individual body and the collective body, collaborating and experimenting with the materiality of presence. The past could no longer be left to sit in the wardrobe, for it was in the process of unraveling. Used clothing represented a different type of distress.

The hope of community-style design opened this chapter, with designers and collaborators piecing together textile remnants to make something new. In the thrift store, as I have written in a different context, "the souls of people who made or once wore those clothes remain forgotten, as these are the human counterparts to the discarded realities along the supply chain." The designers of 12-na, however, actively engaged in a recovery project of those textiles deemed by thrift stores to have such little value or no value these were then bundled together as discards on discount. The name 12-na, or *docena* in Spanish, references that very stack of a dozen pieces of textile waste. Playing with the design concept itself, upcycling through a type of cooperation, the Tecnópolis workshop

Figure 13.2 The Chicos del 12-na make their masks and ponchos from textile fragments. Sometimes these designs become collaborative festivals that bring together people who work together to make new collective dress to be worn by several people together at a time. Photographs courtesy of Chicos del 12-na.

pondered fragments past, imagined ancient masks and the profound hope of the human spirit, and created new myths for Argentinian fashion on that cold, rainy day.

Notes

1. MICA or the Mercado de Industrias Creativas Argentinas, as it is known, was launched by the Secretaría de Cultura de la Nación and held between April 11 and 14, 2013. Notes taken by the author on April 12, 2013.
2. The Mothers of the Plaza de Mayo are a courageous group of women who began to circle the revolutionary monument in commemoration of Argentinian independence on April 30, 1977, to make visible their quest for information about their missing loved ones. Their presence is noted by their white headscarves, originally the cloth diapers of their children who were no longer at home because they had gone missing, which eventually were embroidered with the names of their missing loved ones.
3. Hebe de Bonafini remembers a box of buttons in which she selected each with care when repairing shirts and aprons. Upon opening the box, she thinks of her

grandmother's voice describing each button's color and size. "Do you know…? This brown button was taken from the jacket of your grandfather who died a long time ago, this red one came from a singer's blouse, the white one is from my mother's wedding dress, the small light blue ones, from your brother's little coat" (Bonafini 1997, 11). The translation is mine.
4 I analyze the history and symbolism behind this shawl in Root (2010: 238-239).
5 The translation is mine. This is a collective text by the Association for the Mothers of the Plaza de Mayo (1997: 72).

Bibliography

Asociación Madres de Plaza de Mayo. 1997. "Plaza tomada: Con este pañuelo blanco." In *El corazón en la escritura*, 71-72. Buenos Aires: Ediciones Madres de Plaza de Mayo.

Bennett, Jill. 2005. *Empathic Vision: Affect, Trauma, and Contemporary Art*. Stanford: Stanford University Press.

Forastelli, Fabricio. 2005. "Scattered Bodies, Unfashionable Flesh." In *The Latin American Fashion Reader*, edited by Regina A. Root, 283-289. Oxford and New York: Berg.

Franco, Jean. 1990 (2001). "Introduction." *In a State of Memory*, edited by Tununa Mercado. Translated by Peter Kahn, xii-xiv. Lincoln: University of Nebraska Press.

Mercado, Tununa. 2001. *In a State of Memory*. Translated by Peter Kahn. Lincoln: University of Nebraska Press.

Root, Regina A. 2010. *Couture and Consensus. Fashion and Politics in Postcolonial Argentina*. Minneapolis: University of Minnesota Press.

Root, Regina A. 2013. "Mapping Latin American Fashion." In *The Handbook of Fashion Studies*, edited by Black, Sandy et al., 391-407. London: Bloomsbury.

Saulquin, Susana. 2010. *La muerte de la moda, el día después*. Buenos Aires, Paidós.

Taylor, Diana. 1997. *Disappearing Acts: Spectacles of Gender and Nationalism in Argentina's "Dirty War."* Durham and London: Duke University Press.

Taylor, Diana. 2003. *The Archive and the Repertoire: Performing Cultural Memory in the Americas*. Durham and London: Duke University Press.

14

From Low to High: Fashion, Reggaeton, and Latino Male Idols

William Cruz-Bermeo

Over the past two decades, the reggaeton genre, a vernacular Latin American music expression, has gone global. Its male performers have become active participants in the fashion establishment, both in their home countries and abroad. The reggaeton industry in Medellín, Colombia has played a key role in this process. There, historically, masculinity and fashion have been opposing concepts, as evidenced by the social scorn that the first manifestations of dandyism underwent at the beginning of the twentieth century. Reggaetoneros seem to have in common with those dandies a sensitivity to fashion. However, overcoming rejection and living in a new era, this sensitivity is celebrated and embraced, and serves as a boundary-pushing device in young, urban male fashion. This marks an important change in a conservative society where fashion-conscious men were seen as morally suspect. Since fashion literature focuses primarily on the urban fashions of the Global North, this chapter aims to contribute to the study of urban men's fashion in a region of the Global South, with particular attention to Medellín, Colombia.

In the early twentieth century, Romualdo Gallego, a chronicler from Medellín, Colombia, wrote a brief piece titled "A Man of The Land" (1991, 234). In this piece, Gallego discusses the changing appearance of men in Medellín because of the city's modernization process. The transition from a rural lifestyle to industrialization and urbanization prompted a shift in men's clothing choices, with traditional rural garments like *ruanas* being replaced by more urban attire such as suits, tailcoats, blazers, and any other novelty in dress. As a result, the relationship between men and their clothing underwent significant changes during Medellín's modernization process. This led to the emergence of local dandies that were heavily criticized by chroniclers such as Gallego, because of their fascination with fashion. In a society that valued conservatism, fashion and masculinity were seen as contradictory concepts. Thus, these new dandies, derogatorily labeled as *filipichines*, were associated with effeminacy.

The etymology of the word *filipichín*, in singular form, remains unclear even to La Real Academia de la Lengua, the governing body of the Spanish language, defining it as a synonym for "fop" or "effeminate," and as a type of "printed wool fabric" (RAE 2024). A dictionary of idioms from Bogotá, Colombia, associates the term with a type of checkered fabric utilized during the colonial era (Ospina 2012). This association with clothing suggests that the flamboyant use of suits crafted from checkered fabrics in the late nineteenth century, contrasting with the prevailing plain black suits in men's fashion, may have given rise to the term *filipichín*, as it was used by Gallego during his time.

Gallego (1991) even described *filipichines* as men who wore makeup, corsets, and carried flowers in their jacket pockets—all elements that were traditionally associated with femininity and women's fashion. Gallego went so far as to assert that these *filipichines* were unable to engage in physical activities like sports because they were too flamboyant and weak, and sports were a very mannish pleasure. However, as Giuseppe Scaraffia (2009) states in his dictionary of dandyism, "The femininity of the dandy's beauty shows his profound humanity, in a world and an era of systematic, individual, and social aggression. Once his feminine part is liberated, the dandy affirms his will to seduce through beauty and not through force" (147). In Medellín, the *filipichines* appeared to challenge the standards of acceptable masculinity. Although the poet Tartarín Moreira did not refer to them as *filipichines*, he did mention in his writings a type of men which was becoming more visible in the city in bars, theaters, and salons. There, Moreira (1934) scorns their refinement about their body movements, manners of gazing, and again, their use of corsets. In another passage Moreira (1985) describes men who have effeminate attitudes and fashion choices, parading confidently and attracting admiration. They do not wear hats; instead they use a large amount of perfumed brilliantine on their hair, creating a shiny appearance. Their manicured nails shine brightly, and they shape their eyebrows into thin lines. They move in a seductive and feminine manner, with a swaying motion in their hips and the nape of their necks. Despite their appearance, ironically observes Moreira, it is important to note that "they are still men" (211).

Despite his homophobic comments, Moreira was depicted as a well-dressed dandy in the local media at the time (Anonymous 1926). Photographer Benjamin de la Calle styled Moreira through his queer eye, and captured him wearing makeup and dandyish attire, posing closely with one of his male friends. As historian Guillermo Antonio Correa (2017) argues, De la Calle openly expressed his sexual orientation through his photography. He not only normalized the idea of professional relationships with someone considered *sexually deviant*, but also familiarized the public with his personal aesthetic brand, creating iconic images and preserving a photographic record. By examining photographs at the time, such as those in the collection of Biblioteca Pública Piloto, one can find queer and camp attitudes in terms of pose and attire.

Regardless of their sexual orientation, the *filipichines* were young men proud of their appearance and convinced of their aesthetic superiority. If *filipichines* engaged in same-gender relationships, crossdressing, or any drag practices, is still to be examined, and is not within the scope of this chapter. Still, any evident and public crossdressing practice was strongly marginalized and criminalized in modern Medellín. While there are visual records of cross-dressed men as early as 1910s, these photographs were captured in the privacy of photography studios and intended for personal contemplation. Photographer Benjamin de la Calle contributed to this collection, but his images did not always portray marginalized individuals. Instead, they often depicted privileged men who were shielded from public scorn by their social status, like De la Calle himself. In contrast, there existed a distinct group of trans individuals who resorted to prostitution, theft, begging, and humor as means of livelihood, as affirmed by scholarly documentation (Betancur Gómez 2000; Correa 2017).

The *filipichín* was a social archetype, not a marginalized one, and identified as man. Gallego (1991) recognized that the image of *filipichín* had multiple nuances. Some of them were of beautiful and lofty spirit, others breathed distinction and an exquisite, good taste. Others were real bums, or an artificial product of a weak and presumptuous civilization. Additionally, Gallego observed that a certain type of naïve *filipichín* was the result of the transformation from village to city that Medellín was undergoing. Like Charles Baudelaire's dandy, the *filipichín* flourished in a time of transition. Baudelaire (1974, 79–124) wrote that dandyism appeared in periods when "democracy is not yet omnipotent" and "the aristocracy is partially indecisive and debased" (122). Putting Baudelaire's words in its historical context one would say that the dandy was an individual who appeared in modernity. Although Medellín did not have an aristocracy connected to bloodlines, its own modernity gave rise to another kind of aristocracy, one based on money and personal achievement, a new social class whose bourgeois lifestyle enlivened dandyish spirits.

But not all men's new attitudes to fashion were criticized or suspected of undermining masculinity. Besides those dandies who loved fashion and embraced the sophistication of the perfumes, the gleaming lacquered hairdos, and who used

Figure 14.1 The image of Marco A. Jaramillo Z. gives us an idea of how local dandies of Medellín, Colombia fashioned themselves. By Benjamín de la Calle, Medellín, 1915. ©Biblioteca Pública Piloto de Medellín para América Latina.

to collect a myriad of gloves for unique occasions such as dancing, strolling, visiting, or riding in their carriages (Gallego 1991), there were other men adopting suits more casual and suitable to their everyday life and work. However, their dress was not derided or rejected, instead it was valued and regarded as modern, civilized, hygienic, and straightforward evidence of progress. Suit jackets and pants made of the same fabric, dark-colored boots, black leather belts, loose light-colored shirts with extremely high collars, ties with contrasting hues, and canotiers and Aguadeño hat, were all considered very refined, proper, and masculine. Wearing these clothes was the opposite to wearing bowlers, top hats, canes, patent shoes, frock coats, gloves, having manicured hands, donning a powdered face, and wearing perfumes, or smoking cigarettes, since it was seen as bourgeois, dandyish and, therefore, effeminate. Nevertheless, most people reluctantly accepted the usage of these clothes by men involved in high society, intelligentsia, arts, and entertainment.

It can be argued that men in the fields above mentioned historically had more freedom to experiment with their own image compared to men in other fields. This can be seen in the phenomenon of dandyism, where individuals like Beau Brummell, Lord Byron, or Oscar Wilde, among others, were famous for their fashion sense and innovative attire, and in turn, influenced other men. In the twentieth century and beyond, the rise of mass culture has allowed male musicians to experiment with their appearance, pushing the boundaries of men's fashion as dandyism did in its day.

Medellín has seen a surge in cultural production over the past twenty years, primarily due to the emergence of urban music and its transformation into a global hub for producing urban music and music videos, particularly in the reggaeton genre. The origins of reggaeton are a subject of debate, but it is believed to have originated in Panama and then spread to Puerto Rico, where it faced criminalization in the 1990s and early 2000s. The genre was later embraced by the music industry and gained popularity throughout Latin America in the early and mid-2000s (Herrera 2021). Colombia, specifically the city of Medellín, is credited with the genre's rebirth and global influence. This has given rise to several male idols of the genre who, like the dandies of the past, enjoy experimenting with fashion, influencing the way other men dress, and taking part in the fashion industry.

During the late 1980s and early 1990s, Medellín, along with other major urban centers like Bogotá and Cali, faced the challenges of the government's war on drugs. Unlike the rural areas of the country, which had been dealing with Marxist guerrilla groups since the 1960s, the drug war was concentrated in these urban areas. This situation created mixed feelings among the population about the mafia bosses. People, particularly the relatives of the mobsters' victims, demanded justice. However, there were others who admired the mobsters for their ability to rise from poverty and gain control over their lives, even if it meant controlling the lives of others. The power to challenge the established order was also admired, along with their preferences in architecture, cars, women, and of course, their fashion choices.

According to Gabriel Tarde's theory of emulation, individuals only imitate those they perceive as superior and unique (Monneyron 2006). Thus, the admiration for the mobsters' aesthetic resulted in imitators and created recurring imagery in *narco novelas* and TV series like *Narcos*. However, this imagery is more fiction than reality and has little to do with the clothing aesthetic of male reggaeton idols. It is important to note that the fashion associated with reggaeton music should not be mistaken for an imitation of the fictional image of narco-gangsters from Mexico or Colombia, which is often portrayed in Hollywood films with white suits and shiny shirts.

As historian Katelina Eccleston (2021) describes, reggaeton is not just a culture, but a lived experience. It embodies the sexy essence of *perreo*, joyful music, and resistance. So, its sartorial style is distinct from the glamorized *narco-aesthetic* depicted in the media. Instead, it draws inspiration from hip-hop and its streetwear, as well as the flashy bling-bling style. The genre also embraces a strong affinity for sneakers, caps, jewelry, and other symbols of group status. Additionally, the polished aesthetic of pop music has also influenced the male fashion style within the reggaeton genre.

Fashion has become part of the lyrics in reggaeton and other urban music genres like rap and trap. For instance, Puerto Rican singer Ozuna references the allure of the Balenciaga brand in his song "Balenciaga," highlighting how it helps him catch a girl's attention. Colombian reggaeton icon J Balvin collaborates with María Becerra in a song where they praise the Nike brand, singing, "Those Nike's look nice on you." Similarly, Colombian singer Ryan Castro incorporates fashion into his song "Jordan," mentioning the emblematical Nike sneaker model from 1985. These examples echo the connection that has long existed between urban music and fashion, reminiscent of Run DMC's 1986 hit "My Adidas." Significantly, now lyrics such as those of Monastery song, by Ryan Castro and Feid, mention a namesake local fashion brand, putting it on the same symbolic level of Valentino.

It is precisely this connection that has been strongly preserved in Medellín, Colombia, especially through reggaeton male icons Maluma and J Balvin. Such a statement by no means implies overlooking other artists of urban music who have been involved in the Colombian fashion scene. Then, is it valid to say that both Maluma and J Balvin, and other rising reggaetoneros embody the image of the local dandy in its contemporary version? Are they exhibiting a new kind of *filipichín*, a "man of the land?"

Unlike the *filipichines* of the early twentieth century, male reggaeton idols are not questioned about their sexual orientation or gender identity based on their fashion choices, as their masculinity is assumed. Their appearance is not the object of mocking scrutiny but of fashionista scrutiny. Hence, they enjoy the social consent to play with their own image as the dandies of the past did, since they are protected by their status as male music stars. These circumstances turn them into a type of modern Latino dandies who personify a new masculinity in which virility is fused with a strong fashion consciousness. This image is epitomized by performers Maluma and J Balvin. They are often featured in fashion magazines, advertisements, and high-profile fashion events, and have even partnered with renowned fashion brands, both at home and abroad. All of these give them the status of global fashion icons, while they continue to strive to be recognized as Colombian, highlighting their cultural heritage, and paving the way for other Colombian urban music stars such as Sebastián Yatra, Manuel Turizo, and Karol G. Clearly, Maluma, and J Balvin belong to a society that is more accepting and progressive compared to that of the earlier generations of dandies. Hence, their status as fashion icons can be attributed to an era of change marked by various transitions, such as the shift from an analog to a digital society, a transition from a local textile-focused industry to a fashion-oriented one, and a shift from a luxury fashion sector targeting a select elite to one that caters to a society driven by spectacle, immediacy, and influence.

If urban music, such as reggaeton, spread throughout Latin America thanks to analog cassettes and DJs who took the risk of playing it on their radio stations, the digital era allowed young people to produce their own music and make it known to others through platforms such as Myspace. This was true for Medellín, where DJs such as El Gurú del Sabor or Semáforo introduced the rhythm to the popular communes of the city, making it part of everyday life in the *barrios*.[1] I remember the youngest of my brothers in his early teens attending *noisy* reggaeton parties, where the flow of "Dembow" by Yandel or "Gata Salvaje" by Hector & Tito was playing, while I was into alternative rock, grunge and the Bristol sound. Then, Internet allowed the download and diffusion of reggaeton coming from Puerto Rico, but also the production and circulation of the first tracks of the genre by local stars such as Buche, Thio, Shawn and Pope, the members of Tres Pesos, the first reggaeton group created in Medellín (Arango Duque 2023). They opened the door for the city to be considered the reggaeton capital two decades later.

At the beginning of 2000s, Medellín already had an established fashion trade fair, Colombiamoda, which was the result of gathering the textile manufacturers' effort to face the competition derived from a new economics policy based on the opening of markets instead of protectionism that ruled from the 1930s (Cruz Bermeo 2018b). Textile manufacturers looked for transition from a textile-based industry to a fashion-based industry. Colombiamoda, in addition to being a platform for business, is a meeting place for the country's fashion culture. For three decades, diverse cultural trends in the country have converged on its catwalks, including music and specifically the local reggaeton fever. In 2014, the up-and-coming Maluma took the stage at the conclusion of Non Stop, a Colombiamoda fashion runway aimed at highlighting emerging talent. The sponsors of this runway had seized the opportunity to promote the singer. However, this promotional strategy did not go over well with certain members of the Colombian fashion set (Varela 2014). Reggaeton, it seemed, was considered too mainstream and populist to coexist with the fashion world. Or, conversely, so powerful that it could overshadow the designers. Bad reviews were made off the record.[2] This reaction illustrates the prejudices attached to reggaeton, due to its mistaken association with felony, sexual behavior, drug dealing and other social panics. But also, expose the reactions of *aporophobia* and classism that arise in social circles to which people often feel privileged to belong.

At the time, few local fashion insiders seemed to sense Maluma's potential to be a fashion persona. But later, he would be taking the stage for the finale of Dolce & Gabbana Fall 2018 menswear show in Milan. In 2019, he attended the MET gala as Moschino brand ambassador. One year later, Maluma partnered with creative director at Balmain, Olivier Rousteing, to design a capsule collection, and came back to the MET gala doing his entrance with Donatella Versace, and then again, in 2023, as Boss brand ambassador.

As time went by, fashion and reggaeton were a perfect mix-and-match on Colombiamoda's runways. The path preconized by Maluma would be followed by brands that brought reggaeton stars onto their catwalks, as Joy Staz did in 2017 when it opened its runway show with the up-and-coming—now mega star—Karol G. And then in 2018 with Puerto Rican performers Zion & Lennox. This cocktail of reggaeton and fashion cultures really shook up the Colombian fashion establishment. In these fashion shows, the audience consisted of devoted followers of the brand, who displayed great enthusiasm upon meeting their beloved idols. Simultaneously, the usual occupants of the front row seemed to vanish mysteriously. Consequently, this prime seating area was filled by local reggaeton enthusiasts who were also fans of the brand (Cruz Bermeo 2018a).

But reggaetoneros were not only singing on stage, now they were collaborating with local streetwear brands, lending their style as inspiration for fashion collections designed to mass markets. The year 2018 could be considered as the moment when reggaeton esthetic finally conquered the Colombian fashion establishment. Performer J Balvin partnered with GEF, a long-lived casual and underwear brand, for a collection designed under the guidelines of his sense of style. This was a prime-time show, with a huge budget and attended by all kinds of influencers and traditional media, occupying the front row. The reactions were incredibly different from when Maluma in 2014 had performed on the Non Stop runway, with just claps and buenas vibras ("good vibes").

J Balvin's stardom in the fashion show business was already set by 2018. A decisive year was also 2016, when he was invited to Paris to attend the Chanel Pre-Fall 2017 show and was featured on the Latin-American *Vogue Hombre* edition. Then, CFDA[3] named J Balvin as ambassador to NYFW[4] Men's runway shows, and The Coveteur site featured him as fashion collector, featuring part of his one-of-a-kind and rare pieces of clothing. Once approved by global fashion circles, he was acclaimed by those in his own country. However, when J Balvin posted on his Instagram account the invitation from Chanel the backlash was not absent, perhaps because he was a reggaetonero stepping on the sacred fields of couture? Even so, in 2023, J Balvin was awarded as Latin American Fashion Icon by the recently created Latin American Fashion Awards.

Chanel's video showing J Balvin's arrival at the Ritz echoes French literary tradition. The scene shows a stunned J Balvin looking at the Ritz and then entering to be groomed and dressed, transformed into a Chanel boy. This is reminiscent of the stories of provincial boys who arrived in Paris and then became dandies posturing through the salons of Parisian high society, like those depicted in Balzac's work (Steele 2017). But why would an artist from a once marginalized musical genre receive such a welcome from high fashion and the luxury fashion industry? Obviously, there are promotional forces behind it, but from a cultural point of view it has to do with the industry's drive for survival, and this involves adapting its narratives to the social climate of the times to stay culturally relevant. Multiculturalism and inclusivity are major social concerns, and new generations have the power of interaction via social media, expressing their support for individuals who they believe embody their own identities. As rapper A$AP Rocky declared, "it is important for this generation to see people that look like them or that inspire them, because fashion isn't for the elite anymore" (Morency 2018, 59). Maluma and J Balvin are now part of the elite, and the clothes they wear are far from being accessible to the majority. However, for both the old-fashioned elite and the masses they represent a touch of Latinidad and *barrio*.

The fashion influence of Maluma and J Balvin may be prevalent now, but young people in Medellín have been imitating reggaeton idols for over two decades. Reggaeton's pioneers set fashion trends before the emergence of these current icons. It means that the style of dress for reggaetoneros has evolved over time. There is not a single style, as it varies among performers, but there are consistent features within the genre's sartorial vocabulary. Music videos serve as a popular platform to highlight these features. But in any attempt at analysis, it is important to distinguish when artists are portraying a character within the

Figure 14.2 In 2018 the reggaeton performer J Balvin collaborated with GEF, a long-standing local brand for a collection based on his sense of style. Medellín, Colombia. Photo courtesy of Inexmoda.

video's storyline versus playing themselves. In both cases the sartorial terms are not the same.

Local performers such as Tres Pesos, then Fainal, Shako, Reykon, Yelsid, or Gran Chester, "[…] all began singing in bars, in barbershops, on neighborhood corners dressed as if they were Puerto Ricans, wearing big chains, caps with flat, backward-facing visors, and excessively oversized clothing" (Arango Duque 2023). In addition, they wear finely shaped haircuts and impeccably groomed beards and eyebrows, with diamond earrings in both ears, and shades. By the early 2000s, a toned body was less than a problem. Progressively, as the reggaeton genre touched the borders of pop, tattoos, and toned bodies began to enter its imagery. By 2012, for example, J Balvin had become an athletic guy, as seen in the music video *Tranquila*, dressed more in the vein of Justin Bieber but adding his own flow to the look. It was also the moment when the music videos of a still untattooed Maluma began to give cameos to his barely under construction torso.

Historically, clothes and accessories that shape the style of reggaetoneros have been criminalized, just because they come from once marginalized social contexts. Nonetheless, these have been embraced by the masses and symbolically sanitized by the power of image and the fashion industry. They come mainly from the urban streetwear universe, and especially from hip-hop culture which, in terms of fashion, is one of the most influential all over the world. However, other references continue being incorporated into the stylistic system of reggaeton, sometimes as unrelated to it as punk or the acid colors of house music esthetic. One evidence of this is the use of brightly colored dyed hair by some reggaeton artists, like the more contemporary artist Blessd, who has made of his blue colored hair a distinctive style.

This progressive incorporation of new elements into the reggaeton's style sartorial bases, illustrates the theory of style as *bricolage*, used by sociologist Dick Hebdige (1979) to explain how subcultural styles are constructed. According to this, individuals can create their own systems to think of their own world, assembling elements implicitly coherent but explicitly bewildering. But these are not monolithic systems since, as Hebdige writes, "they are capable of infinite extension because basic elements can be used in a variety of improvised combinations to generate new meanings within them" (103). So, sneakers being an essential part of the reggaetonero style, Balvin's collaboration with Nike is based on tuning up the Air Force 1 model, printing on them his "vibes," more than reinventing them. In the meanwhile, jewelry has not the same bling-bling as it had in times of, let us say, the rapper Slick Dick, though ostentatious, yellow gold has been replaced by white gold or platinum, and diamonds studding forms such as crosses, bunnies, or pets.

This begs us to ask: have reggaeton male artists contributed to pushing gender boundaries in terms of dress? It is not an easy question, just because the genre milieu is strongly heteronormative. When Bad Bunny, the Puerto Rican artist, confidently dons skirts and long painted nails on the red carpet, it is important to remember that such appearances are a spectacle and might not reflect his everyday attire. Even so, there is a possibility that this bold fashion statement *trickles-down*, reaches the men's fashion trends, and gradually challenges traditional notions of masculinity in dress. However, it becomes clear that male reggaeton idols share with those dandies of the past an enthusiasm for fashion and an awareness of their own image. This opens to them a broad framework to challenge conventions. Daniela Riaño (Teams message to author, February 5, 2024), who has been fashion stylist for male urban musicians such as the legend and pioneer of Spanish rap Vico C. or Colombian reggaetonero Feid, notes that male artists, particularly the "new school" of reggaetoneros tend to be reluctant to use make-up. The long-experienced make-up artist Carolina Lebrun (In conversation with author, January 26, 2024) agrees but finds other male artists more open to the habit of make-up. Lebrun and Riaño afree that some male music stars are highly conscious of their facial image. On the one hand, mobile phones work as mirrors which let them check their faces for how they will look on screens, Lebrun reflects. On the other hand, they have strong confidence in their barbers, and the preparations for a video shooting grooming could take more time than dressing, says Riaño. In the period of Western modernity, make-up, as it is known, was mainly a matter of femininity. However, apparently in postmodern times, of genderless trends and gender freedom, makeup is still a contentious field for heteronormativity.

Riaño highlights her preference for styling male urban artists because they are more open to the stylist's proposals and have strong self-confidence. Possibly, Riaño reflects, this is because society demands more controlled standards of beauty from women than from men. Although standards for masculinity also exist, they are less constrained, and self-confidence plays in favor of setting fashion trends inside the limits of the music genre itself. More importantly, they push boundaries into mainstream urban fashion. Namely, when in 2022 the design team at GEF company created a collection under the sign of Maluma's style, this validation by a figure who proudly experiments with fashion, led them to propose a set of genderless and male body revealing garments. In conservative societies like those in Medellín and Latin America at large, this is considerable progress.

Finally, it is inevitable to ask what makes Medellín an attractive center for the reggaeton industry and the production of its music videos. The reception of the genre by youth attracted the arrival of many artists from Puerto Rico seeking to produce in a city where factors such as weather, affordability, and talented teams of directors, producers, writers, models, make-up artists, stylist, and fashion designers are abundant and became highly attractive for its stories, locations, and fashions. All these in the middle of an exceedingly kind ambiance, characterized by the charm of the *paisas*, the demonym given to people from Medellín, who proudly remark on its origins. "Hi, everybody, my name is Karol G. I am from Medellín, Colombia," started the artist in her acceptance speech at the 2024 Grammy Music Awards.

Notes

1 There are numerous versions about, but these press articles content the most accepted version. See Carlos Andrés Arango Lopera, "¿Por qué el reggaetón floreció en Medellín?" *Razón Pública*, November 26, 2023. Also see Fucsia, "Así llegó Medellín a convertirse en el corazón de la música urbana," *Fucsia.co*, May 5, 2022.
2 I attended the show in person, so being in the front row allowed me to gather opinions from fashion insiders about Maluma's presence at the close of this fashion show.
3 Council of Fashion Designers of America.
4 New York Fashion Week.

Bibliography

Anonymous. 1926. "Sexo feo." *El Bateo*, August 28, 1926.

Arango Duque, Jaime Horacio. 2023. "La historia del reguetón paisa contada por cuatro generaciones." *El Colombiano*, June 8, 2023. https://www.elcolombiano.com/cultura/historia-del-regatonen-medellin-jbalvin-karol-g-maluma-CM21696037

Baudelaire, Charles. [1863] 1974. "El pintor de la vida moderna." In *El dandismo,* edited by Salvador Clotas, 79–124. Barcelona: Anagrama. Translated by Joan Giner.

Correa, Guillermo Antonio. 2017. *Raros: Historia cultural de la homosexualidad en Medellín 1890–1980.* Medellín: Editorial Universidad de Antioquia: Fondo Editorial FCSH de la Facultad de Ciencias Sociales y Humanas.

Cruz Bermeo, William. 2018a. "El desfile como espectáculo. Joy Staz." *Fashion Radicals*, July 26, 2018. https://www.fashionradicals.com/el-desfile-como-espectaculo-joystaz/.

Cruz Bermeo, William. 2018b. "Institutional Roles in the Development of Fashion Design in Colombia." Conference paper presented at 10th+1 Conference of the International Committee of Design History and Design Studies, Barcelona, October 10, 2018. https://www.researchgate.net/publication/331287564_Institutional_Roles_in_the_Development_of_Fashion_Design_in_Colombia

Eccleston, Katelina. 2021. "'Loud' Podcast highlights the History of Reggaeton." KQED´s Forum. Podcast audio, August 20, 2021. https://open.spotify.com/episode/5Ei5y7Alx U5tDOOR64gC73?si=JVYJAkvLTdytlENeyHFBow&nd=1&dlsi=cea61190bcf74028

Gallego, Romualdo. 1991. *Novelas, cuentos y crónicas.* Medellín: Ediciones Autores Antioqueños.

Gómez, Jorge Mario Betancur. 2000. *Moscas de todos los colores. Historia del barrio Guayaquil de Medellín. 1894–1934.* Medellín: Ministerio de Cultura.

Hebdige, Dick. 1979. *Subculture: The Meaning of Style.* London: Taylor & Francis.
Herrera, Isabelia. 2021. "Reggaeton's History Is Complex. A New Podcast Helps Us Listen That Way." *New York Times*, August 11, 2021. https://www.nytimes.com/2021/08/11/arts/music/reggaeton-loud-podcast.html?bgrp=a&smid=url-share
Monneyron, Fréderick. 2006. *50 respuestas sobre la moda.* Barcelona: Gustavo Gili.
Moreira, Tartarín. 1985. "Tierra de dañados." In *Cancionero, verso y prosa.* Medellín: Ediciones Extensión Cultural Departamental, 1985.
Moreira, Tartarín. 1934. "n. t." *El Bateo*, July 28, 1934.
Morency, Christopher. 2018. "The New Kings and Queens of Fashion." *The Business of Fashion*, Special Edition, No 11, May 2018.
Ospina, Andrés. 2012. *Bogotálogo I. Usos desusos y abusos del español hablado en Bogotá: A-Luqueado.* Bogotá: Instituto Distrital de Patrimonio Cultural.
Real Academia Española. 2024. "Diccionario de la lengua española, 23.ª ed." Accessed February 26, 2024. https://dle.rae.es.
Scaraffia, Giuseppe. 2009. *Diccionario del dandi.* Madrid: A. Machado Libros.
Steele, Valerie. 2017. *Paris Fashion: A Cultural History.* London: Bloomsbury.
Varela Rodríguez, Jeniffer. 2014. "Non Stop en Colombiamoda: el talento le ganó al reguetón." *Moda 2.0*, August 2014. http://www.modadospuntocero.com/2014/07/non-stop-en-colombiamoda-el-talento-le.html

Part 4

Creative and Collective Agency

15

The Fashion of Face Masks in Mexico: Protest, Culture, and Identity during the COVID-19 Pandemic

Andrea A. Gaytán-Cuesta

On March 17, 2020, an article in *The New York Times* declared that "The surgical face mask has become a symbol of our times" (Friedman 2020), reflecting on how this protective accessory was becoming a fashion trend worldwide. Although the use of protective masks dates to the Middle Ages, the emergence of the COVID-19 pandemic led to the widespread use of face masks as personal protective equipment (PPE), mainly due to the guidance of the World Health Organization and enforcement by local governments. Besides its medical use, the concept of PPE face masks has been analyzed in fashion theory as an intersection of identity, culture, societal norms (Lurie 1981), communication, cultural affiliation, and even artistic advocacy (Barnard 2013). In the case of Mexico, the global shortage of surgical face masks created a market in which cloth masks were manufactured domestically to counter the scarcity of the product. The creation of cloth face masks pushed individual households, Indigenous communities, social entrepreneurship entities, and local artists to develop a re-signified accessory of unique designs that re-interpreted Indigenous traditions, embodied feminist slogans, and even became markers of social status in niche "Mexican brands."

Through the lens of critical fashion studies which, according to Natalya Lusty, analyzes the "material, aesthetic and ethical practices of fashion with cultural studies approaches" (2021), this chapter explores the cultural use of the mask as a fashion device for hyperbolic communication during the COVID-19 pandemic in Mexico. My analysis also considers decolonial sustainability and resilient practices in pandemic fashion, which has been a non-explored topic. I examine four cases: the lucha libre face mask as a contradictory product of the pandemic; the artisanal face mask as a revindication of Indigenous identity (in particular, the Zapatista mask); the face mask as a symbol of feminist protest in Mexico; and the face mask as a niche product of the "Mexican Brand." The study of face masks within the context of cultural identity is part of a broader discussion on decolonization in Mexico, where communities assert their cultural heritage against colonial influence, explore new health practices, and create unique cultural artifacts. Face masks in Mexico as a material culture are artistic expressions of resistance that defy dominant narratives and promote solidarity and symbols of public activism during protests. This chapter is divided into three sections. The first part delves into a historical philosophy of masks in Mexico, as well as the symbolic relation between face masks and illness during the COVID-19 pandemic. Then, I explore specific case studies of face masks produced and used during the pandemic, ending with a brief conclusion about face masks and their future in Mexican fashion.

Máscara or "mask" is a word with a diverse origin that derives from the Arabic *máshara* (joker, disguise, or new face); the German *masca* (darkness or a witch); and the French *mascotte* or charm (Perez-Bustamante 1990). Thus, the aspects of magic, darkness, or the supernatural were since the beginning linked to its definition. Masks as objects hide or manifest a different "face" and mediate the relationship between the individual and society. They hide an identity while they represent a different one, and in that sense, they can dehumanize, or give a superhuman value to those who use them.

In Mexico, masks have existed since pre-Columbian times resembling humans or animals, being attributed a superhuman value. As part of traditional and ceremonial attire, the creation and use of masks are part of a collective and community decision and process. After colonization, masks were worn in Mexico in folkloric dances to mock *conquistadores*, as well as images of devils, surreal creatures, and even governors or people in positions of power. Masks were also used as a key device to Catholic evangelization in *pastorelas* or nativity representations, carnivals, and at Easter. Ritual masks are present in almost any cultural event, the Day of the Dead, parties at the end of the year, or traditional dances influenced by African culture, on the coasts of Guerrero and Oaxaca.

In philosophy, Mexican masks have been a highly explored topic. In the *Labyrinth of Solitude*, Octavio Paz explained: "[The Mexican is] a person who shuts himself away to protect himself: *his face is a mask and so is his smile*.[1] In his harsh solitude, which is both barbed and courteous, everything serves him as a defense: silence and words, politeness and disdain, irony, and resignation" (Paz 1985, 28–29). This idea of wearing masks as defense and protection motivated Rodolfo Usigli's analysis of the three masks present in Mexican idiosyncrasy: the

Indigenous, the Spanish, and the *mestizo*.[2] In the search for the original Mexican,[3] he says, the only legacy Mexicans have *is their masks*[4] which confront them with a world that can only survive in a symbolic form. Living through this symbol allows the introverted Mexican many contradictory and diverse interpretations of the self (Usigli 2007, 137). And it is here where Mexicans also trace their modern experience with masks, which evokes the symbolic masking of the constant fear of scarcity, need, and death, but also serves as a playful device of expression.

The face mask, as an extension of the ritual mask, is portrayed not as a metaphor, but as a protection against the pandemic, but cannot avoid being a depiction of Mexican identity. Face masks become effective and representational devices. They are also devices that reflect fears, as in the debates about which face mask will be the safest to wear. We use a face mask to differentiate ourselves or make ourselves part of a community, as a marker, to get us out of solitude as Octavio Paz asserts, in a failed experiment to approach the "modern" unattainable experience.

While we construct the symbol of the face mask as protection, it is also useful to understand the metaphors that surround the construction of COVID-19 as a global and local phenomenon. Old metaphors of illness can also represent new metaphors for new illnesses. For Susan Sontag, epidemic diseases have been conceived in history as a "common figure for social disorder" (Sontag 1979, 42). The reaction towards them is an examination of the moral character of a person, the occasion finally to behave well. In the case of COVID-19, both the sickness and the use of the mask were examinations of moral character that, in being politicized, depicted fear, solidarity, or a lack of trust. Sontag explains how in the use of the illness as a metaphor, individuals realize that "the disease is the evidence of the treachery of the body, the recognition of our organic nature, and a special way of demarcating 'dangerous' people and between nations, and a way to spread and construct fear" (1979, 37). The fear Sontag refers to is even more evident during a pandemic, allowing us to feel it as an uncertainty shared by the whole world. In her analysis of the outbreak narratives in popular culture and the use of zombies, Dahlia Schweitzer explains that the pandemic fear dwells in its effect on humans: "It is a specific kind of fear and anxiety created by events with no endpoint or temporal dimension" (Schweitzer 2018, 33) and for which there are six key thematic tropes that have shaped visual depictions of infectious diseases on and off screen: the idea of the necessary accident, the othering, the establishment of policing security where those others pose a threat, the process of unifying against them (the infected versus the non-infected), making the invisible visible, and fear of progress, with globalization as a form of progress (Schweitzer 2018, 40).

The approach to illness throughout history has been characterized by these metaphors that exist as guilt, punishment, or the ghost of the apocalypse and the end of society. Face masks, in this case, are the most immediate individual solution to an unknown global/public problem. Masks divide individuals, opposing the healthy and the sick, the doctor and the patient, the detractor, and the good citizen, and the infected suspects from those who suspect them. Suddenly, the exclusion and avoidance of a guilty or infected suspect has a physical and tangible barrier that divides and becomes part of regular life, highly interconnected. For Susan Sontag: "Illness is the night side of life, a more onerous citizenship. Everyone who is born holds dual citizenship, in the kingdom of the well and the kingdom of the sick. Although we all prefer to use only the good passport, sooner or later each of us is obliged, at least for a spell, to identify ourselves as citizens of that other place" (1979, 42).

In the case of the COVID-19 pandemic, this dual citizenship was shortly expressed by the measures of protectionism, the rhetoric game of using the virus as a "foreign virus" and even the "Chinese virus" as expressed by the US government at the beginning of the spread. A virus is always an invisible and unwanted foreigner, therefore, aligning a special characteristic or nationality (different from the personal), allowing one to achieve a basic idealization of protection.

While containment, the closure of national borders, and travel restrictions were the temporary state measures used to stop the spread of the COVID-19 virus, masks were and continued to be the main individual response and protection to a public and international problem until the official end of the pandemic. In the use of face masks, another increase in inequality between nations and income sources was demonstrated, causing poorer nations to look for creative ways of protection with homemade masks of diverse materials. Several videos on how to make face masks out of kitchen cloth, cotton, or even vacuum cleaner bags (with a filtering capacity of 95 percent) were consulted worldwide, but it was only a matter of time before the fashion industry and people would include special patterns and individualized functions to the PPE cloth (Rivera 2020).

Personalizing face masks humanized a situation in "which people can't see your face" (Trebay 2021), as Alexandra Lord, a historian of medicine and the chair of the Smithsonian Museum's Medicine and Science Division, explained. The capacity of a personalized face mask, not only in marking an item but also as a humanizing experience, became a playful opportunity for expression, a symbol of distinctiveness and culture, a material object of belonging, and a creative agent of significance.

Face masks during the COVID-19 pandemic were more than shields of virus defense: they became, like any other fashion objects, pieces of resistance, revelry, markers of status, gender-bending devices, and sources of income in a moment of uncertainty and scarcity. In the case of their production and use in Mexico, they were also instruments of oppression, demure, and control, as much as sources of liberation, as evidenced by the following case studies.

The first example I want to explore is how the lucha libre mask became a face mask with the outbreak of COVID-19. Mexican lucha libre or Mexican freestyle wrestling was declared by UNESCO as an "Intangible Cultural Heritage of Mexico City" for its special characteristics of flashy costumes, high-flying, fast maneuvers, and being a spectacular urban sport. Popularized in Mexico at the beginning of the twentieth century, the lively ambiance attracted the enthusiastic inhabitants of the city, particularly men belonging to economically depressed sectors of society. The use of masks was introduced in the 1930s but was massively popularized around the 1950s, with the use of cinema as a main source of promotion. The phrase *Máscara contra cabellera* (mask against hair) was commonly used in matches in which the wrestler who lost would be unmasked or his hair would be cut. lucha libre masks resembled the hypermasculine hero that covered his identity as the savior of humanity. The most famous masked wrestler, El Santo, fought against monsters, zombies, Aztec mummies, vampire women, and even aliens. His fame surpassed the confines of Mexico, becoming a global hero and symbol of justice, never unmasked until a final televised interview. Shockingly, he would die one week after his unmasking and his massive funeral would admire the body with the masked face.

The Mexican philosopher Carlos Monsiváis believed that lucha libre masks were the greatest "theatrical resource." For Monsiváis, the most important fact about these masks was that they created an intimidating and mocking reaction, allowing the spectator to imagine the faces behind the mask, their grimaces, and gestures throughout the fight (Ocampo 2012). The mask also hid the signs of fear or pain that the wrestlers might experience, allowing the audience to empathize, but also to ignore their human suffering.

With the onset of the COVID-19 pandemic, the traditional lucha libre shows were suspended, creating a need for wrestlers to stream live shows online, but also find other sources of income. One of the actions was to support the "wear a face mask" campaigns, providing masks purchased by themselves and forcing customers in plazas, markets, or schools to use them. Amid the COVID-19 pandemic, these displays were often streamed and made viral through TikTok, YouTube, and Facebook, and broadcast in international news such as *The Guardian*, Forbes, CNN en Español, and local news. In a video streamed by Telemundo in the US, Bandido, and Espectrito, two *luchadores* (lucha libre wrestlers) of Mexico City confronted the buyers and sellers who refused to wear the face mask at the Central de Abastos market. In the video, the wrestlers grabbed a young man who refused to wear a mask. Shouting expressions such as "¡Póntela! ¡póntela!" [Wear it! Wear it!], and "¿Qué, muy machito?" [What, you think you are so macho?] (Telemundo 2020), the wrestlers bought and gave away masks. As a public culture demonstration, this performance depicted the act of being masked in a carnivalesque way and masking others, and portrayed a truthful exercise of solidarity and commitment to public health.

By 2021, with the appearance of the COVID-19 vaccine, lucha libre wrestlers were hired by the government to support vaccination campaigns, for example, to entertain elderly people while they were waiting for the vaccine. To fight the unemployment caused by the cancellation of public shows, many wrestlers, like El Hijo del Soberano (Kahn 2020) decided to focus their efforts on producing cloth face masks that resembled their own and selling them to support their families, through the internet and expanding them as cultural products. The action of both producing the mask and engaging public space to improve public health comprises what Doris Sommer has called "conscientious cultural agency [which] requires the collaboration of various skill sets to hitch stale and unproductive social patterns to the motor of unconventional interventions" (Sommer 2014, 7). By engaging the audience in a public health action through their shows, masked wrestlers of lucha libre were performers, producers, and agents of change, wielding and brandishing a cultural artifact as a device of solidarity and protection. Turning citizens into luchadores against the pandemic, lucha libre wrestlers also questioned traditional Mexican masculinity by taking a job, traditionally done by women, to enforce care. The expressions referred to in the Telemundo video: "Wear it! Wear it!" and "What, you think you are so macho?" also produced in the receiver and passerby a gender transgression of the sexist culture of Mexico in which protection—even to a dangerous virus such as COVID-19—is an expression of weakness or femininity. By wearing face masks, producing face masks, and encouraging their use, lucha libre wrestlers were creating a much-needed culture of health, solidarity, and awareness.

The second case I would like to explore is the artisanal production of face masks in Indigenous communities. Indigenous textiles in Mexico have been long studied, as a part of the historical narrative and the cultural heritage of native peoples. The use of a mask for Indigenous peoples is a spiritual connection with ancestors and a product of historical heritage. Indigenous peoples, in particular Nahua, Mazahua, Purh'épecha, Otomí, and Maya K'iché, were also impacted in their production due to the COVID-19 pandemic. In the case of these communities, there was a change directed towards the market needs for repurposing products. Instead of producing shirts or dresses, they manufactured face masks massively which, although at a lower price, allowed them to recover some of the loss caused by the lack of tourism and the decline in the purchase of other products.

A particular case is the Zapatista mask or balaclava (knitted black mask), which became an expressive element, an item that not only offered symbolic information but also an ideological message. At the break of dawn of 1994, the first postmodern revolution of the twenty-first century emerged in Mexico by the Zapatista Army of National Liberation (EZLN). Its spokesperson, the self-named Subcomandante Marcos, wrote from the depths of the jungle the diverse Declaraciones de la Selva Lacandona, strongly influenced by the Indigenous thought of the Tzotzil, Tzeltal, Tojolabal, Chol, Mame, and Zoque communities. Regardless of the fight, a particular element drew the public's attention and the government's disdain: the black masks or balaclavas used to preserve the anonymity of the rebels also protected them from the dust, the wind, and the cold. The Zapatista masks soon became the most iconic and visible element of the movement. Their provocation of anonymity unveiled the struggles of a previously ignored population. It allowed us to read and see the faces of the peoples of Chiapas, their displacement, and their isolated lives, overseen by the Mexican State. It revealed, above all, a new text, that of social justice.

By 1994, in Chiapas, a change happened with the increase of "revolutionary tourism" in the region: the rise of NGOs that were established in the region, the interest of foreign press and international organizations, which supported the "Caracoles" or rebel enclaves by consuming products that inspired and support the revolutionary cause. Zapaturismo or Zapatourism was the name of this phenomenon, which soon changed to a commerce focusing on Zapatista merchandising, from coffee to literature, and of course, a change from the traditional dolls or "chamulitas" to figures of Subcomandante Marcos riding a horse (Hemispheric Institute 2018). Masks became a material historical testimony of conflict, and through their use allowed the rest of the population to identify with a cause, to create solidarity with face coverings.

With the start of the COVID-19 pandemic, a shift in the production of traditional toys, shirts, or dresses, led to the appearance of masks inspired by the masked Zapatista fighters in Chiapas. Although there is no clear figure for the income or profits of this industry, since most of the production has been in the informal market, many Facebook sites such as "El bordado de Ramona," and international stores online including Etsy and Redbubble have included the sale of Zapatista face masks, to support and sustain the Zapatista cause and communities. The users of these masks, in many cases with several layers of protection and filters such as the PM4, demonstrated an ideological statement that, through a political souvenir, supported the cause.

The political use of the face mask was also repurposed by the feminist struggle in Mexico. Feminist and anti-abortion protests had already spread across Latin America in the previous five years, with the expansion of the #MeToo movement and the mobilizations in South America. In Argentina and Chile, the use of a green or purple bandana, sometimes covering the mouth, was used also as a way of solidarity, expression of sorority, and as a protection of identity during demonstrations and political actions.

In Mexico, some of these trends were replicated, in abortion decriminalization protests, demonstrations against femicide, forced disappearances of women, and domestic violence. According to the International Amnesty report, "Mexico: La era de las mujeres. Estigma y violencia contra mujeres que protestan" (2020), face masks in demonstrations surpassed the use of pandemic protection, to be also a communication device. Slogans such as "Ni una menos" [Not one less], "Nos están matando" [They are killing us], "¿Dónde están?" [Where are they?] y "¡Somos el grito de las que no tienen voz!" [We are the outcry of those women without voice!] were also improvised in surgical face masks marked with sharpies or sometimes embroidered or printed. In the report, masked demonstration participants suffered a different source of violence after being detained by police officers in Mexico City without a warrant: they were forced to unmask, to show their faces; risking being infected and identified. The face mask, then, became a hyperbolic threatening symbol in many instances: it was not only threatening because of its message and because of who wore it, but because it reflected a denial of women's human rights.

Within the popular use of face masks as everyday fashion items, some of the most popular feminist figures in Mexican culture were also used in masks, spreading a message of Mexican liberation and representation. Embroidered or printed images of Frida Kahlo and Sor Juana Inés de la Cruz, or cartoon versions of them, decorated face masks that became popular among teenage girls and women in Mexico. More than a protection product or a souvenir device, these masks have become cultural objects that make it possible to inform—through a piece of clothing and a traditionally feminine activity such as embroidering—a call for justice. The purple bandana is still used in protests every March 8 (International Women's Day), even after the end of mask enforcement in Mexico. It has shown how a seemingly temporary device has become highly representative of this movement.

As communication devices, masks would also make an impact in the high-fashion industry, as luxury items or products of consumption. In an interview with Tere Pérez, former Brand Manager of El Palacio de Hierro, Etro, Slowear, and Pineda Covalín, among others, the Mexican fashion industry, like many other industries in the world, was not prepared for a pandemic. In Mexico, the use of face masks was restricted to surgical use, and its regular wear was not common. Soon, in the outbreak of the pandemic, Mexican high fashion brands tried to make statements, matching clothing and masks, but in many cases, not paying attention to or following the regulations about thread count or filters by the World Health Organization.

Masks as a "luxury" item or "niche" market were an opportunity for the reaffirmation of a "Mexican Brand." *Vogue México* dedicated space to a digital spread that included original designs, by Mexican producers, along with information of support for associations that produced face masks. *Harper's Bazaar* also wrote on masks and sustainability, showcasing sustainable workshops and non-traditional fashion brands. In this report, we can see the products of Carla Fernández, who does a meta-creation of face masks with prints of traditional masks; the brand Marfil, a factory located in Tijuana that manufactures face masks made out of spare fabric; and even Operación Calma, a project made by unemployed seamstresses from Ciudad Nezahualcóyotl in Mexico.

In this regard, the struggle of local artists and producers for survival attempted to compensate for the massive imports from China. High-end fashion masks were, of course, markers of income, of social class and status, but they also revealed community belonging and commitment with social causes, following the green label or a social-responsibility brand. Their designs, however, surpassed in most cases the prices of masks fabricated in an artisanal way, but their prints were usually inspired by Indigenous designs or Mexican traditions. This niche market is usually advertised through social media networks for international consumers or exclusive retailers. Their advertisements, aimed at restricted segments of the population, limited both the consumption and marketing of the brands, raising prices and creating pieces as art, rather than as utility.

The discussion of the impact of face mask production in Mexico has been insufficient because of the lack of information of a highly informal market, as well as a lack in representation of this type of business. More than 350,000 jobs in the textile sector were lost in 2020 and it was a similar number in 2021 (Garduño 2021). According to a report on Textiles Panamericanos, the states that lost the most jobs were Quintana Roo, Nuevo León, and Mexico City, making approximately 56 percent of the loss. The National Chamber of Textile Industry (CANAINTEX) declared that before the pandemic, the textile industry contributed 3.2 percent to the national GDP, and was 60 percent nurtured by national supplies. After the contraction of the market, in which fashion clothing diminished by 35 percent, the production of medical products, such as hospital bed sheets, medical gowns, and face masks, were a "breath of fresh air" that allowed the industry to survive, showing the importance of the local market and supplies (Davis 2020). The high demand of face masks was due to the greatest perception of risk, topping the surveys of face mask wearing countries. In a study conducted by the University of Maryland and Carnegie Mellon in collaboration with Facebook, it was found that 88.7 percent of Mexicans had opted for the use of face masks compared to only 64.5 percent, by February of 2022 (Núñez 2022). Besides the approved perception of the face mask, the COVID-19 pandemic showed the need for attention to the national market and supplies of the Mexican textile and fashion industry, which was made obvious by the shortage in supplies, unable to cover the national market during an emergency.

The scarcity of face masks at the beginning of the COVID-19 pandemic became a symbol of the fragility of medical systems throughout the world, but thanks to improvisation, creativity, and care, it was also a fertile space for other means of cultural expression, through a fashion-useful device. The end of the COVID-19 pandemic and the lift of the face mask mandate caused a substantial decrease in its demand. In 2024, according to the "Market Analysis Report" of Grand View Research, globally, the fashion face mask market was estimated at 465.4 million dollars in 2019 and is expected to grow by a percentage of 22.7 from 2020 to 2027 (2022). In Mexico, "repurposed uses" include the use of face masks as protection against pollution in big cities like Mexico City, Guadalajara, and Monterrey; its continuous use as a shield from respiratory illnesses such as flu (and Covid-19, as it is a latent menace); but also as a fashion item: as a souvenir or token for tourists, and, of course, as a way of protest and identity. According to news reports, for some, mask-wearing has become "a habit . . . an act of courtesy" (Peralta 2022), worn by people in service, waiters, drivers, and caretakers, but also as a solidarizing artifact that is an expression device. Wearing a face mask is not only a health-conscious act but it is also nurtured by sociological, psychological, political, and ideological motivations.

Masks in Mexico have been a performative instrument that allows the people behind them to be, not themselves, but the character they want to represent them. In this chapter, we have seen the pandemic as a metaphor for containment as proof of moral character, but also as an example of solidarity, resilience, expression, and resistance. We have scientific evidence of the efficiency of face masks in containing the spread, which should be reason enough to continue encouraging their use, even in the absence of a world pandemic. In addition, the expressive capacity of the masks can allow a creative catharsis that produces strength, as a symbol of unity. COVID-19 and the appearance of face masks as symbolic devices has opened a small opportunity for expression, which not only balances the socioeconomic loss but also creates a cultural change, through the empowering of disenfranchised groups through a tool that is used to cover the mouth and nose but speaks and breathes protest, identity, and fashion.

Notes

1. Italics mine.
2. Broadly described as the son of a Spaniard man and an Indigenous woman.
3. In his writing Octavio Paz talks about "the Mexican" using third person masculine pronouns, which is the standard in the Spanish language to refer to groups of people.
4. Italics mine.

Bibliography

Al Rojo Vivo. 2020. "Luchadores castigan a quienes no usen mascarilla en México." Telemundo. YouTube, September 11, 2020. www.youtube.com/watch?v=K8dEltaD4wQ

Amnistía Internacional. 2021. "México: La Era de las Mujeres." https://amnistia.org.mx/contenido/index.php/mexico-la-era-de-las-mujeres/

Ávila, Isabel. 2020. "Conoce a los diseñadores mexicanos que enamoran con estos versátiles cubrebocas." *Vogue México*, July 9, 2020. www.vogue.mx/moda/articulo/cubrebocas-con-diseno-de disenadores-mexicanos

Barnard, Malcolm. 2013. *Fashion as Communication*. London: Routledge.

Cantera, Sara. 2020. "Manos mexicanas dan color a cubrebocas." *El Universal*, September 6, 2020. www.eluniversal.com.mx/cartera/manos-mexicanas-dan-color-a-cubrebocas.

Davis, Rachael. 2020. "El papel de Canaintex durante la pandemia." *Textiles Panamericanos*, October 12, 2020. https://textilespanamericanos.com/textiles-panamericanos/2020/10/el-papel-de-canaintex-durante-la-pandemia/

El bordado de Ramona Facebook Page. 2020. "Zapatista Face mask." August 16, 2020. www.facebook.com/El-Bordado-De-Ramona-1427071247591253/photos

Equipos de Lucha en la Laguna Facebook Page. 2020. "Face masks." March 28, 2020. www.facebook.com/photo/?fbid=1607266826095602&set=pb.100004368997154.-2207520000

Friedman, Vanessa. 2020. "The Mask." *The New York Times*, March 17, 2020. www.nytimes.com/2020/03/17/style/face-maskcoronavirus.html?searchResultPosition=1

Garcia, Lorenza and Ana Soberón. 2020. "Protégete ayudando: cubrebocas hechos en México." *Harper's Bazaar*, June 11, 2020. www.harpersbazaar.mx/moda/protegete-ayudando-cubrebocas-hechos-en-mexico/

Garduño, Mónica. 2021. "Industria textil pide al gobierno combatir ilegalidad y costos de energía competitivos." *Forbes México*, March 24, 2021. www.forbes.com.mx/negocios-industria-textil-gobierno-combatir-ilegalidad-

Grand View Research. 2022 "Fashion Face Mask Market Size, Share & Trends Analysis Report By Product (Anti-pollution, Non Anti-pollution), By Distribution Channel (Offline, Online), By Region, And Segment Forecasts, 2020–2027." *Grand View Research Fashion Face Mask Market,* January 16, 2022. www.grandviewresearch.com/industry-analysis/fashion-face-mask-market

Hemispheric Institute. 2018. "Critical Introduction on Zapaturismo." *Hemispheric Institute*, April 9, 2018. https://hemisphericinstitute.org/es/su10-tourism/item/878-su10-critical-intro-zapaturismo.html

Kahn, Carrie. 2020. "A Mexican '*lucha libre*' Wrestler Is Sewing Masks to Fight Coronavirus." NPR, April 30, 2020. www.npr.org/sections/coronavirus-live-updates/2020/04/30/848215046/a-mexican-lucha-libre-wrestler-is-sewing-masks-to-fight-coronavirus

Lucas, Dave. 2021. "Mexico's *lucha libre* Wrestlers Fight against COVID." *Reuters*, March 12, 2021. www.reuters.com/news/picture/mexicos-lucha-libre-wrestlers-fight-again-idUSRTXACI26

Lurie, Alison. 1981. *The Language of Clothes*. New York: Random House.

Lusty, Natalya. 2021. "Fashion Futures and Critical Fashion Studies." *Journal of Media & Cultural Studies*. Taylor and Francis Online, March 12, 2021. www.tandfonline.com/doi/full/10.1080/10304312.2021.1993568

Núñez, Alfonso. 2022. "Mexico Tops North America in Use of Face Masks." *Mexico Business News*, February 22, 2022. https://mexicobusiness.news/health/news/mexico-tops-north-america-use-face-masks

Ocampo, Ernesto. "Carlos Monsiváis y la lucha libre, a dos años de su partida." Superluchas, June 19, 2012. https://superluchas.com/carlos-monsivais-y-la-lucha-libre-a-dos-anos-de-su-partida/

Paz, Octavio. 1985. *The Labyrinth of Solitude*. Translated by Lysander Kemp, Yara Milos, and Rachel Phillips Belash. New York: Grove Press.

Peralta, Eyder. 2022. "How Masks Became a Habit in Mexico City." *Morning Edition NPR,* November 24, 2022. www.npr.org/2022/11/24/1139147082/how-masks-became-a-habit-in-mexico-city

Pérez-Bustamante, Anasofía. 1990. "Saga y fugas de un símbolo: la máscara." *Actas del IV Seminario del Carnaval*, Cádiz, Ayuntamiento, pp. 113–121.

Rivera, Selene. 2020. "Descubren las mejores y las peores telas para hacer el cubrebocas en el hogar." *Los Angeles Times*, April 22, 2020. www.latimes.com/espanol/california/articulo/202-04-22/las-mejores-y-las-peores-telas-para-hacer-el-cubrebocas

Schweitzer, Dahlia. 2018. *Going Viral: Zombies, Viruses, and the End of the World*. New Brunswick: Rutgers University Press.

Sommer, Doris. 2014. *The Work of Art in the World: Civic Agency and Public Humanities*. Durham and London, Duke University Press.

Sontag, Susan. 1979. *Illness as Metaphor*. London: Allen Lane.

Trebay, Guy. 2021. "The Hidden Language of Masks." *The New York Times*. May 15, 2021. www.nytimes.com/2020/05/15/style/the-hidden-language-of-masks-smithsonian.html?smid=url-share.

Usigli, Rodolfo. 2007. "Las máscaras de la hipocresía" In *Anatomía del mexicano*. ed. Roger Bartra. México, D.F.: Debolsillo, pp. 131–145.

16

Transnational Experiences in Fashion: The Work of Equihua, Barragán, and Ricardo Seco

Tanya Meléndez-Escalante

In 2018, Los Angeles-based designer Brenda Equihua mused about the relevance of her Mexican background in her work as a fashion designer in a feature in *Vogue*, "I came to a place in my life where I realized how powerful, how unique and beautiful the world I came from was" (Kim 2018). She alluded to the inexplicable feeling of belonging in two countries, which involves a perennial state of transition. Having a dual origin can be disorienting, perhaps even isolating, but it is also very enriching. For many designers, their work is intrinsically intertwined with their identity and for those who are binational, they have a double source of inspiration in their experiences. For instance, Council of Fashion Designers of America finalist Víctor Barragán asserted in 2020, "Being able to learn how to navigate culture clashes sparks creation" (Browchuk 2020); while fashion creator Ricardo Seco, succinctly described the ethos of his work as a "touch of Mexico in New York style" (Lim 2014). These designers favor complex narratives in their streetwear brands, incorporating transnational lived experiences to fashion.

Based in the United States and of Mexican heritage, Equihua, Barragán, and Ricardo Seco engage with issues of blended ethnicities and the porosity of borders in gender, culture, and politics. Their binational experiences and heritage are essential to their practice: cultural hybridity is central in their collections. In their work, the power and weight of the immigrant experience is palpable. It is layered, intense, and runs deep. The joy and suffering of a transnational identity feed their creativity. These Mexican American designers are players in the fashion system in the United States. Rather than assimilating to the narratives of dominant culture through their commercial and marketing activities, they propose that Chicano aesthetics and immigrant experiences can be aspirational.

In this process, they diversify the fashion system in the United States, creating spaces where dual identities are made explicit and are incorporated into fashion.

Tomás Ybarra-Frausto's seminal text *Rasquachismo: A Chicano Sensibility* proposes a framework within which to consider an aesthetic particular to Mexican Americans. The Spanish word *rascuache* is a colloquial term that indicates low value or low quality.[1] Ybarra-Frausto (1989) describes *rasquachismo* as the sensibility of the downtrodden, which "mirrored the social reality of the majority of Chicanos who were poor, disenfranchised and mired in elemental daily struggles for survival." Linking this sensibility with class, the point of view of those in a disadvantaged financial position reshuffles and gives new meanings to vernacular art forms in visual terms. Ybarra-Frausto explains, "Signs and symbols which those in power manipulated to signal unworthiness and deficiencies [are] mobilized and turned about as markers of pride and affirmation" (Ybarra-Frausto 1989). In other words, *rasquachismo* celebrates what dominant culture might consider bad taste, and because of its association with financial distress, it also values the full use of resources, deriving in zero-waste practices. Therefore, when analyzing Mexican Americans' work in fashion, *rasquachismo* facilitates our understanding of the aesthetics that radiate from their binational life experiences.

Building on the work of Ybarra-Frausto, Stacy I. Macías uses *rasquachismo* to engage with fashion. In a text grounded in personal experiences and observations from popular culture, Macías describes how Latina women create their own styles and adorn themselves with tastes that stand apart from the fashion system and its trends. She explains: "Chicana/Latina self-styling and fashion practices [...] resist normative white femininity and disembodied subjectivity" (Macías 2020, 262). She argues that Chicanas utilize *rasquache* aesthetics in fashion to generate their own fashion trends which are racially charged and distinct from styles that emerge from milieus of privilege. Macías's thesis is compelling in that it locates Mexican American styles as self-generating and linked to personal experience. It also demonstrates how Ybarra-Frausto's essay can be useful when discussing fashion, even if she did not address the work of fashion designers who are operating within the fashion system in the United States.

In this chapter, I will rely on *rasquachismo* as a framework to discuss the work of Equihua, Barragán, and Ricardo Seco. Macías's analysis of how Latinx styles are informed by race and ethnicity and deviate from dominant culture shed light on the designers' work in fashion. I will also refer to the history of queer activism and studies of disidentification in queer performativity. These ideas will be useful tools to situate the designers' binational and marginal identities within society in the United States and to describe how they resist assimilation to mainstream fashion, while operating within the American fashion system.

In 2017, after working in the fashion industry for over a decade in brands such as Monique Lhuillier, Tadashi Shoji, Juan Carlos Obando (James 2021), Brenda Equihua found herself at a crossroads regarding her own brand. The designer wanted to unlearn what she had learned in fashion school and in the fashion industry. When attending a prominent fashion school, she felt that references were all "white. They were based on an industry that hadn't been inclusive [...] You're not supposed to bring about change. People would say 'everything in fashion has been done,' I can't tell you how many times I've heard that. Even by supposed visionaries. I don't subscribe to that. Everything has been done if you operate from [just] one angle."

And thus, she started brainstorming in places she had not gone before: her personal history and Mexican heritage. She made lists of classics in fashion and a separate list of items that were meaningful to her growing up. Initially both lists were unrelated, but one day, during a family outing she saw the connection. Equihua thought of the *colchas San Marcos*, puffy blankets originally produced in Aguascalientes, Mexico and that can be found in a large number of Mexican American homes. Those intimate objects, meant to be used in the most private of contexts, were the perfect material for what would become her collection of "New Classics" (Brenda Equihua, interview with the author, June 23, 2021).

A notable design is a bomber jacket featuring a tiger, the most well-known pattern of the San Marcos blankets. She titled it "The Tigers of the North." The name of the jacket is a humorous nod to the emblematic Mexican band Los Tigres del Norte who are known for lyrics that narrate stories of Mexican immigrants to the United States. It is a bomber jacket, an American classic of military origin, a derivation of the Ike jacket. According to the National Museum of American History, "General Dwight Eisenhower wanted a style which could be worn by itself or over a shirt. [...], Eisenhower wanted the jacket to be 'very short, very comfortable, and very natty looking.' The 'Ike jacket' became standard issue for U.S. troops beginning in November 1944" (National Museum of American History, n.d.). The Tigers of the North jacket expressed the designer's dual identity. It juxtaposed fashion's and Latinxs' aesthetic by mixing the bomber jacket with an iconic object in Mexican American culture.

Another design that brings together a well-known garment with an iconic symbol of Chicano identity is Equihua's Devotion coat, also designed in 2018. It is an ankle-length, straight coat, with a zipper closure and a hood, a mix of a coat and a hoodie: "The hoodie to me—explains Equihua,—is one of the most

Figure 16.1 Brenda Equihua, Tigers of the North Cobija jacket, 2018. Photographer and Stylist: Keyla Marquez. Model: Rhyan Anthony Santos. Courtesy of Brenda Equihua.

democratic of garments, it exists in all social classes." The back of the coat is emblazoned with the likeness of the Virgin of Guadalupe. This piece of outerwear is an exploration of the cultural impact of Catholicism and its iconography in the Latino community. According to the Catholic Church, the Virgin of Guadalupe appeared to San Juan Diego (the first Indigenous man to be canonized) in 1531 in the outskirts of Mexico City. Called the "Virgen Morena," her story was a potent tool in evangelization and in later the construction of national unity of what would become Mexico. As early as the eighteenth century, the images of the Virgin of Guadalupe were a popular memento for Europeans who had spent time in

New Spain, a symbol of a remote part of the world (Alcalá et al. 2017, 40). During the war of Independence, a banner of the Virgin of Guadalupe became the emblem of independentists. Later that century, in 1845, she became "the official patron of all Latin America" and has been called "the Lady of national history, the mother of a Mexico mestizo, and the Queen of Mexico" (Napolitano 2009).

Brenda Equihua selected the Virgin of Guadalupe as a motif because of the deeply intimate religious, maternal, and nostalgic connections that she has with the symbol, as many people do. The designer muses that some probably "connect it to Los Angeles because she is everywhere. Even if you are not religious" (Brenda Equihua, interview with the author, June 23, 2021). The designer also noted that she considers the Virgin of Guadalupe in color very Mexican, while on black and white it reads Chicano. Perhaps as when tattooed on someone's body.

This garment has resonated with many, including the popular reggaeton Puerto Rican performer Bad Bunny, who wore it in Paris Lollapalooza in 2019 and in the video "Cuidado por Ahí." Brenda Equihua explained that many clients have reported that items from the "New Classics" are their first luxury purchase. In 2021, the artist rafa esparza painted a portrait of poet and activist Yosimar Reyes and his grandmother, who wears her grandson's Equihua "Pray for 'Em" jacket. Reyes describes the look of the jacket as "fancy." He explains, "Poor people do not like to look poor, honey; we like to show out. I think that's become the symbolism of these very decadent *cobijas*.[2] We like the flashy as a symbol of our aspirations" (James 2021). In this instance, the wearer appreciates the significance of fashion and establishes a connection with class. He alludes to what Tomás Ybarra-Frausto describes as *rasquachismo's* "bicultural sensibility among Mexican Americans. On both sides of the border, it retains an "underclass perspective" (Ybarra-Frausto 1989). Esparza's artwork, painted onto mudbrick, which Indigenous peoples in the Americas use for building, is in consonance with Equihua's point of view. As the press release for his exhibition at Commonwealth and Council explains, "In placing these Brown and Black individuals on surfaces derived from California dirt, esparza underscores their fraught relationship to the land—stolen from its original occupants; where many labor in exploitative situations and are denied shelter and support" (Commonwealth and Council 2021). Brenda Equihua, as a designer, aims to incorporate the lived experience of migrants to the United States fashion industry through the materials and symbols that make up the garments.

Another designer whose work explores the crossing of borders in fashion is Víctor Barragán. When fashion and pop culture icon Kim Kardashian visited the Vatican during the summer of 2021, she wore a dress by Barragán. A daring choice by a professional of reality television, the dress is body conscious, has cutouts that reveal skin in various parts of the body, and importantly, was designed to reference the "Mexican Inquisition and the persecution of brujas and brujos, witchcraft practitioners whose beliefs were deemed heretical by the Catholic Church. 'The collection is about sexuality as power and protection from widespread patriarchal domination as used in brujería in the sixteenth century, which may still resonate today,' said the designer" (Okwodu 2021). The dress was provocative and political, two words that define Barragán.

Víctor Barragán is one of the most successful Mexican fashion designers in the United States currently. While living in Mexico, the designer dropped out of industrial design to devote his attention to fashion. However, his first work found limited success in his country and in 2015, Barragán moved to New York where his urban aesthetic was quickly appreciated. Barragán designs for a marginal and hedonistic nightlife, transgressing gender boundaries, disregarding institutions, and favoring subcultural references.

Per the designer's interview with the blog *Something Curated*, the spirit of the brand is "a space of constant experimentation, creating and collaborating with diverse artists" (Something Curated 2018). The Instagram accounts of the designer and brand are instrumental in communicating his aesthetic. From these social media posts, it could be argued that Barragán's collections are about himself and about his own sexuality. He explained to Mexican magazine *Gatopardo* that his clothes are "sex positive, seeing sex as something good. You don't have to be naked or showing a lot of skin to be sexually attractive" (Mereles Gras 2019, 64). In his brand, there are no borders, identity is redefined, and old binaries like male and female or Mexican and American are irrelevant. José Esteban Muñoz studied the performance of politics in queer people of color. He proposed disidentification as a prevalent strategy in the creative production emanating from members of this intersectional community. Muñoz explains that in their hybrid representations, "Identity markers such as *queer* (from the German *quer* meaning "transverse") or *mestizo* (Spanish for "mixed") are terms that defy notions of uniform identity or origins. *Hybrid* catches the fragmentary subject formation of people whose identities traverse different race, sexuality, and gender identifications" (Muñoz 2019, 31–32).

A review of Barragán's Spring/Summer 2018 collection noted, "His Instagram feeds (both his personal and work accounts) are filled with trade, and jacked dudes with cheesy tattoos who you just might see in porn. Much of his SS18 Barragán show felt like a tribute to them" (Office Magazine 2017). The designer celebrates representations of gay culture. He regularly incorporates nods to the sexualized male body *for* the male gaze. For Barragán, "fashion is a site of gay cultural construction," borrowing the language of Valerie Steele who co-curated with Fred Dennis the exhibition "A Queer History of Fashion" (Steele 2019).

The brand's clothes have been described as "basics in irregular variations. Barragán creates new silhouettes out of old ones" (Sijbers 2021). These staples, however, hypersexualize the human figure in an unsettling androgyny. His designs intentionally highlight sexual organs, including penises, vaginas, and breasts. These garments sometimes uncover body parts, through cut outs or transparencies, or highlight them using bold patterns, designs or colors. Through vulgarity, the designer seeks to separate himself from mainstream society (both in Mexico and in the United States), proudly pronouncing himself an outcast. He opposes good taste, and again, *rasquachismo* comes to mind. As Tomás Ybarra-Frausto explained, this aesthetic has "connotations of vulgarity and bad taste, a sense of being *cursi*. [Ybarra-Frausto's italics]" (Ybarra-Frausto 1989). Barragán sees value in an alternative aesthetic that borrows symbols from drug paraphernalia, graffiti, and pornography.

A fashion presentation for Barragán's Fall/Winter 2018 collection was titled "Home Decor," and it included a series of performances by male and female models pretending to be enjoying an evening out, including dancing, romantic encounters, and drug use. Víctor Barragán is interested in performativity and fashion shows have been opportunities for him to disidentify with patriarchal heteronormative society through humor and vulgarity. In his performances, fashion as an embodied practice serves as a strategy of resistance to ever-shifting narratives about power: "instead of buckling under the pressures of dominant ideology (identification, assimilation) or attempting to break free of its inescapable sphere (counter identification, Utopianism), this working 'on and against' is a strategy that tries to transform a cultural logic from within, always laboring to enact permanent structural change while at the same time valuing the importance of local everyday struggles of resistance" (Muñoz 1999, 11–12).

For his Fall 2021 collection, Barragán presented various versions of footwear inspired by clown shoes. He explained to *Vogue* that the brand proposed, "A decontextualized version of what being a 'clown' means [. . .] We shouldn't take ourselves seriously and fashion should be about having fun with a positive message" (Satestein 2021). Fun as it may be, the clown is an ambiguous character. These gender-neutral entertainers are contradictory in nature as the identity of the person remains anonymous and yet they seek attention. In Mexican social media, the clown is used to mock naiveté in romantic relationships and conveys sexual and amorous humiliation. Thus, the Barragán shoe might be fun but it's also an unsettling image of sexual gratification through ambiguity and humiliation.

During the fashion show of Barragán's Fall 2021 collection titled *Humildad* (Humility), models and the designer himself wore contact lenses of pastel colors, but also of the flags of the United States and Mexico. Barragán was literally seeing the world from the vantage points of the United States and Mexico. In 2017, he explained to Fashionista, "I like to reference the streets in Mexico City or here in New York" (Bauck, 2017). Those two cities also play a concrete role in his production process: all the fabrics are sourced in New York City, while the garments are produced in his hometown of Mexico City: "I really like to show my own culture, too. I'm tattooed; these flame graphics that we used on the last collection are really popular [in Mexico]. I tried to show them in a different way on the garments" (Bauk n.d.). The designer pledges alliance with both countries, through his manufacturing processes and through the ideas expressed in his collections. He remains connected with both New York City and Mexico City. This is in tandem with what José Esteban Muñoz describes as the migrant status, which "can be characterized by its need to move back and forth, to occupy at least two spaces at once" (Muñoz 1999, 32).

For Barragán, fashion is a place of experimentation that can be slippery and ambiguous: "Disidentification is a step further than cracking open the code of the majority; it proceeds to use this code as raw material for representing a disempowered politics or positionality that has been rendered unthinkable by the dominant culture" (Muñoz 1999, 31). The brand problematizes how the binational experience of identity can be fractured and split. The designer's work sheds light on the contradictions of belonging in two worlds but only partially and uncomfortably. Discomfort is central to Barragán, full of discovery, wonder, and growth.

The designer Ricardo Seco had been a golden boy of Mexican fashion when in 2011 he decided to try his luck in New York City. Once relocated, a few Mexican nationals working in fashion warned him to "not let people know that I was from Mexico. I was shocked and disheartened. I've always been proud of where I come from. I realized that after a successful career in Mexico, I was going to have to start from scratch here" (Ricardo Seco, interview with the author, January 26, 2021). Over the years, Seco has met allies in New York who appreciate his point of view; but staying true to the vision of celebrating his heritage took resilience and perhaps a dose of stubbornness. In fashion in 2021 there is a renewed interest in voices from outside dominant culture, but when Seco was new to New York, the environment was very different. The designer understood the trials and tribulations of immigrants through his own experiences, but also through those of the many people he met in his new city. Seco decided to be a designer who brings visibility to immigrant issues. Only four years after his arrival, Ricardo Seco was firmly positioned in the United States fashion system and was one of the designers invited to the inaugural Menswear New York Fashion Week.

Seco creates garments that function as moving billboards that point at current events as they unfold. Oftentimes, he dissects the complicated political dance between Mexico and the United States. In 2016, after Donald Trump had launched his presidential bid by disparaging Mexicans, Seco presented his collection which featured black and white looks accompanied by garments that celebrated sarapes, the colorful and iconic Mexican shawl. But he also included a t-shirt featuring Donald Trump and the caption "I'm Mexico. Who is Trump?" In a contentious time, Seco affirmed his alliance with other Mexicans who suffered increased discrimination during the Trump presidency (Canizales and Agius Vallejo 2021).

Months later, as Seco prepared the collection "Together," in which he addressed binational relations between Mexico and the United States, he remembers being told, "Don't do it, you're going to get deported" and "You're turning into an activist, a designer wouldn't do that" (Reina 2017). Instead of backing out, Seco presented a series of looks where he intermingled the Mexican and American flags and multiple garments with embroidered phrases in the vein of "Together we can bring down in-visible walls." His use of flags was reminiscent of garments sold in inexpensive markets in Mexican border towns such as Tijuana and Ciudad Juárez. Seco's *rasquachismo* confronts hegemonic attitudes by incorporating binational symbols of the person who migrates seeking a better life, and by celebrating their struggle. In this instance, the flags are an affirmation of national origin that directly confronts anti-immigrant racism and classism, where the immigrant poor are portrayed as disorderly, due to their lack of wealth, but also because they grew up in the wrong milieu, didn't have a proper upbringing, and thus lack good taste. Through his press and marketing activities, Seco counters these assumptions and presents the aesthetic from the border as fashionable, making the immigrant experience visible.

For pride month in 2020, Seco designed a T-shirt with the pride flag that simply read "Latinx." A particularly contentious term, *Latinx* is a gender-neutral term for *Latino*. The use of the letter "X," which is derived from the English language, is controversial to many who consider it a concession to mainstream

Figure 16.2 Ricardo Seco, Juntos/Together jacket, FW 2017. Photographer: Enrique Figueroa. Courtesy of Ricardo Seco.

America. Just as when addressing immigrant experience in his collections, Seco did not shy away from the controversy surrounding the word. For Seco, the gender neutrality of the term is particularly important, as he is openly gay.

His use of T-shirt as vehicles of political discourse is heir to twentieth-century queer activism. Scholar Jonathan D. Katz traces the history of queer political t-shirts from the 1970s, when lesbians wore t-shirts that read "Lavender Menace" during the NOW Congress to Unite Women, through 1987 when activists wore black t-shirts with the slogan "Queer and Present Danger" to the steps of the

Supreme Court in protest of the *Bowers v. Hardwick* decision that ratified the illegality of homosexuality, to the 1990s when ACT UP popularized t-shirts with slogans that served as activism and fundraising for the organization (Katz 2013, 225). Seco's use of these inexpensive garments that can be printed to express alliance to particular political and cultural ideas is not dissimilar to these predecessors. Katz explained, "the rise of sloganeering in activist fashion can be tied to two key developments, the beginning of mainstream media coverage of queer protests, and the development of a truly collective queer politics" (Katz 2013, 222). In turn, Seco uses social media to communicate his ideas. His coats and t-shirts with political slogans are disseminated by the designer and his followers and clients, advancing his political messaging.

In an intersectional impulse, Seco juxtaposes the pride flag with the term "Latinx," highlighting two marginal communities. Words such as *Mexican American, Chicano, Hispanic, Latino, Latinx* categorize groups of people as an alternative to the term "Hispanic Origin" used in the United States census.[3] Related to these terms is Latinidad, a feeling of belonging in the Latino group, which according to author Patricia L. Price, is "a scale-shifting identification of the individual and his or her immediate zone of inhabitance—a block, a neighborhood, a street—to nations and world regions that are hemispheric in scale," with shifting alliances based on heritage, life experiences, and politics (Price 2007). Hence, Seco's "Latinx" t-shirt is an affirmation of his double alliance. As in previous examples of queer political t-shirts, it is predicated on the development of a new historical identity, one that embraced the forthright declaration of visible difference as a strategic political advantage" (Katz 2013, 222). The designer is proud of his Latinidad and of his status as a gay man in America. From these examples, it can be concluded that Ricardo Seco's work in the United States has been strongly committed to providing visibility to marginalized communities. He has relied on the use of slogans to express ideas related to gender, ethnicity, and politics. He sees his role in fashion as a form of advocacy and his collections as political action.

To conclude, in fashion, boundaries can be dynamic and porous. This discipline strips and reshuffles the cultural significance and meaning of dress and distills aesthetic properties that can be turned into trends. The three designers discussed in this chapter embrace their Latinidad and turn it into cool, wearable clothes. They establish their voices in the US fashion system by drawing on their personal experiences. Brenda Equihua celebrates the richness of growing up Chicana in the United States. Her signature design, outerwear inspired by

Mexican San Marcos blankets, is a nod to family and heritage. With humor and intimacy, Equihua juxtaposes objects and symbols imbued with memories and nostalgia for the Mexico of times past. Víctor Barragán problematizes the shifting borders of identity, proposing fashion as a place to negotiate sexual and national binaries. The designer actively creates paths within the fashion system for dissenting voices. His practice is a form of resistance from within the hegemonic structures. Ricardo Seco expresses his political ideas by integrating fashion and advocacy through slogans, emphasizing layered identities. He gives intersectionality a central stage in his collections. Over the course of his career in the United States, he has relentlessly remained a steadfast vocal ally for immigrants, clearly expressing points of view of the political landscape in the United States.

The work of Equihua, Barragán, and Ricardo Seco is exemplary of the fashion emerging from Mexican American culture. The designers are devoted to their craft and are active members of the fashion industry in this country. As Brenda Equihua expressed, there are many stories yet to be told in fashion. Víctor Barragán argues that diversity sparks creativity. Seco proposes that immigrant voices should be heard. Their work is representative of the Latinx experience, but it is also fashion that is sought out by consumers and has been validated by the system at large. They are able to retain their voice, claim their heritage and participate in the fashion industry. Through their urban streetwear, they propose an aesthetic of *rasquachismo*, where the Mexican American appreciation for making do and a certain degree of kitsch, are a slap in the face to prim-and-proper high fashion. Their work is a form of resistance against erasure from mainstream culture and inequity.

Notes

1 "Rascuache 1. adj. coloq. El Salv., Hond. y Méx. Dicho de una persona o de una cosa: De mala calidad o de poco valor." Real Academia de la Lengua website, https://dle.rae.es/rascuache viewed on July 6, 2021.
2 *Cobija* is the Spanish word for blanket.
3 According to the United States Census Bureau, "Hispanic origin can be viewed as the heritage, nationality, lineage, or country of birth of the person or the person's parents or ancestors before arriving in the United States. People who identify as Hispanic, Latino, or Spanish may be any race." United States Census Bureau website, www.census.gov/topics/population/hispanic-origin.html viewed on June 26, 2021.

Bibliography

Alcalá, Luis Elena. Jaime Cuadriello, Ilona Katzew, and Paula Mues Orts. 2017. "Printed in Mexico, 1700–1790: *Pinxit Mexici.*" *Painted in Mexico, 1700-1790: Pinxit Mexici*, ed. by Ilona Katzew. Los Angeles, Mexico City, Munich: LACMA, Fomento Cultural Banamex, Del Monico Books.

Bauk, Whitney. (2016) "Up-And-Coming Label Barragán is the Antidote to your Boringly Pretty Feed." *Fashionista*. October 16, 2017. https://fashionista.com/2017/09/barragan-fashion-label

Bauk, Whitney. n.d. 2021 "Up-and-coming Label Barragán Is the Antidote to Your Boringly Pretty Insta Feed." Fashionista.com. https://fashionista.com/2017/09/barragan-fashion-label

Browchuk, Eliseé. 2020. "Barragán: Spring 2021 Ready-to-Wear." *Vogue Runway*. www.vogue.com/fashion-shows/spring-2021-ready-to-wear/barragan

Canizales, Stephanie L. and Jody Agius Vallejo. 2021. "Latinos & Racism in the Trump Era." *Dædalus*. www.amacad.org/sites/default/files/publication/downloads/Daedalus_Sp21_10_Canizales-%26-Vallejo.pdf

Commonwealth and Council. 2021. "Press Release of Exhibition. 'keeping.'" https://commonwealthandcouncil.com/exhibitions/keeping/press

Katz, Jonathan D. 2013. "Queer Activist Fashion." *A Queer History of Fashion*. New Haven/London: Yale University Press.

James, Julissa. 2021. "The L.A. Designer Who Remade the Cobija into Luxury Fashion." in *LA Times*.com. www.latimes.com/lifestyle/image/story/2021-05-26/brenda-equihua-turned-cobija-into-luxury-jackets-for-lil-nas-x-young-thug

Kim, Monica. 2018. "These Graphic Blanket Coats, Made From San Marcos *Cobijas*, Celebrate Latino Culture." *Vogue*.com. www.vogue.com/article/equihua-san-marcos-cobijas-blanket-coats

Lim, Michelle. 2014. "Ricardo Seco, Spring/Summer 2015." *Washington Square News*. https://nyunews.com/2014/09/10/ricardo-seco-springsummer-2015/

Macías, Stacy I. 2020. "(Ad) Dressing Chicana/Latina Femininities: Consumption, Labor, and the Cultural Politics of Style in Latina Fashion." In *MeXicana Fashions: Politics, Self-Adornment, and Identity Construction*, edited by Aída Hurtado and Norma E. Cantú. Austin: Texas University Press.

Mereles Gras, Louise. 2019. "Un mexicano en Nueva York: Un perfil de Víctor Barragán." *Revista Gatopardo, Especial de Moda*.

Muñoz, José Esteban. 2019. *Disidentifications: Queers of Color and the Performance of Politics*. Minneapolis/London: University of Minnesota Press.

Napolitano, Valentina. 2009. "The Virgin of Guadalupe: A Nexus of Affect." In *The Journal of the Royal Anthropological Institute* 15 (1): 99.

National Museum of American History. 2021. "Eisenhower Jacket." Eisenhower Jacket. https://americanhistory.si.edu/collections/search/object/nmah_1218893

Office Magazine. 2017. "Barragán Spring/Summer 2018." September 14, 2017. http://officemagazine.net/barragán-springsummer-2018

Okwodu, Janelle. 2021. "Kim Kardashian's Vatican Dress Sends a Message." *Vogue*.com. www.vogue.com/article/kim-kardashian-vatican-visit-barragan-dress

Price, Patricia L. 2007. "Cohering Culture on Calle Ocho: The Pause and Flow of Latinidad." *Globalizations*. Vol. 4, Num 1. DOI: 10.1080=14747730701245632

Reina, Elizabeth. 2017. "Designer's "Mexican pride" Wear Popularizes Anti-Trump Fashion." *El Pais*. https://english.elpais.com/elpais/2017/04/05/inenglish/1491402094_785915.html

Satestein, Liana. 2021. "Lourdes Leon Stars in Barragán's Erotic-Thriller Lookbook." www.vogue.com/article/barragan-lookbook-lourdes-leon-mayan-toledano-ally-bo

Sijbers, Nicole. 2021. "Víctor Barragán – Blurry Line Between Fashion and Art." *Metal Magazine*. https://metalmagazine.eu/en/post/interview/victor-barragan-blurry-line-between-fashion-and-art

Something Curated. 2018. "Interview: In The Studio with Víctor Barragán." https://somethingcurated.com/2018/07/16/interview-studio-victor-barragan/

Steele, Valerie. "A Queer History of Fashion." June 25, 2019. The Museum at FIT Fashion Culture Podcast. 23 min. https://podcasts.apple.com/us/podcast/the-museum-at-fit-fashion-culture-podcast/id1434306168

Ybarra-Frausto, Tomás. 1989. "Rasquachismo: a Chicano Sensibility." In *Chicano Aesthetics: Rasquachismo*. 5–8. Exh. cat. Phoenix: MARS, Movimiento Artístico del Rio Salado. https://icaa.mfah.org/s/en/item/845510#?c=&m=&s=&cv=3&xywh=-1992%2C364%2C5459%2C3055

Interviews

Brenda Equihua. Interview conducted by Tanya Meléndez-Escalante. June 23, 2021.
Ricardo Seco. Interview conducted by Tanya Meléndez-Escalante. January 26, 2021.

Research Note

This chapter uses interviews conducted via Zoom by the author with designers Brenda Equihua and Ricardo Seco. They provided authorization to be quoted in this text only. The recordings of the interviews are not available for other researchers.

17

The National Movement of Maya Weavers and Neocolonialism in Fashion Intellectual Property

Kedron Thomas

> Our weavings are the books the colonizers could not burn. *(Nuestros tejidos son los libros que la colonia no pudo quemar.)*
> —Asociación Femenina para el Desarrollo de Sacatepéquez

Handwoven textiles are integral to the lives of many Indigenous Maya people in Guatemala. Produced on backstrap looms, a technology that predates the Spanish invasion of Maya territories, the intricately designed *-pot* (blouses, or *huipiles* in Spanish) that many Maya women wear are potent cultural symbols of ethnicity, place, and belonging.[1] The figures, color combinations, and weaving techniques used to create garments and accessories encode important cultural knowledge and represent connections to past generations of artists and weavers. They also constitute contemporary relationships across communities of design, production, and use.

Traditional textiles are aesthetically, culturally, and politically significant for Maya people. They are also creative works that require immense artistry, time, and labor to produce. The people, mostly women, who weave at backstrap looms across the Guatemalan highlands often begin learning this skill at a young age.[2] An expert designer-weaver may spend three months or more on a single blouse. Traded in local markets, purchased by tourists and collectors, and incorporated into fashion lines in Paris and New York, handwoven textiles have considerable economic value as well. Photographs of Indigenous women adorned in brightly colored -pot and *-uq* (skirts, or *cortes* in Spanish) are the primary means by which the Guatemalan government attracts tourism dollars. Yet Maya weavers see very little of the money made from their work. While exporters and online retailers, non-Indigenous fashion designers, and the owners of tourism and travel companies reap significant financial benefits from the appropriation of Maya women's dress styles and creative work, Indigenous weavers are often paid very little or nothing at all for their art and images. Deeply entrenched anti-Indigenous racism and patriarchy within and beyond Guatemala mean that although traditional textiles are valuable commodities, the women who produce them are treated as highly exploitable.

This chapter focuses on the collective efforts of Maya weavers to rectify this situation of deep inequality. In 2014, a group of Kaqchikel Maya women from the Department of Sacatepéquez, which encompasses several large municipalities and dozens of Indigenous-majority towns and hamlets, launched a political movement to regain control over the textile designs they create and produce. Since that time, the Asociación Femenina para el Desarrollo de Sacatepéquez (AFEDES, the Women's Association for the Development of Sacatepéquez), has brought together thirty Indigenous organizations from eighteen different linguistic communities (Eulich 2019) to form the Movimiento Nacional de Tejedoras Ruchajixik ri Qana'ojabäl (the National Movement of Maya Weavers: Guardians of Our Knowledge; hereafter "National Movement").[3] AFEDES boasts more than 1,000 members (Meares Cohen 2016), and hundreds of women have participated in the National Movement's coordinated events, from protests outside government offices to hearings inside the courtrooms of the nation's highest judicial body.

The National Movement has made important strides toward protecting textile designs from unauthorized and unremunerated reproduction and sale. They have made a series of formal appeals to the Guatemalan government based on the country's participation in the globalized system of intellectual property (IP) rights that includes copyright, trademark, and patent law. One aim in this chapter is to document the ongoing work of National Movement coordinators to secure copyright protections for their work. If the movement succeeds, Indigenous communities in Guatemala will be legally recognized as the collective authors of traditional textile designs and have the right to determine who is and is not permitted to produce and sell this work. This would be an important victory in the fight for Indigenous rights across Latin America.

Another aim is to advance decolonial approaches in fashion studies through critical consideration of the neocolonialism that structures the IP regime that Maya weavers are strategically employing to protect their designs. Drawing on long-term, ethnographic research with Maya fashion and textile producers in highland Guatemala, I connect scholarly debates surrounding IP rights with conversations in fashion studies about diversity and coloniality. As many others have argued, fashion studies too often privilege a Western definition of what constitutes "fashion" (Eicher, Evenson, and Lutz 2000; Kaiser and Green 2012; Jansen and Craik 2016; Gaugele and Titton 2019; Cheang, Rabine, and Sandhu 2020), understood as a product of European invention, Western modernity, and industrial capitalism introduced to the rest of the world through colonialism and globalization. As anthropologist M. Angela Jansen (2020) notes, "Other ways and systems of fashioning the body continue to be included in the global fashion conversation within the modernity/coloniality framework, rather than in their own right, on their own terms and with their own definitions, esthetics and epistemological frameworks" (816).

It is imperative that Maya weavers and other Indigenous producers of textiles and apparel be centered in the global fashion conversation. The labor and creativity inherent in the production and circulation of style in Maya communities constitutes a vibrant fashion system with wide-ranging resonances and influences. This fashion system involves histories, epistemologies, and aesthetics that are distinct from those that characterize fashion systems that have manifested in other times and places. Maya fashion also emerges from property relations and ideas of authorship and creativity that differ from the Western models on which copyright law is based. To protect their textile designs, the National Movement must frame their weaving practices in terms that are easily legible to the Guatemalan state and aligned with the IP framework. The decolonization of fashion studies must involve attention to fashion's deepening relationship to IP law, which places burdens of assimilation and concession-making on Indigenous peoples, even as their activism reshapes IP law in new directions.

The quote that begins this chapter is the title of a book that AFEDES published in Spanish (AFEDES 2020), which describes the history of the National Movement, the reasons for its struggle, and the group's specific demands. The phrase "Our weavings are the books the colonizers could not burn" appears frequently in their other public communications as well. It captures so much of what is at stake for Indigenous weavers. The analogy between books and textiles is important. The National Movement asserts that copyright law—the same legal framework that protects authors' rights to control the reproduction and circulation of books—should also extend to Indigenous weavers and their traditional textile designs. This is not just a matter of fairness; rather, the denial of these rights to Maya weavers can be understood as part of a long history of non-Indigenous people enacting material and symbolic violence on Indigenous populations. In the sixteenth and seventeenth centuries, this violence included book burnings. Colonial authorities set fire to texts written by Maya inhabitants of present-day Mexico and Central America, including books of history, mythology, genealogy, science, ritual, and religion. Historians agree that in "burning the books, the Spanish invaders and inquisitors were attempting to Christianize the native population and to eradicate their culture and history" (Ovenden 2020, 86). In their narrow understanding of inscription, however, Spanish colonizers misrecognized textiles as mere adornment (Brumfiel 2006; Maxwell 2015). They failed to comprehend that weaving is a form of literacy, and that the stylized features of textile design and construction powerfully communicate and, indeed, bring to life the culture, knowledge, and history of Maya people (Chacón 2020). Indigenous women have worked tirelessly to maintain these *text*-iles across generations. Today, they seek to protect them from a new set of challenges.

On June 28, 2016, representatives of the National Movement appeared before the Guatemalan Constitutional Court to argue for the legal recognition of the collective authorship of Indigenous weavers over traditional textile designs. A month prior, the group had filed a legal action with the country's highest court challenging the constitutionality of the omission from national law of specific rules that would extend collective copyright protections to Maya textiles. The National Movement is coordinated by Angelina Aspuac, a Kaqchikel Maya woman, community leader, and AFEDES member from Santiago Sacatepéquez. As the Court debated the merits of the Movement's arguments, Aspuac described to journalists the significance of collective IP protections: "We must protect our textile knowledge just as we protect our territories ... intellectual property protection is a fundamental dimension of autonomy" (quoted in Picq 2017). International law recognizes the right of Indigenous communities to ownership and possession of their lands and to decide how natural resources on those lands are used and managed. In recent decades, multinational mining companies (with the support of the Guatemalan government) have attempted to establish operations in Maya territories throughout the Western highlands. Community members have repeatedly thwarted these incursions by staging large-scale protests and holding formal community consultations to voice their opposition to extractivism (Xiloj 2019). In drawing a parallel between territorial sovereignty and copyright protections, Aspuac builds on the momentum of the anti-mining movement to affirm the power of Indigenous political activism. She also uses the tangible example of territory to emphasize that the struggle for Indigenous political, cultural, and economic autonomy—part of the broader agenda that

AFEDES promotes—must include sovereignty over the ancestral wisdom and shared knowledge that weaving practices and textile creations embody.

In early 2017, the Movement won an important victory. The Comisión Presidencial contra la Discriminación y el Racismo contra los Pueblos Indígenas en Guatemala (CODISRA, the Presidential Commission on Discrimination and Racism against Indigenous Peoples in Guatemala), presented a formal complaint to the attorney general's office, asking the public prosecutor to investigate a possible case of discrimination related to the sale of *trajes típicos* (Indigenous dress styles) by a company that was using the term, María Chula, in their marketing. The name "María" is a racial epithet used by non-Indigenous Guatemalans to homogenize and stereotype Maya women as uneducated, subservient, and inferior. Accompanied by the adjective "chula," meaning *cute* in Guatemalan Spanish, the retailer was selling Maya women's artistic works under a racist and derogatory brand name. CODISRA issued the complaint after AFEDES brought the issue to the Commission's attention and led an extensive social media campaign to draw public attention to the retailer's marketing practices.

A year later, the Movement achieved an even greater success. After a public hearing attended by an estimated 500 female weavers (Horizons of Friendship 2022), the Constitutional Court issued a resolution recommending that the National Congress take action to protect the collective IP of Indigenous Guatemalans by recognizing Maya communities as the authors of traditional textiles and related goods. Movement leaders, with support from the United Nations Human Rights Office in Guatemala and a team of legal and policy experts, had already sent a bill to the Congress in November 2016 that would reform existing national law to include the necessary provisions. Bill No. 5247 was formally introduced in February 2017 with the endorsement of sixteen legislators and the congressional Commission on Indigenous Peoples. Political scientist Manuela Picq (2017) summarized the bill's content as follows:

> The bill has two objectives. First, it calls for a recognition of a definition of collective intellectual property, which is linked to the right of Indigenous Peoples to administer and manage their heritage. Second, it asks that Indigenous nations be recognized as authors, in which case they would automatically benefit from intellectual property law. Recognizing Indigenous nations as authors just like individuals or companies means that corporations that benefit from the export of Maya hand-woven goods will have to pay royalties to the communities who are the authors of huipiles.[4]

Even though the Constitutional Court ruling underscored the importance of the bill's passage, Movement leaders anticipated a number of obstacles. In particular, they expected push back from the economic elite involved in the export and tourism industries—two sectors that benefit greatly from the unfettered reproduction and sale of Maya textiles and images of Maya women dressed in traje (Walsh 2018, 7–8). The bill has stalled in the Congress since 2017.

The National Movement's congressional supporters introduced a second bill in September 2022 that takes a more focused approach by instituting collectively held copyright protections specifically for Indigenous textiles and clothing.[5] Beginning in 2018, weavers worked alongside representatives from the National Congress, CODISRA, the national Intellectual Property Registry, Institute of Interethnic and Indigenous Peoples Studies at the University of San Carlos of Guatemala (Guatemala's public university), congressional Commission on Indigenous Peoples, national office of the Human Rights Ombudsman, American Chambers of Commerce, and Lawyers without Borders (among others) to develop the legislation. On April 26, 2022, World Intellectual Property Day, a delegation led by Angelina Aspuac met with the Commission on Indigenous Peoples for a formal review of the draft, asking for the commission's official support. The Commission held a press conference to discuss the finalized bill on September 5 (International Indigenous Women's Day), and the bill was formally introduced in the Congress on September 22, 2022. Movement leaders continue to advocate its passage.

Favorable resolutions issued by the Constitutional Court and shows of support from government agencies and commissions must be understood against the backdrop of the Guatemalan government's own appropriations of Maya textile traditions. Consider the example of a recent official visit to Guatemala by the president of Mexico, Andrés Manuel Lopez Obrador. The Instituto Guatemalteco de Turismo (INGUAT, the Guatemalan Tourism Institute, a government agency) arranged a spectacular welcome for the dignitary at Guatemala City's La Aurora International Airport on May 5, 2022. Lopez Obrador was thoroughly impressed, according to reports from INGUAT on social media, where he was quoted as saying, "So much culture, so much art, what a unique reception, Guatemala!" (INGUAT 2022). Along the hallways leading from the international arrival gates to immigration and customs, living dioramas featured men and women adorned in dress styles from various towns and Mayan linguistic communities. A woman representing the Tz'utujil Maya-majority town of Santiago Atitlan, a favorite tourist destination on the shores of picturesque Lake Atitlan, carried a large ceramic pitcher on her head, resting just above her colorful hair wrap, and another tucked under her arm. A string of gourds and bunches of carnations dressed the dugout canoe in which she stood. Typical of dress styles created and worn by many Tz'utujil Maya women in Santiago Atitlan, she wore a three-panel -pot featuring purple stripes and multicolor, embroidered birds, together with a red ikat skirt and woven belt. A striped shawl draped over her right shoulder and a long ikat scarf affixed to the wall on her left framed her figure. In acknowledgment of the COVID-19 public health emergency, the woman wore a mask crafted from the foot loom-woven fabric used for -uq in many highland towns.

On INGUAT's Facebook page, these curated representations of Maya culture received mixed reviews. Alongside the "likes" and "loves," there were several dozen angry emojis. Scattered among the comments expressing praise—"blessings beautiful ladies," "such precious trajes típicos, a lovely reception"—also appeared biting critiques. One Facebook user commented, for example:

> I don't fault our fellow citizens for the fact that INGUAT makes them pass as Indigenous people, but it leaves a lot to be desired on the part of the institution that claims to promote the culture and Indigenous traje that belongs to the [Indigenous] people before the eyes of the world, when it uses people who are not Indigenous and who do not know how to properly wear Indigenous traje. Who don't know the true history of the peoples they represent, and even worse, don't live in those towns. They should have given the opportunity to people who are really Indigenous because they would not have to pretend to be Indigenous . . .

The idea of dressing non-Indigenous women in traje, surrounding them with artisanal and agricultural products, and staging them as a representation of Guatemala's national identity—something that INGUAT has, in fact, done repeatedly—is both offensive and distressing given Maya peoples' ongoing and systematic marginalization, exclusion, and exploitation at the hands of the country's political and economic elite. More than five centuries of settler colonialism marked by forced cultural assimilation, forced labor, and warfare, including a genocidal campaign carried out by the Guatemalan military from 1978 to 1983, now involves meager assurances of basic rights for Indigenous Guatemalans, but no real governmental efforts to ameliorate entrenched inequalities and ongoing forms of discrimination.

The National Movement has taken legal action against INGUAT to challenge the constitutionality of the agency's use of images of Maya women without securing their permission or providing remuneration. Movement leaders decry the tourism industry's treatment of Maya culture as a national brand and Maya women and their traje as objects of folklore. As noted in a Movement communique shared on social media: "Folklorization as an expression of racism is a form of violence against Indigenous women because they use us as a tourist attraction, stripping us of our humanity, and making us into exotic objects for public exhibition" (National Movement 2020). The Movement filed an appeal for protection (*amparo* in Spanish) with the Constitutional Court in December 2017 on the grounds that INGUAT's unauthorized use of images of Maya women for marketing and communications violates the rights of Maya people. Movement leaders spoke at a public hearing on the issue in March 2019, and, in November 2020, the Constitutional Court sided with the Movement.

To accompany the legal action and build public support, AFEDES had organized a series of protests outside the INGUAT headquarters and other government offices in Guatemala City, demanding that the government stop using Maya women's images and Maya traje to promote the economic interests of a state that refuses to address the needs and demands of Maya citizens. These protests have powerfully shaped nationwide conversations about the state's cultural and economic appropriation of Maya people's likenesses and material culture. In response to INGUAT's Facebook post showcasing the Mexican president's reception, a user who identifies as a Kaqchikel Maya university student commented: "And what about the author's rights of the Maya weavers? *Kaxlanas* [Kaqchikel Mayan term for non-Indigenous people] turning our clothing into folklore, it's racism . . . Our clothing is not a costume, it embodies struggle, history, and resistance." Another user identifying as a male weaver from the Kaqchikel Maya-majority town of Sololá commented on a different series of national events: "Why does INGUAT always put people [in its publicity] pretending to pass as Indigenous? Why the need to dress them in Indigenous clothing? Could it be that Indigenous people are not permitted to present their own creations, their work, art, cosmovision, and clothing in these spaces? These actions could be labeled as cultural genocide. The State and Guatemalan leaders insist on eliminating the presence of Maya people" (INGUAT 2022).

IP rights are gaining importance worldwide as fashion brands and retailers increasingly utilize legal protections to ensure competitiveness and grow profitability, whether through copyright protections for designs or trademark protections for brand names and logos.[6] As IP law's reach expands, the regime often works in favor of resourced populations and against marginalized groups (Bettig 1996; Poblete and Goldgel-Carballo 2020; Tehranian 2012; Thomas 2016; Vats 2020). Firms that have the economic resources and symbolic capital to invest in crafting and promoting a brand image and the time, money, and forms of expertise to defend themselves against design "piracy" exert considerable control over the fashion industry, including the global trade in traditional textiles and clothing. For example, non-Indigenous Guatemalan designers Anita Lara and Alida Boer market products that feature Maya textiles to an international audience, with items retailing for upwards of $500 (Abbott 2016, 6–7). These designers invest in brand promotion and marketing messages intended to give their items an "authentic," yet decidedly cosmopolitan, feel. Internationally celebrated fashion brands including Isabel Marant, Missoni, and Valentino have produced clothing lines featuring textile designs from Indigenous peoples in Mexico and Guatemala, marketed to elite consumers who are no doubt drawn to the "native" look and "ethnic" flair of these garments. The production of -pot is also being mechanized in and beyond Guatemala using computerized embroidery machines and dye-sublimation printers to drastically reduce the time and cost of producing textiles with the look and feel of traje. Maya weavers say "they have not benefited from this international, commercial interest in their communities' work" (Walsh 2018, 4–6). Instead, people who are structurally positioned to take advantage of legal protections and investment opportunities are finding ways to further disadvantage Maya weavers and marginalize their contributions to the textile trade and fashion industry. The globalization of IP rights contributes to the deepening of "racial and neo-colonial inequality" (Vats and Keller 2018, 735) as Indigenous people are more often confronted with IP law as "violators" than as beneficiaries (Thomas 2016).

Indigenous peoples' struggles for IP protections tend to emerge, therefore, from situations where claiming exclusive rights to their creative work becomes the only viable means to counter ownership claims made by people from outside the community (Brown 1998; Coombe 1998; Strathern and Hirsch 2004). This is the case with the National Movement in Guatemala. Maya weavers had been lamenting the appropriation of their textiles by government agencies and private enterprises for many years, but the need to take legal action became acute and urgent around 2014, as Angelina Aspuac recounts,

> ...when two designers threatened AFEDES weavers who were producing huipiles for them. And when they delivered [the huipiles] and were paid for them, [the two designers] demanded exclusive rights to those pieces. Those [huipiles] contained ancestral symbols, they are huipiles that women weavers have made forever. The companies want exclusive rights to particular pieces, but along with their demands for exclusivity, there is the risk that weavers could go to jail if they weave that same huipil again.
>
> Quoted in Chiquitó 2022

Aspuac and other AFEDES members were appalled that companies who were contracting with weavers to produce textiles to sell to tourists and collectors would claim exclusive rights to specific designs. The book published by AFEDES further explains this context. It was becoming commonplace, the authors recount, for companies to request textiles "with certain changes in the figures and colors," and then for the companies to claim that their employees were the real "designers" of the fabrics, "even when these changes were minimal" (AFEDES 2020, 17). In other words, non-Indigenous firms began to assert IP rights over designs that had long been elaborated and produced by Maya weavers. They were claiming authorship based on minor design inflections as a means of monopolizing control over potentially lucrative commodities. AFEDES members were concerned that Guatemalan IP law would legitimate those claims but delegitimize counterclaims by Maya weavers to collective authorship and ownership. Indeed, this was precisely the legal imbalance that the Constitutional Court acknowledged when it issued its 2018 recommendation.

Maya weavers have developed their knowledge and practice for a long time without the need for formal, government-backed rules regarding authorship and ownership. As anthropologist Carol Hendrickson (1995) explains, Maya weavers work within a tradition where imitation has been understood as a productive part of the creative process. Knowing which figures and symbols to reproduce and in which combinations is a matter of pride for weavers. Adding creative inflections to these designs is also important, in that it demonstrates a weaver's particular skills and expands the field of design possibilities for future generations. My research (2016) affirms that fashion design and production in Maya communities happens within a relatively open system of shared knowledge, skills, and techniques. Textile and clothing designers acknowledge the economic and moral legitimacy of borrowing ideas from one another within an Indigenous community of producers. A powerful sense of shared ethnic identity and a commitment to economic fairness underwrite this iterative, collaborative, and intergenerational process. Among Kaqchikel Maya people who make and sell clothing—whether -pot or the nontraditional sweaters, sweatshirts, and jeans that I have more closely analyzed—the ideal fashion marketplace is one where everyone benefits from a community-based system of shared resources, fair pricing, and mutual support.

This is not the marketplace that is imagined in IP law. A set of rules that largely originated in eighteenth-century England, copyright was standardized in Guatemala in line with international agreements in the 1990s and 2000s.[7] Social scientists debate the benefits and drawbacks of an expanding IP regime.

Anthropologists have emphasized that IP frameworks are often incommensurable with the ways of being and knowing evident across different societies. Although Indigenous communities can now (under certain circumstances) claim exclusive rights to specific cultural forms and creative works, successful claims often require that they conform their cultural norms and practices to Western logics of property and ownership. Copyright law is grounded in a concept of authorship that privileges individual autonomy and fixed identity. It does not easily align with the norms and practices of communities who recognize collective agency, or who view artistic production as a temporally fluid process that stretches back through time (Scafidi 2005). International institutions involved in the development and administration of IP law have negotiated rules that purport to take communal forms of ownership and Indigenous relationships to knowledge and natural resources into account. These rules focus on the protection of traditional knowledge and folklore and management of biodiversity. In this regard, the IP regime reflects stereotypical assumptions about who Indigenous people are and what they do, as if their activities and interests are limited to areas such as ritual, agriculture, and ecology, as if Indigenous people are *not* central to the dynamic sphere of fashion and other "modern" pursuits. Assessing these dynamics, scholars have argued that IP law functions less as a tool of empowerment and more as a neocolonial tool of forced assimilation, one that extends Euro-American hegemony into new realms (Aoki 1998; Correa 2000; Rahmatian 2009).

The National Movement's struggle for copyright protections is a fight for recognition—as authors, creators, and, indeed, as a vital and valued presence in Guatemalan society. Achieving these rights and recognitions would be an important step, the Movement's leaders argue, toward recuperating and maintaining forms of knowledge and material culture, modes of expression, and ways of life that colonial and neocolonial regimes have attempted to eradicate. Maya weavers are also reshaping the IP framework by pushing for official recognition of Indigenous communities' collective rights.[8] And rather than stand by and wait for the Guatemalan National Congress to pass the proposed bills, the National Movement is forging ahead by organizing Consejos de Tejedoras (Weaving Councils) in Kaqchikel Maya-majority municipalities. These elected representatives are charged with administering and defending the community's collective rights to their textile designs. If the Guatemalan government does institutionalize these rights, it should not be the state's nor the international community's only answer to the conditions of racism and inequality that Maya women face. Nor should the copyright fight overshadow AFEDES's other demands. It is crucial to understand this effort as just one part of the organization's broader set of goals and strategies for improving the lives of Maya women.

AFEDES has been an active organization for more than 30 years.[9] Its leaders have worked on numerous issues, including gender-based violence and the chronic malnutrition that disproportionately affects Indigenous women and children in Guatemala. In the 1990s and early 2000s, one of the organization's principal activities was providing small loans and technical training to support women's entrepreneurship. In 2006, the organization reached a turning point:

> As time passed, and as we continued to empower ourselves on the basis of our rights, we realized that the problems we face are structural in nature and have to do with patriarchy, capitalism, and colonialism. The ways our actions were contributing to abolishing patriarchy were clear. But there were contradictions and inconsistencies in relation to our economic activities. We came to understand that we were working within capitalist logics rather than truly contributing to the economic welfare [*la economía*] of women.
>
> AFEDES 2022a

AFEDES's leadership reoriented their efforts "toward a process of political and ideological formation" to understand the root causes of the problems affecting their communities. After a period of reflection and analysis, they determined that their collective actions should promote women's holistic wellbeing and worth given that their lives and labor are fundamentally devalued within hegemonic systems and structures. They committed to building a "new economy," or what could "better [be] described as reclaiming and recuperating the ancestral principles and practices of our grandparents," including principles of food sovereignty, political autonomy, economic solidarity, and an autonomous, "feminist economy that calls into question the gendered division of labor." The organizational transition that leaders undertook in 2007 was arduous and costly. AFEDES lost members to lenders who did not demand the same level of commitment and participation, and many women who had previously received microloans from the association defaulted.

These challenges gave rise to new directions in planning and organization, including more studied consideration of issues of race and ethnicity. In 2014, association leaders began to emphasize more concertedly that its membership is Kaqchikel Maya. AFEDES now defines its core mission as "promoting the harmony and equilibrium of the web of life through the recuperation of our historical memory and identity and the defense of our territories, science, and knowledge, constituting ourselves as political subjects and subjects of rights within a framework of political autonomy for our people." They describe their core objective as the realization of Utz' K'aslemal, a Kaqchikel Mayan phrase denoting "a life of abundance and happiness," a good life. In this context, the phrase also refers to a way of life that is distinctively Indigenous, informed by and realized through intergenerational knowledge sharing and practice, including the weaving of textiles.

In public communications, AFEDES celebrates its landmark accomplishments in the struggle for collective IP rights alongside other important initiatives. The association operates weaving schools in a number of Kaqchikel Maya-majority communities, where hundreds of women have learned to weave or shared their knowledge and skills. The association sponsors workshops on agroecological knowledge and organic farming practices and public conversations on anti-Indigenous racism. They are involved in efforts to provide clean water for Indigenous communities and address the environmental contamination resulting from plastics. AFEDES members collaborate in many forms of feminist and Indigenous political activism. In 2022, they advocated the release of three Q'eqchi' Maya women who were sentenced to prison for alleged involvement in the deaths of heavily armed Guatemalan soldiers who had been sent to intimidate community leaders opposing the incursions of a large agro-industrial firm operating in the area (AFEDES 2022b). And, in 2023, members of AFEDES and the National Movement were vocal opponents of the Guatemalan attorney general's attempts to delegitimize the political party of anti-corruption presidential candidate Bernardo Arévalo.

The fight for copyright protections for traditional textiles draws more attention from national and international media than other aspects of AFEDES's work. The aesthetic richness of the textile designs and the scale of National Movement protests that have drawn hundreds of Maya women to Guatemala City's plazas and streets yield compelling images and narratives. Western liberalism encourages the view that Indigenous women participating in the Movement are being empowered through an international legal regime that guarantees their rights, such that media coverage of the Movement often takes on a celebratory, even self-congratulatory, tone. A close look at the situation confronting Maya weavers helps us to comprehend, however, that the expansion of IP rights as part of a globalized system of capitalist economic development has helped to produce the very conditions in which Indigenous women must now demand rights to their own ancestral knowledge and creative work. The need to secure copyright protections arises from a context in which Indigenous women's creativity and labor—including their work as fashion designers and artists—has been systematically devalued by colonial and neocolonial regimes of commodification and extraction. These are the kinds of structural issues that AFEDES leaders aim to ameliorate, understanding that realizing a "life of abundance" will require the restoration of Indigenous autonomy rather than the mere deepening of Maya people's political and economic relationships to systems that are not of their own design.

Notes

1 I prefer the Kaqchikel Mayan term for a woven blouse because my own knowledge and experience of Maya fashion is a result of the generous amounts of time that members of Kaqchikel Maya communities in Guatemala have contributed to my research over many years. The Mayan Language Academy of Guatemala (Academia de las Lenguas Mayas de Guatemala) recognizes 22 distinct languages and linguistic communities of Maya peoples in Guatemala. Kaqchikel Mayan is spoken by more than 500,000 people who reside mainly in the central highlands.

2 As Susan Kellogg (2005) explains, "Weaving . . . constitutes an important part of women's work across the highlands and is an activity that serves as a source of both income and pride. Tzotzil Maya comment through song that women weave because they are women. In other words, men and women see weaving as part of the very essence of being a woman. While highland men have woven from the colonial period on, women specialize in weaving and wearing the most valuable items" (113).

3 The organization's official moniker includes both Spanish and Kaqchikel Mayan phrases. In my translation, I have added a colon to separate the two phrases. The Kaqchikel Mayan phrase selected by the Movement's leaders, especially the polysemous term, qana'ojabäl, emphasizes that weaving is an embodied practice through which collective and inherited wisdom, artistic forms, and technical abilities are transmitted and shared among Maya people. Thank you to Paola Lux Sacbaja for contributing to this translation.

4 The bill proposes a set of reforms to the Law of Authorship Rights and Related Rights (No. 33–98) and the Law of Industrial Property (No. 57–2000).

5 As described by reporters, "The proposed bill would prohibit the importation of similar products or copies of the textiles of the Indigenous communities of Guatemala; reproduction, sublimation, or printing without the free and informed consent of the Indigenous community; the reproduction, via printing or embroidery, of items that alter the ceremonial traje of Indigenous peoples and communities; imprisonment and fines for violators" (Bello 2022).

6   For detailed studies of the current role and future possibilities for expanded intellectual property rights in the fashion industry, see Jankowska 2024 and Cerchia and Pozzo 2020.
7   I refer here to Guatemala's participation in the World Trade Organization's (WTO) Trade-Related Aspects of Intellectual Property Rights (TRIPS) Agreement. Signed in 1995 by nearly 130 nations, Guatemala had until January 1, 2000, to implement the required set of laws. TRIPS violations are subject to review under a WTO system that allows for significant trade sanctions against countries not abiding by or enforcing IP protections, which creates a powerful incentive for national governments to promote compliance and criminalize violations. In the aftermath of TRIPS, the United States continued to push for even tougher IP regulations and enforcement procedures through a series of bilateral and multilateral free trade agreements, including the Dominican Republic-Central America Free Trade Agreement (DR-CAFTA), which the Guatemalan government implemented in 2006.
8   There is precedence in Latin America for the protection of the collective IP rights of Indigenous peoples over their traditional knowledge. In Brazil, Costa Rica, Panama, Peru, and Venezuela, for example, laws recognizing the collective rights of Indigenous peoples to intellectual property protections are already in place (Gutiérrez 2020). Acknowledging the region's innovations in the promotion of collective rights can contribute to the "provincialization" of IP law (Geismar 2013; cf. Chakrabarty 2000), where peoples and regions commonly considered peripheral to the development of IP law come to be seen instead as integral to shaping the regime. In a public roundtable sponsored by the Institute of Interethnic and Indigenous Peoples Studies at the University of San Carlos of Guatemala, Angelina Aspuac explained the Movement's tendentious relationship to IP law as follows: "We are not here to defend the intellectual property framework as such, but rather to make it known that there are also other logics that emerge from Indigenous peoples, that we have our own forms of knowledge, our own practices, our own creations, and so it is in this context that we talk about collective intellectual property, because we are part of a collective." (IDEIPI 2022)
9   The history that I relate here is based on information available on the AFEDES website (AFEDES 2022a), which is published in both Spanish and English. For stylistic reasons, I have chosen to work from the Spanish version; thus, the English translations that appear in quotation marks throughout the remainder of this chapter are my own.

Bibliography

Abbott, Jeff. 2016. "Opposing Corporate Theft of Mayan Textiles, Weavers Appeal to Guatemala's High Court." *Truthout*, August 14, 2016. https://truthout.org/articles/

opposing-corporate-theft-of-mayan-textiles-weavers-appeal-to-guatemala-s-high-court/

Aoki, Keith. 1998. "Neocolonialism. Anticommons Property, and Biopiracy in the (Not-So-Brave) New World Order of International Intellectual Property Protection." *Indiana Journal of Global Legal Studies* 6 (1): 11–58.

Asociación Femenina para el Desarrollo de Sacatepéquez [AFEDES]. 2020. *Nuestros Tejidos Son Los Libros Que La Colonia No Pudo Quemar: El Camino del Movimiento Nacional de Tejedoras Mayas de Guatemala.* Guatemala City: AFEDES.

Asociación Femenina para el Desarrollo de Sacatepéquez [AFEDES]. 2022a. AFEDES Website. https://mujeresdeafedes.wordpress.com.

Asociación Femenina para el Desarrollo de Sacatepéquez [AFEDES]. 2022b. "Comunicado a favor de las mujeres maya q'eqchi sentenciadas a 75 años de prisión incnmutables." Facebook, April 22, 2022. www.facebook.com/mujeresafedes/posts/pfbid02TUzq9tGyn2N67Ly1TKZM2NsVuBmoskoUbJkxSn2zxxBika4sY31u7Lqot6GVJbADl.

Bello, Nelyabith. 2022. "Tejedoras mayas piden reconocer propiedad intelectual de sus tejidos." *TN23*. April 26, 2022. www.chapintv.com/noticia/tejedoras-mayas-piden-reconocer-propiedad-intelectual-de-sus-tejidos/

Bettig, Ronald V. 1996. *Copyrighting Culture: The Political Economy of Intellectual Property.* Boulder: Westview Press.

Brown, Michael F. 1998. "Can Culture be Copyrighted?" *Current Anthropology* 39 (2): 193–222.

Brumfiel, Elizabeth. 2006. "Cloth, Gender, Continuity, and Change: Fabricating Unity in Anthropology." *American Anthropologist* 108 (4): 862–877.

Cerchia, Rossella E., and Barbara Pozzo, eds. 2020. Special Issue, The New Frontiers of Fashion Law. *Laws* 9 (1).

Chacón, Gloria E. 2020. "Material Culture, Indigeneity, and Temporality." *Textual Cultures* 13 (2): 46–69.

Chakrabarty, Dipesh. 2000. *Provincializing Europe: Postcolonial Thought and Historical Difference.* Princeton, NJ: Princeton University Press.

Cheang, Sarah, Leslie Rabine, and Arti Sandhu. 2020. "Decolonizing Fashion [Studies] as Process." *International Journal of Fashion Studies* 9 (2): 247–255.

Chiquitó, Elsa A. 2022. "Sublimados, una Amenaza a las Tejedoras." *No-Ficción Guatemala*, podcast audio, May 19, 2022. www.no-ficcion.com/project/sublimados-amenaza-tejedoras.

Coombe, Rosemary J. 1998. *The Cultural Life of Intellectual Properties: Authorship, Appropriation, and the Law.* Durham, NC: Duke University Press.

Correa, Carlos. 2000. *Intellectual Property Rights, the WTO and Developing Countries: The TRIPS Agreement and Policy Options.* London: Zed Books.

Eicher, Joanne B., Sandra L. Evenson, and Hazel A. Lutz. 2000. *The Visible Self: Global Perspectives on Dress, Culture, and Society.* 2nd edition. New York Fairchild.

Eulich, Whitney. 2019. "Pride and Profit: Why Mayan Weavers Fight for Intellectual Property Rights." *Christian Science Monitor*, March 17, 2019. www.csmonitor.com/World/Americas/2019/0327/Pride-and-profit-Why-Mayan-weavers-fight-for-intellectual-property-rights.

Gaugele, Elke, and Monica Titton, eds. 2019. *Fashion and Postcolonial Critique.* Berlin, Germany: Sternberg Press.

Geismar, Haidy. 2013. *Treasured Possessions: Indigenous Interventions into Cultural and Intellectual Property.* Durham, NC: Duke University Press.

Gutiérrez, Nicolás. 2020. "How Latin America Countries Protect their Traditional Knowledge through IP." European Commission, January 16, 2020. https://intellectual-property-helpdesk.ec.europa.eu/news-events/news/how-latin-america-countries-protect-their-traditional-knowledge-through-ip-2020-01-16_en.

Hendrickson, Carol. 1995. *Weaving Identities: Construction of Dress and Self in a Highland Guatemala Town.* Austin: University of Texas Press.

Horizons of Friendship. 2022. "Project Summary: Conservation and Protection of Mayan Textile Art of the Indigenous Women of Guatemala." www.horizons.ca/mayan-textile-art-of-indigenous-women.

Instituto de Estudios Interétnicos y de los Pueblos Indígenas [IDEIPI]. 2022. "Conocimientos ancestrales y propiedad intelectual." Facebook, April 26, 2022. www.facebook.com/usacideipi/videos/5149698241754592.

Instituto Guatemalteco de Turismo [INGUAT]. 2022. "#VisitaOficialMx." Facebook, May 5, 2022. www.facebook.com/inguat/posts/pfbid0MNq8Bra2WLzVcngGY9FagDkgvcXhbkdc9Sein7dQLE2cGvbHRyhMdmSs7KQ6RtYol.

Jankowska, Marlena. 2024. *Intellectual Property Rights, Copynorm and the Fashion Industry: A Comparative Analysis.* Abingdon, UK: Routledge.

Jansen, M. Angela, and Jennifer Craik. 2016. "Introduction." In *Modern Fashion Traditions: Negotiating Tradition and Modernity through Fashion*, edited by M. Angela Jansen and Jennifer Craik, 1–21. London: Bloomsbury.

Jansen, M. Angela. 2020. "Fashion and the Phantasmagoria of Modernity: An Introduction to Decolonial Fashion Discourse." *Fashion Theory* 24 (6): 815–836.

Kaiser, Susan B., and Denise N. Green. 2012. *Fashion and Cultural Studies.* 2nd ed. New York: Berg.

Kellogg, Susan. 2005. *Weaving the Past: A History of Latin America's Indigenous Women from the Prehispanic Period to the Present.* Oxford: Oxford University Press.

Maxwell, Judith M. 2015. "Change in Literacy and Literature in Highland Guatemala, Precontact to Present." *Ethnohistory* 62 (3): 553–572.

Meares Cohen, Alison. 2016. "Indigenous Women Fight to Protect Rights of Woven Guatemala Textile Design." *Ecowatch*, August 16, 2016. www.ecowatch.com/guatemala-textile-design-1975198164.html.

Movimiento Nacional de Tejedoras Ruchajixik ri Qana'ojbäl [National Movement]. 2020. "Corte de constitucionalidad: ¡Otorga amparo a favor de las tejedoras! En contra del INGUAT." Facebook, November 6, 2020. www.facebook.com/Movimiento

NacionalTejedoras/posts/pfbid02omxP5GhEeydrGXZdYtuLuBphHvdFTvEj6h4pn1ozvCFkDLp1dhjXRFw7NC6VEKkbl.

Ovenden, Richard. 2020. *Burning the Books: A History of the Deliberate Destruction of Knowledge.* Cambridge, MA: Harvard University Press.

Picq, Manuela. 2017. "Maya Weavers Propose A Collective Intellectual Property Law." *Intercontinental Cry*, March 15, 2017. https://intercontinentalcry.org/maya-weavers-propose-collective-intellectual-property-law/.

Poblete, Juan, and Víctor Goldgel-Carballo, eds. 2020. *Piracy and Intellectual Property in Latin America: Rethinking Creativity and the Common Good.* New York: Routledge.

Rahmatian, Andreas. 2009. "Neo-Colonial Aspects of Global Intellectual Property Protection." *Journal of World Intellectual Property* 12 (1): 40–74.

Scafidi, Susan. 2005. *Who Owns Culture? Appropriation and Authenticity in American Law.* New Brunswick, NJ: Rutgers University Press.

Strathern, Marilyn, and Eric Hirsch. 2004. "Introduction." In *Transactions and Creations: Property Debates and the Stimulus Of Melanesia*, edited by Eric Hirsch and Marilyn Strathern, 1–20. New York: Berghahn Books.

Tehranian, John. 2012. "Towards a Critical IP Theory: Copyright, Consecration, and Control." *Brigham Young University Law Review* 2012 (4): 1233–1289.

Thomas, Kedron. 2016. *Regulating Style: Intellectual Property Law and the Business of Fashion in Guatemala.* Berkeley: University of California.

Vats, Anjali. 2020. *The Color of Creatorship: Intellectual Property, Race, and the Making of Americans.* Stanford, CA: Stanford University Press.

Vats, Anjali, and Deidre A. Keller. 2018. "Critical Race IP." *Cardozo Arts and Entertainment Law Journal* 36 (3): 735–795.

Walsh, Aisling. 2018. "How Mayan Women in Guatemala are Fighting to Protect their Designs—and their Identity." *Open Democracy*, August 8, 2018. www.opendemocracy.net/en/5050/how-mayan-women-in-guatemala-are-fighting-to-protect-their-designs-and-identity/.

Xiloj, Lucía. 2019. "Implementation of the Right to Prior Consultation of Indigenous Peoples in Guatemala." In *The Prior Consultation of Indigenous Peoples in Latin America*, edited by Claire Wright and Alexandra Tomaselli, 243–260. New York: Routledge.

18

Design as Natural Healer

Maria Carolina Garcia

Thinking collaboratively, several artists, designers, and entrepreneurs worked to bridge social isolation and minimize its effects on human emotional health during the COVID-19 pandemic in Brazil. This, in turn, has impacted a broader audience of students, self-employed workers, and retired citizens, who have notably applied their learning to what are now post-pandemic years. As the World Health Organization (WHO) officially declared a Coronavirus pandemic in the first quarter of 2020, activities considered non-essential were halted across the creative economy sector. Such a situation lowered the level of per capita income and employment in the creative industries throughout Brazil; in particular, São Paulo and Rio de Janeiro, two states that together represent half of the creative jobs offered in the country, found themselves deeply impacted.[1] Because the Brazilian creative economy has become an engine of income and social inclusion, the worst moment of the confinement in 2020 was devastating. As a result, Brazilian fashion designers quickly developed strategies to respond to the crisis on their own terms, reviewing handcrafted innovations with technological experiments to move forward. It would appear that design, art and its relationship to nature have fueled new social practices and have empowered small fashion businesses connecting people through participatory experiences in order to provide a renewed sense of well-being. A series of sustainable practices led by The Flower Punchers, a collaborative printing design project that emerged from the isolation of the pandemic into a post-pandemic version of citizen science, began to imagine how the general public might work alongside professional scientists, artists and designers, to collect, analyze, conserve, and apply data in the natural realm amidst urban life. The Flower Punchers initiative has woven local natural forms from the warp and weft of ancestral textile techniques, the obsolescence of disposable debris, and the experimental sounds of comforting music in order to create meaningful experiences. Hence, this experiment adopted the vision of sustainable fashion to promote ideas like wellbeing and planetary health.[2] Transcending health and food insecurity issues, which seat in the basis of planetary health concerns, this concept lays out the contemporary moment through the lens of ecological emergencies and aims to change existing patterns like "fast fashion" consumption and obsolescence. Within this frame, design itself might be considered as a collective tool for healing. Feeling the impacts of the COVID-19 pandemic profoundly, as Brazilian lives lost reached tragic proportions and the living contemplated an entire creative economy on the verge of collapse, the evolution of The Flower Punchers project joined this venture on planetary health on both a national and international scale. In a sense, fashion was being reinvented when perhaps it always is a reinvention taking to task historical perceptions and scientific advancements. In a sense, one might consider this as the intersection of participatory culture, ontological design and a circular economy to reimagine new paths in the "Do it yourself" (DIY) movement that now united a very real "Face it together" style of solidarity.

In *Designs for the Pluriverse*, Arturo Escobar argues that potentially everybody can design. Under mandatory social isolation, many paid more attention to their immediate surroundings, which led to inventories of unusual resources such as food waste, dried leaves, cloth rags, old tools, and forgotten objects. Among these items, accumulated debris stood out as a potential resource, particularly what many began to gather in balcony planters and private gardens. The random leaves from early autumn winds began to pile. As lockdowns implied virtual searches, such as those conducted through online shopping or social media exchanges, there appeared to be a new potential for imagining fresh opportunities for fashion design entrepreneurship on a small-scale.

During the initial days of the pandemic lockdowns, the appeal of simple techniques not requiring special skills nor equipment seemed paramount and was not lost on a growing community such as The Flower Punchers. Considering that these professionals had to reinvent their own workflows and processes, reorganizing their system as a form of resilience and survival effort, practitioners created an informal network of unusual supplies based upon collaboration. Research data edited by Amaral, Franco, and Lira (2021) under the UNESCO office in Brasília revealed the need for networking as a potential way to address growing economic issues. Observing the scenario in Brazil, De Jesus (2020) indicates that the creative sector's new models integrated innovation as a response to increase resilience and continue some form of production during the pandemic (1135). Even with the creation of new products, funding sources, digital solutions and online workshops, daily life in Brazil seemed to resemble a form of science fiction, and yet, from this chaos one felt more desperate to hope.

The Flower Punchers project gathered these thoughts and dreams with a newly found respect for Brazilian nature and materials that were now caringly sourced from the heart of a big metropolis like São Paulo. Participants from this community group of design practitioners began to experiment with plant remnants that could serve as raw materials for natural dyes and eco-prints. This process was followed by online discussions. Practitioners acquired a collective knowledge through the exploration of natural residues—understood by most people as garbage—that could then be transmitted to a broader audience through a range of formats. During these unfolding online sessions, a less-known technique called flowerpounding, also called *hapa zome*, or *tataki-zome*[3] in Japan, emerged as an interesting creative expression all would enact spontaneously. Flowerpounding is a Japanese printing technique that does not use heat nor any sort of chemicals. It consists of gentle punches which transfer fresh plant pigments onto natural fabrics, such as organic cotton, linen, and wool. Therefore, it can be easily performed at home, since it does not require any sophisticated materials or unusual tools: just plants, a hammer or a similar utensil, and cloth or paper. Participants relished in the transformation of fallen autumn leaves into a circular resource for design printing.

The Flower Punchers held six online workshops between May and October 2020, each comprised of no more than twelve people to allow for close attention to each individual's unique creation. Storytelling enabled a kind of living knowledge exchange, which soon caught the eye of social media followers. At first, those affiliated with The Flower Punchers printed textile goods; those following the initiative on social media were encouraged to learn the techniques, never alone (DIY), but together, as kindred spirits. Considering that items adorned with natural dyes are affected by light, washing, and the passage of time, what seemed like potential disadvantages for flowerpounded creations became the beginning of a given garment's journey. Design participants brought out items they wished to repair. Colors could be altered or fade over time. There was even a kind of recipe exchange, to learn from one another's experiments. As word spread, the number of participants grew. Many seemed intrigued by this design initiative's circular economic principles, such as the embellishment or refreshing life given to secondhand clothing. Others seemed to embrace a new hobby to enhance their emotional wellbeing, in particular the desire to become closer to nature as the pandemic's social isolation predominated. The distribution

Figure 18.1 This sample shows details of a single leaf of *Plectranthus barbatus*, a plant commonly found in urban gardens and sidewalks in Brazil, hand printed on felted wool. Courtesy of The Flower Punchers.

of benefits and challenges among various groups of people also offered a path to minimize inequalities.

The Flower Punchers workshops concentrated efforts on equal opportunities across generations. In the workshop scenario, anyone over the age of eight through senior citizens could engage activities. However, vulnerable groups were specifically encouraged not to use heavy or metal hammers, giving instead preference to small gems or rocks as a safeguard. These items were previously checked by the instructor through pictures and specifications exchanged with the participants. For safety issues, each stone had to be covered fully by the participant's fingers around it, leaving no more than two inches stone-free in order to hammer the plant on the selected surface of either a page of paper or textile. Hands-on investigations in local gardens and the creation of individual herbaria[4] created the basis for a local knowledge of native plants. With the shadows of deforestation and climate change ever threatening the Amazon and

Central Brazil regions, a call to individual action provided an urgent yet soothing sense from which to consider sustainable principles.

The slow pace of making with nature allowed for an important direct relationship to native plants within this participatory design process. Because technology was facilitating these new connections, workshops quickly enrolled across Brazil, from Belém do Pará to Curitiba (or from north to south). Although conducted in Portuguese, participants from around the globe soon joined the creative process, sharing and altering with care the projects at hand.

The selection of flowers through their local symbolic meanings, colors, textures, formats, and healing powers evoked memories of craft practices that several expressed they had not engaged since childhood. Moreover, participants benefited from each other's knowledge of the remedies of plants, herbs, and flowers in teas and healing baths. Given that this all took place within a virtual venue, collaborative practices coincided with commonly held notions that everyone is able to design and share their experiences (Escobar 2018). The Flower Punchers initiative developed inclusive modes of knowledge exchange, reflecting on the use of natural resources and empowering co-creation. The only guiding principle was to invoke the well-known trio of rethink, recycle, and reuse of leaves and debris found in street gutters and private gardens as raw materials for textile printing. Precisely, an ontological approach to design reinforces practices that allow the creators to revisit their own ancestry and culture, crucial at this juncture in what is imagined as a circular economy. By regenerating natural systems, using materials to their full extent and re-using waste for the purposes of design seemed to evoke the loss of biodiversity and cultural diversity at large.[5]

The Flower Punchers group members began by stabilizing stocks relative to their flows, that is, noting which plants were available each month and documenting neighborhood areas where weeds proliferated during public maintenance service disruptions. Prints made exclusively of plant surfaces and natural dyes spoke to the local knowledge found just outside of one's home. Rhythmic patterns, color charts, multifaceted shapes and textures made each creation a unique process of discovery. If one specific leaf or flower was not available due to its expired life cycle, it could be substituted by a digital version or different species to move forward with a whole new approach.

Innovation seeks to implement invention, potentializing the creation and usage of something new (Mohd Zawawi et al., 2016). In other words, innovation can add layers incrementally, adding variable uses to materials, objects and practices (88). As nature became a regular guest to workshops, imprinting the crossroad between traditional knowledge and emerging technologies, The Flower Punchers realized that the hammering of flowers and herbs in open-air might allow the participant to reflect on social distancing and center healing, if only for an hour of joy in a new daily routine to enhance emotional health. Since most members had never met and were joining workshops from around the world, these virtual meetings were also spaces with which to meet kindred spirits and share values. The common denominator, however, was that all members had connections to the creative economy impacted by the pandemic. These dedicated innovators were led by the vision that design projects engage and reward all participants with "a sense of ownership," at the same time maintaining vital ties to more collective results (Escobar 2018; Garcia 2010).

On the other hand, technology is a differential. Once printed, pieces of paper or textiles were used as markers for augmented reality (AR) elements, inviting the user to create digital patterns inspired by physical prints. First, the user received instructions on how to download a free app. After downloading, the mobile device camera was directed towards the printed marker, providing the user with an extra visual layer complete with filters, films, and even music, adding value to the experience. As a result, handmade and digital floral goods transformed elements mainly considered without logical use—remnant stones, herbal debris, flower residues, weeds found in gutters—into meaningful objects. The iconic plant that would come to represent The Flower Punchers, *Talinum paniculatum*, first appeared as a print on organic cotton. *Talinum paniculatum* is an edible weed that grows wildly in gutters and sidewalks all over Brazil and throughout most of Latin America; it serves as a symbol of resilience, growing widly and yet full of vitamins and minerals like magnesium, zinc, and iron.

Twenty numbered textile samples made up the first collaborative collection, with analogic mood boards containing elements recycled from the process to promote zero waste. The inspirational box that comprised this mood box brought together images, candles, soaps, potpourris, or natural incense, among other digital goods inspired by the particular plants gathered. Designs could become matrices for digital printing or as a base for activities like embroidery, painting, or sewing. Through social media, customers engaged sales amidst instructions on varying colors and textures that might emerge after four to six months. Because time inevitably transforms flower pounded textiles, we wondered how to turn disadvantages into a positive outcome. The ephemeral nature of some

Figure 18.2 *Talinum paniculatum* was the plant chosen to create a print for an augmented reality marker for Cris Romagna's song launch. Courtesy of The Flower Punchers.

dyes seemed like an opportunity for others to engage this process and refresh the flower pounding themselves, thus building upon the sense of community among artisans and designers. Designs evolved as a hybrid combination of material and immaterial states, moving towards what has become a continuous collaboration. In essence, design as a natural healer.

Instagram filters, which promoted playful social media engagement while bringing local biodiversity into home interiors, applied to items as ordinary as the kitchen tablecloth. This trend was primarily spread by free apps such as Acute Art,[6] which represents works by prominent contemporary artists. Architect Solimar Isaac applied a combination of software technologies to allow for digital flower modeling to match textiles by The Flower Punchers. She created the filters *Purple Flowers* and *Hibiscus*, so that participants could display and share digital flower bouquets atop said tablecloths, matching prints according to taste or mood. Eventually, there were new virtual environments, including a 360-degree showroom with augmented reality elements that produced additional layers of meaning atop the handcrafted flowerpounded prints. A multidisciplinary team of creators including an art director, 3D designer, graphic designer, journalist and musicians brought this all together in an immersive showroom that simulated an art gallery installed in a tropical garden. Solimar Isaac, who can be credited for the design of this immersive garden, imagined a visitor following a pathway through which the stories of each and every print also played an entire soundtrack developed by music producer Neto Francatto. *Dancing Flowers*, digital artwork elaborated in partnership with 3D designer Letícia Motta from Studio Acci made for a fluid and interactive experience.[7] During weekly meetings at which leadership changed according to expertise, participants distributed tasks, showed their results, and voted on the next steps. At the same time, smaller groups connected daily to prepare details implied with each step. A two-month period of collaborative work emphasized the data analysis, experimentation, and tests required of the final digital design for this virtual garden. This was ultimately displayed during Inspiramais, Latin America's only innovation and materials design exhibit.[8] The Flower Punchers showroom arguably affirmed its environmental commitment with this immersive garden and the artistic series of digital textiles titled *Dancing Flowers*, which included original 3D prints by Letícia Motta, such as the series on *The Black Halfeti Rose* alongside a specially composed musical rhythm.

Bringing together digital technologies with artisanal craft techniques, which allowed for a new approach creation through user participation, uncovered changes in the design field that were akin to collaborative problem-solving. Unlocking the development of different forms of expression, this approach was perceived as what has been explained in another context as "collaborative, plural, participatory, and distributed" (Escobar 2018). With the integration of the very collaboration that the pandemic would have seemed to destroy, design imagined a circular flow close to ontological design (Escobar 2018). At a time when people needed hope the most, design as a form of natural healing reinforced the idea of adaption to new practices that promised a groundedness in wellbeing and the collaborative.

Delivery methods also expanded the project's ethos. Because non-digital mail had made a steady decline in recent decades, the pandemic created an even greater sense of urgency in connecting people. The Flower Punchers and Studio Acci co-sponsored a collaboration presenting an exclusive at-home audiovisual experience for fans of Brazilian singer Cris Romagna and songwriter Fernanda

Martins. A postcard that activated augmentative reality through a handcrafted print allowed people to connect in new ways with art, music and culture in Brazil. Graphic design effects aligned with a digital hologram on the front of the postcard, part of an app activated by the user. With mandatory shelter-in-place measures, those who received the postcard were able to place the virtual singer anywhere in their homes or garden for a picture and social media engagement, not to mention the sheer pleasure of listening to a preview of what was slated to become a popular song.

The pandemic likely accelerated technological innovations. The ability to create narratives across multiple modalities, respecting diverse perspectives and engaging alternatives whenever possible, may have resulted in what has become known as a "pluriversal" design perspective. While theoretical and all too soon to understand fully the roles and impact of participatory designs that have been the source of many experiments throughout the Americas, it is perhaps beneficial to engage its potential as a Latin American fashion process for healing. In diversifying cultural expression, which in this case was manifested through experimentation in the realm of augmented reality, graphic design, textile printing and music, the collaborative learning and development of skills during the pandemic may just have revealed some of the potential for empowering a more sustainable future. Might the experience of flowerpounding have reoriented the elements of fashion design to "make do" with what one could gather in an emergency and create with nature at a time during which so many of our countries had undergone draconian lockdowns?

Planetary health values inspired the participants of The Flower Punchers to continue their evolution as local citizens and global agents. A pandemic may have exposed the silver lining that created fertile ground for a previously unknown participatory culture. While monitoring of fruit-bearing plants and their flowers in Brazilian urban areas, designers imagined the properties and integration of native botanical species, many of which could be found in parks and along sidewalks, that in turn inspired new textile prints and practices. Contemporary fashion design in the post-pandemic era brings to fore these lessons, such as interior design that centers native plant-based textile printing using an Urban Orchard database facilitated by a network of Brazilian scientists (Soares *et al*, 2024). Gaining knowledge on the medicinal and nutritional properties of Brazilian botanicals and using augmented reality resources added all the more to textile developments.

Collaborative design as a form of healing may have become indispensable to Brazilian participatory design during the global pandemic. Social connections among practitioners reinforce that each contribution matters, that civic engagement and design justice prevails at significant historical junctures. We might add that the preservation of nature and awareness in what might be a more circular economy in light of climate change remains paramount. During the pandemic, Root and Saunders (2021) argue, Latin American creative industries transformed their platforms and frameworks to take on new meaning (94). The process that The Flower Punchers allowed important ways in which to experiment and rethink the way in which fashion design practices embraced alternatives and shifting values from distinct fields and geographical locations. Through digital networking, design as natural healing reimagined the tools of the trade in order to cross disciplinary bounders and even borders as the world locked itself into place. While participatory design seemed to enact a profound state of vulnerability, its collaborations activated important connections and fostered a "pluriverse" within and outside of the creative economy sectors. It was as if, perhaps for a moment, we were reimagining our individual and collective role in bringing about nature's nourishment and design justice amidst planetary change. It was, in other words, a solidarity-inspired moment calling us to "Do It Together."

Notes

1   When discussing the Brazilian creative industries landscape, this work uses the classifications adopted by the Federation of Industries of Rio de Janeiro (FIRJAN), which are presented in the mapping of the creative industry in Brazil. According to FIRJAN (2019), São Paulo is one of the most relevant markets for the creative sector in Brazil, providing 328,700 jobs, followed by Rio de Janeiro with 88,900 jobs (5). The updated mapping of 2022, also provided by FIRJAN, encompasses the years from 2017 to 2020. It shows 380,300 jobs provided by the creative industries in São Paulo, followed by 95,700 jobs in Rio de Janeiro. Therefore, both states were responsible for 50.9 percent of the formal creative jobs in the country in 2020. For more information, please refer to the original documents (in Portuguese): https://casafirjan.com.br/sites/default/files/2022-07/Mapeamento%20da%20Ind%C3%BAstria%20Criativa%20no%20Brasil%202022.pdf
2   For more information on this topic and global initiatives, the author suggests the access of Planetary Health Alliance, a growing consortium of universities, non-governmental organizations, research institutes and government institutions from more than 60 countries. Available at: https://www.planetaryhealthalliance.org/

3 In Japan, flowerpounding technique is mostly known as *tataki-zomé*, or a botanical print that does not use heat, vapor or hot water immersion. *Tataki* means hammering in Japanese, and *zomé* means to dye. India Flint, Australian-born textile artist, coined the term *hapa-zome*, also applied to refer to this technique. *Hapa* is the Japanese word for leaf, reflecting the essence of the process.

4 An herbarium is a collection of dried plant fragments *(exsiccata)* that are systematically dated, registered, classified, and preserved to provide botanical knowledge on local species and document flora biodiversity for future reference.

5 For more in-depth information on this concept, the author suggests the access of The Circular Economy Hub (CE-Hub), a network for sharing and collaborating that brings together various stakeholders. Available at: https://ce-hub.org. Moreover, the database provided online by the Ellen McArthur Foundation, the largest non-profit international organization devoted to engaging businesses, institutions, governments, cities, universities to set policies towards such goals, can be of interest. Available at: https://ellenmacarthurfoundation.org/

6 Acute Art is a digital project directed and curated by Daniel Birnbaum. Visual artworks in Virtual Reality (VR), Augmented Reality (AR), and Mixed Reality (MR) are signed by international artists and can be accessed through a free app available for both Android and IOS systems at Google Play and App Store. Moreover, the creative collaborations can also be seen in exhibitions that took place in public areas of Basel, London, Moscow, New York, and Venice. See the Acute Art website: http://www.acuteart.com

7 The Flower Punchers garden showroom briefing was conceived by the whole multidisciplinary team, while the development and implementation were led by architect Solimar Isaac, graphic designer Gabriela de Laurentis, and this author.

8 Inspiramais is held twice a year to launch around 600 different materials, which are seen by over 10 thousand visitors. After 20 physical editions held in São Paulo, the event had to migrate to a virtual environment in August 2020, considering the sanitary barriers and the necessary social distance.

Bibliography

Acute Art. 2021. "Artists." https://acuteart.com/

Amaral, Rodrigo Correia Do; Franco, Pedro Affonso Ivo, and Lira, André Luís Gomes (ed.). 2021. *Pesquisa de percepção dos impactos da COVID-19 nos setores cultural e criativo do Brasil: resumo*. The United Nations Educational, Scientific and Cultural Organization (UNESCO), and the UNESCO Office in Brasília. Available at https://unesdoc.unesco.org/ark:/48223/pf0000375069. © UNESCO 2020. Reproduced under a Creative Commons Attribution -ShareAlike 3.0 IGO (CC BY-SA 3.0 IGO) License.https://creativecommons.org/licenses/by-sa/3.0/igo/

De Jesus, Diego Santos Vieira. 2020 "Necropolitics and Necrocapitalism: The Impact of COVID-19 on Brazilian Creative Economy." *Modern Economy* 11: 1121–40. Available at https://doi.org/10.4236/me.2020.116082 © by authors and Scientific Research Publishing Inc. 2024. Reproduced under a Creative Commons Attribution 4.0 International License (CC BY 4.0). https://creativecommons.org/licenses/by/4.0/

Di Giulio, Gabriela Marques, Eliseu Alves, Waldman, João Nunes, Paulo Buss, Jaime Marchiori, Patrícia Constante, Tereza Campelo and Helena Ribeiro. 2024. "Saúde Global e Saúde Planetária: Perspectivas para uma transição para um mundo mais sustentável pós-COVID-19." *Ciência e Saúde Coletiva* (2021/Sep). http://www.cienciaesaudecoletiva.com.br/en/articles/saude-global-e-saude-planetaria-perspectivas-para-uma-transicao-para-um-mundo-mais-sustentavel-poscovid19/18184?id=18184. © by authors and Ciência e Saúde Coletiva – Revista da Associação Brasileira de Saúde Coletiva 2021. Reproduced under a Creative Commons Attribution 4.0 International License (CC BY 4.0). https://creativecommons.org/licenses/by/4.0/

Ellen MacArthur Foundation. 2021. "The Nature Imperative: How the Circular Economy Tackles Biodiversity Loss." https://ellenmacarthurfoundation.org/biodiversity-report

Escobar, Arturo. 2018. *Designs for the Pluriverse: Radical Interdependence, Autonomy, and the Making of Worlds*. Durham: Duke University Press.

Garcia, Carol. 2010. *Imagens errantes: ambiguidade, resistência e cultura de moda*. São Paulo: Estação das Letras e Cores.

Mapeamento da indústria criativa no Brasil / Firjan – 2022. Rio de Janeiro: Firjan. https://casafirjan.com.br/sites/default/files/2022-07/Mapeamento%20da%20Ind%C3%BAstria%20Criativa%20no%20Brasil%202022.pdf

Mohd Zawawi, Nur Fadiah, Sazali Abd Wahab, Abdullah Al-Mamun, Abu Sofian Yaacob, Naresh Kumar Al Samy, and Syed Ali Fazal. 2016 "Defining the Concept of Innovation and Firm Innovativeness: A Critical Analysis from Resource-Based View Perspective." *International Journal of Business and Management* 11 (6): 87–94. https://doi.org/10.5539/ijbm.v11n6p87 © by authors and International Journal of Business and Management 2016. Reproduced under a Creative Commons Attribution 4.0 International License (CC BY 4.0). https://creativecommons.org/licenses/by/4.0/

Root, Regina. A. and Stephanie N. Saunders 2021. "Refashioning Collaborations: Crossing Borders During the Pandemic." *Middle Atlantic Review of Latin American Studies* 5 (1): 88–96. https://doi.org/10.23870/marlas.361 © by authors and Middle Atlantic Review of Latin American Studies 2021. Reproduced under a Creative Commons Attribution 4.0 International License (CC BY 4.0). https://creativecommons.org/licenses/by/4.0/

Soares, Filipi Miranda, Luís Ferreira Pires, Maria Carolina Garcia, Maria Carolina, Lídio Coradin, Natália P. Ghilardi-Lopes, Rubens Rangel Silva and, Aline Monteiro de Carvalho. 2024. Supporting data for "Citizen Science Data on Urban Forageable Plants: A Case Study in Brazil" [Data set]. *GigaScience Database*. http://dx.doi.org/

10.5524/102499 © by authors and Oxford University Press GigaScience 2024. Reproduced under a Creative Commons Attribution 4.0 International License (CC BY 4.0). https://creativecommons.org/licenses/by/4.0/

World Health Organization. 2023. data.who.int, WHO Coronavirus (COVID-19) dashboard \> Cases [Dashboard]. https://data.who.int/dashboards/covid19/cases https://doi.org/10.5539/ijbm.v11n6p87 © World Health Organization 2023 Reproduced under a Creative Commons Attribution 4.0 International (CC BY 4.0) https://creativecommons.org/licenses/by/4.0/

Index

Note: Page numbers in italics indicate figures.

Abey, 80
ableism, 153
ACAB (All Cops Are Bastards) clan, 175
Acapulco, Mexico, 39, 47
accessories, 151. *See also specific accessories*
    material culture of fashion and, 39–55
    nation-building and, 42
    for protesting, 174–179, 184n11
Aching, Gerald, 126
ACT UP, 238
activism, 8, 229, 238, 245, 254. *See also* protests
Acute Art, 266, 270n6
Adichie, 16
adornments, 36, 95–96. *See also* accessories
advertisements, in Peru, 6–7
Affonso, João, *Três Séculos de Moda*, 18
Africa, *quitandeiras* in, 99
African Americans, racist depictions of, 114–115
African-descent Peruvians, 111–113
Africans, enslaved, 93
Afro-Brazilian culture, 93–107
Afro-Brazilian identities, 105n1, 136–144, *141*
Afro-Brazilian styles, 93–107
Afro-Brazilian women, 6, 93–107, 97–99, *97*, *98*
Afro-Cuban culture, 80
Afro-descendants, 95, 109
Afro-Peruvian women, 6–7, 108–119
Afro-Peruvians, 108
agency, 9–11, 149
Aguadeño hats, 201
Aguardientes Vargas advertisement, 115
Agudelo, Carolina, 11n1
AIDS epidemic, 8, 159, 161–162, 163, 164, 167
alabaster, 33

Alessandri, Pilola, 162
Almagro, Manuel, 96–97
alternative femininities, 147
Alvarado Perales, Isabel, 18
Amador, Fernán Félix de, 128
Amaral, Rodrigo Correia Do, 261
Amaral, Tarisola do, 132n2
Ancízar, Manuel, 62
Andalusia, 43, 43–44, 46–47, 49, 50, 51n13
Andeans, 33–35, 118
Andes, 32–33, 64, 118
Andrade, Oswald de, 132n2
Andrade, Rita Morais de, 4, 6, 15–24, 22n6
Andre, María Claudia, 7–8
Angola, 99
Angrand, Léonce, 109
anonymity, 8, 103
anti-*encapuchados* law, 181
anti-Indigenous racism, 10
anti-mining movement, 245
Antioquia, Colombia, 65
anti-racism, 139
apus, 33–34, *34*, 35
Aragón, Alba F., 7
archives, 4–6, 15–24, 120–121
    in Brazil, 15–24
    colonialism and, 15–16
    consolidation of, 20
    creation of, 20
    decolonialization and, 19–20
    defense of, 4, 15–24
    inclusivity and, 19–20
    personal, 136–144
Archives Matter, 21n2
Archivio Istituto Luce online, 18
Arévalo, Bernardo, 254
Argentina, 8, 222
    cultural fragments and recycled identities in, 188–197
    dictatorship in, 188–197, *194*, 196n2

historiography of fashion in, 193–194
independence movement in, 121
textile recycling in, 188–197
transition to democracy in, 195
arpilleras, 8, 164
Arriaga, Pablo José de, 34
artisan carving tradition, 32–36
artisans. *See also* craftsmanship
   educated, 63
   pre-Columbian, 32–35
Asia, 40, 43, 49–50
Asociación Femenina para el Desarrollo de Sacatepéquez (AFEDES, the Women's Association for the Development of Sacatepéquez), 242, 243, 245–246, 249, 250–254, 256n9
Aspuac, Angelina, 245–246, 247, 250, 256n8
augmented reality (AR), 265, *266*, 270n6
Augustinians, 29
Aunt Jemima advertisements, 113–114, 115
authoritarianism, 8
authorship, 244
   collective, 245–246, 256n8
   individual, 252
autobiographical narrative, 184n10
Avianca Airlines, 66–67
Axid (Andrés Ramos), 166
Aymara women, 7–8, 147–157, 151
Aztecs, 28, 30, 32

Babel, Anna M., 150
Bad Bunny, 208, 232
Bahia, Brazil, 93–107, 96–97, 99
balaclavas, 174, 176–177, 181, 184n7
Balandre, 57
Balenciaga, 18, 203
Ballesteros, Adolfo Montiel, 128–129
Balmain, 205
Balzac, Honoré de, 206
bandanas, 184n11, 222, 223
Bantu, 99
Barragán, Víctor, 10, 228, 228–241, 229, 232–235, 239
barras bravas, 173
barrio(s), 204, 206
Batá, 80

Batos, 83
Baudelaire, Charles, 200
beauty, 80–82, 147–157
Becerra, María, 203
belts, 201
Bennett, Jill, 190
Bensaid, Norbert, 193
Berlin Wall, fall of, 74
Betancur, Adriana, 11n1
Biblioteca Nacional catalog, 97
Biblioteca Pública Piloto, 200
binationalism, 228–241
Black bodies, 94, 95
Black communities, in Brazil, 21n22, 22n3
Black diaspora, 137, 141, 143
Black femininity, idea of, 94
Black heritage, family photographs and, 136–144
Black Lives Matter Movements, 21n2, 168n12
Black women, 98–99
   commodification of images of, 93
   dress practices of, 93–107
   exploitation of images of, 93
   identities of, 104–105
   images of, 93–107
   photographs of, 100–103
   resistance against objectification, 104–105
   stereotypes of, 99
   visibility of, 93
blackness, 115
Blacks, 16, 19, 61, 63, 64, 65, 105n1, 149
   enslaved, 93, 96–97, 98–99
   free, 96–97, 98–99
   marginalization of, 93
   ruanas and, 58–59, 66
Blanco, Alda, 47
Bleichmar, Daniela, 41
Blessd, 208
blindfolds, 179–180, 181, 184n11
blouses, 242, 255n1
the body/bodies
   Black bodies, 94, 95
   bodily experiences, 56
   body expressions, 8
   colonization of, 59
   politics of, 173
   racialization of, 59

as territory, 123
textiles and, 104
Boer, Alida, 249
Bogotá, Colombia, 56, 68, 202
Bois de Boulogne, 128
Bolivia, 7–8
   caste system in, 149–150
   Constitutional Assembly, 154
   House of Deputies, 154
   women in, 147–157
bomber jackets, 230
Bonafini, Hebe de, 192, 196n3
Bonnaffé, A.A., 6, 108–109, 114
   La Chichera, 109–110
   La Marinera, 110
   Recuerdos de Lima: tipos, trajes, y costumbres, 109
   La Zamacueca/La Marinera, 109, 116–117
books
   book burnings, 245
   objectification of, 126
boots, 201
borderlessness, 233
borders, 10
Boucher, François, 19
boundaries, porous, 233, 238
Bourbon Reforms, 59
Bowers v. Hardwick, 238
bowler hats, 150, 153–154
brands
   brand names, 74, *79*
   brand themes, 76–78, *77*
   in Cuba, 73–89, *79*
   Cuba's strategic use of, 84
   foreign, 86n7
   licensing of, 75, 84
   logos, *77*, 82–83, 84
   "Mexican Brand," 215, 216, 223
   national identity and, 83
   quality and, 83–84
   semiotic approach to brand identity, 74–75, 85
   as semiotic engines, 74–75, 85
   as tools of statecraft, 74–75
Brazil
   African presence in, 94
   Afro-Brazilian identity, 136–145
   Afro-Brazilian style, 93–107

archives in, 15–24
Black peoples in, 22n3, 93–107, 136–145
colonial period in, 7
coloniality in, 93–107
COVID-19 pandemic in, 260
dress in, 15–24, 93–107
expatriation of cultural assets from, 16–17
fashion designers in, 260–272
museums in, 15–24
museum's statute law (*Estatuto de Museus – Lei* 11904/09, 2009) in, 20
national imaginary shaped by coloniality, 95
nationalism in, 20
portraiture in, 93–107
race in, 22n3, 93–107
repatriation of cultural assets to, 17
slavery in, 93, 136–144
societal formation process in, 105n1
women of, 93–107
Brazilian identity, 19, 136–145
Breccia, Mariano, 188–197
bricolage, 208
Buche, 204
Buenos Aires, Argentina, 189–190, 193, 195
Burke, Peter, 99
Butler, Judith, 184n9

Cabral, Alliny Maia, 6, 46–47
Cabral Agudo Bejarano, Manuel, *46*, 47, 51n12
Cabrera Arús, María A., 5–6
cachacos, 62
Cacique, 76–77, 82
cajón, 108
Calanca, Daniela, 18
Cali, Colombia, 202
camisa, 57
Campt, Tina M., 138
Candomblé, 99, 105n3
Canizales, Akhil (Piiciis), 166
canotiers, 201
Canton, China, 40
The Canvas (Brooklyn, New York), 85
capisayo, 58
capitalism, 244, 254

capuchas, 173–174, 176–179, 180, *180*, 181–182, *181*
Carnival, 151
Carrera, Magali, 47
Cartagena de Indias, Colombia, 2
cartes de visite, 95
Casa da Hera, 20
Casa Mappin, 18
casaca, 65
Casas, Francisco, 165
Cassatt, Mary, 51n12
Castro, Estiven, 68
Castro, Ryan, 203
Castro y Ordóñez, Rafael, 6, 93–107, *96*, *97*, 97–98, *97*, *98*, 99, 100
Catholic reliquary lockets (*medallones relicarios*), 5, 25–38
Catholicism, 5, 28–30, 34, 35, 37, 231
chamanto, 57
Chamberlain, Henry, 98
Chanca, 33
Chanel, 206
Chavín civilization, 32–33
Cheang, Sarah, 4
Chiapas, 221
Chicano aesthetics, 228–241
Chicanos, 238–241
Chicos del 12-na, *196*
Chile, 222
  abortion movement in, 178
  anti-*encapuchados* law in, 181
  COVID-19 pandemic in, 182
  dictatorship in, 179–180, 184n8
  feminist movement in, 175–179, 178, 184n8
  independence movement in, 121
  loca community in, 8
  under Pinochet, 158–159, 161
  politics of clothed body in, 172–187
  protests in, 8, 172–187, 183n4, 184n11
  social outburst in, 172–187
  trans representation in, 158–171
  transition to democracy, 159, 161
China, 40, 43, 223
chinas poblanas, *rebozos* (Mexican scarves) and, 48–49
Chinese luxury goods, 44–45
chinoiserie, 45
chintz fabric, 104

choice, lack of, 10
cholas/cholitas, 8, 147–157,156n11
  cholitas paceñas, 150
  discrimination against, 152
  embracing Indigenous roots, 153–154, 155n1, 155n5
  empowerment of, 152
  ethnicity and, 153
  femininity and, 147–157
  participation in masculine sports, 151–152
  undomesticated femininity of, 151–152
cholos/as, 149. *See also cholas/cholitas*
Chorographic Commission, 61, 70n4
Christianity, 28–30, 31, 32, 35, 37. *See also* Catholicism
Circular Economy Hub (CE-Hub), 270n5
citizenship, dress and, 121
Ciudad Nezhualcóyotl, Mexico, 223
Clandestina, 84–85
class, 8, 42, 44, 47, 48, 147, 149–150, 150
Clearly, Karol G., 204
clothing, 8, 95–96. *See also specific items of clothing*
  accessibility of, 73
  Afro-Brazilian identities and, 136–145
  class and, 8, 47, 150
  in Cuba, 73
  expressions through, 173
  informally produced, 86n16
  in Mexico, 47
  names of, 73–89
  personal style and, 8
  protective, 174–175, *181*
  rationing of, 73–74, 76
  region and, 8
  resistance and, 172–187
  second-hand, 156n8
  as space for inherited identity, 7
  used, 8, 163–164, 191–192
  as whitening tool, 59
clown shoes, 234
Coatlicue, 30
coats, 230–231. *See also* jackets
Cobb, Julia Symmes, 159
Colectivo Complejo Conejo, 177
collars, 201
collections, personal, 136–144

collective agency, 9–11
Collective Las Tesis, 179, 184n11
collectivism, 73
Colombi, Beatriz, 123
Colombia, 8–9, 56–72, 159, 168n12, 198–211, 203
   Augustinians, 70n1
   Autonomous Period, 57, 58
   emerging national textile industry in, 63
   human rights violations in, 166
   independence of, 60
   national fashion system in, 67
   national identity in, 60–61
   textile industry in, 204–205
   war on drugs in, 202
Colombiamoda, 204–205
colonial identity, 5
colonialism, 4, 17, 25–38, 41, 43, 44, 137
   aesthetics of, 56
   development of archives and museums during, 15–16
   racialization and, 94–95
coloniality, 3, 58, 95, 103, 244
   Black bodies and, 94
   in Brazil, 7, 93–107
   feminine identity and, 147–157
   the gaze and, 147–157
   gender and, 147–157
   of power, 57, 59–60
   Quijano's theory of, 93
   theory of, 6
colonization, 25–38
   Catholicism and, 28–30
   cultural appropriation and, 29–30
   European narratives of, 27
colonized dialectics, 149
El Comercio
   advertisements in, 111–115, *117*
   "Bailando 'La Marinera'" advertisement in, 111
Cometa, 82
Comisión Presidencial contra la Discriminación y el Racismo contra los Pueblos Indígenas en Guatemala (CODISRA, the Presidential Commission on Discrimination and Racism against Indigenous Peoples in Guatemala), 246

Commission on Indigenous Peoples (Guatemala), 246, 247
commodity culture, 124
communism, in Cuba, 73
community, 8
conopa, 33, 34–35, 37
conquest, 25–38
conquistadors, 28–29, 31–32, 216, 245
Consejos de Tejedoras (Weaving Councils), 252
conservation, prioritizing, 4, 15–24
consumer goods, access to, 150
consumerism, 63, 126
   modernist disavowal of, 126–127
   women and, 122
Consumir lo que el país produce es hacer patria (To Consume what the Country Produces Builds the Fatherland), 73
consumption, in Cuba, 73–74
contact zones, 27–28, 31
Continental, 80
conversation, 10
conversion, 28–29, 32, 34–36, 37
coolhunting, 190
Coordinadora Feminista Universitaria (Cofeu) (Feminist University Coordinator), 175–176
copyright protections, 244–246, 251–253
Cordovez, José María, 62–63
Corpus Christi festivities, 50
Correa, Guillermo Antonio, 199–200
corsets, 199
Cortés, Hernán, 31
Corujo-Martín, Inés, 5
cosmopolitanism, 122, 127
costumbrismo, 6, 41–43, *46*, 47, 49, 51n12, 109
Cota, 68
cotton, 48, 58
Council of Fashion Designers of America (CFDA), 206
The Coveteur, 206
COVID-19 pandemic, 4, 10–11, 15–24, 139, 159, 169n18, 182, 248
   blurring of public and private boundaries during, 2–3

in Brazil, 260
in Chile, 182
face masks and, 9–10, 215–227
in Guatemala, 248
impact of, 4
metaphors surrounding, 217–218
Mexico and, 215–227
shortages due to, 10–11
craftsmanship
artisan carving tradition, 32–36
digital technologies and, 260–272
as racialized labor, 65–66
social mobility and, 65
creative agency, 9–11
creativity, 7, 58, 244
creole elites, 60
Cromos, 67
cross-cultural approaches, 20–21
crossdressing, 200
Cruz-Bermeo, William, 9
Cuba, 43, 110
brands in, 73–89, *79*
clothing in, 73
communism in, 73
consumer agency in, 73
consumption in, 73–74
Decree-Law No. 68, 76
fashion boom in, 84–85
footwear industry in, 73
foreign influences and, 77–78
independence movement in, 121
informally produced and sold clothing in, 86n16
Ministry of Domestic Commerce, 75
National Office of Inventions, Technical Information, and Trademarks (ONIITEM), 74, 76
nationalism in, 78–80, *79*
nationalization in, 5–6, 76
Obama's visit to, 85
principle themes in brandscape, 76–78, *77*
rationing of industrial goods in, 73–74, 76
reorientation of fashion toward the utilitarian in, 81
scarcity in, 73
Soviet Union and, 73, 74, 76
strategic use of fashion branding, 84

textile industry in, 73, 78
transformation of brandscape after 1989, 84
Cuban Bureau of Industrial Property (OCPI), 5–6, 74
Cuban Revolution, 5–6, 73, 75
Cubartesanía, 83
cultural appropriation
colonization and, 29–30
mantones de Manila, 44–45
cultural assets, expatriation and repatriation of, 16–17
cultural assimilation, forced, 248, 252
cultural heterogeneity, 36
cultural hybridity, 30–31, 49, 228–241
cultural identity, 122–123
"cultural otherness," 44
culture, 215–227
empowering lens of, 6–7
theme of, 80–82
Cumming, Valerie, 22n
Cundinamarca, Colombia, 68

Dahl, Ulrika, 155n2
dandyism, 8–9, 198–211, *201*
Darío, Rubén, 7, 120, 121, 123, 132n3, 133n6
"Balada sobre la sencillez de las rosas perfectas" (Ballad on the simplicity of perfect roses), 124, *125*
De Greef, Erica, 4
De Jesus, Diego Santos Vieira, 261
De la Calle, Benjamin, 199, *201*
deaccessioning, 22n10
Dean, Carolyn, 30–31
Debret, Jean-Baptiste, 98
Declaraciones de la Selva Lacandona, 221
decolonial sustainability, 215
decoloniality, 3
decolonialization, 5, 36, 154, 216
of fashion, 56–72
of fashion practices, 69
fashion studies and, 243–244
defiance, 94
Denmark, 17
Dennis, Fred, 234
department stores, 5–6, 127
derbies, 151

design, 8, 260–272
  community-style, 188–189, 195–196
  design crisis, 9
  design interventions, 8
  design thinking, 9
  as natural healer, 260–272
designers, 10
  in Brazil, 260–272
  designer education, 9
  international, 10
  Mexican American, 228–241
d'Espagan, Pierre, 62
Devotion coat, 230–231
devotional objects, 25–38
D'Gala, 81, 82
Di Girolamo, Greta, 177, *180*
Diana, 80
Diego, Jeannine, 84
digital humanities, 4
digital technologies, artisanal craft techniques and, 260–272
Dirty War, 189, 191
discourse, 9, 115
discrimination, 8, 153, 155n5, 156n10
  ethnic, 94–95
  institutionalized, 155n5, 156n7
  national, 94–95
disidentification, 233, 235
12-na, 188–197, *196*
Dolce & Gabbana, 205
Dom Pedro II, Emperor, 96, 97
domestic labor, 6–7, 113–114
Dominican Republic-Central America Free Trade Agreement (DR-CAFTA), 256n7
Dominicans, 29
dress, 95–96
  in Brazil, 93–107
  citizenship and, 121
  collection of, 20
  vs. fashion, 122
  national, 41, 44
  photography and, 100
  political agency and, 121
  social perceptions and, 94
dress history, 9
  of Brazil, 15–24
  decolonial perspective, 15–24
  photography and, 94

dressing
  agency embedded in act of, 6
  dress practices, 56
  as space for inherited identity, 7

Earle, Rebecca, 47
earnings, 10
earrings, 151
Earth Goddesses, Indigenous, 29–30, 35
Eastern Europe, state socialist countries in, 74–75, 76
Eccleston, Katelina, 203
Ecuador, 58
Edwards, Louise, 44
Eisenhower, Dwight, 230
El Gurú del Sabor, 204
El Hijo del Soberano, 220
El Museo Universal, 96
El Santo, 219
elegance, 66
Elegancias (Elegances), 7, 120, 124–125, *125*, 127, 130, *131*, 132–133n5, 132n3
ELLE Brazil, 139
Ema Klabin Museum, 20
emancipation, 142
embroidery, 47
Empire of Brazil, 96
encapuchados, 174, 181
enslaved peoples, 58–59, 93, 96–99, 108–118, 142
entravée, 128
Entwistle, Joanne, 160–161
environmental devastation, 9
Equihua, Brenda, 10, 228, 229, 230–231, *231*, 232, 238–239
eroticism, 152
Escobar, Arturo, 261
Escola Nacional de Belas Artes, 18
esparza, rafa, 232
essentialism, 148, 152, 153
Estrella, 77
ethnicity, 44, 105n1, 238
  cholas/cholitas and, 153
  commodification of, 153
  ethnic discrimination, 94–95
ethnographic photographers, 95
eugenics, 59, 66
Eurocentrism, 5, 16, 154

Europeans, 95–97
evangelization, 216, 231–232
Evans, Caroline, 164
exoticism, 45, 94, 128, 153
explorers, 31–32. *See also* conquistadors
expression, 10
extractivism, 245
eye gear, 174

face coverings. *See* face masks
face masks, 9–10, 10, 173–180, *180*, 181–182, *181*, 215–227. *See also* masks
    after colonization, 216
    anti-abortion protests and, 222
    as communication devices, 223
    cultural history of, 9–10
    cultural identity and, 216
    as defense or protection, 216–217
    fashion and, 223, 224
    feminist movement and, 222–223
    illness and, 216, 217–218
    Indigenous artisan production of, 220–221
    Indigenous peoples and, 220–221
    as "luxury" or "niche" items, 223, 224
    as metaphor for Mexican character, 9–10
    in Mexico, 9–10, 215–227, 216
    as performative instrument, 225
    personalizing, 218–219
    as playful device of expression, 217
    political use of, 174–179, 222–223
    pre-Columbian, 216
    ritual, 216–217
    scarcity of, 224
    sustainability and, 223
    "wear a face mask" campaign, 219–220
    Zapatista movement and, 221–222
failure, queer art of, 148–149
Fainal, 207
Fals-Borda, Orlando, 57–58
family histories, 136–144, 143
family photographs, 7, *141*
fashion, 120–135, 150
    Black personal stories and, 141
    cholas/cholitas and, 147–157
    colonial narrative of what counts as, 56
    commercialization of, 81
    criticized as instrument of capitalist exploitation and class division, 73
    as dangerous practice, 128
    decolonialization of, 56–72
    vs. dress, 122
    face masks and, 223, 224
    femininity and, 7–8
    gender and, 120–135
    hegemonic, 57
    historiography of, 193–194
    hybridity and, 48
    image and, 7
    literary style and, 120–135
    masculinity and, 198–211
    material culture of, 39–55
    as means of domination or resistance, 16
    politics and, 42–43
    silenced voices and, 4
    terms of representation and, 4
    trans representation and, 158–171
    transnational experiences in, 228–241
    utilitarian reorientation of, 81
fashion boom, in Cuba, 84–85
fashion boutiques, in Cuba, 5–6
fashion columns, in newspapers, 193
fashion cycles, 3
fashion discourse, 10
fashion history, 5, 9, 18, 18–19, 39–55, 56–72
    fashion historiography, 18–19
    fashion history archive, 17
    representation of, 4, 15–24
fashion imaginaries, 1–2
fashion industry
    COVID-19 pandemic and, 10–11
    in Cuba, 73–89
    nationalized in Cuba, 76
fashion intellectual property, 242–259
fashion magazines, 7, 120–135. *See also specific magazines*
fashion practices, decolonialization of, 69
fashion shows, 205, 206, *207*, 234–235
fashion studies, 3–4, 7–8, 147
    decolonial approaches to, 243–244
    Latin American, 3–4
fashion studies research, 2
featherwork, 19–20

Federation of Industries of Rio de Janeiro (FIRJAN), 269n1
fedoras, 150
Fehérváry, Krisztina, 75
Feid, 203, 208
Felipe II, 58
Félix, María, 165
Felski, Rita, 132n2, 133n7
female body, as territory, 123
female readership, 122, 127
feminine identity, 44
    coloniality and, 147–157
    Indigenous reconfigurations of, 147–157
    Spanish, 44
feminism, 120–135
femininity, 50, 120–135, 199, 220. *See also* feminine identity
    alternative femininities, 147
    bourgeois, 163
    cholas/cholitas and, 147–157, 151–152
    constructs of, 154
    fashion and, 7–8
    ideal, 48–49
    normative constructs of, 147
    patriarchal, 148
    queer femininities, 147
    racialized, 147–157
    stereotypes and, 6
    traditional, 128
feminist movement, 120–135, 130, *131*, 216
    in Chile, 175–179, 184n8
    face masks and, 222–223
feminist theory, 147–157
femme, definition of, 148
femme identities, 147–157
femme studies, 147–157, 154
femme theory, 7–8
femmebodiments, 148, 155n2
femmephobia, 148
Ferdinand, 28
Feria de Sevilla (the Seville Fair), 50
Fernández, Carla, 223
Fernández, Carmelo, 61–62
Fernandez, Leire, 85
Fernández Cifuentes, Luis, 44
Fierro, Francisco "Pancho," 109
filipichines, 199–203, *201*

The Flower Punchers, 10–11, 260–272, *263*, *266*, 270n7
flower pounding, also called *hapa zome*, or *tataki-zome*, 260–272, 268, 270n3
flowers, 199
folklorization, 249
food shortages, 8
footwear, 49, 82–83, 137, 141, 142, *142*, 156n6, 234–235
    rationing of, 73–74, 76
    as symbol of freedom, 142
footwear industry, in Cuba, 73
Forastelli, Fabricio, 161
Ford, Tanisha, 143
Fotografía Rodríguez, 66
Foucault, Michel, 121
found textiles, 8
fragrance advertisements, 124
Francatto, Neto, 267
France, 17
Franciscans, 29
Franco, Pedro Affonso Ivo, 261
free Blacks, 96–97, 98–99
Frente Patriótico Manuel Rodríguez, 174
Freyre, Gilberto, 19
fringes, 39, 40, 44, 45, 48, 51n17, 63

Gage, Kelly, 104
Gaitán, Jorge Eliécer, 66
Gallego, Romualdo, 8–9, 198, 199, 200, 201
Garcia, Carol, 10–11, 11n1
García, Sandra E., 166
Garvey, Ellen Grumber, 127
gas masks, 175
Gatopardo magazine, 233
Gauguin, Paul, 51n14
Gauthier, Mélissa, 163
Gaytán Cuesta, Andrea A., 9–10
the gaze, 64, 94, 95
    colonial, 147–157
    coloniality and, 147–157
    male, 176, 234
    mestizaje, 151
    white, 57
GEF, 205, *207*, 208
gender, 7–8, 42, 44, 147–157, 238
    celebratory non-binary representations of, 166–167

coloniality and, 147–157
commodification of, 153
fashion and, 120–135
gender codes, 154
gender discrimination, 148
gender empowerment, 8
gender norms, 9
gender performance, 148
gender roles, 7–8
gender violence, 9
Indigenous reconfigurations of, 147–157
literary style and, 120–135
nationalism and, 42–43
gender identity, 5, 50
    changes in terminology, 159–160
    Indigenous, 149
gender violence, 9
Germans, 97
Gill, Leslie, 150
Girón, Lázaro María, 61–62
global encounters, 39–55
global networks, 41
Global North, 9, 165, 198
Global South, 198
global studies, 42
globalization, 244
gloves, 175, 201
goggles, 174, 175
gold thread, 48
Goldgel, Víctor, 121
Gómez, Ángel, 56
Gómez, Francisco, 67, 68
Gómez Carrillo, Ernesto, 120, 127, 130
Gonzales, Lélia, 22n3
González-Stephan, Beatriz, 123
Grammy Music Awards, 209
Gran Chester, 207
grand magasins, 127
Granziera, Patrizia, 29
Grinberg, Miguel, 193
Guajardo Rives, Verónica, 18
Guam, 43
Guatemala, 10, 28
    Bill No. 5247, 246–247, 255n4, 255n5
    Congress, 246–247
    Constitutional Court in, 245, 246–247, 251
    COVID-19 pandemic in, 248
    government's appropriation of Maya textile traditions, 247–248, 248
    Indigenous textile design in, 242–259
    Intellectual Property Registry, 247
    Law of Authorship Rights and Related Rights (No. 33-98), 255n4
    Law of Industrial Property (No. 57-2000)., 255n4
    Maya weavers in, 242–259
    National Congress, 252
    protests in, 245
    tourism in, 10, 242–259
    tourism industry in, 247–249
    women in, 10, 242–259
Guatemala City, Guatemala, 247, 249
Guayaquil, Ecuador, 34
Guerrero, Nicolas, 168n12
Guevara, Che, *181*
Guirior, Manuel de, 59
Guizio, Danielle, 167
Gutiérrez Nájera, Manuel, 126

hairstyles, 150
Halberstam, Jack, 148–149
Halberstam, Judith, 147
Hanneken, Jaime, 122–123
Harper's Bazaar, 223
Harrison, Brian F., 166
Harrod's, 193, 195
Hart, Stephen, 133n6
Hartman, Saidiya, 137
hats, 150, 151, 153–154, 201. *See also specific kinds of hats*
haute couture, 8, 10, 20
Haynes, Nell, 152, 153
headscarves, of Mothers of the Plaza de Mayo, 190, 196n2
headwraps, 94, 102–103, 103, 105
Hebdige, Dick, 208
Hector & Tito, 204
helmets, 174–175, 175
Hendrickson, Carol, 251
Heroína, 83
Hiner, Susan, 41
hip-hop, 203, 208
Hispano-Arab cultural exchange, 48
Hispano-Arab culture, 44
Holm, Olaf, 34
Holy Week, 50

homosexuality, 238
hoodies, 230-231. *See also* jackets
hooks, bell, 140
Hoskin, Rhea A., 148, 154
Huamanga stone, 33-34, 34, 35-36, 36, 37
Huari, 32-33
Huarpa, 33
human rights, 8, 222
Human Rights Ombudsman, 247
Human Rights Watch, 166
humor, 234
Hungary, 75
hybridity, 30-31, 31, 35-36, 36-37, 41, 44, 48, 233. *See also mestizaje*
    cultural, 49-50
    hybrid dress, 44
    positive valuation of, 46-47
    racist stereotypes of, 49
    in Spanish national discourse, 46-47

Ibáñez, Laura, 176
iconization, 153
iconography, 231
identity/identities, 215-227
    cholas/cholitas and, 147-157
    gender, 5
    identity formation, 104, 105n1
    inherited, 7
    national, 5
    racialized, 5
    shifting, 45
    shifting borders of, 228-241
ikat technique, 48
Ike jacket, 230
illas, 33-34
illness, masks and, 217-218
images
    fashion and, 7
    meaning constructed through, 99-104
immigrant experience, 228-241
imperialism, 41, 43
improvisation, 29, 30, 31, 36-37
Incas, 28, 30, 32, 33, 57, 58, 64
inclusivity, 206
independence movements, 37, 43, 60, 95, 121, 232
Indigeneity, 25-38
    symbols of, 153
Indigenous communities, 10

Indigenous cultures, 27
Indigenous dress styles, 246
Indigenous garments, 56
Indigenous groups
    contact zones among, 28
    dress designs by, 9
Indigenous heritage, theme of, 76-77, 84
Indigenous identities, 149, 215
Indigenous material culture, 32-36
    survivance of, 32
Indigenous metallurgy traditions, 37
Indigenous peoples, 16, 61, 63, 95, 242-259
    in Andean highlands, 118
    conversion of, 28-32, 34
    face masks and, 220-221
    ruanas and, 57-58
Indigenous Peoples Day, 2
Indigenous rights, 10, 19
Indigenous roots, embracing, 154
Indigenous women, 242-259
industrialization, 9
innovation, 264-265
Inspiramais, 267, 270n7
Instagram, 206
Institute of Interethnic and Indigenous Peoples Studies at the University of San Carlos of Guatemala, 247
Instituto Guatemalteco de Turismo (INGUAT, the Guatemalan Tourism Institute, a government agency), 247, 248-249
intellectual property rights, 10, 242-259. *See also* copyright protections
    collective, 256n8
    as neocolonial tool of forced assimilation, 252
    "provincialization" of, 256n8
intercultural work, 20
interiority, 126
International Amnesty report, 222
International Woman's Day, 182
intersectionality, 161, 238
invisibility, 93
Iny-Karajá peoples, 15, 21, 21n1
Isaac, Solimar, 266
Isabel II of Spain, 96
Isabel Marant, 249
Isabella of Spain, 28
IXEL Moda, 2-3

J Balvin, 203–206, *207*, 208
jackets, 230
Japan, 262, 270n3
Jaramillo Z., Marco A., *201*
jaspe technique, 48
jeans, 251
jewelry, 5, 49, 151. *See also specific types of jewelry*
    devotional, 25–38, *25*, *26*
jewels, 151
Jiquí, 83
Jobim, Sophia, 18–19, 20
John the Baptist, 31
Juan Diego, San, 231
Juana Inés de la Cruz, Sor, 222
Judex, 80
Juntos/Together jacket, *237*
jupe-culotte, 128, 129
Jurey, 80
jute, 128

Kahlo, Frida, 165, 222
Kaqchikel Maya, 243, 245, 249, 251, 253–254, 255n1
"Karajá Presence," 17
Karaminas, Vicki, 165, 169n17
Kardashian, Kim, 232–233
Karol G., 205, 209
Karush, Matthew B., 114–115
Katz, Jonathan D., 237, 238
keffiyah, 183n6
Kellogg, Susan, 255n2
Kenzo, models of, 193
Kessler, Marni Reva, 41
kitanda, 98–99
Klemm, Federico Jorge, 191
Krenak, 16
Krenak, Ailton, 22n4
Krenak ethnic group, 22n4
Kutesko, Elizabeth, 104

La Cariñosa, Juanita, 152
La Opinión magazine, 193, *194*
La Tercera newspaper, 162
labor, 11
Lara, Anita, 249
Latin America
    mantones de Manila in, 47
    social unrest in, 7–9

Latin American Academic Council of Fashion, 2, 11n1
    "Manifesto of Cartagena," 2, 9
Latin American Fashion Awards, 206
The Latin American Fashion Reader, 1
Latin American identity, 122–123
Latin American literature, 120–135
latinoamericanismo, 123
Latinidad, 206, 238
Latinos, 198–211, 236–237, 238
Latinx, 229, 230, 231, 236–237, 238. *See also* Latinos
laundresses, 139
Laver, James, 19
Lazarte, Silvia, 154
Lebrun, Carolina, 208
Lehman, Ken, 152
Leibsohn, Dana, 30–31
Lemebel, Pedro, 8, 158–171
    "The Death of Madonna," 165
    Loco afán, 161–162
León, Samuel, 56
Leroux, Gaston, 124
LGTBQIA+ communities, 153, 158–171, 166
Lhuiller, Monique, 230
liberation, 149
lifestyle, 8
Lima, Peru, 108–109, 110, 111, 118
Lira, André Luís Gomes, 261
literary magazines, 6, 7
literary marketplace, 130
literary style
    fashion and, 120–135
    gender and, 120–135
literary texts, as commodities, 124, 126
lithography, 49, 60, *61*
llikllas (shawls), 150
loca community, 8
local production, 10
lockets, 5, 25–38
logos, *77*, 82–83, 84
Londoño, Marcelino, 64, *65*
Londoño, Pedro, 66
Loof, Sergio de, 195
López, José María, 65
Lopez Obrador, Andrés Manuel, 247
Lord, Alexandra, 218–219
Los Tigres del Norte, 230

low theory, 148
Loza, Remedios, 154
Luanda, 99
lucha libre face mask, 215, 219–220
luchadores libres (pro-wrestlers), 9–10
Luján, Argentina, 192
Lusty, Natalya, 215
luxury goods, surcharges on, 73

Macías, Stacy I., 229
Macro-Jê group, 22n4
Madonna, 165
magasin, 124
magazines, 7, 120–135. *See also specific magazines*
Maison, 83
Major, John S., 45
makeup, 199
makuñ, 57
male readership, 124
Maluma, 203–204, 204–205, 206, 208
Mamani, Cristina, 154
Manila Galleons, 39–40, 48, 50
Manila shawls. *See mantones de Manila* (Manila shawls)
mantles, 58, 68
mantones de Manila (Manila shawls), 5, 6, 39–55, *40*, *46*, 51n12
  alteration of, 44
  Asian motifs on, 44–45, 48
  Asian roots of, 49–50
  cultural appropriation, 44–45
  democratization of, 43, 47
  as emblem of national sentiment and purist traditionalism, 50
  evolution of, 44
  fringe of, 44–45
  Hispano-Arab cultural exchange and, 44
  hybridization of, 49–50
  identified with Andalusia, 43–44
  Indigenous motifs in, 47
  Latin America, 47
  as marker of femininity, 50
  Mexican adaptation of, 47
  national pride and, 47
  in New Spain, 47–48
  as object in flux, 45
  in Peruvian dress, 51n15
  Philippines, 47
  popularity of, 43, 44
  Spanish adaptation of, 44–45
  Spanish national identity and, 41–45, 47
  Spanish vs. Chinese motifs, 44
  spread throughout Hispanic world, 47
  in travelogues, 51n14
Mapuche people, 57, 58
Mapuche-Huilliche, 58
Marcos, Subcomandante, 184n7, 221
Marfil, 223
"María Chula," 246
Mariposa, 82
marketplace, resistance to, 126
Martin, Meredith, 41
Martínez, José María, 126
Martínez, Mechi, 188–197
Martínez-Carreño, Aida, 58
Martin-Márquez, 43
Martins, Fernanda, 267–268
Marxism-Leninsim, 73
máscara, 216
masculinity, 66
  fashion and, 198–211
  Mexican, 220
masks. *See* face masks
mask-wearing, 10–11. *See also* face masks
material culture, of fashion, 39–55
Mathieux, Viviane, 161
maxi-ruana, 67
Maya, 28, 32, 242–259
Mayan women, unauthorized images of, 247–249
Mayor, Alberto, 65
Mbembe, Achille, 120–121
McKinley, Catherine, 143
"Me Too" movement, 175
medallones relicarios, 25–38, *25*, *26*
Medellín, Colombia, 64, 65, 198–211
Meléndez-Escalante, Tanya, 10
Mello e Souza, Gilda de, 19, 143
memories, 136–144, 239
memory, 190–191, 192
men
  dandyism and, 8–9, 198–211, *201*
  dress practices of, 57
Menswear New York Fashion Week, 236
Mercado, Tununa, 192–193

Mercado de Industrias Creativas Argentinas (MICA), 196n1
merchants, 66
mestizaje, 156n9
mestizos/as, 47, 58, 60, 63, 113, 115, 149, 150, 151, 155n4, 217, 233
    mestizo identity, 111
    rebozos (Mexican scarves) and, 48, 49
MET gala, 205
metal, 34
#MeToo movement, 222
Mexican Americans, 228–241
Mexican nationalism, femininity and, 48–49
Mexican Revolution, 9–10
mexicanidad, purist, 48–49
Mexico, 5, 10, 28, 39, 41, 48, 203, 247
    Asian influence on, 49–50
    clothing and class in, 47
    COVID-19 pandemic and, 215–227
    Indigenous textile design in, 249
    masks in, 215–227
    national identity and, 48–49
    protests in, 215–227
    silk and shawl embroidery in, 47
    Zapatista movement in, 10
Mexico City, D.F., Mexico, 235
Michelson, Melissa R., 166
Michoacán, Mexico, 48
migrants, 66
Milagro-Quevedo culture, 34
Miller, Lesley, 18
Mirzoeff, Nicholas, 6, 93
miscegenation, 46–47, 105n1. *See also* hybridity
misrepresentation, 10
Missoni, 249
Moda Paula, 162
modern/colonial paradigm, 56
modernism, 132n2
modernismo, 7, 120–135, 132n2, 133n6
modernist literature, 120–135
modernistas, 120–135, 133n6
modernité, 132n2
modernity, 3, 7, 41, 62, 81, 122, 132n2, 133n7, 244
    racialized notions of, 66
    visual culture of, 123

modernization, 17, 122, 198–199
Monastery, 203
Monsiváis, Carlos, 9, 219
Montalva, Pía, 8
Moore, Robin, 110
Moorish culture, 43–44, 46–47, 51n13
Moors, 28
Morales, Evo, 152
Moreira, Tartarín, 199–200
Moritz, Johann (Juan Mauricio) Rugendas, 109
Moschino, 205
motherhood, 8
Mothers of the Plaza de Mayo, 192, 196n2
    headscarves of, 190, 192, 196n2
Motta, Letícia, 267
Movimiento Nacional de Tejedoras Ruchajixik ri Qanaʼojabäl (the National Movement of Maya Weavers: Guardians of Our Knowledge; hereafter "National Movement"), 243. *See also* National Movement of Maya Weavers (Guatemala)
mudanza de traje, 191
Muisca Council of Cota, 68
Muisca people, 58, 67–68
mujeres de pollera (pollera women), 154
multiculturalism, 206
multidisciplinarity, 20
Mundial Magazine [Worldwide Magazine], 120, 122–124
Muñoz, José Esteban, 233, 235
Murillo, Marcela, 151, 155n5, 156n9
Museo Histórico Nacional de Chile, 18
Museu do Traje e do Textil de Salvador, 20
Museu do Traje e Indumentária de Salvador, Bahia, 20
The Museum Within the Museum, 56
Museums. *See also specific museums*
    in Brazil, 15–24
    colonialism and, 15–16
    consolidation of, 20
    creation of, 20
    deaccessioning and, 22n10

Ña Pancha, 115
Nahuas, 29–30
NAMES project AIDS quilt, 163, 164

naming, 5–6
Napier, Alison, 5
narco novelas, 202
narco-aesthetic, 203
narco-gangsters, 203
narrative, 100, 137. *See also* slave narratives
　narrative style, 137
　travel, 96–97
　visual, 95–96
National Chamber of Textile Industry (CANAINTEX), 224
national dress, 41, 44
national formation, 50
National Historic Archive (Brazil), 16
National Historical Museum, 20
national identity, 5, 50, 165
　brands and, 83
　in Colombia, 60–61
　Mexico and, 48–49
　of Spain, 41–44
National Movement of Maya Weavers (Guatemala), 10, 242–259, 255n3
National Museum (Denmark), 17
National Museum of American History, 230
National Museum of Brazil, 4, 15, 15–24
National Museum of Colombia, 56
national pride, 62
National Zapatista Liberation Army, 184n7
nationalism, 5–6, 41, 73, 84
　in Brazil, 20
　in Cuba, 78–80, *79*
　gender and, 42–43
　rise of, 40
Nationalmuseet (Denmark), 17
nation-building, 156n9
　accessories and, 42
　dress and, 44
　ruana incompatible with, 60–61
native survivance, 5
Nawe, 84
Negreiros, Hanayrá, 7, 136–144
Negreiros, Zeferino, 137, *142*
neocolonialism, fashion intellectual property and, 242–259
Nervo, Amado, 126
New Granada, Viceroyalty of, 57, 59, 62. *See also* Peru

New Spain, Viceroyalty of, 43, 47, 231–232. *See also* Mexico
　mantones de Manila in, 47–48
New York City, New York, 85, 206, 235–236
New York Fashion Week (NYFD), 206, 236
New York Times, 215–227
newspapers, fashion columns in, 193
Nice, system of, 5–6
Nice Classification, Class 25, 74
Nike, 203
Non Stop, 204–205
nostalgia, 136–144, 239
Nova (Felipe Velandia), 166
novels, 43, 51n12
Novik, Laura, 11n1
NOW Congress to Unite Women, 237–238

Oaxaca, Mexico, 48
Obama, Barack, 85
Obando, Juan Carlos, 230
"object in motion," 41, 48
object-based research, 41–42
objectification, resistance to, 104–105
office wear, ditching of, 3
Órbita, 82, 83
Operación Calma, 223
oppression, 152, 153
Ordinance of the Viceroy of Nueva Granada, 5
Orientalism, 44, 45
Otero-Claves, Ana Maria, 63
Ozuna, 203

Pachamama, 30
paintings, 49, 51n12, 61–62, 108
paisas, 208–209
Palaversich, Diana, 163
Panama, 202
pano da costa, 99, 101, 103, 105, 105n4
pantskirts, 128, 201
Para Ti magazine, 191
Paris, France, 7, 123
Parra, Violeta, 165
past, reconstruction of, 8
pastorelas (nativity representations), 216
patchwork tapestries, 8
Patiño, Silvia, 67, 68
patriarchy, 10, 154
patron saint medals, 37

Paula magazine, 162
Paulista Museum, University of São Paulo, 15, 16, 18, 20
Paz, Manuel María, 64
Paz, Octavio, 9, 216, 217, 225n3
peasants, 57, 61, 62, 63
pectoral forms, 32
pendants, 32, 36
"perceptecide," 191
Pérez, Louis, 114–115
Pérez, Tere, 223
Pérez Galdós, Benito, 51n12
Perfection Stove Company, advertisement for, 111–115, *117*
performance, trans representation and, 158–171
performance art, 166
performativity, 29, 30, 35–37, 229, 234
periodicals, 120–135
Perón, Eva, 165
perreo, 203
personal histories, 136–144
personal protective equipment (PPE), 215–227, 218
personal style, 8
perspective, 100
Peru, 28, 33, 159
    advertisements in, 6–7
    Afro-Peruvian women, 108–119
    mantones de Manila in, 51n15
    polka dots in, 108–119
Petrópolis Museum, 20
Philippines, 39, 43, 47
photography, 6, 7, 64, 65–66, *65*, *69*, 93–107, 123
    dress and, 94, 100
    meaning constructed through, 99–104
    personal collections, 136–144
    studio, 64
    study of, 143
Picq, Manuela M., 149, 246
Piisciis (Akhil Canizales), 166
Pinochet, Augusto, 161
Planetary Health Alliance, 269n2
"Plaza de la Dignidad" *Dignity Square*), 182
Plaza Pública CADEM poll N°228, 176
"pluriversal" design perspective, 268

Poiret, Paul, 128
political agency, dress and, 121
    politics, 42–43, 121, 238
polka dots, 6–7, 108–119
polleras (full-pleated skirts), 150, 151–152, 151n1, 153
polytheism, 28–29
popular knowledge, 148
portraiture, in Brazil, 93–107. *See also specific media*
Portugal, 17
Portuguese, 97
-pot, 241, 251
pots-and-pans demonstrations, 8
poverty, 10, 57, 58, 59, 60, 61, 66
power, 58, 67, 121
    coloniality of, 57, 59–60
    defiance against, 94
    power dynamics, 95
    power mechanisms, 27, 31
    resistant sites of, 7–8
Pratt, Mary Louise, 3, 27
precarity, 58, 66
Price, Patricia L., 238
pride, 236, 238
primitivism, 94
print culture, 121, 122
printing, serialized, 122
professional choices, 8
professions, 8
progress, 73
protectionism, 204, 218
protests, 9, 58, 222–223, 238
    accessories for, 174–179
    in Chile, 8, 183n4, 184n11
    in Guatemala, 245
    in Mexico, 215–227
Providencia, Chile, 182
public access, prioritizing, 4, 15–24
public discourse, women and, 120–135
public health, 9–10
public sphere, women in, 7
Puebla, Mexico, 48, 49
Puerto Rico, 43, 202, 204, 205, 207, 208
Pussy Riot, 176

quality, brands and, 83–84
Quechua people, 7–8, 70n2, 147–157
Quechuan women, 7–8, 147–157

queer activism, 229
queer failure, theory of, 147
queer femininities, 147
queer performativity, 229
queer studies, 7–8, 147, 154
Quijano, Aníbal, 6, 93, 94–95
quitandeiras, 6, 93–107, *97*, *98*
Quitrín, 83

race, 42, 48, 93–107, 105n1, 140
racial hybridity. *See also* miscegenation,
   positive valuation of, 46–47
   in Spanish national discourse, 46–47
racial politics, 66
racialization, 5, 50, 57, 58, 59, 63, 96–97, 99
   colonialism and, 94–95
   process of, 110
racism, 10, 140, 153, 249
racist stereotypes, of hybridity, 49
Radar, 82
Radcliffe, Sarah A., 118
Rama, Ángel, 122
Ramos, Andrés, 166
Randall, Kimberly, 49
rascuache, 10, 229, 234
rasquachismo, 229–230, 232, 236, 239
Raul y Tamara, 174
rayon, 48
Rayos, Rosa Isabel (Mrs. Booggie), 167, 169n18
Real Academia de la Lengua, 199
rebozos (Mexican scarves), 41, 48, 51n17
   Asian motifs on, 48
   Asian roots of, 49–50
   china poblana and, 48–49
   as emblem of national sentiment and purist traditionalism, 50
   hybridization of, 49–50
   as marker of femininity, 50
   mestizos/as and, 48, 49
   Mexican nationalism and, 48–49
   purist *mexicanidad* and, 48–49
   as typical Mexican female garb, 50
Recreo, 80
recycled clothing, 8
"Red Ruana," 66
reggaetoneros, 9, 198–211
region, 8
regional imaginaries, 2

reino interior, 126
Reis, João, 103
reliquary lockets, 25–38, *25*, *26*
representation of, 140
resilient practices, 215
resistance, 7–9, 94, 103, 152, 153–154, 193, 216
   clothing and, 172–187
   dandyism and, 9
   through failure, 148–149
   genealogies of, 56–72
   to marketplace, 126
   to objectification, 104–105
   trans representation and, 158–171
Reyes, Yosimar, 232
Reykon, 207
Riaño, Daniela, 208
Ribeiro, 20
Ribeiro, Berta, 22n6
Richard, Nelly, 163, 165, 169n16
Rio de Janeiro, Brazil, 16, 18, 20, 102–103, 193, 260, 269n1
ritual minatures, 36
ritxoko ceramic dolls, 17
Rivera-Servera, Ramón, 166
Roces, Mina, 44
Romagna, Cris, *266*, 267–268
romanticism, 49
Romero, Fernando, 117–118n1
Root, Regina A., 8, 11n1, 121, 269
ropa americana, 163
Ropero Paula, 162
Rosa, Carmen, 152
Rosas, Juan Manuel de, 193
Rousteing, Olivier, 205
Rowe, Anne Pollard, 58
ruana (voice), 70n2
ruanas, 5
   Black peoples and, 66
   in Colombian imagination, 68–69
   continuity and change and, 64
   detachable collars on, 66
   eradication as strategy of civilization and moral control, 59
   "eternal," 62
   as formal attire, 64
   heritage and, 67
   with high collar, 66
   history of, 56–72

incompatibility with national project, 60–61
mantles and, 68
maxi-ruana, 67
modernity and, 67
politics of use, 67
prohibited in schools, 60
racial and class valuation of, 64
regarded by elites as suspicious, 62–63
rejection of, 67
in rural spaces, 66–67
stylistic richness of, 63–64
stylization of, 64
symbolism of, 67
territorial variation of, 63–64
varieties of, 63
woolen fabrics, 65–66
Rumba, 80
Run DMC, 203
runaway slave advertisements, 101–103, 104, 105n6

Sacatepéquez, Department of, 243
Salazar Celis, Edward, 5
Salvador, Bahia, Brazil, 20
San Marcos blankets, 230, 239
sandals, 150, 156n6
Santa María del Río (San Luis Potosí), 48
Santiago, Chile, 8, 172–187, 182
Santiago Atitlan, Guatemala, 247–248, 248
São Paulo, Brazil, 15, 20, 260, 269n1
sarapes, 236
Sargent, John, 51n12
sartorial decrees, 47
sartorial studies, 136–144
sartorial trends, *chinoiserie* and, 44–45
Saulquin, Susana, 193–195
Saunders, Stephanie N., 8, 139, 269
Sayer, Chloë, 47
Scaraffia, Giuseppe, 199
scarves, 41, 181. See also headscarves; *rebozos* (Mexican scarves)
Schwarcz, Lilia Moritz, 22n3
Schweitzer, Dahlia, 217
Scott, James C., 149
seamstresses, 139–140
Seco, Ricardo, 10, 225n3, 229, 235–236, 237, 239
second-hand clothes, 156n8

seeing, models of, 140
Segato, Rita, 179
self-expression, 9
self-fashioning, 5, 63
Semáforo, 204
Señor Amor, 190
settler colonialism, 248
sevillanas, 45
Seville, Spain, 39, 43
sexism, 153
sexual identity, changes in terminology, 159–160
sexual oppression, 148
sexualities, 7–8, 149, 233, 234
Shako, 207
Shaw and Pope, 204
shawls, 39–55, *40*, 150, 151, 236. See also *mantones de Manila* (Manila shawls)
shields, 175
shirts, 201, 236–238, 238
shoelaces, 150
shoes. See footwear
Shoji, Tadashi, 230
silk, 39–40, 47, 48
"silk trade route," 40, 48
Sillar, Bill, 33
Silva, Josés Á, 127
silver thread, 48
ski-masks, 174
skirts, 128, 129, 147–157, 241,
slave narratives, 104–105
slave trade, 93
slavery, 111, 142
    Afro-Brazilian identities and, 136–144
    in Brazil, 93, 136–144
    nostalgic images of, 114
Slick Dick, 208
sloganeering, 238
social codes, 142
social media, 7, 220, 223, 233, 234, 238, 247, 248, 249, 266–267
social mobility, 65
Social Outburst of 2019, 172–187, 182n1, 182n2
social unrest, 7–9
socialism, 73–74, 74
Society "Organizing Trans Diversities" (OTD Chile), 160

Sommer, Doris, 220
Somos Mhuyscas, 68, *69*
Sontag, Susan, 217, 218
Sorolla, Joaquín, 51n12
Soviet Union
    Cuba and, 73, 74, 76
    disintegration of, 74
Spain, 5, 28–30, 39, 56
    evolution from empire to nation-state, 43
    identity crisis in, 43
    national dress in, 41
    national identity and, 41–44
    national identity of, 41–44
Spanish American *modernismo*, 120–135. *See also modernismo*
Spanish American writers, professionalization of, 122
Spanish conquest, 28–32, 34. *See also* conquistadors
Spanish Empire, 28–30, 31–32, 34, 47
    end of, 43
    evoked in *mantones de Manila*, 45
Spanish feminine identity, 44
Spanish garments, 56, 57, 58
Spanish national discourses
    fin-de-siècle, 46–47
    positive valuation of racial hybridity and miscegenation in, 46–47
Spanish national identity, *mantones de Manila* and, 41–45, 47
Spanish nation-building, 40
Spanish Philippines, 39
Spanish women, characterized as Orientalized and exotic, 45
Spanish–American War, 39, 43
Spanishness, 45
sports, 8, 151–152
status, theme of, 81–82
Staz, Joy, 205
Steele, Valerie, 18, 45, 234
Stein, Stanley, 19
stereotypes, femininity and, 6
stockings, 49, 151
Stokes, Lawrence La Fountain, 160
stone, 33–34, 34–35
storytelling, 137
street vendors, 6
streetwear, 203, 208

Strong, Mary, 32–33
Studio Acci, 267–268
style
    definition of, 94
    human rights and, 8
    narrative, 137
    style sultane (sultana skirt), 128
    subcultural, 9
style narratives, 94, 103–104
    Afro-Brazilian, 101
    Black personal stories and, 141
style sultane (sultana skirt), 128
subalterns, 30–31, 36, 95
subcultural styles, 9
subjectivity, 149
submission, 94
subversion, 30, 30–31, 35
suits, 143, 199, 201
sumptuary laws, 47
survival, 10, 32
survivance, 29, 30, 32, 36
sustainability, face masks and, 223
sweaters, 150, 251
sweatshirts, 174, 251
syncretism, 29–30

tagua nuts, 34, 35–36, 36, 37
tailcoats, 137, 141, *142*
tailors, 139
Taino people, 76–77
Takagi, Yōko, 4
Tarde, Gabriel, 202
tassels, 150
taste, 63
Taylor, Allison, 154
Taylor, Diana, 191
Taylor, Elizabeth, 165
Taylor, Lou, 17–18
technological advancement, theme of, 83
Tecnópolis, Argentina, 188–189, 195–196
Tejada, Arturo, 66
Telemundo, 220
terminology, inconsistencies in, 19–20
territorial sovereignty, 245–246
textile designs
    Indigenous, 242–259
    traditional, 245–246

textile industry
    in Colombia, 204–205
    COVID-19 pandemic and, 10–11
    in Cuba, 73, 78
textile recycling, 188–197
textiles
    the body and, 104
    found, 8
    handwoven, 242–259
    traditional, 10
text-iles, 245
Textiles Panamericanos, 224
Thereza Christina Maria, 97
Thio, 204
Thomas, Kedron, 10
Tiahuanacu, 32–33
Tiendas del Pueblo stores, 73
ties, 201
Tigers of the North Cobija jacket, 230, *231*
Tikuna, Josi, 149
Titton, Monica, 183n6
Toledo de Paula, Teresa Cristana, 18, 22n6
Torres, Diego de, 58
Torres, Heloïsa Alberto, 105n4
Torres, Ramón, 60, *61*
Torres Méndez, Ramón, 64
tourism, 10
    in Guatemala, 10, 242–259
    tourism industry, 247–249
trademarks, 74, 76
trading routes, 39–55
traditionalism, 41, 50
trajes típicos, 246, 248, 249
trans communities, violence against, 8
trans models, 166
trans representation, 158–171
trans resistance, 8
Trans rights, 159
transatlantic cultural exchange, 50
transatlantic studies, 42
transcultural exchange, 39–55
transnational cultural exchange, 50
transnational experiences, in fashion, 228–241
transnational studies, 7–8, 147
transnationality, 228–241
trarikan makuñ, 57
trauma, 191, 192–193
travel narrative, 96–97

Tres Pesos, 204, 207
Tristán, Flora, 51n14
Trump, Donald, 236
t-shirts. *See* shirts
Tulloch, Carol, 94, 141, 183n6
Tupinambá, Glicélia, 17
Tupinambá cloak, 17
Tupinambá people, 17
Turizo, Manuel, 204
Turmequé, 58
Tynan, Jane, 183n6
typology images, 95–96
Tz'utujil Maya, 247–248, 255n2

ultis, 33–34
underwear, 152
UNESCO, 219, 261
uniforms, 73
United Nations Human Rights Office, 246
United States, 17
    Aunt Jemima advertisements in, 113–114, 115
    racist depictions of African Americans in, 114–115
Universidad Austral de Chile, 175–176
unku, 57
upcycling, 188–197
-uq, 241
urban fashions, 9
urbanization, 9
US Supreme Court, 238
used clothing, 191–192
    use of, 163–164
    used clothing industry, 8
Usigli, Rodolfo, 216–217

Valdés, Ana Gabriela, 84
Valdés, Dafne, 179
Valdivia, Chile, 175–176
Valencia de Castaño, 67
Valentino, 203, 249
Van Vleet, Krista, 151, 156n8
Vazquez, Estrella, 169n18
Vázquez Parladé, Joaquín, 51n14
veils, 41
Velandia, Felipe, 166
Veloz, Juan, 167
Veracruz, Mexico, 39, 47
Versace, Donatella, 205

Viceroyalties of New Spain, 41
Vickery, Amanda, 18
Vico C., 208
violence, 8–9
"Virgen Morena," 231–232
Virgin and Child, 31
Virgin Mary, 29–30, 30, 31, 35
Virgin of Guadalupe, 231–232
visibility, 93
visual discourse, 115
visual narratives, 95–96
visuality, 6, 93, 95, 96–97, 100
visuality regimes, 95, 96–97, 100
Vizenor, Gerald, 29
Vogue Hombre magazine, 206
Vogue magazine, 162, 166–167, 169n18, 228, 234
Vogue México magazine, 166–167, 169n18, 223
voices, silenced, 4
vulgarity, 234

Walker, Tamara, 6–7
Walsh, Catherine E., 3
"weapons of the weak," 149, 152, 153–154
weavers, 242–259
weaving, 245, 255n2
Weismantel, Mary, 153–154
whiteness, 56, 58, 115, 153–154
  whites, 60, 113, 115, 151
Willis, Deborah, 138
women
  Aymara, 7–8
  in Bolivia, 147–157
  consumerism and, 122
  in Guatemala, 10, 242–259
  Indigenous, 242–259
  print culture and, 122
  public discourse and, 120–135
  in public sphere, 7
  Quechuan, 7–8
women's fashion magazines, 7
women's rights, 10, 184n8
women's suffrage movement, 184n8
wood, 34
wool, 48
workwear, 73, 78
World Health Organization, 215, 260
World Intellectual Property Day, 247
World Trade Organiztion, Trade-Related Aspects of Intellectual Property Rights (TRIPS) Agreement, 256n7
Worth, Charles Frederick, *194*
wrestling, 151–152, 152–153

Yanaconan Quechuas, 57–58
Yandel, 204
Yatra, Sebastián, 204
Ybarra-Frausto, Tomás, 229, 232, 234
Yelsid, 207
Yucatán, 28
Yucatán Peninsula, 31

zamacueca, 108, 117–118n1
zamacueca performers, 109
Zanardi, Tara, 44
Zapata, Emiliano, 10
Zapatista movement, 10, 176, 184n7, 216, 221–222
zarzuelas (Spanish operettas), 43, 51n12
Zion & Lennox, 205
Zorn, Elaine, 151, 155n4, 156n7